THAT TIME I GOT REINCARNATED AS A

SLIME

5

Author: FUSE

Artist: TAIKI KAWAKAMI

Character design: MITZ VAH

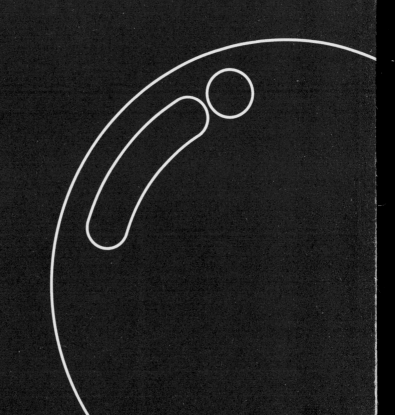

World Map

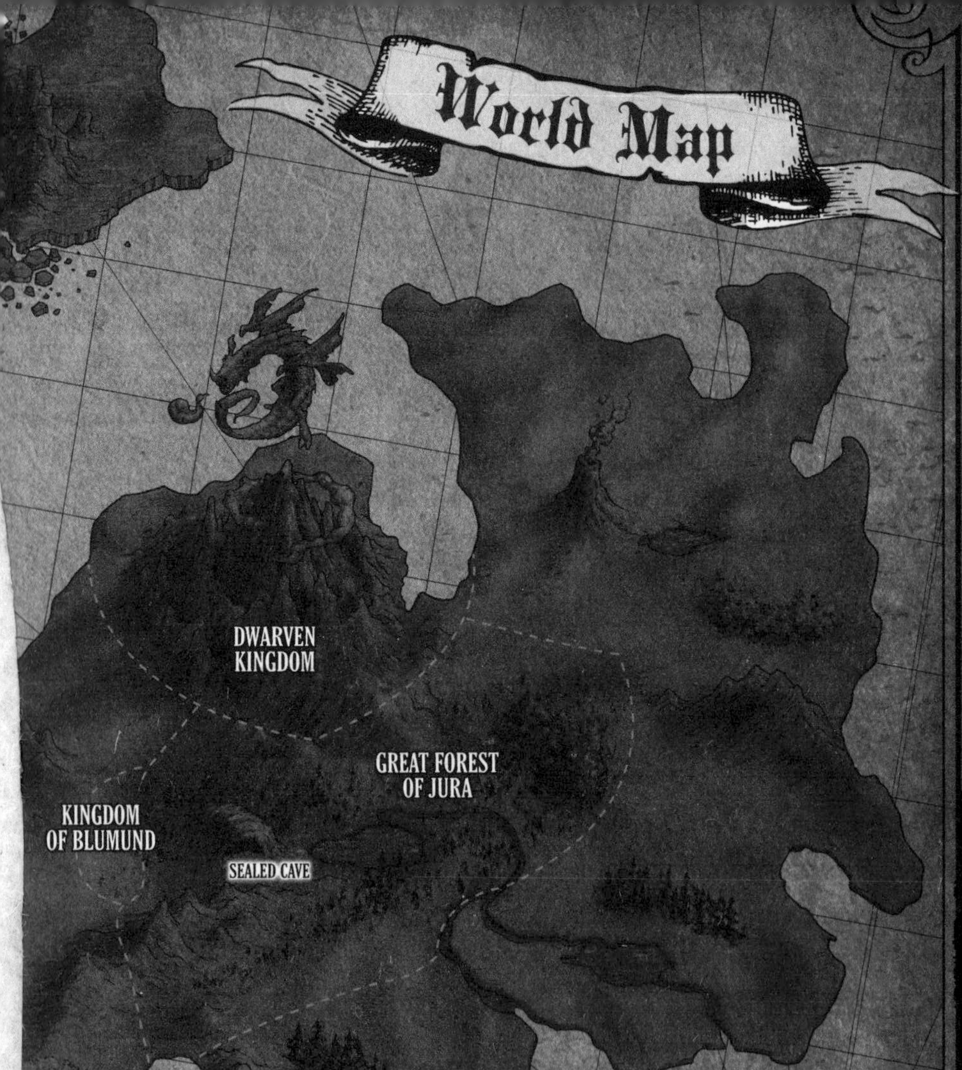
DWARVEN KINGDOM
GREAT FOREST OF JURA
KINGDOM OF BLUMUND
SEALED CAVE

PLOT SUMMARY

The orc lord and his army of 200,000 threaten the Great Forest of Jura. Rimuru had hoped to join forces with the lizardmen of the swamp to fight this menace, but Gabiru the lizardman, underestimating the orc lord's threat, stages a rebellion that accidentally plunges the lizardmen into the threat of extinction. Only the timely arrival of Rimuru's band saves them. The tide is turned against the orcs thanks to the help of Benimaru and the other kijin. This is when the mastermind behind the orcs, Gelmud the majin, takes the field... ▼

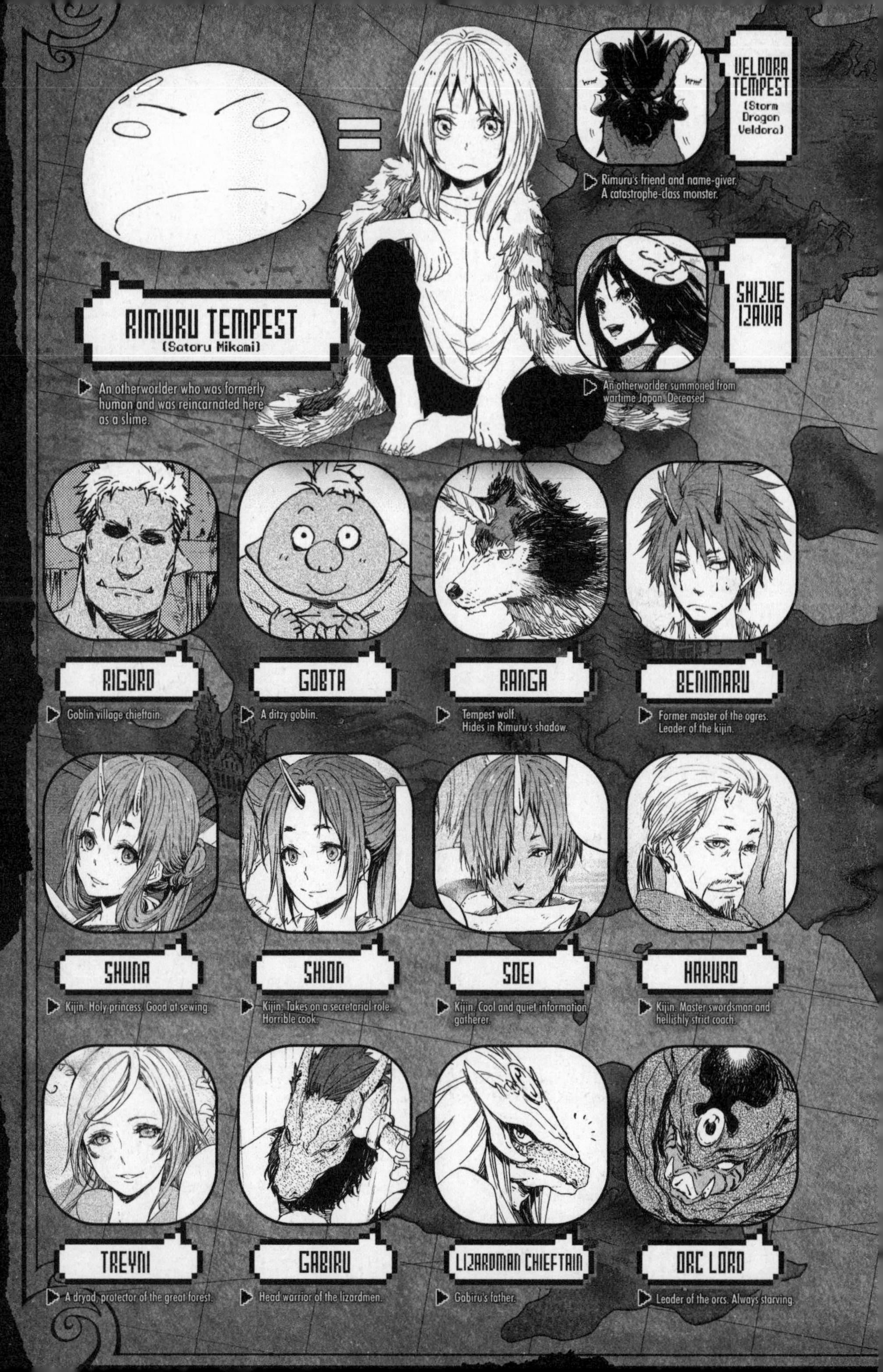
RIMURU TEMPEST
(Satoru Mikami)
An otherworlder who was formerly human and was reincarnated here as a slime.
hrmf
hrmf
VELDORA TEMPEST
(Storm Dragon Veldora)
Rimuru's friend and name-giver. A catastrophe-class monster.
SHIZUE IZAWA
An otherworlder summoned from wartime Japan. Deceased.
RIGURD
Goblin village chieftain.
GOBTA
A ditzy goblin.
RANGA
Tempest wolf. Hides in Rimuru's shadow.
BENIMARU
Former master of the ogres. Leader of the kijin.
SHUNA
Kijin. Holy princess. Good at sewing.
SHION
Kijin. Takes on a secretarial role. Horrible cook.
SOEI
Kijin. Cool and quiet information gatherer.
HAKURO
Kijin. Master swordsman and hellishly strict coach.
TREYNI
A dryad, protector of the great forest.
GABIRU
Head warrior of the lizardmen.
LIZARDMAN CHIEFTAIN
Gabiru's father.
ORC LORD
Leader of the orcs. Always starving.

CONTENTS

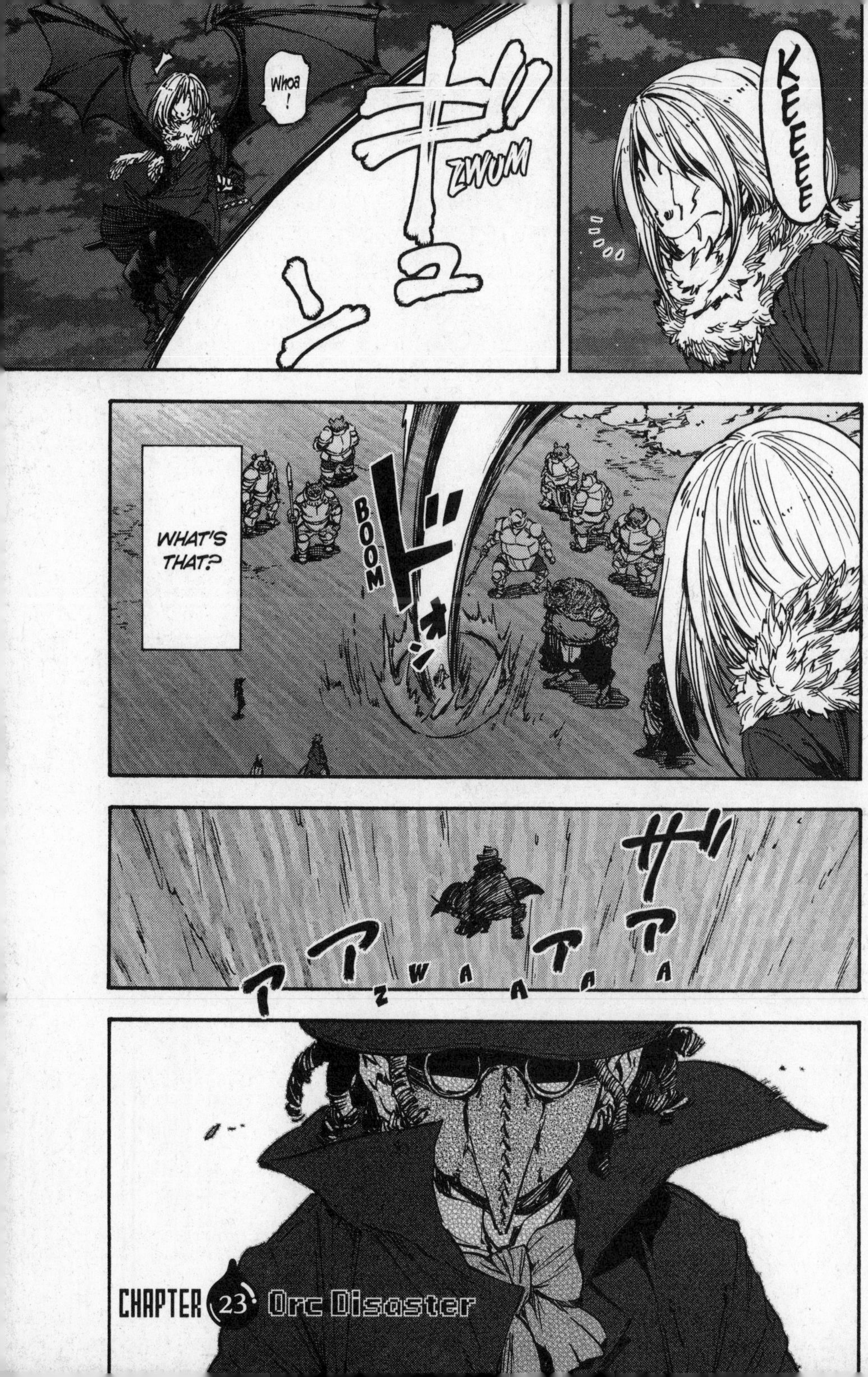
KEEEEE
Whoa!
ギュン
ZWUM
WHAT'S THAT?
ドォン
BOOM
ザァァァァ
ZWAAAA
CHAPTER 23 Orc Disaster

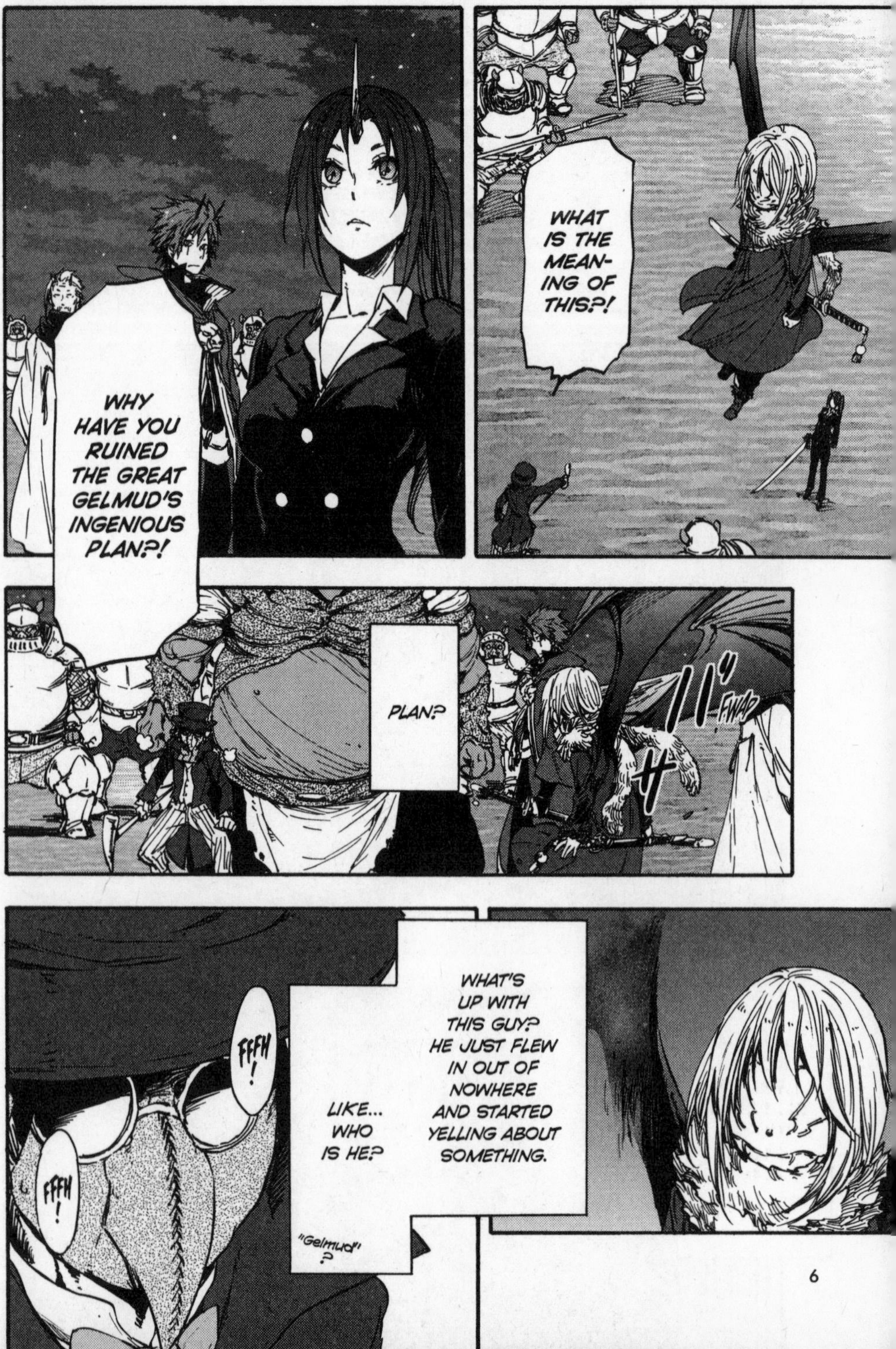
WHAT IS THE MEANING OF THIS?!
WHY HAVE YOU RUINED THE GREAT GELMUD'S INGENIOUS PLAN?!
PLAN?
FWAP
WHAT'S UP WITH THIS GUY? HE JUST FLEW IN OUT OF NOWHERE AND STARTED YELLING ABOUT SOMETHING.
LIKE... WHO IS HE?
"Gelmud"?
FFFH!
FFFH!

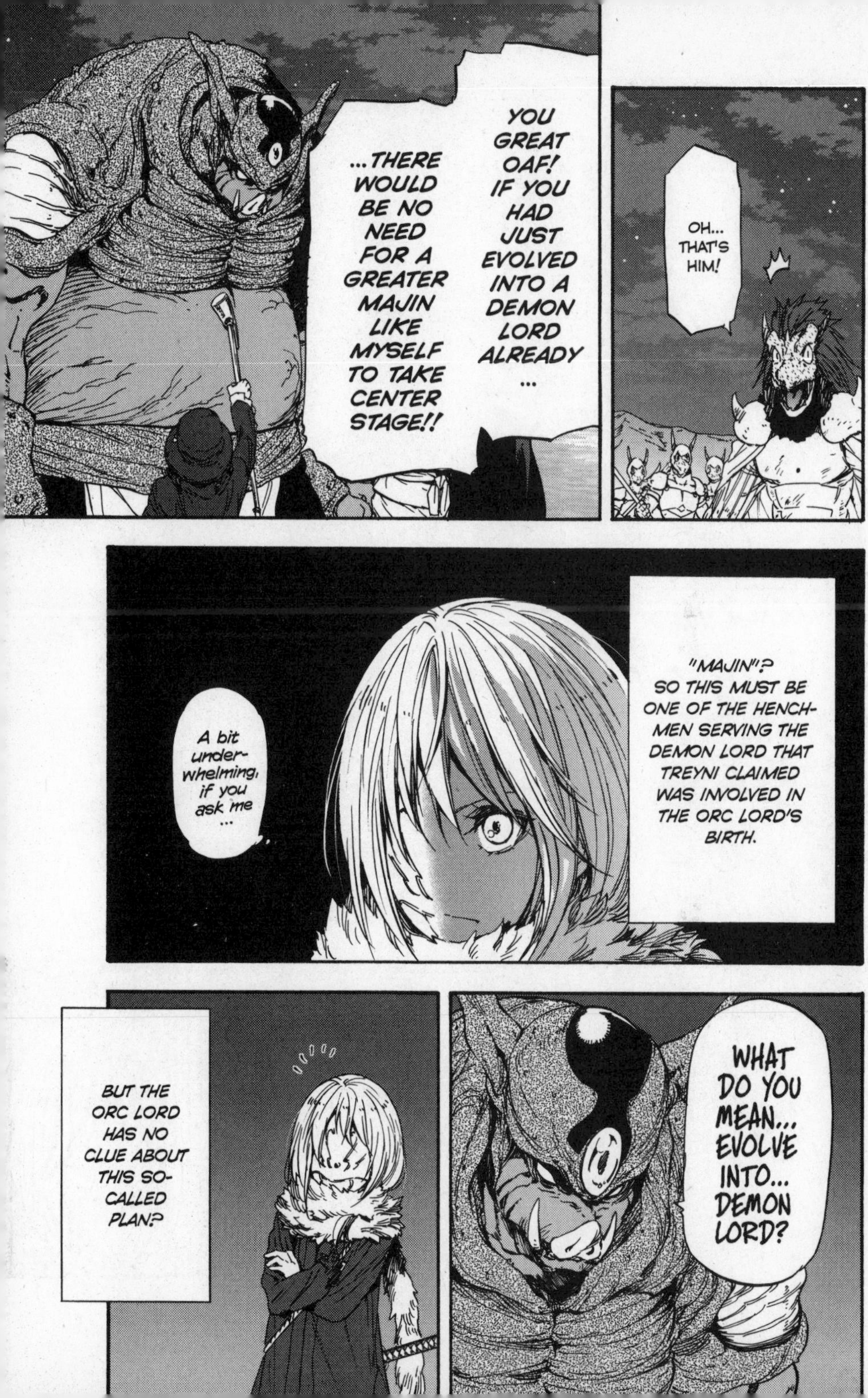
OH... THAT'S HIM!
YOU GREAT OAF! IF YOU HAD JUST EVOLVED INTO A DEMON LORD ALREADY...
...THERE WOULD BE NO NEED FOR A GREATER MAJIN LIKE MYSELF TO TAKE CENTER STAGE!!
"MAJIN"? SO THIS MUST BE ONE OF THE HENCH-MEN SERVING THE DEMON LORD THAT TREYNI CLAIMED WAS INVOLVED IN THE ORC LORD'S BIRTH.
A bit under-whelming, if you ask me...
WHAT DO YOU MEAN... EVOLVE INTO... DEMON LORD?
BUT THE ORC LORD HAS NO CLUE ABOUT THIS SO-CALLED PLAN?

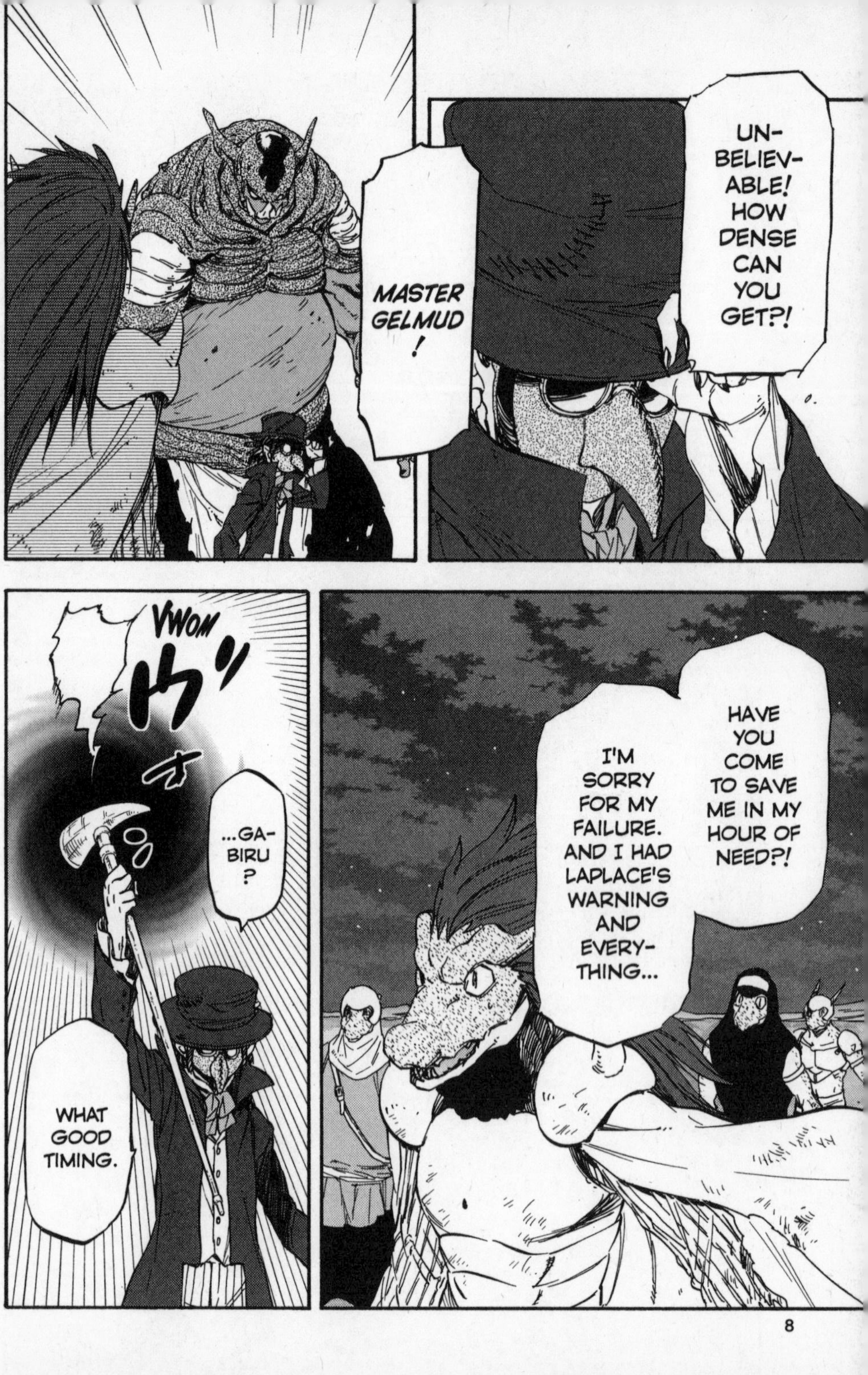
UN-BELIEV-ABLE! HOW DENSE CAN YOU GET?!
MASTER GELMUD!
HAVE YOU COME TO SAVE ME IN MY HOUR OF NEED?!
I'M SORRY FOR MY FAILURE. AND I HAD LAPLACE'S WARNING AND EVERY-THING...
VWOM
...GA-BIRU?
WHAT GOOD TIMING.

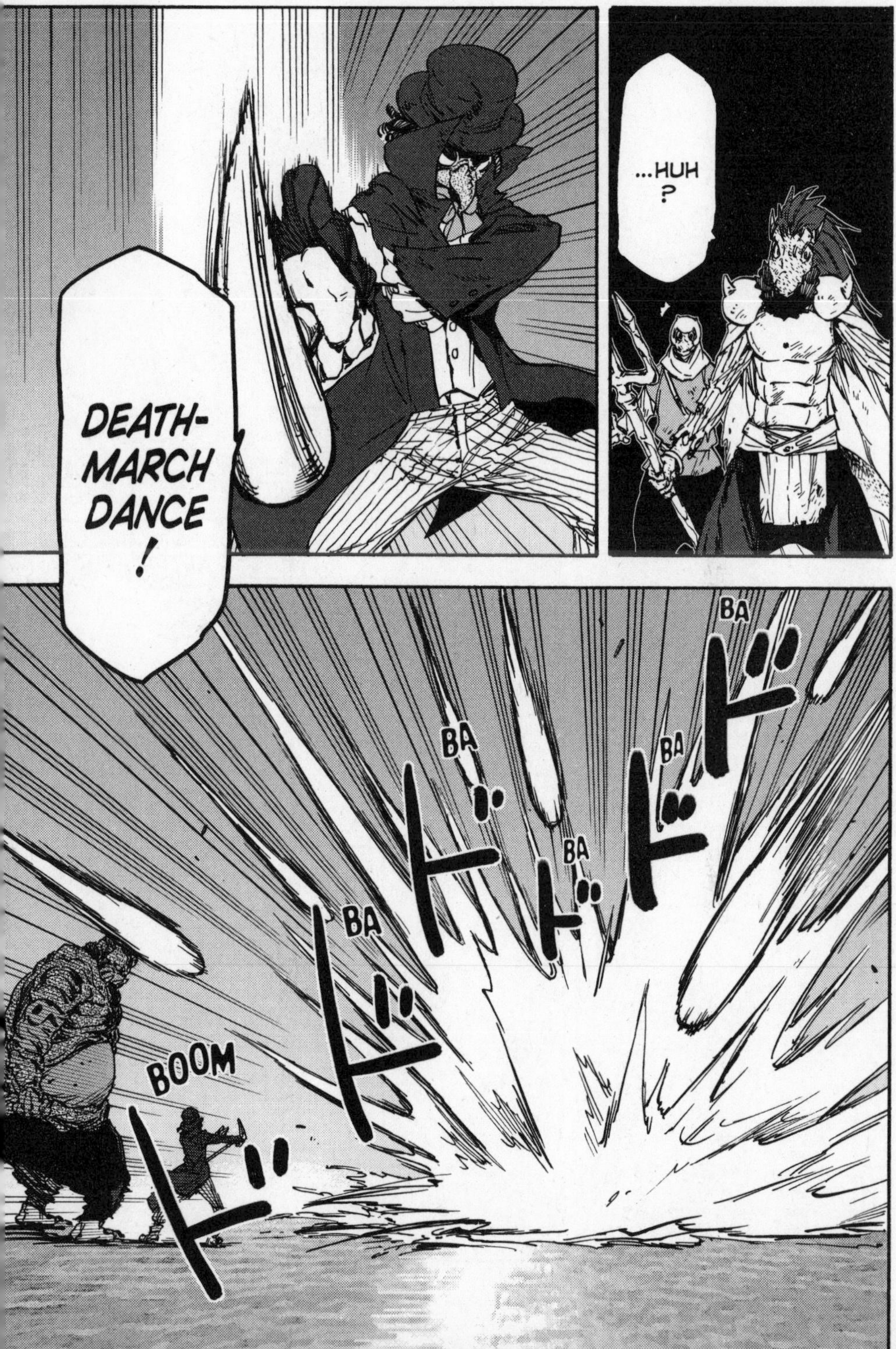

...HUH?
DEATH-MARCH DANCE!
BA
ド
BA
ド
BA
ド
BA
ド
BA
ド
BOOM
ド

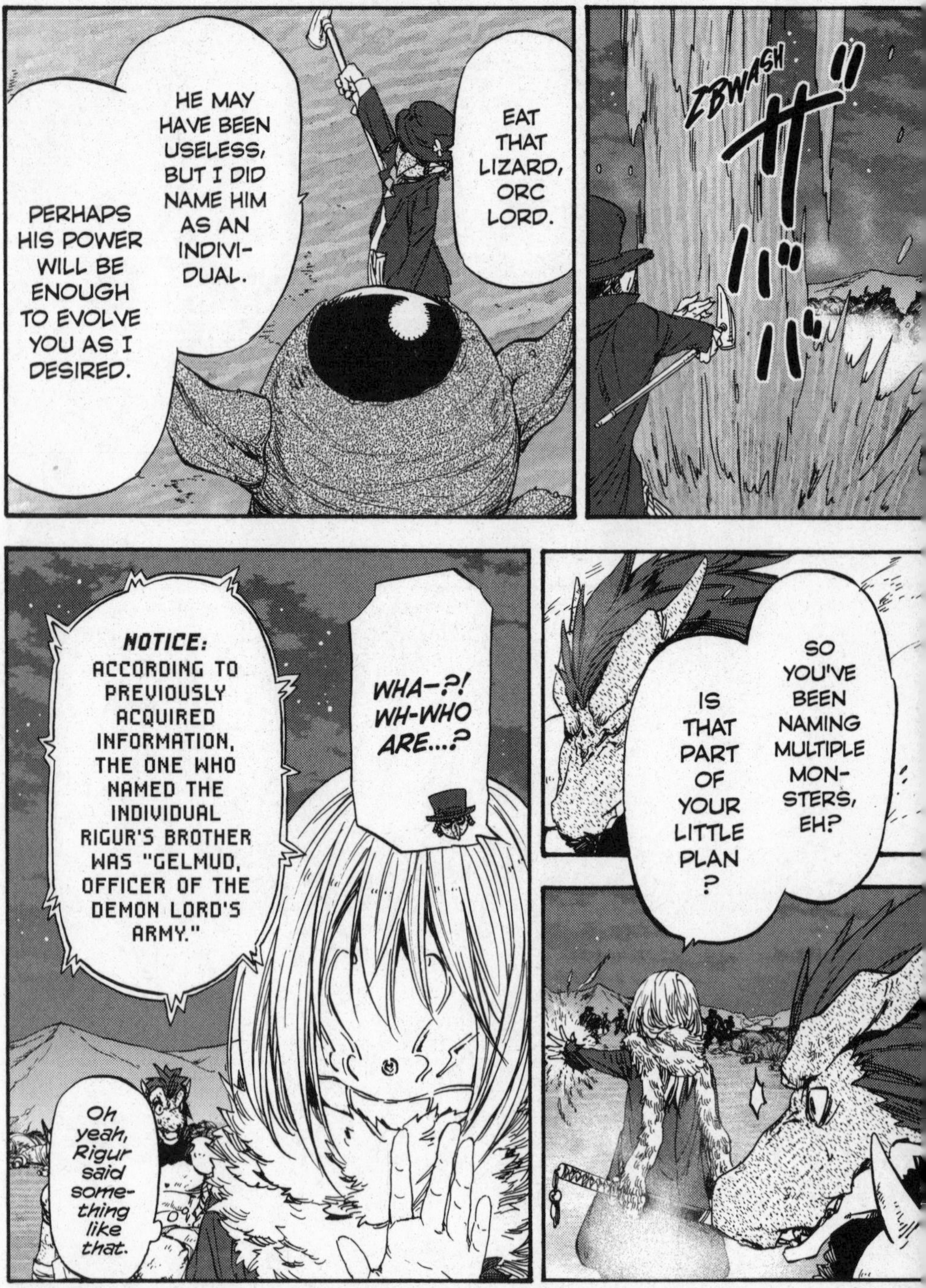
ZBWASH
EAT THAT LIZARD, ORC LORD.
HE MAY HAVE BEEN USELESS, BUT I DID NAME HIM AS AN INDIVIDUAL.
PERHAPS HIS POWER WILL BE ENOUGH TO EVOLVE YOU AS I DESIRED.
SO YOU'VE BEEN NAMING MULTIPLE MONSTERS, EH?
IS THAT PART OF YOUR LITTLE PLAN?
WHA-?! WH-WHO ARE...?
NOTICE: ACCORDING TO PREVIOUSLY ACQUIRED INFORMATION, THE ONE WHO NAMED THE INDIVIDUAL RIGUR'S BROTHER WAS "GELMUD, OFFICER OF THE DEMON LORD'S ARMY."
Oh yeah, Rigur said something like that.

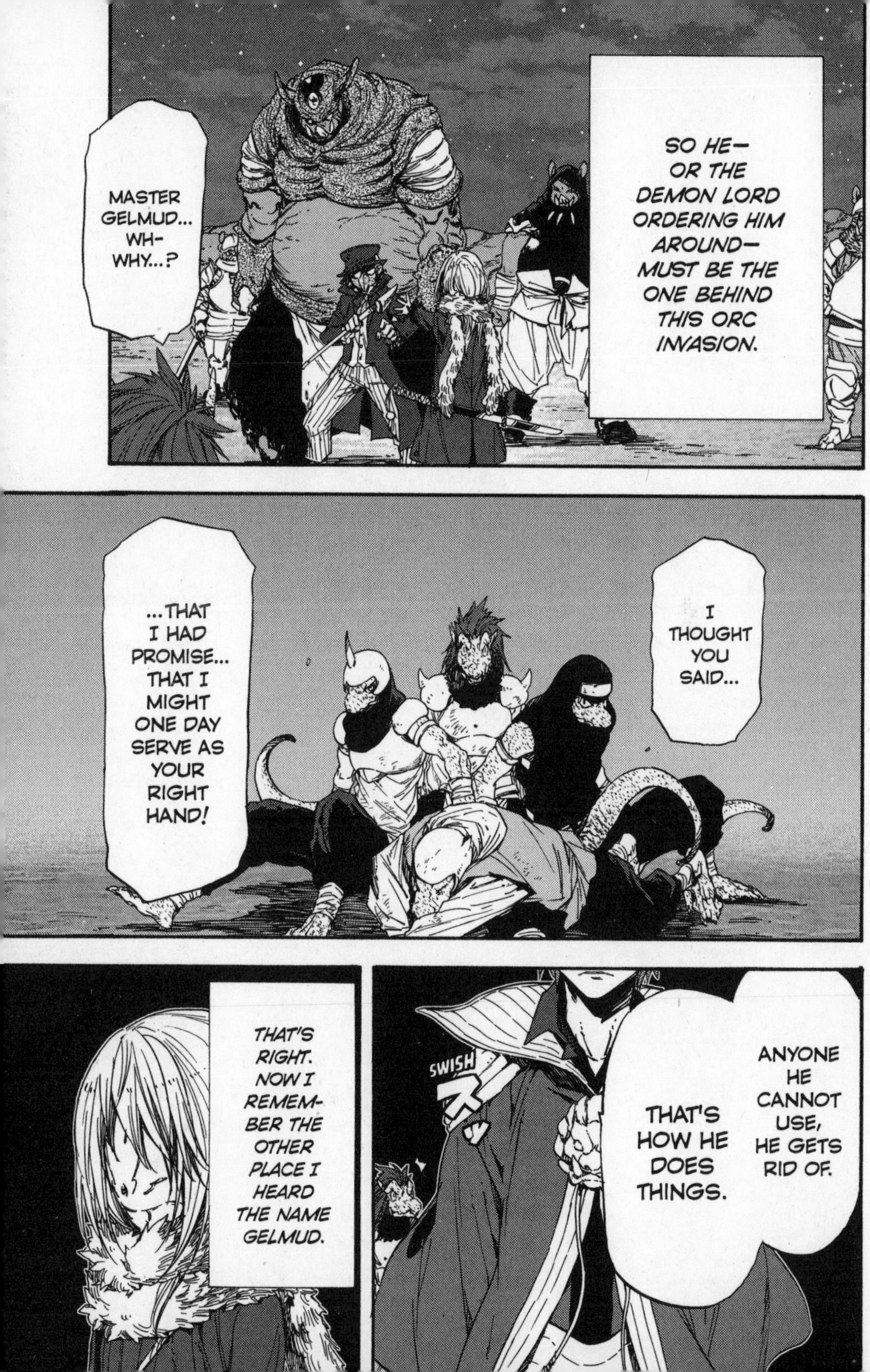
SO HE— OR THE DEMON LORD ORDERING HIM AROUND— MUST BE THE ONE BEHIND THIS ORC INVASION.
MASTER GELMUD... WH- WHY...?
I THOUGHT YOU SAID...
...THAT I HAD PROMISE... THAT I MIGHT ONE DAY SERVE AS YOUR RIGHT HAND!
ANYONE HE CANNOT USE, HE GETS RID OF.
THAT'S HOW HE DOES THINGS.
SWISH
THAT'S RIGHT. NOW I REMEMBER THE OTHER PLACE I HEARD THE NAME GELMUD.

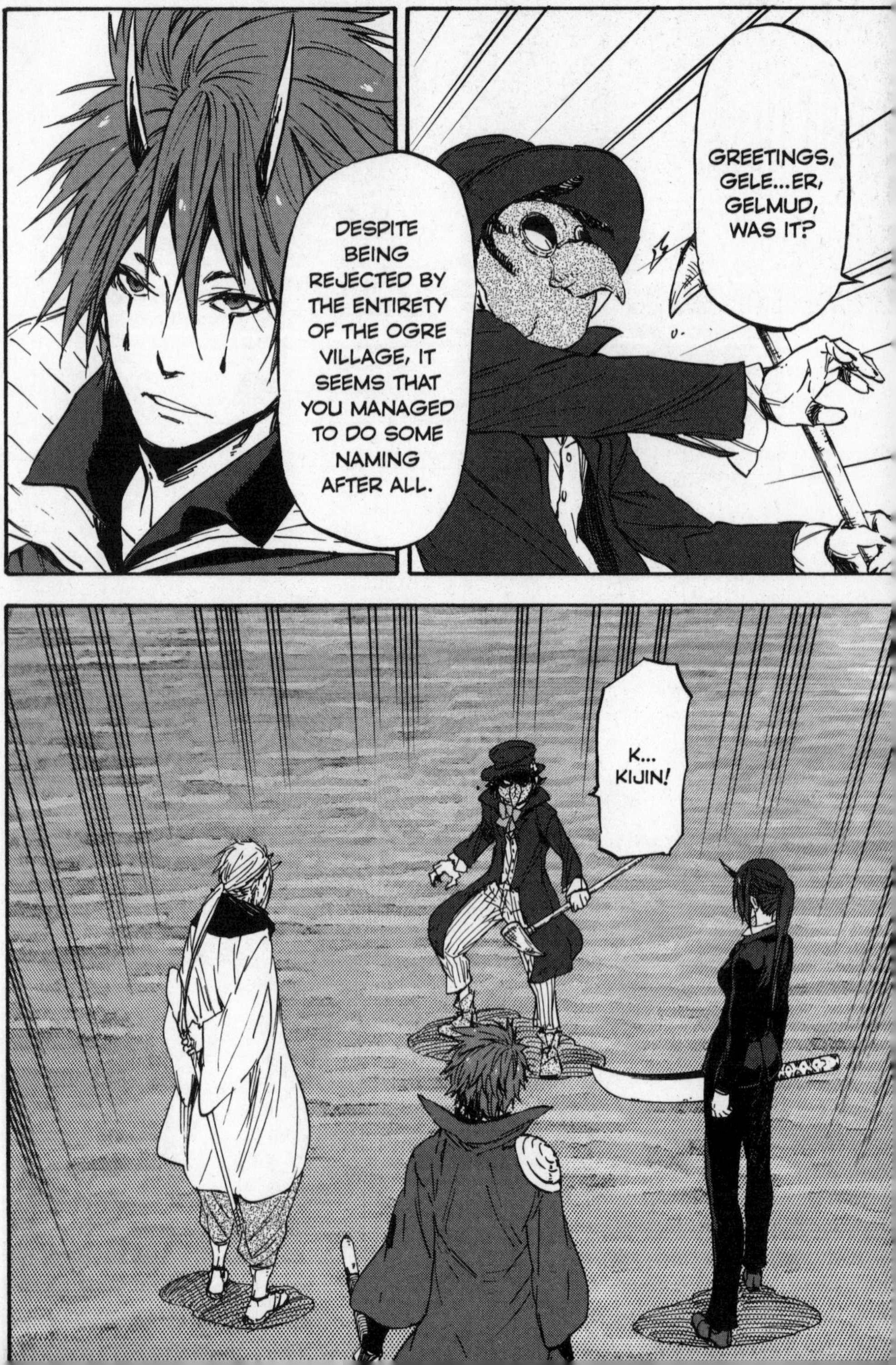
GREETINGS, GELE...ER, GELMUD, WAS IT?
DESPITE BEING REJECTED BY THE ENTIRETY OF THE OGRE VILLAGE, IT SEEMS THAT YOU MANAGED TO DO SOME NAMING AFTER ALL.
K... KIJIN!

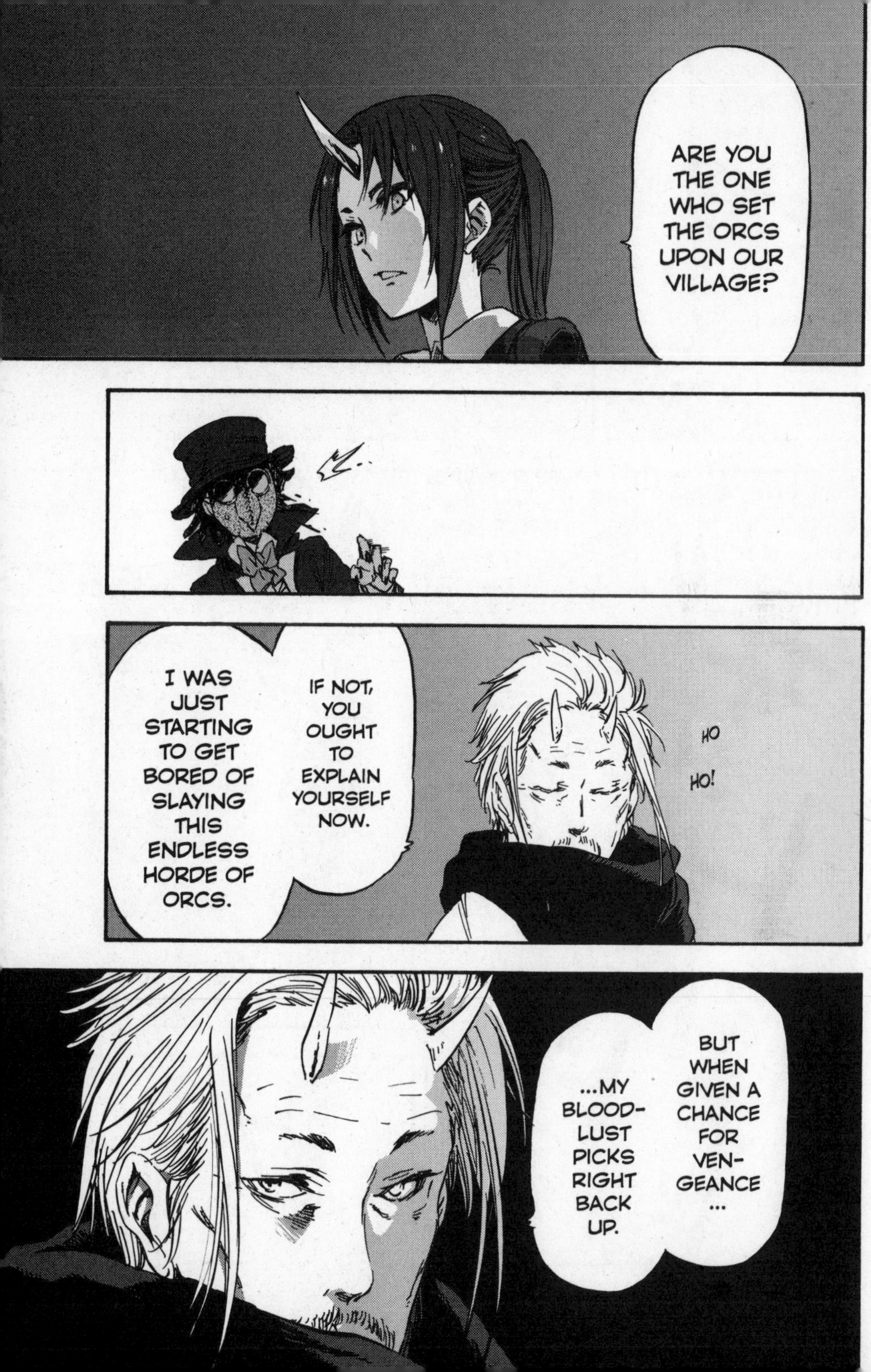
ARE YOU THE ONE WHO SET THE ORCS UPON OUR VILLAGE?
HO HO!
IF NOT, YOU OUGHT TO EXPLAIN YOURSELF NOW.
I WAS JUST STARTING TO GET BORED OF SLAYING THIS ENDLESS HORDE OF ORCS.
BUT WHEN GIVEN A CHANCE FOR VEN-GEANCE ...
...MY BLOOD-LUST PICKS RIGHT BACK UP.

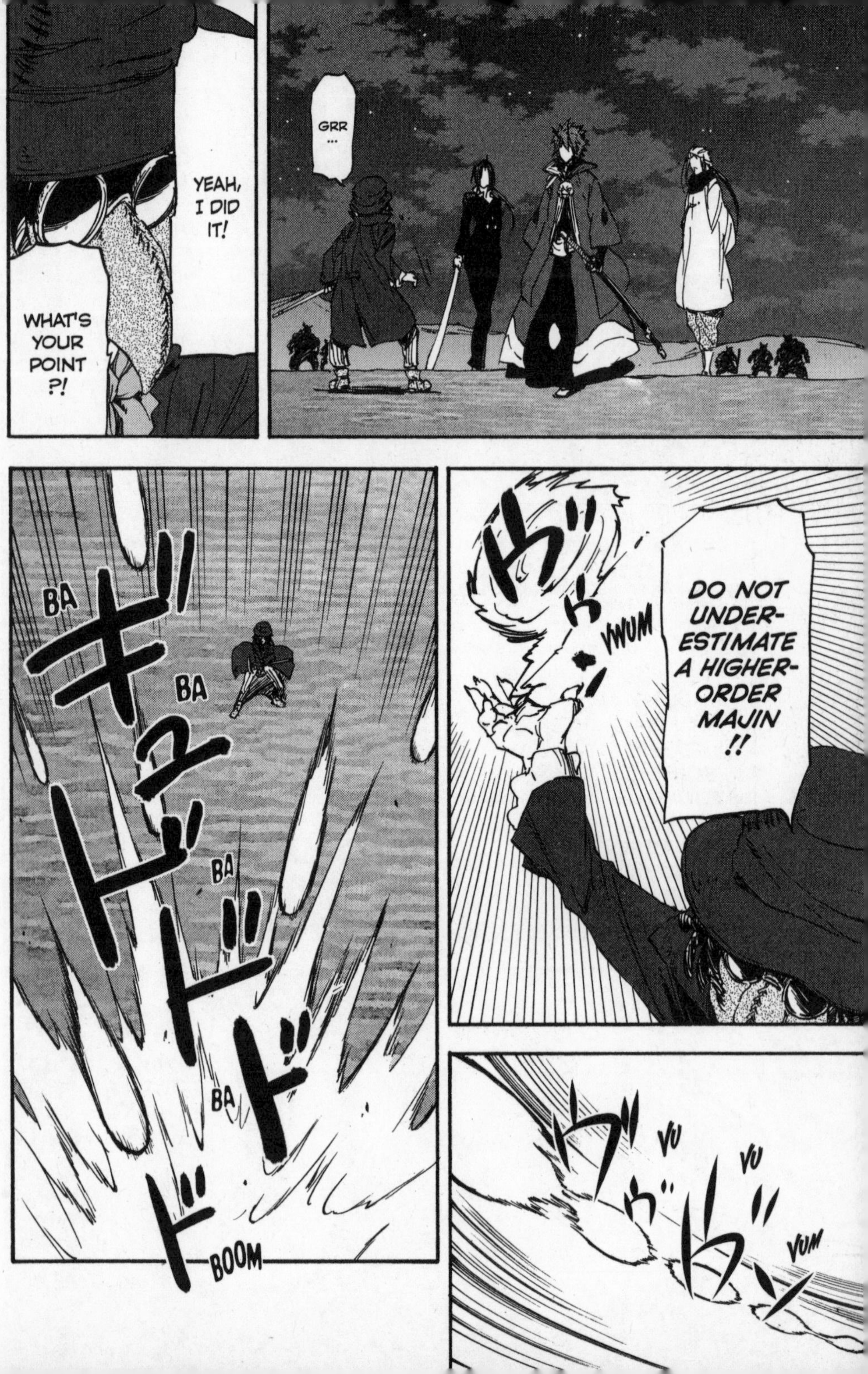
GRR ...
YEAH, I DID IT!
WHAT'S YOUR POINT ?!
VWUM
DO NOT UNDER-ESTIMATE A HIGHER-ORDER MAJIN !!
VU
VU
VUM
BA
BA
BA
BA
BOOM

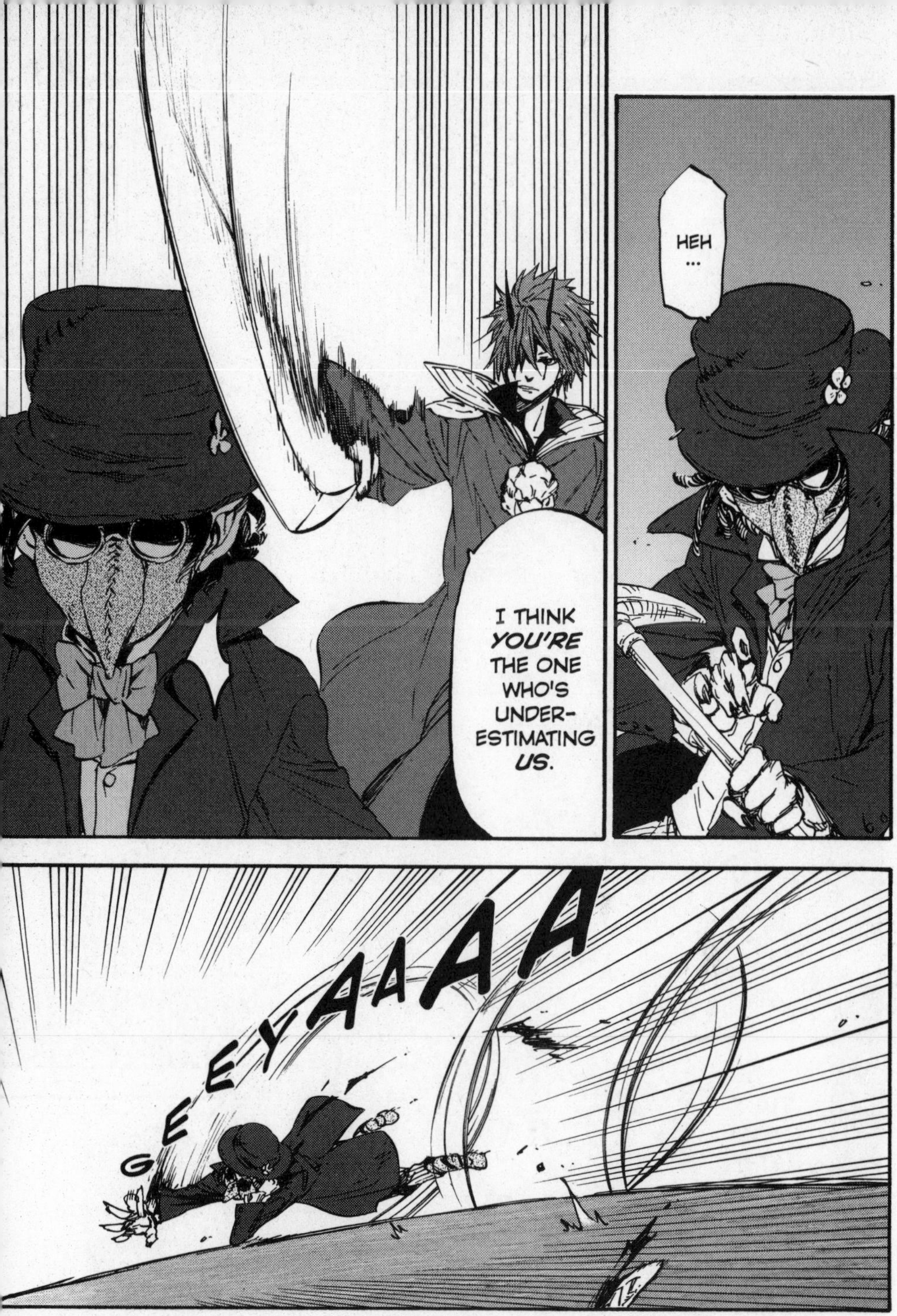
HEH ...
I THINK *YOU'RE* THE ONE WHO'S UNDER-ESTIMATING *US*.
GEEYAAAAA

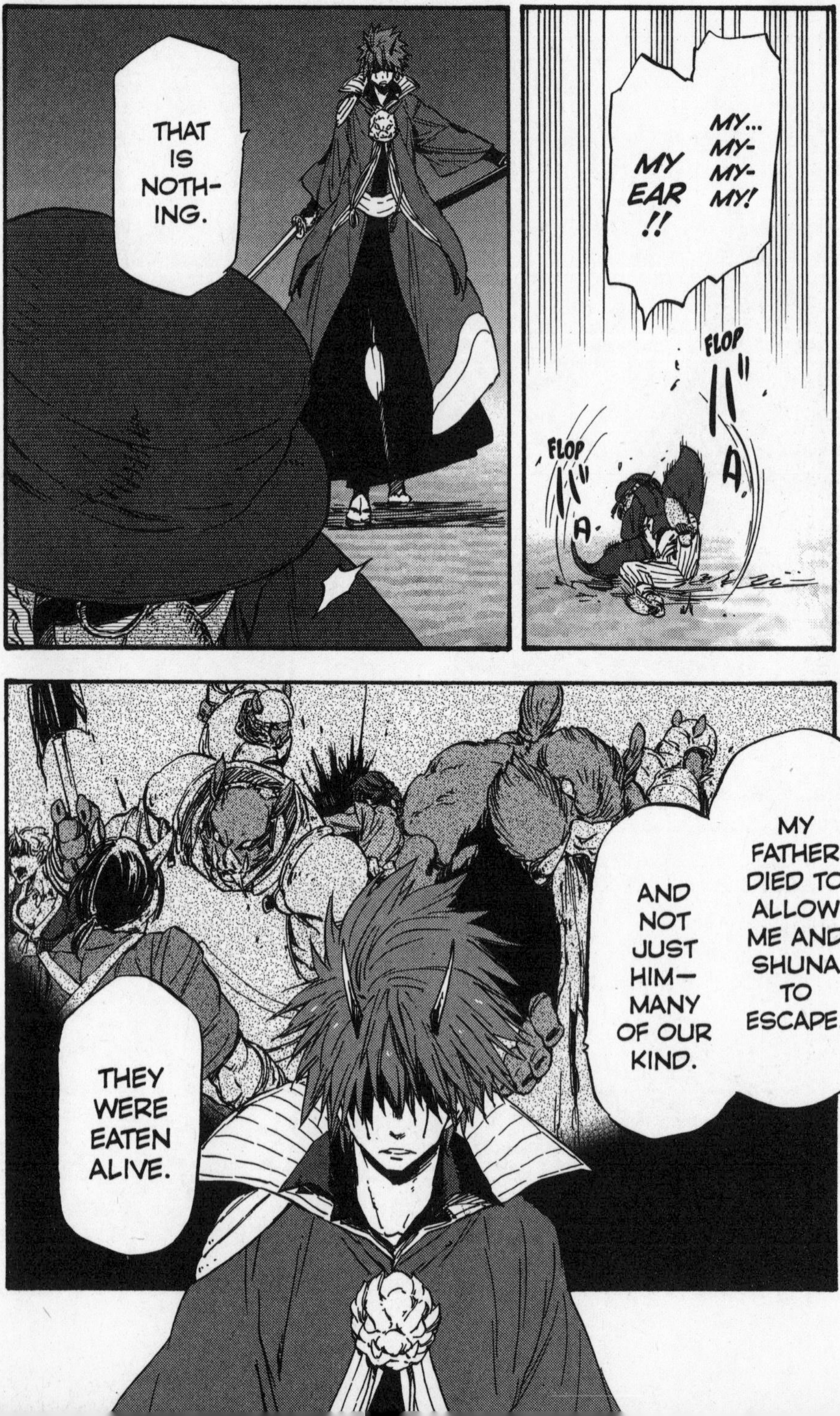
MY... MY-MY-MY!
MY EAR!!
FLOP
A
FLOP
A
THAT IS NOTH-ING.
MY FATHER DIED TO ALLOW ME AND SHUNA TO ESCAPE.
AND NOT JUST HIM—MANY OF OUR KIND.
THEY WERE EATEN ALIVE.

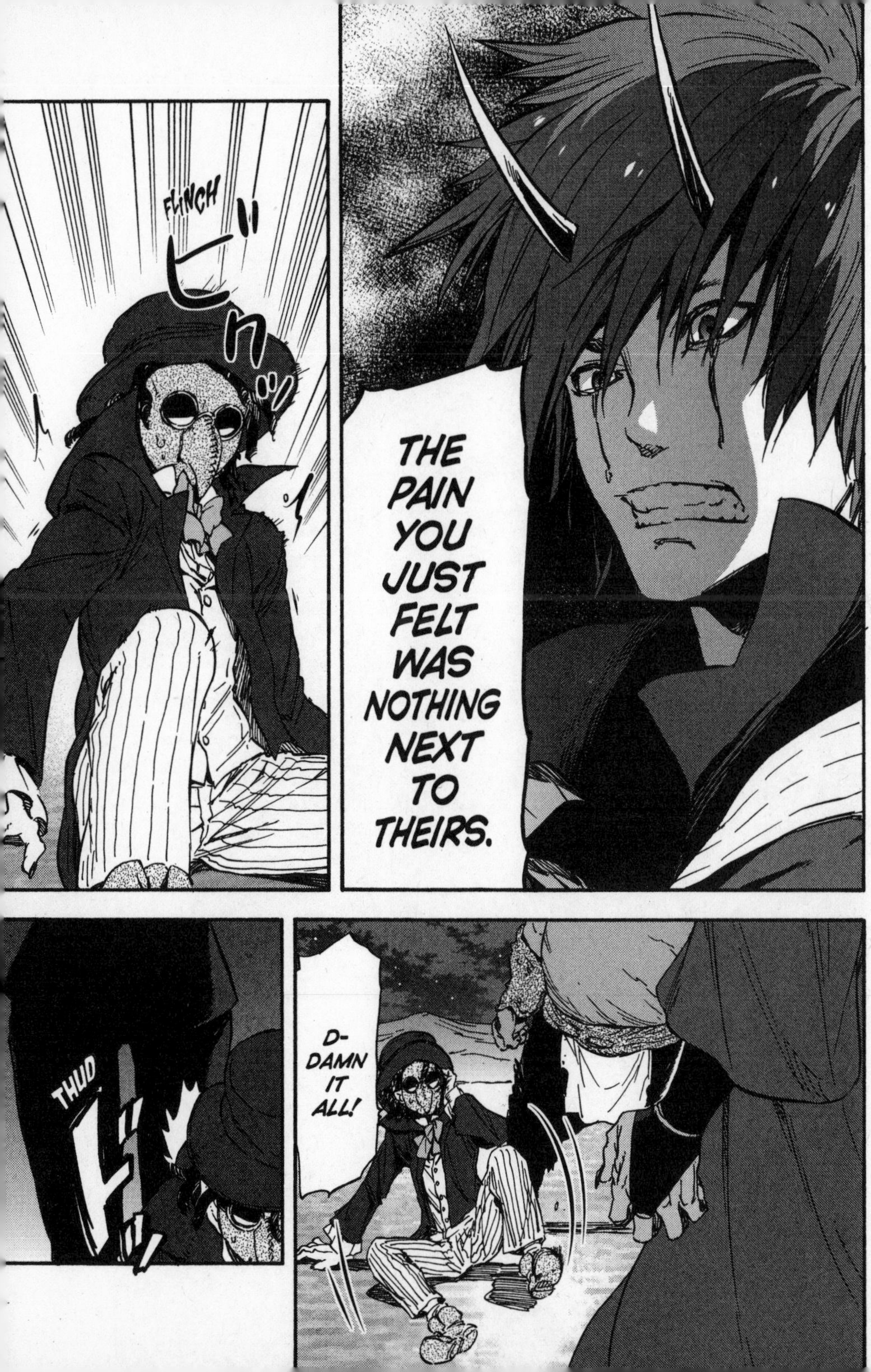
THE PAIN YOU JUST FELT WAS NOTHING NEXT TO THEIRS.
FLINCH
D-DAMN IT ALL!
THUD

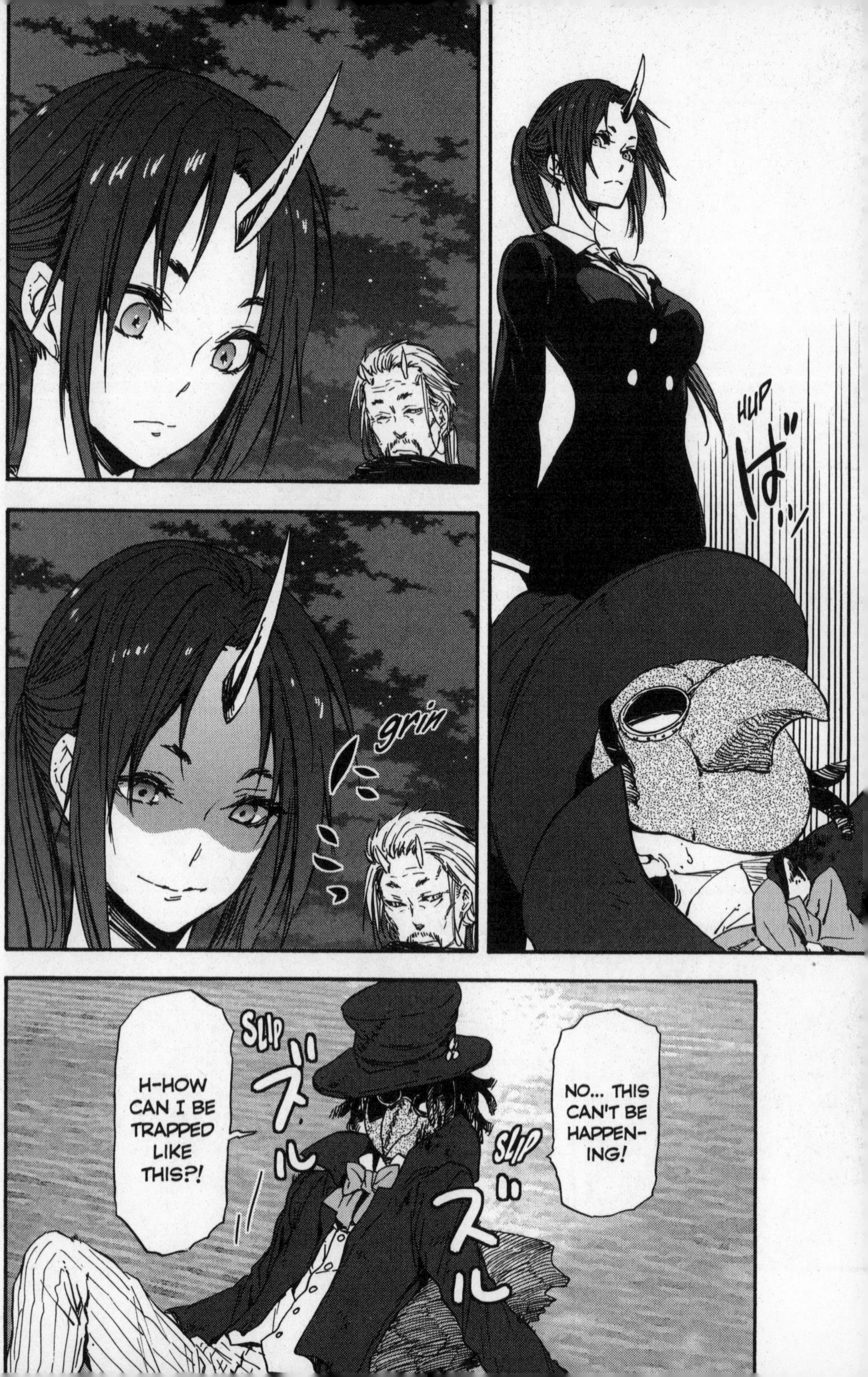
HUP
ばっ
grin
にこっ
NO... THIS CAN'T BE HAPPENING!
SLIP
ズル
SLIP
ズル
H-HOW CAN I BE TRAPPED LIKE THIS?!

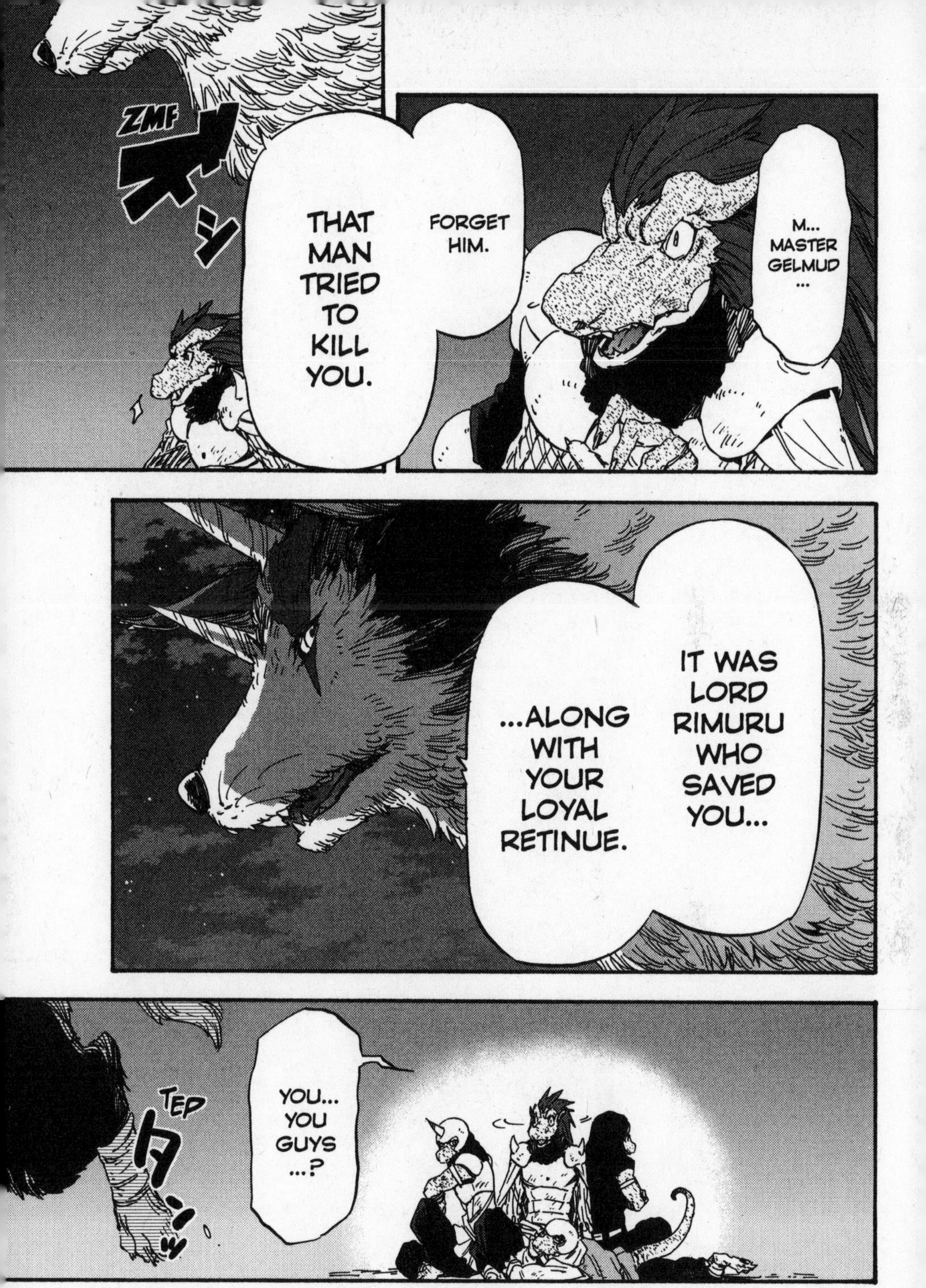
M... MASTER GELMUD ...
FORGET HIM.
THAT MAN TRIED TO KILL YOU.
ZMF
IT WAS LORD RIMURU WHO SAVED YOU...
...ALONG WITH YOUR LOYAL RETINUE.
YOU... YOU GUYS ...?
TEP

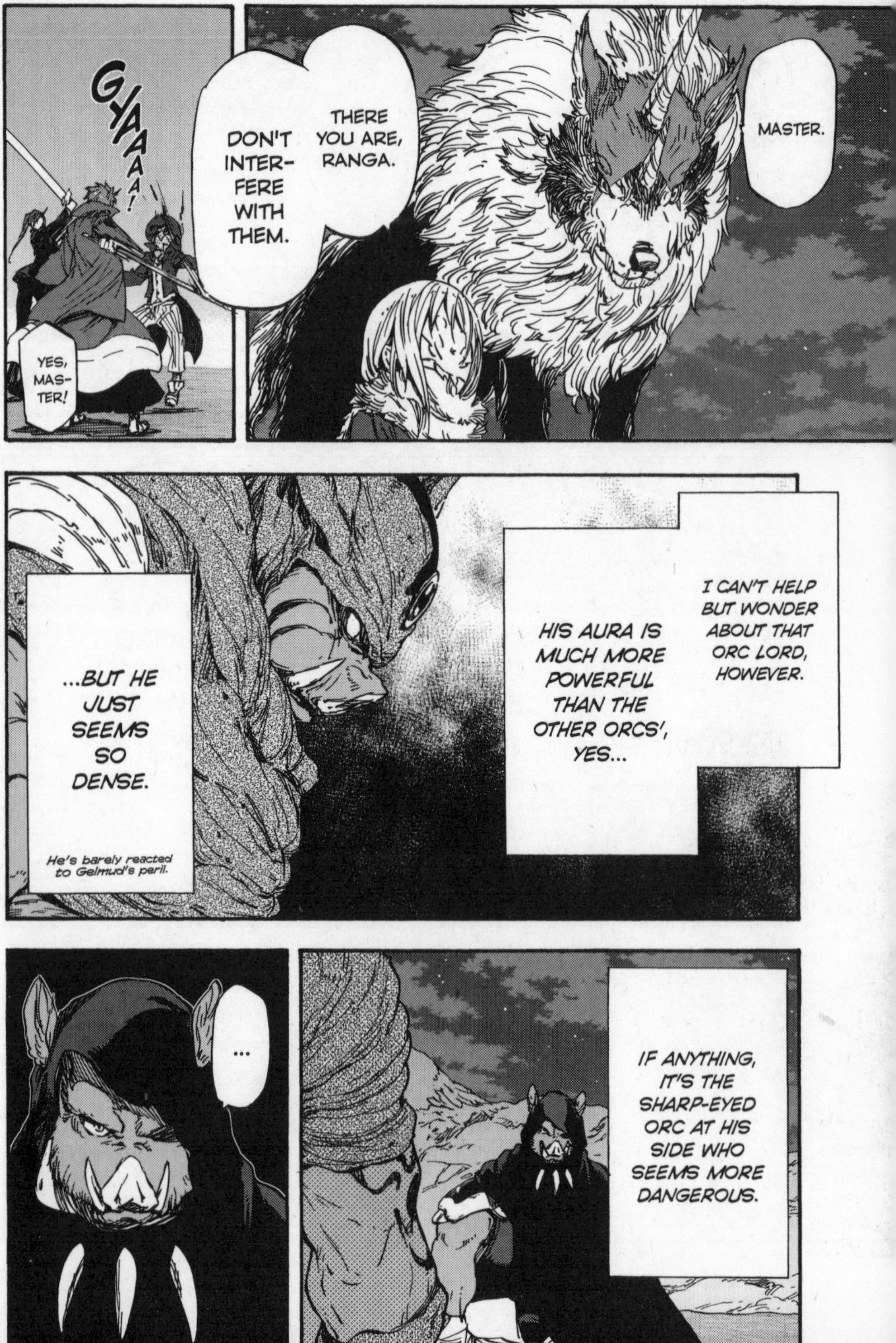
MASTER.
THERE YOU ARE, RANGA.
DON'T INTER-FERE WITH THEM.
GYAAAAA!
YES, MAS-TER!
I CAN'T HELP BUT WONDER ABOUT THAT ORC LORD, HOWEVER.
HIS AURA IS MUCH MORE POWERFUL THAN THE OTHER ORCS', YES...
...BUT HE JUST SEEMS SO DENSE.
He's barely reacted to Gelmud's peril.
IF ANYTHING, IT'S THE SHARP-EYED ORC AT HIS SIDE WHO SEEMS MORE DANGEROUS.
...

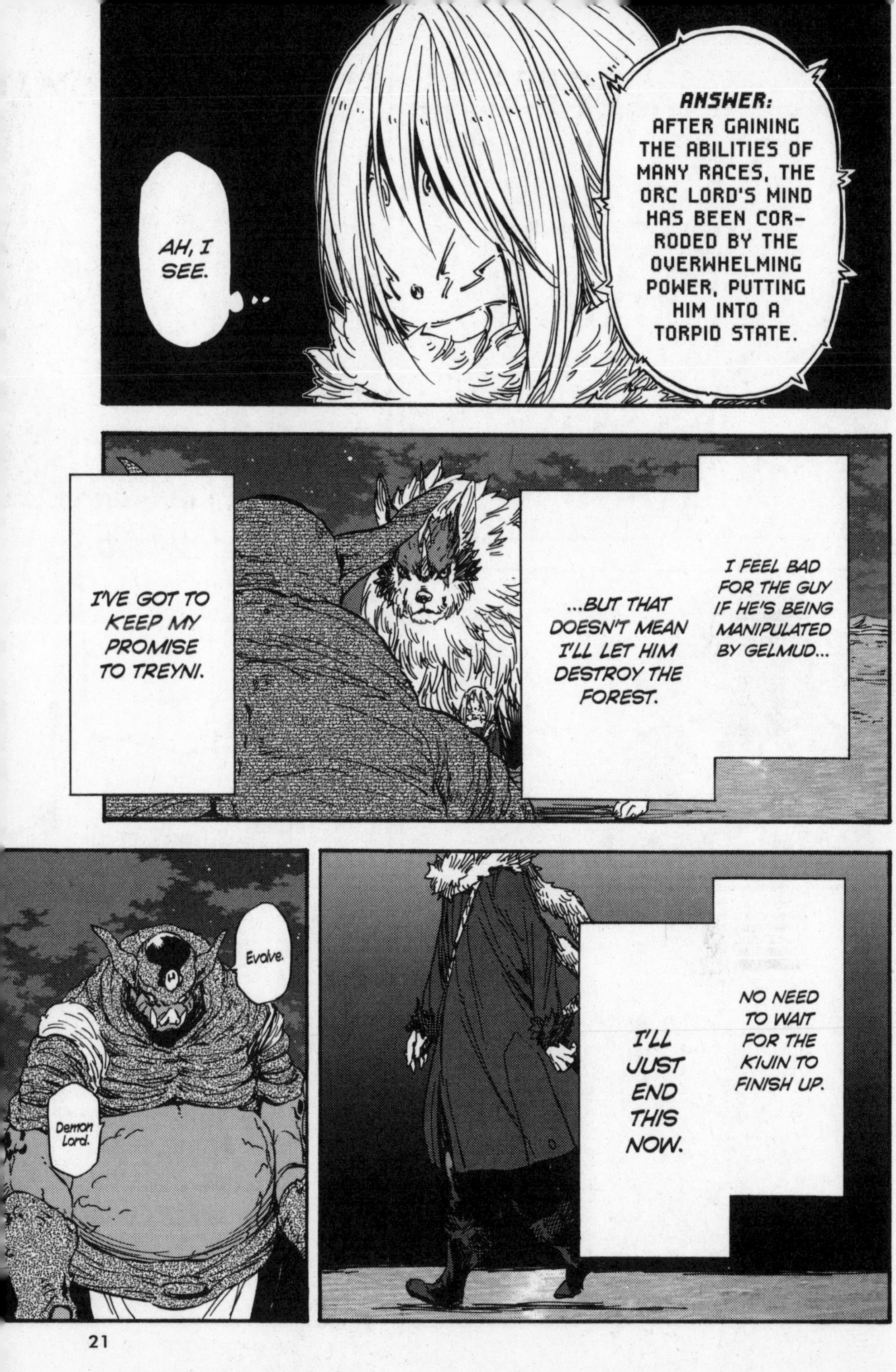
ANSWER: AFTER GAINING THE ABILITIES OF MANY RACES, THE ORC LORD'S MIND HAS BEEN COR-RODED BY THE OVERWHELMING POWER, PUTTING HIM INTO A TORPID STATE.
AH, I SEE. ...
I FEEL BAD FOR THE GUY IF HE'S BEING MANIPULATED BY GELMUD...
...BUT THAT DOESN'T MEAN I'LL LET HIM DESTROY THE FOREST.
I'VE GOT TO KEEP MY PROMISE TO TREYNI.
NO NEED TO WAIT FOR THE KIJIN TO FINISH UP.
I'LL JUST END THIS NOW.
Evolve.
Demon Lord.

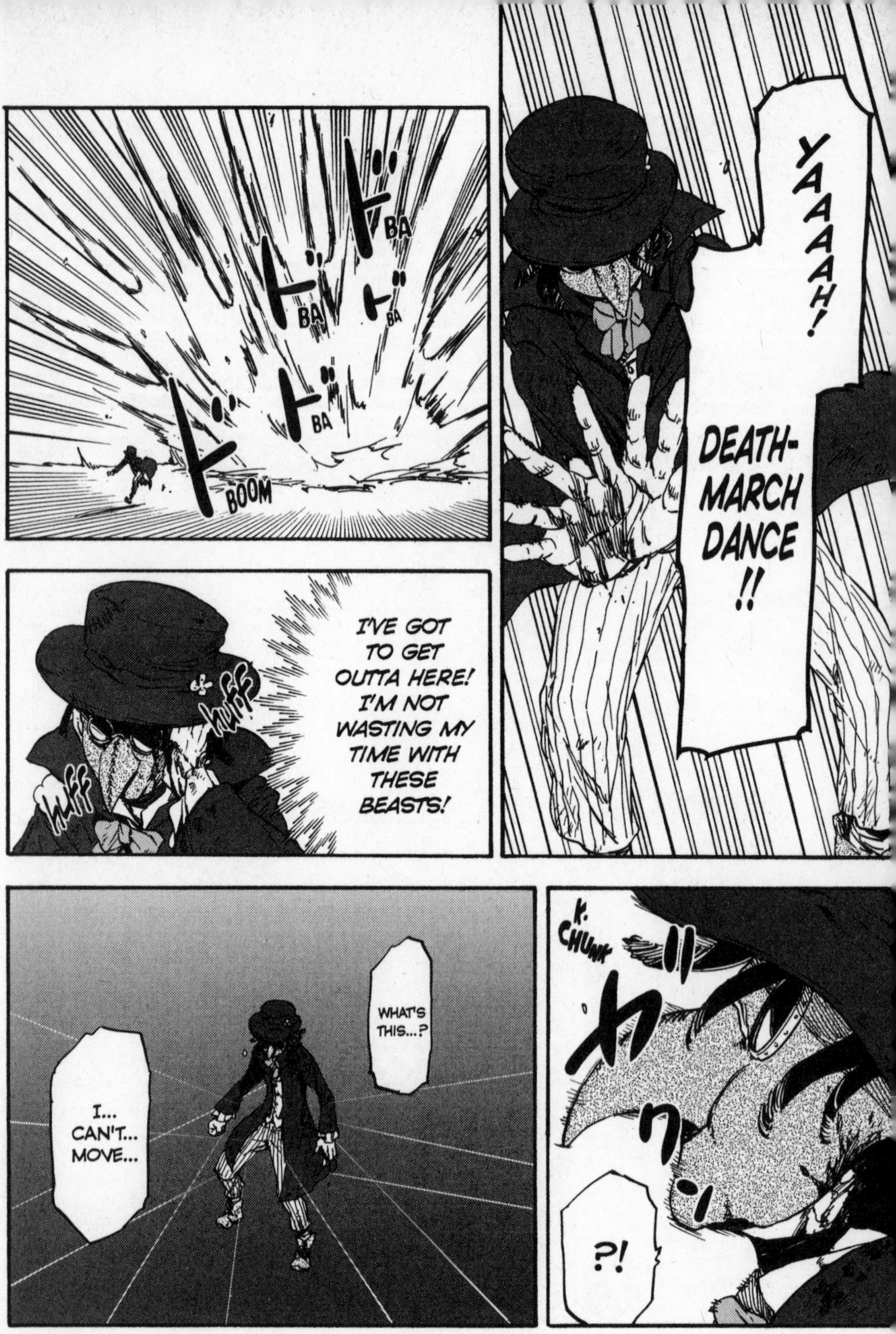
YAAAAAH!
DEATH-MARCH DANCE!!
BA
BA
BA
BA
BOOM
huff
huff
I'VE GOT TO GET OUTTA HERE! I'M NOT WASTING MY TIME WITH THESE BEASTS!
K-CHUNK
?!
WHAT'S THIS...?
I... CAN'T... MOVE...

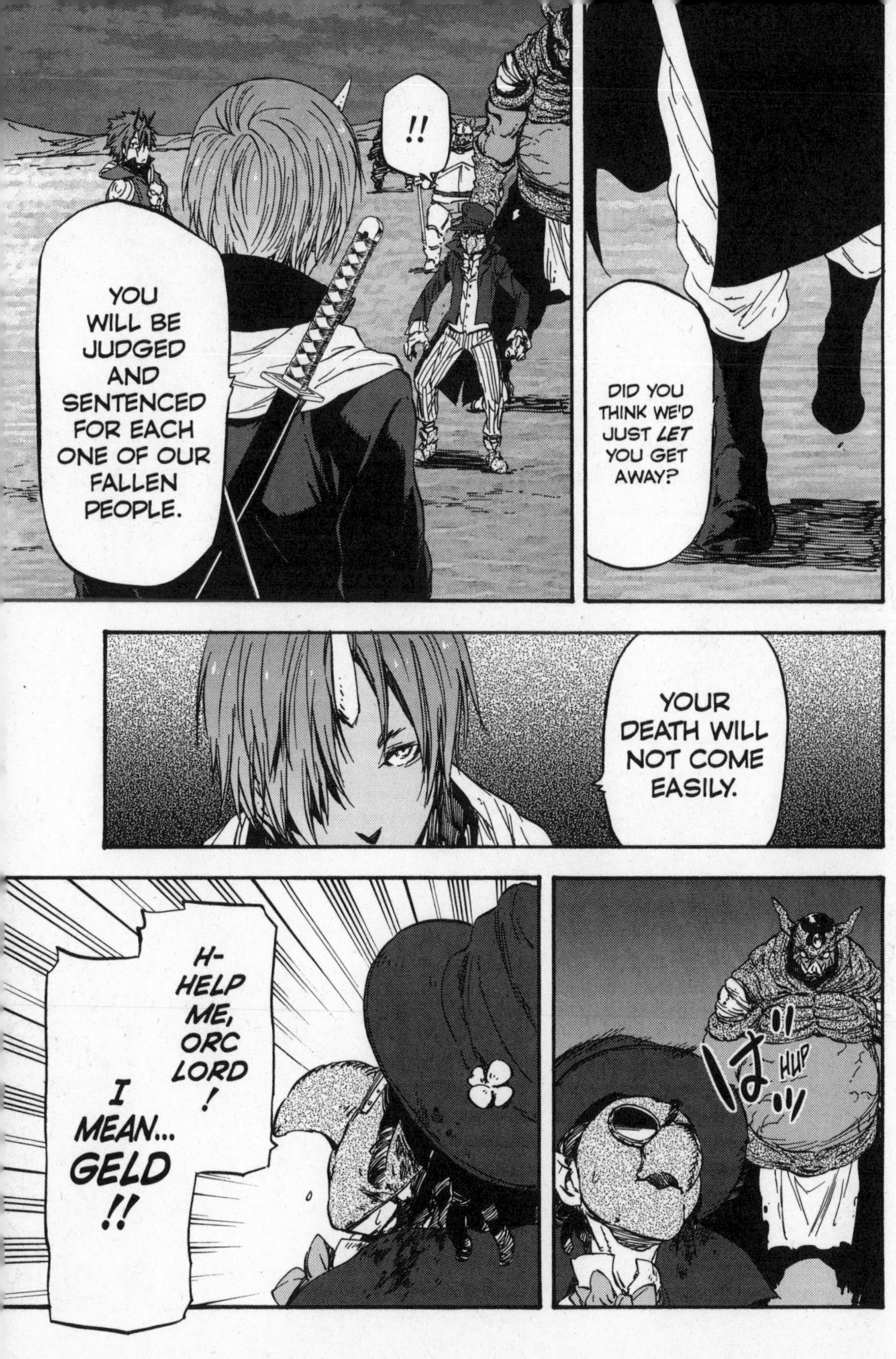
DID YOU THINK WE'D JUST *LET* YOU GET AWAY?
!!
YOU WILL BE JUDGED AND SENTENCED FOR EACH ONE OF OUR FALLEN PEOPLE.
YOUR DEATH WILL NOT COME EASILY.
はッ
HUP
H-HELP ME, ORC LORD!
I MEAN... GELD!!

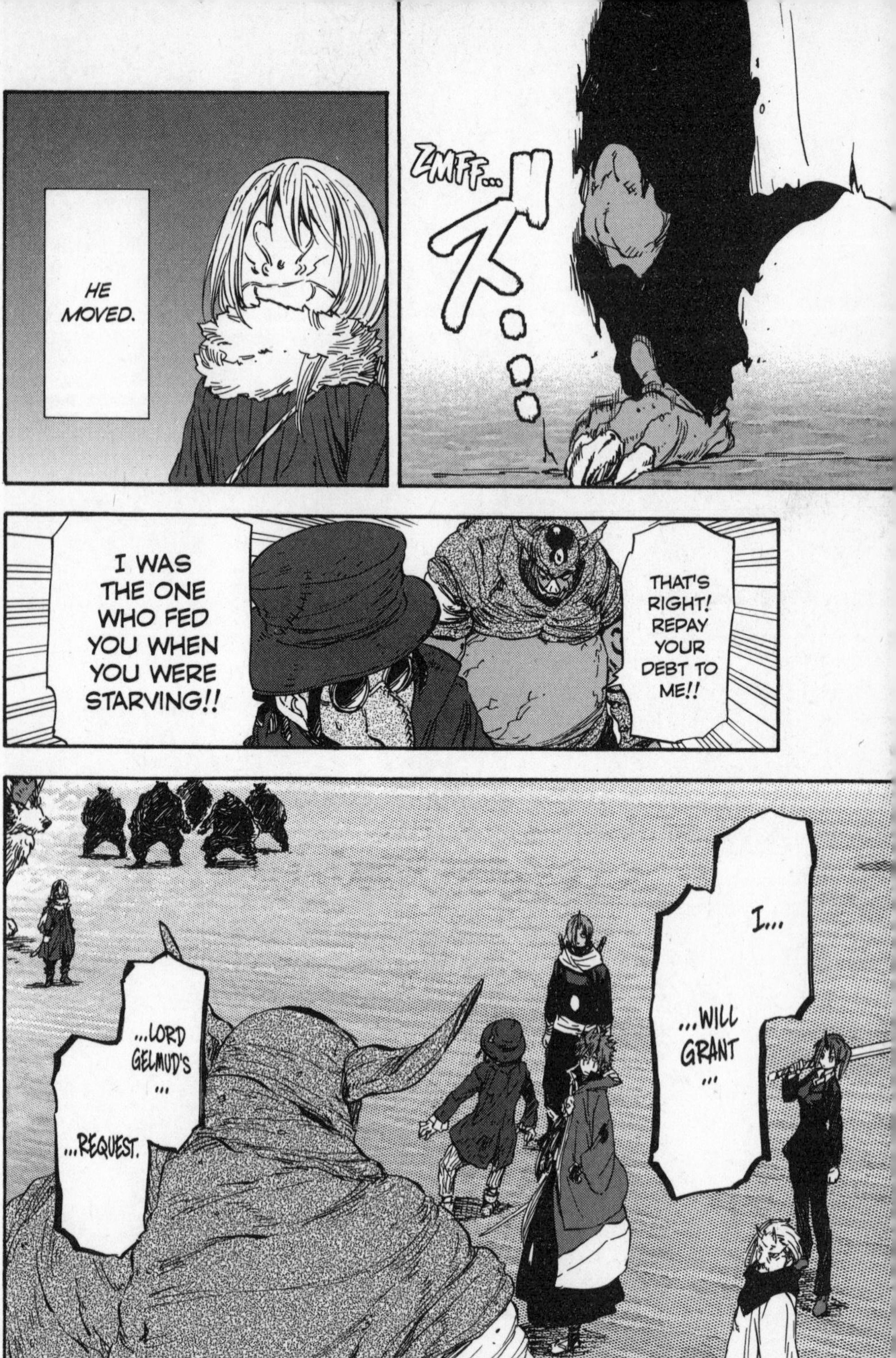
ZMFF...
HE MOVED.
THAT'S RIGHT! REPAY YOUR DEBT TO ME!!
I WAS THE ONE WHO FED YOU WHEN YOU WERE STARVING!!
I...
...WILL GRANT ...
...LORD GELMUD'S ...
...REQUEST.

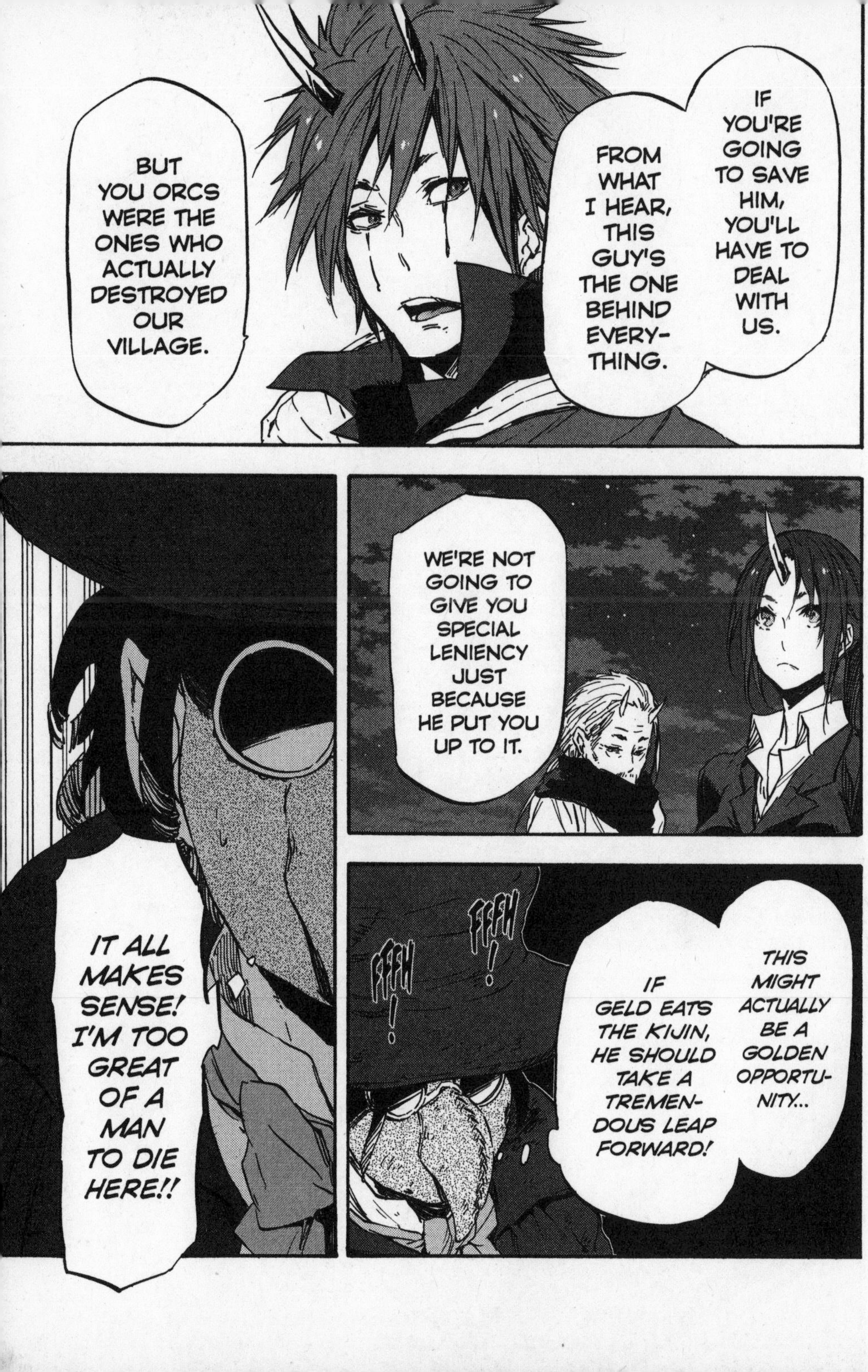
IF YOU'RE GOING TO SAVE HIM, YOU'LL HAVE TO DEAL WITH US.
FROM WHAT I HEAR, THIS GUY'S THE ONE BEHIND EVERY-THING.
BUT YOU ORCS WERE THE ONES WHO ACTUALLY DESTROYED OUR VILLAGE.
WE'RE NOT GOING TO GIVE YOU SPECIAL LENIENCY JUST BECAUSE HE PUT YOU UP TO IT.
FFFH!
FFFH!
THIS MIGHT ACTUALLY BE A GOLDEN OPPORTU-NITY...
IF GELD EATS THE KIJIN, HE SHOULD TAKE A TREMEN-DOUS LEAP FORWARD!
IT ALL MAKES SENSE! I'M TOO GREAT OF A MAN TO DIE HERE!!

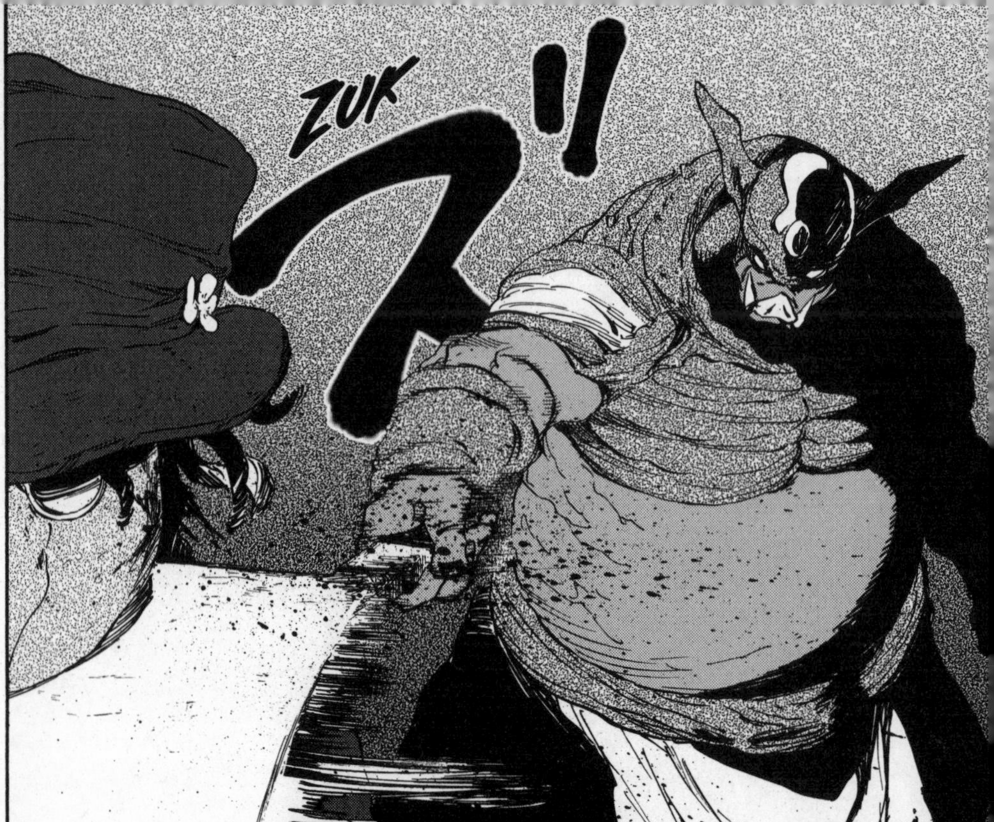
ZUK
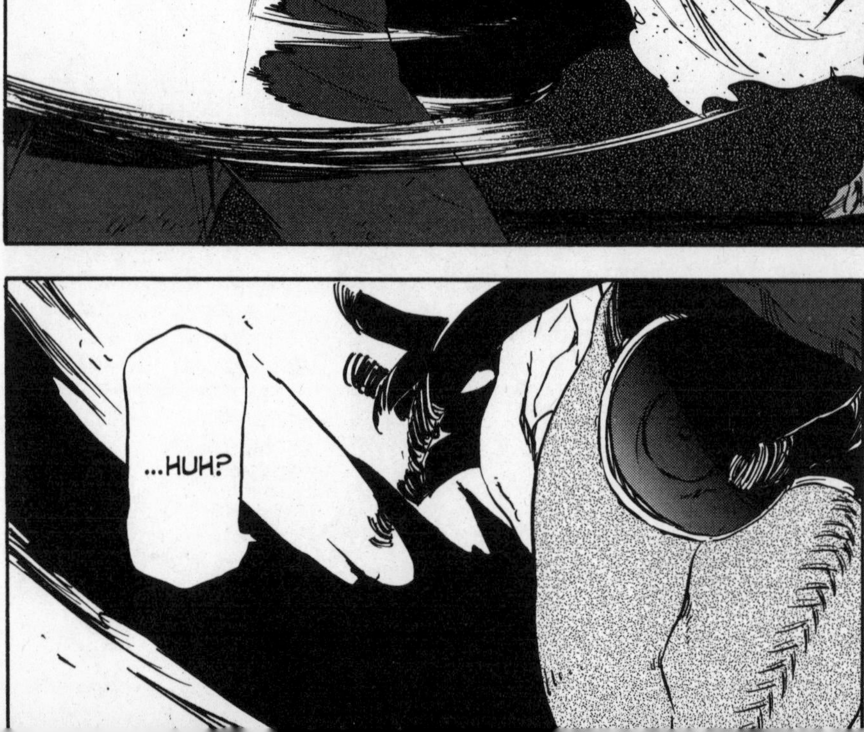
...HUH?

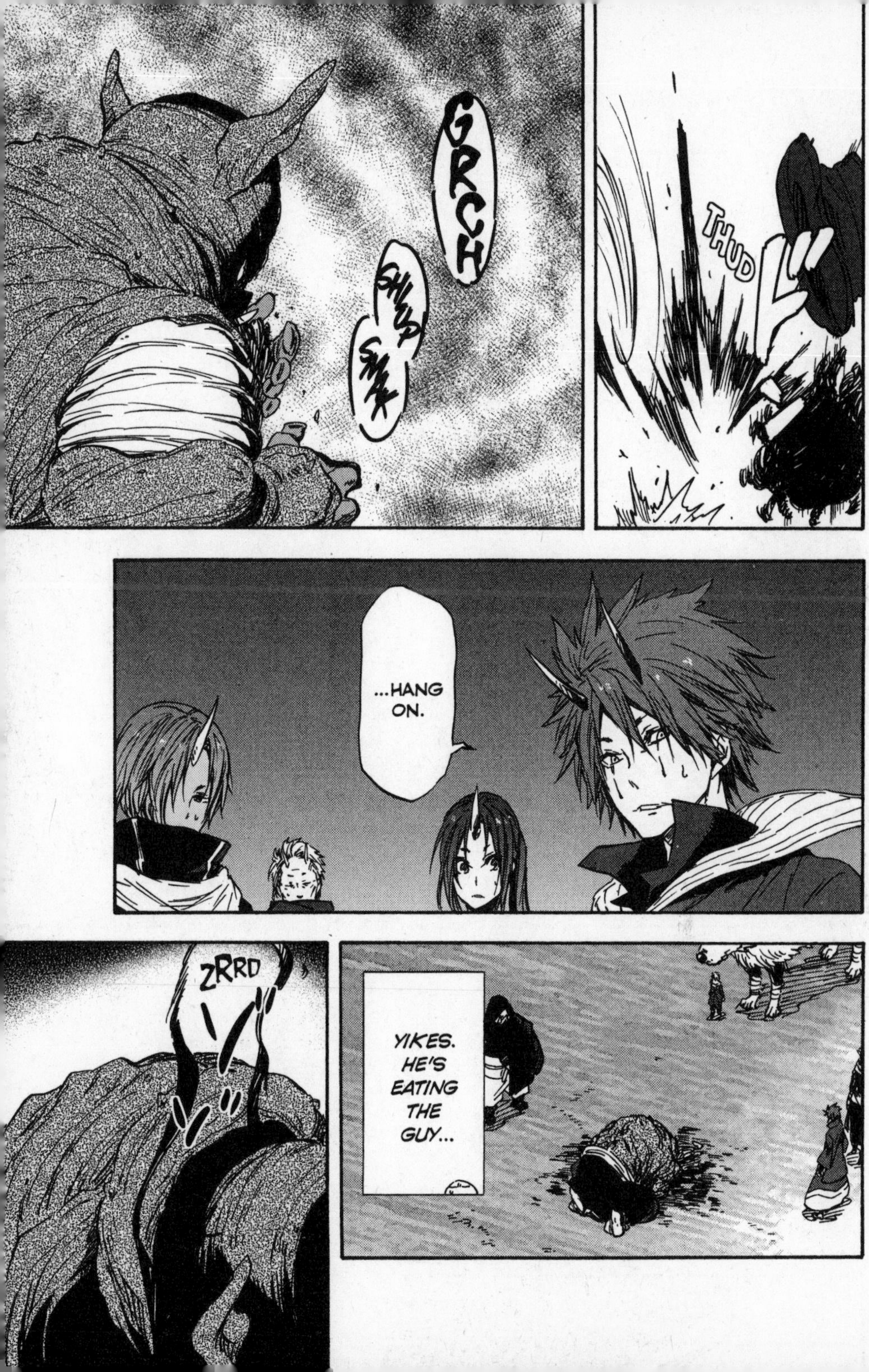
THUD
GRCH
SHLURP
SNAK
...HANG ON.
YIKES. HE'S EATING THE GUY...
ZRRD

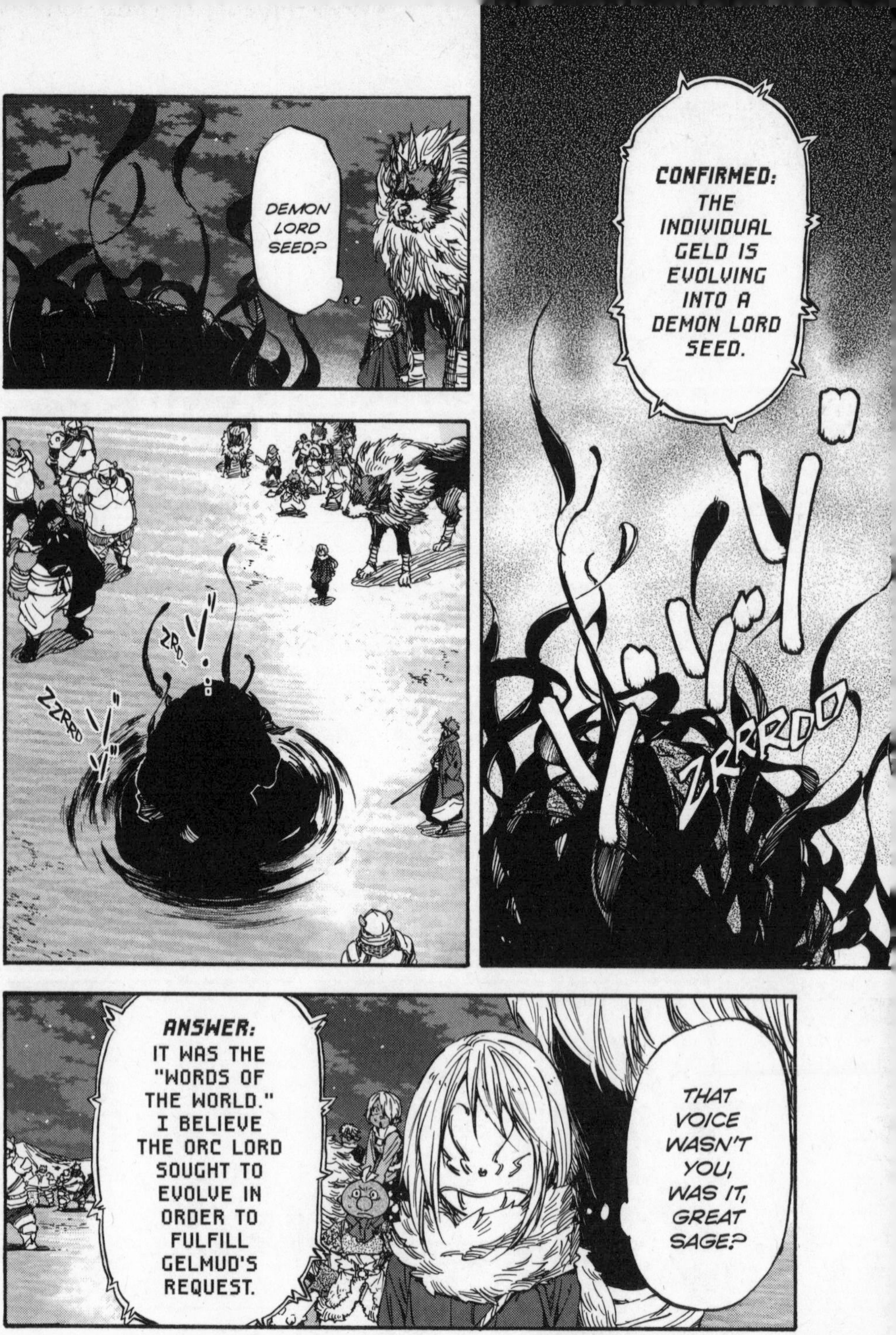
CONFIRMED: THE INDIVIDUAL GELD IS EVOLVING INTO A DEMON LORD SEED.
ZRRRDO
DEMON LORD SEED?
ZRD...
ZZRRD
THAT VOICE WASN'T YOU, WAS IT, GREAT SAGE?
ANSWER: IT WAS THE "WORDS OF THE WORLD." I BELIEVE THE ORC LORD SOUGHT TO EVOLVE IN ORDER TO FULFILL GELMUD'S REQUEST.

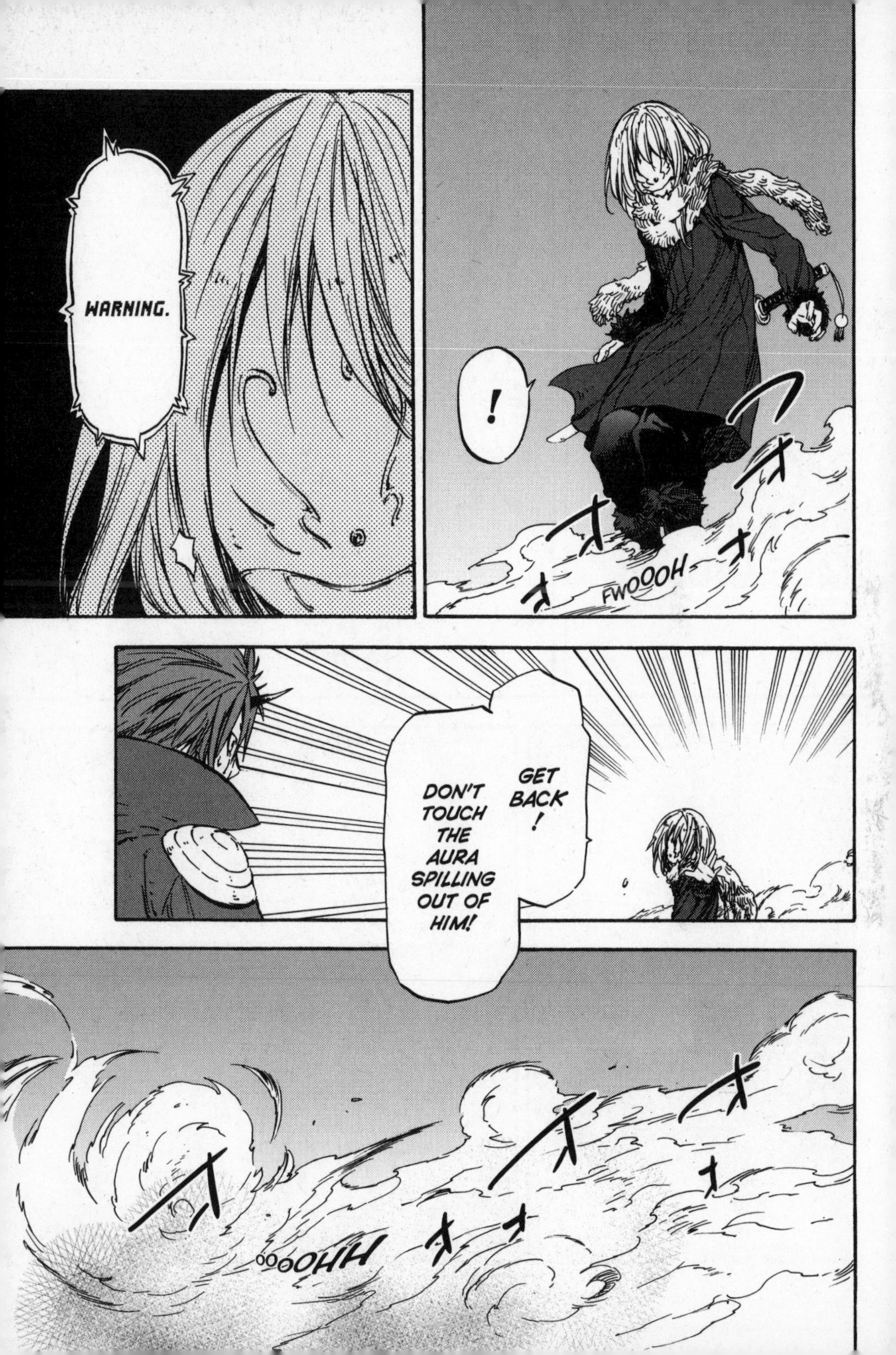
!
FWOOOH
WARNING.
GET BACK!
DON'T TOUCH THE AURA SPILLING OUT OF HIM!

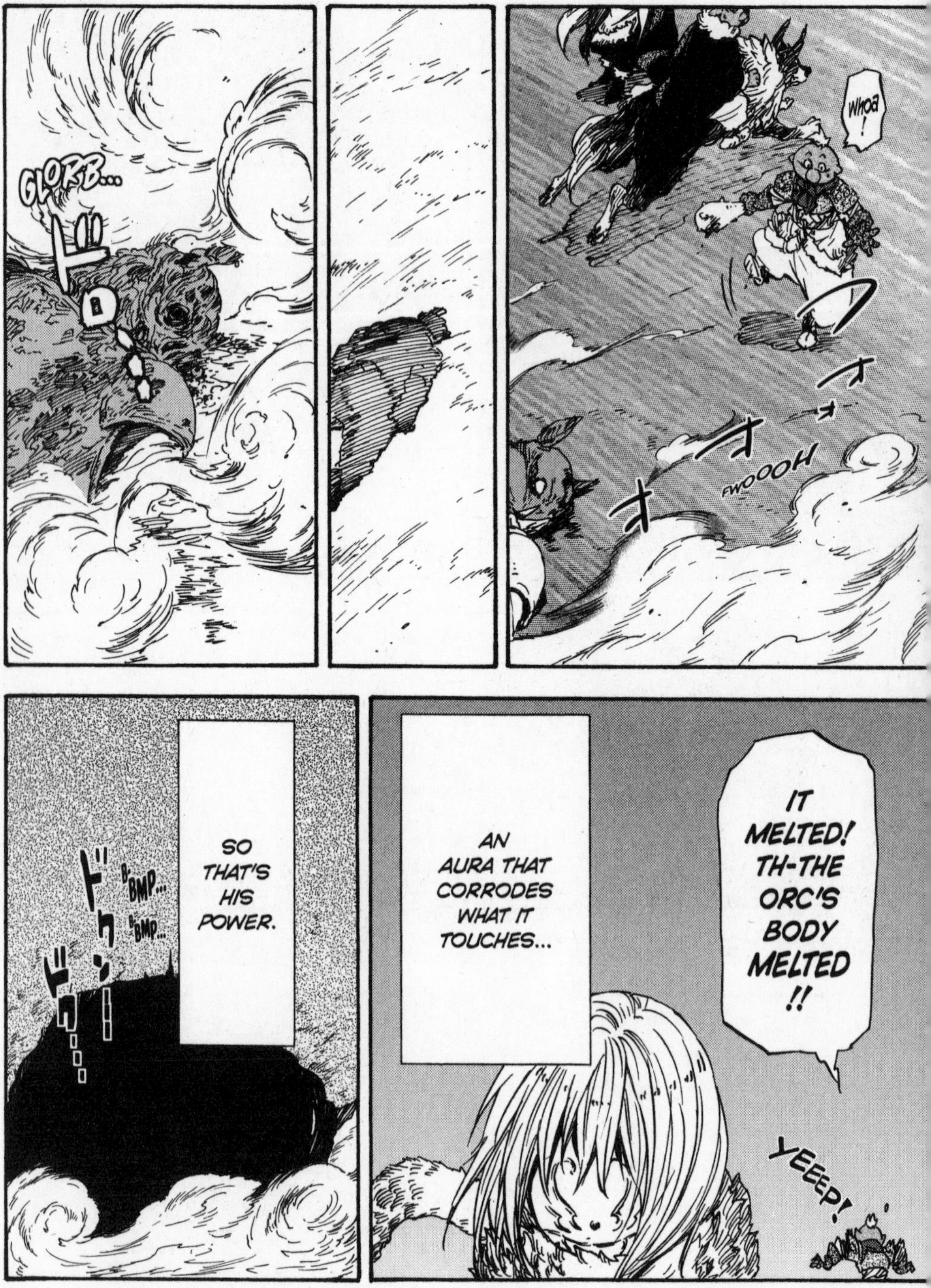
Whoa!
FWOOOH
GLORB...
IT MELTED! TH-THE ORC'S BODY MELTED!!
AN AURA THAT CORRODES WHAT IT TOUCHES...
YEEEP!
SO THAT'S HIS POWER.
B-BMP...
B-BMP...

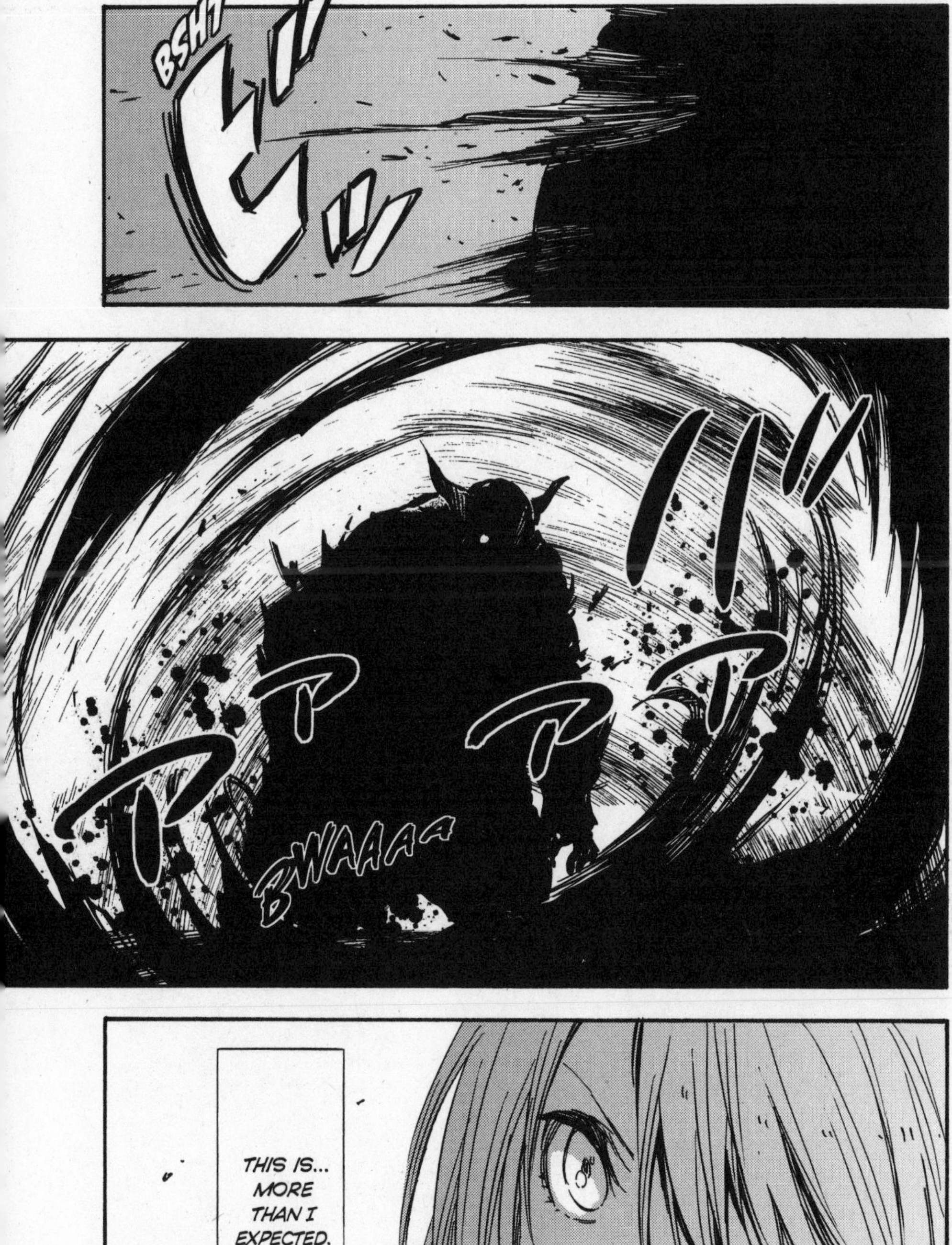
BSHT
BWAAAA
THIS IS... MORE THAN I EXPECTED.

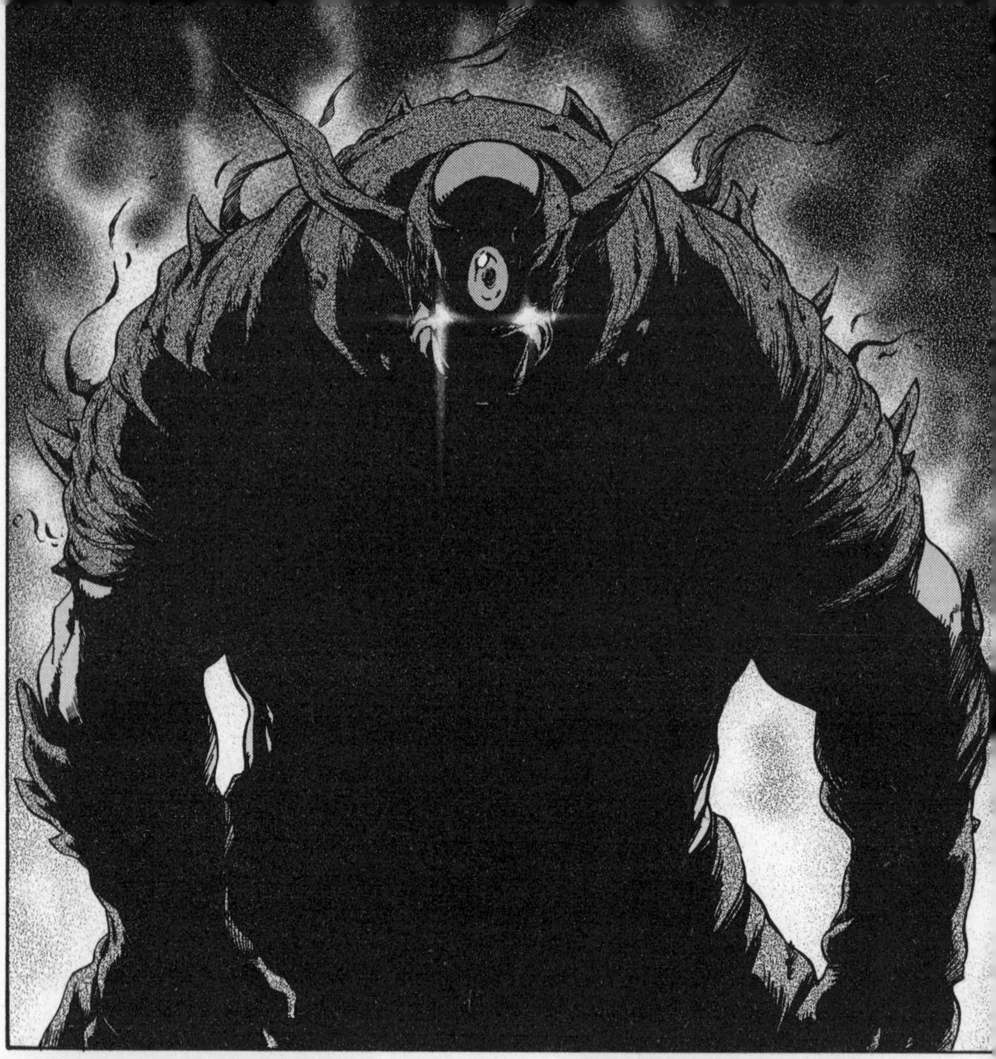

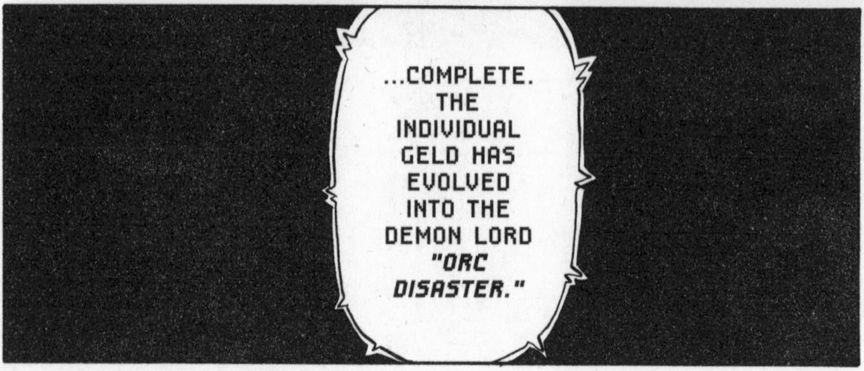
...COMPLETE. THE INDIVIDUAL GELD HAS EVOLVED INTO THE DEMON LORD *"ORC DISASTER."*

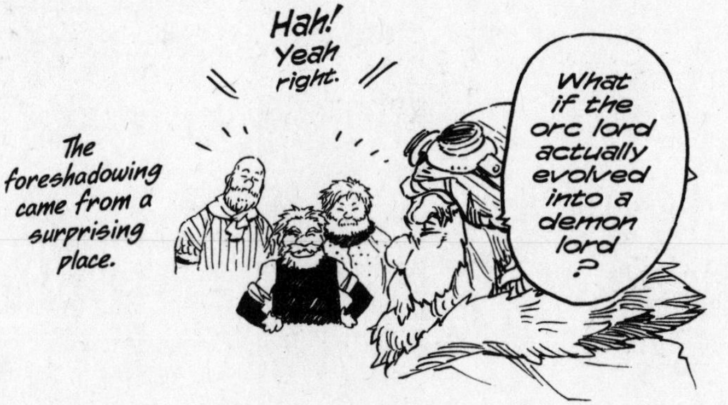
What if the orc lord actually evolved into a demon lord?
Hah! Yeah right.
The foreshadowing came from a surprising place.

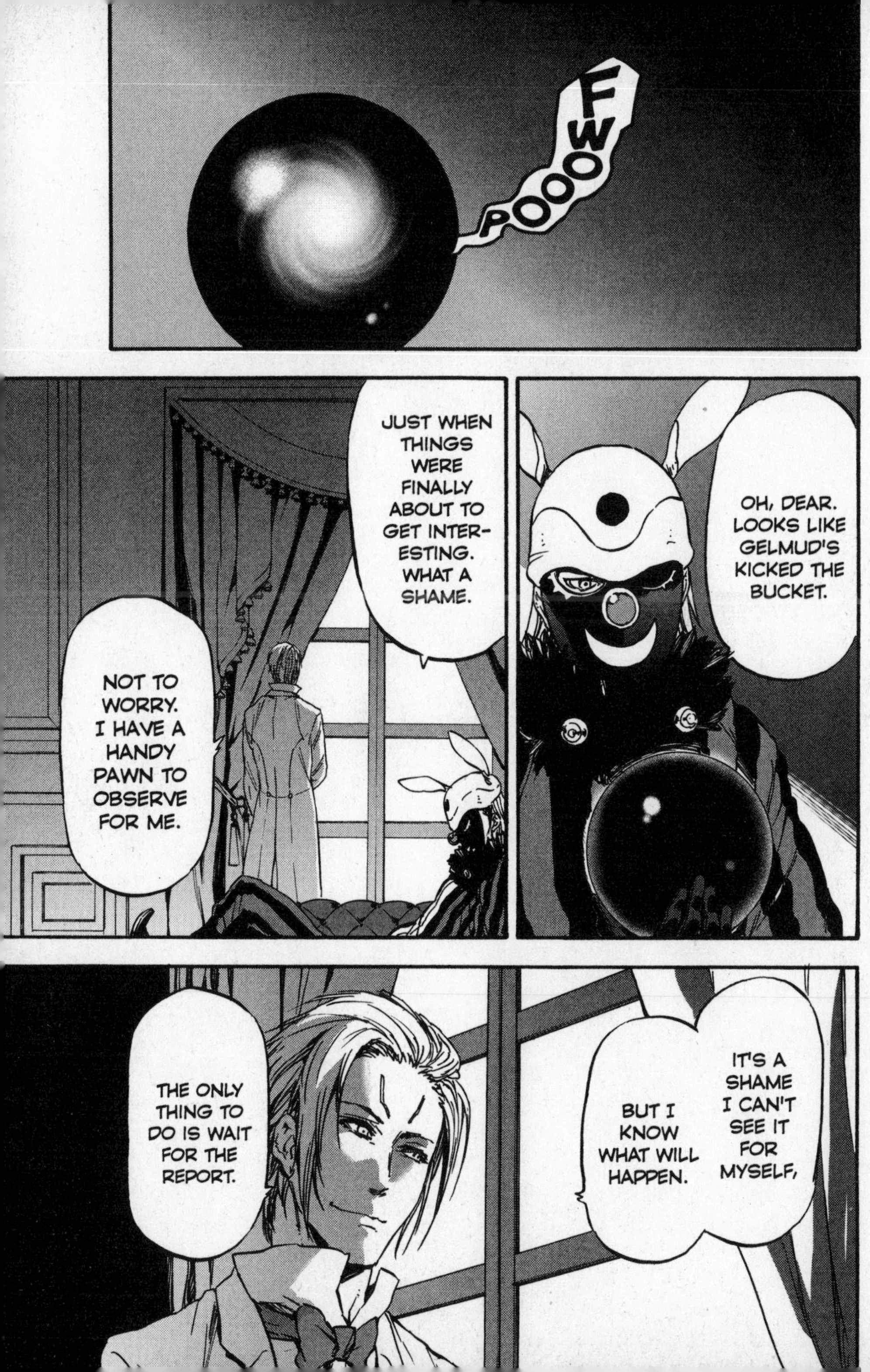
FWOOOP
OH, DEAR. LOOKS LIKE GELMUD'S KICKED THE BUCKET.
JUST WHEN THINGS WERE FINALLY ABOUT TO GET INTER-ESTING. WHAT A SHAME.
NOT TO WORRY. I HAVE A HANDY PAWN TO OBSERVE FOR ME.
IT'S A SHAME I CAN'T SEE IT FOR MYSELF,
BUT I KNOW WHAT WILL HAPPEN.
THE ONLY THING TO DO IS WAIT FOR THE REPORT.

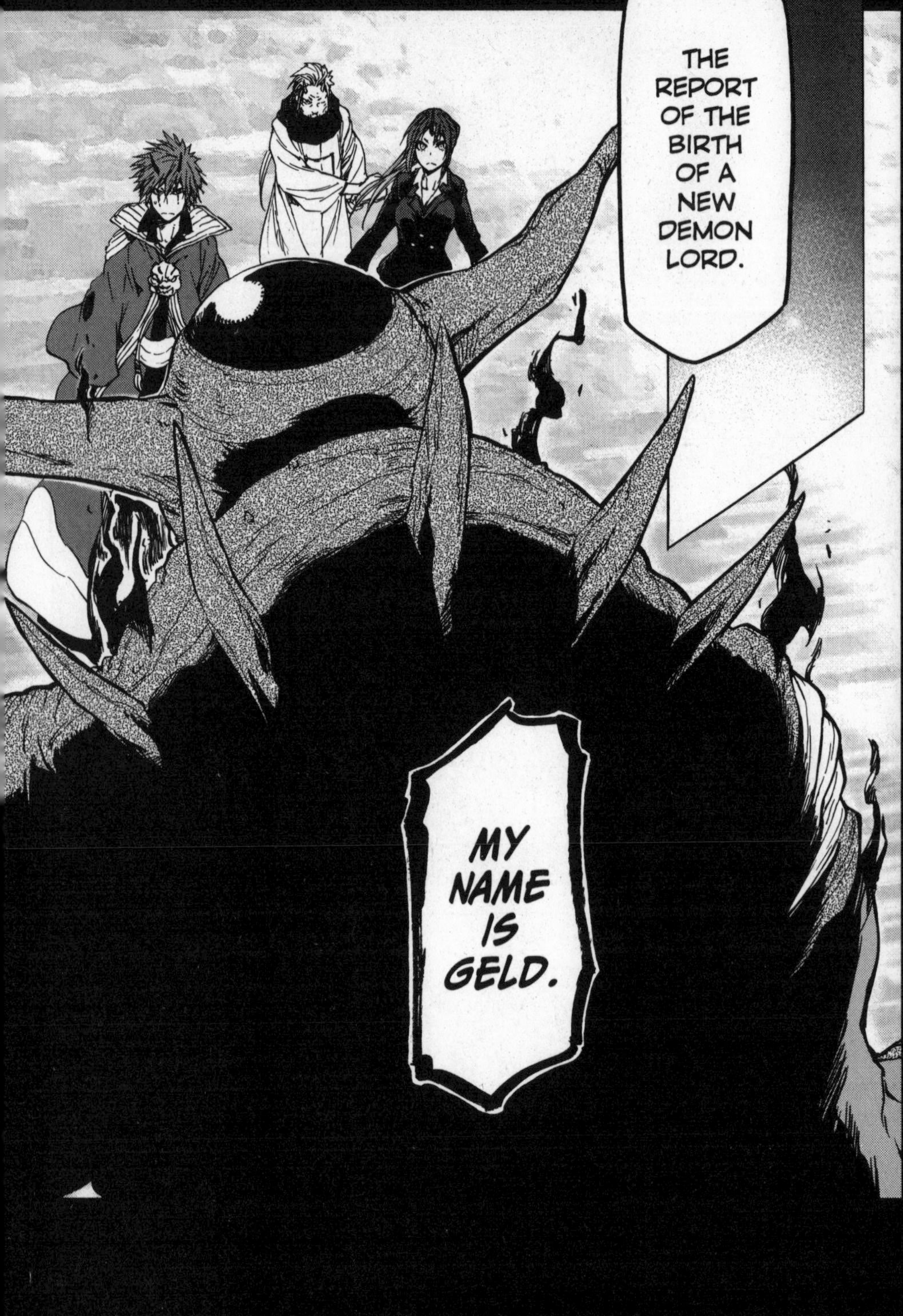
THE REPORT OF THE BIRTH OF A NEW DEMON LORD.
MY NAME IS GELD.

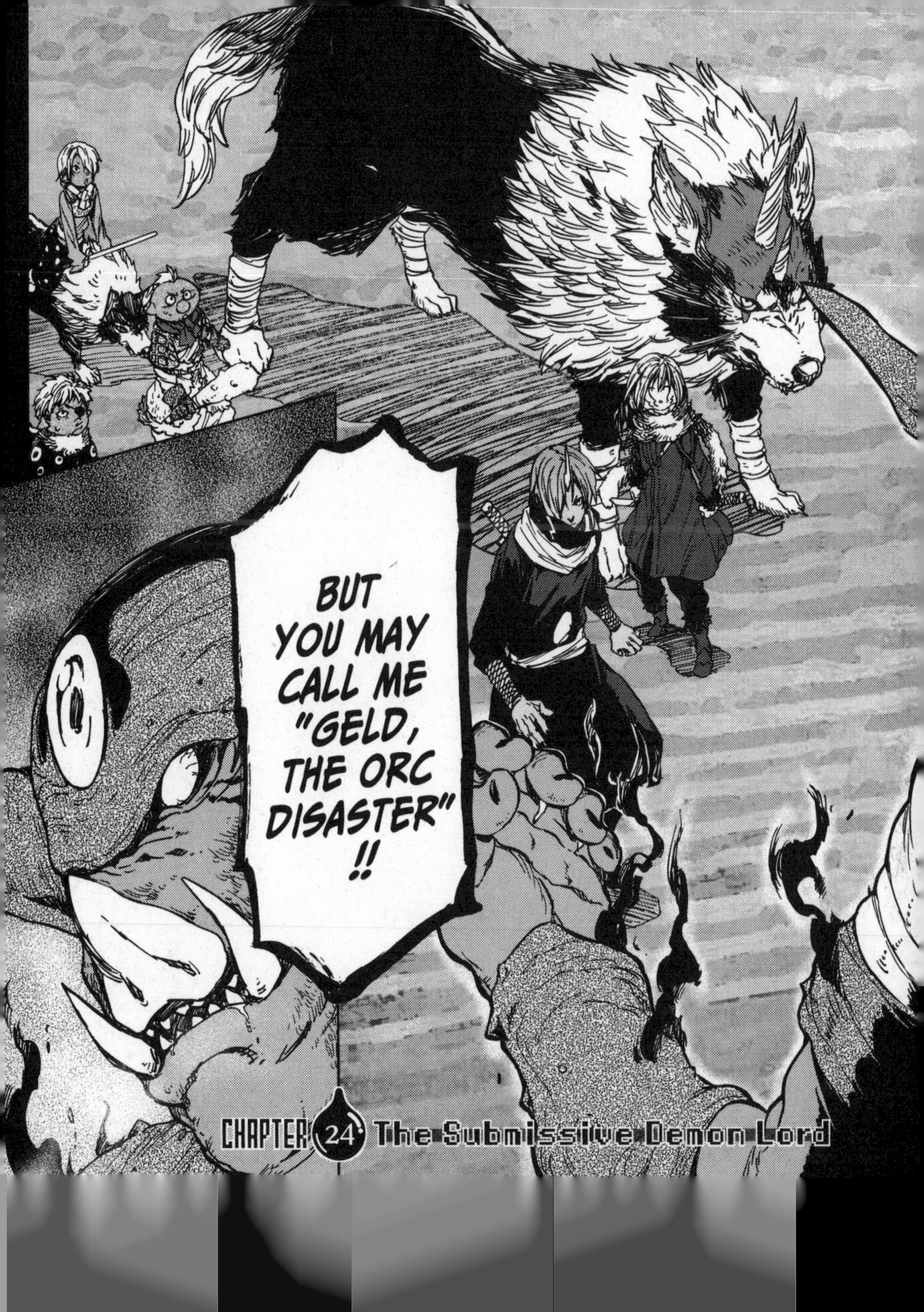
BUT YOU MAY CALL ME "GELD, THE ORC DISASTER" !!
CHAPTER 24 The Submissive Demon Lord

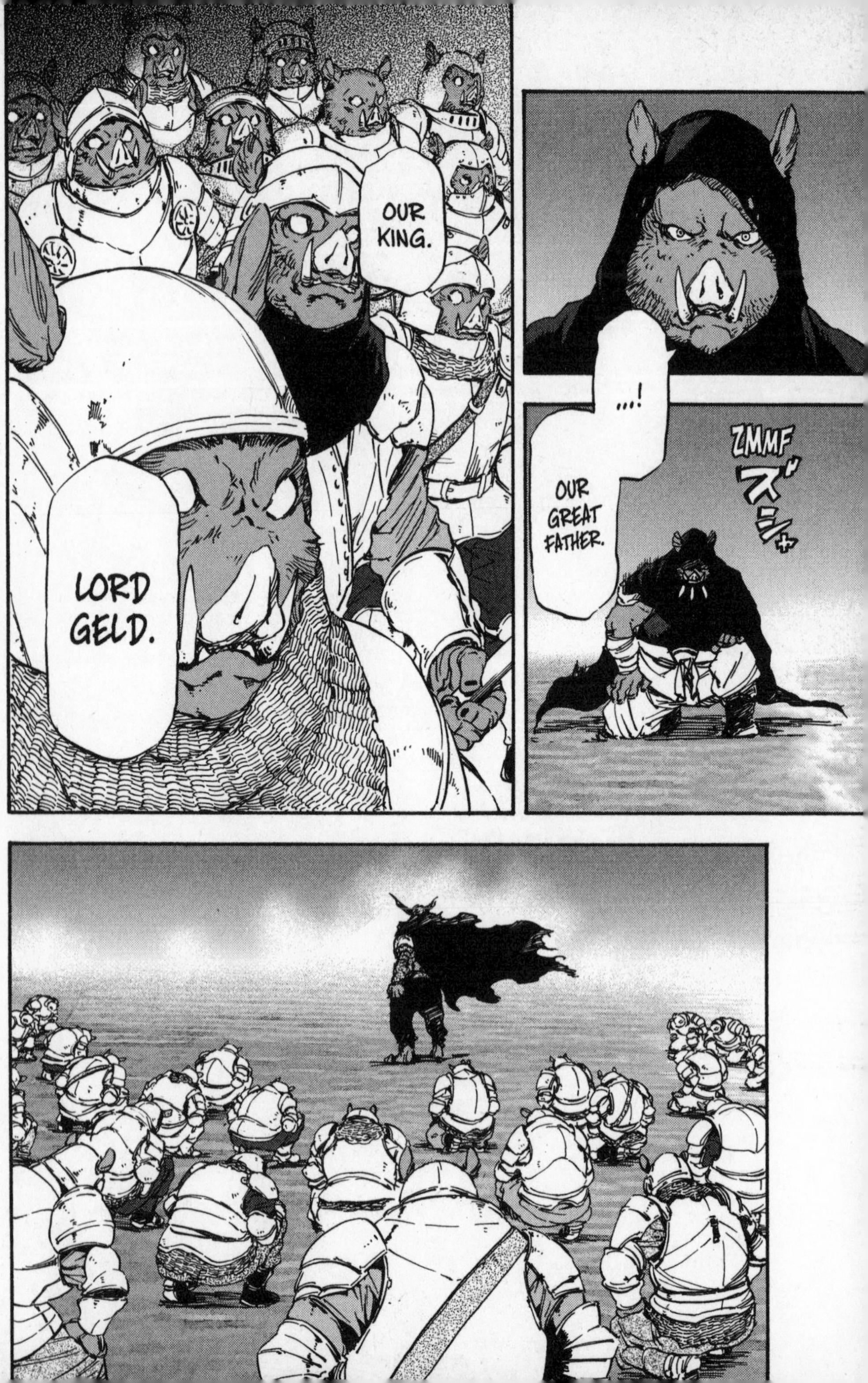
...!
OUR GREAT FATHER.
ZMMF
ズシャ
OUR KING.
LORD GELD.

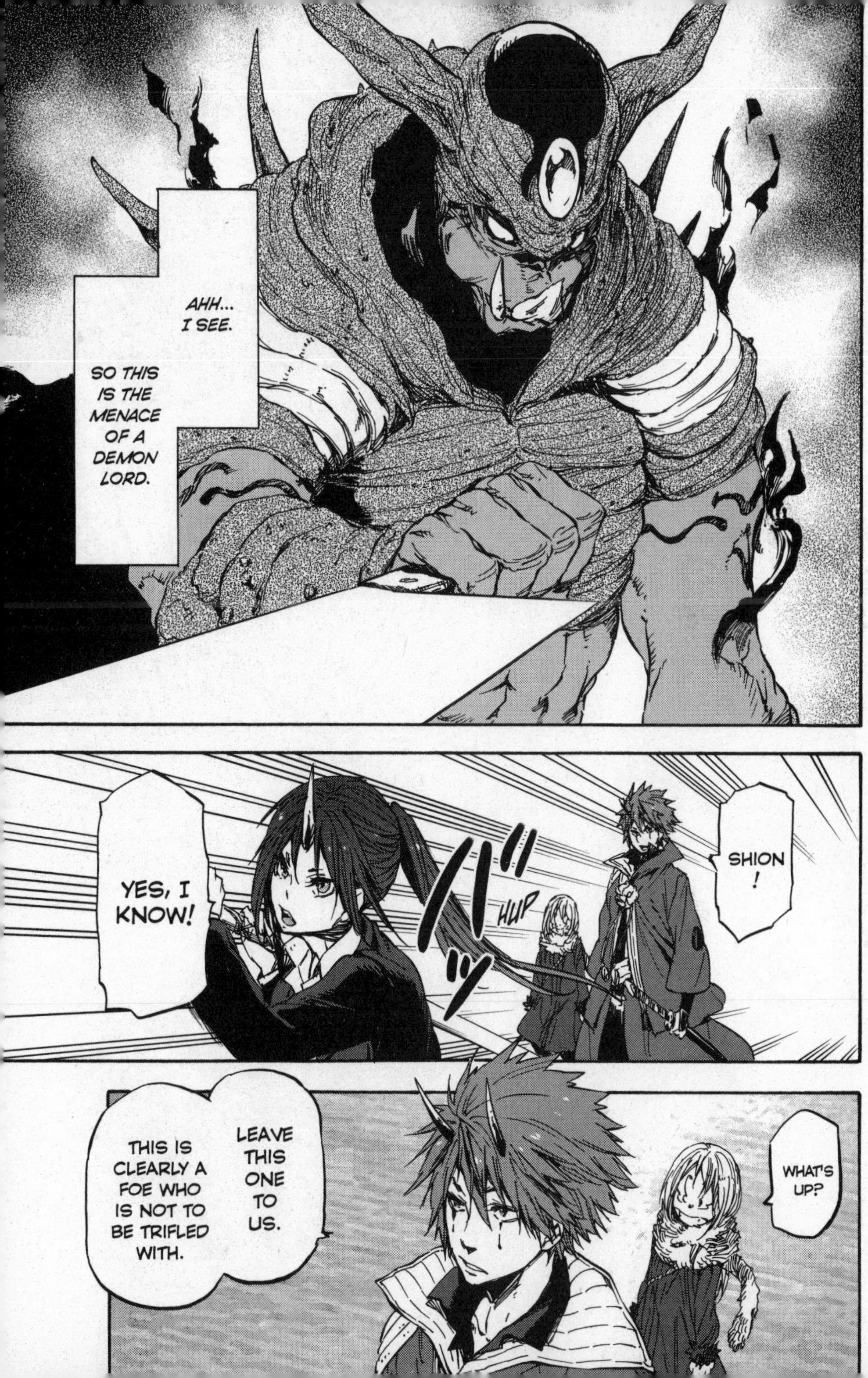
AHH... I SEE.
SO THIS IS THE MENACE OF A DEMON LORD.
SHION!
HUP
YES, I KNOW!
WHAT'S UP?
LEAVE THIS ONE TO US.
THIS IS CLEARLY A FOE WHO IS NOT TO BE TRIFLED WITH.

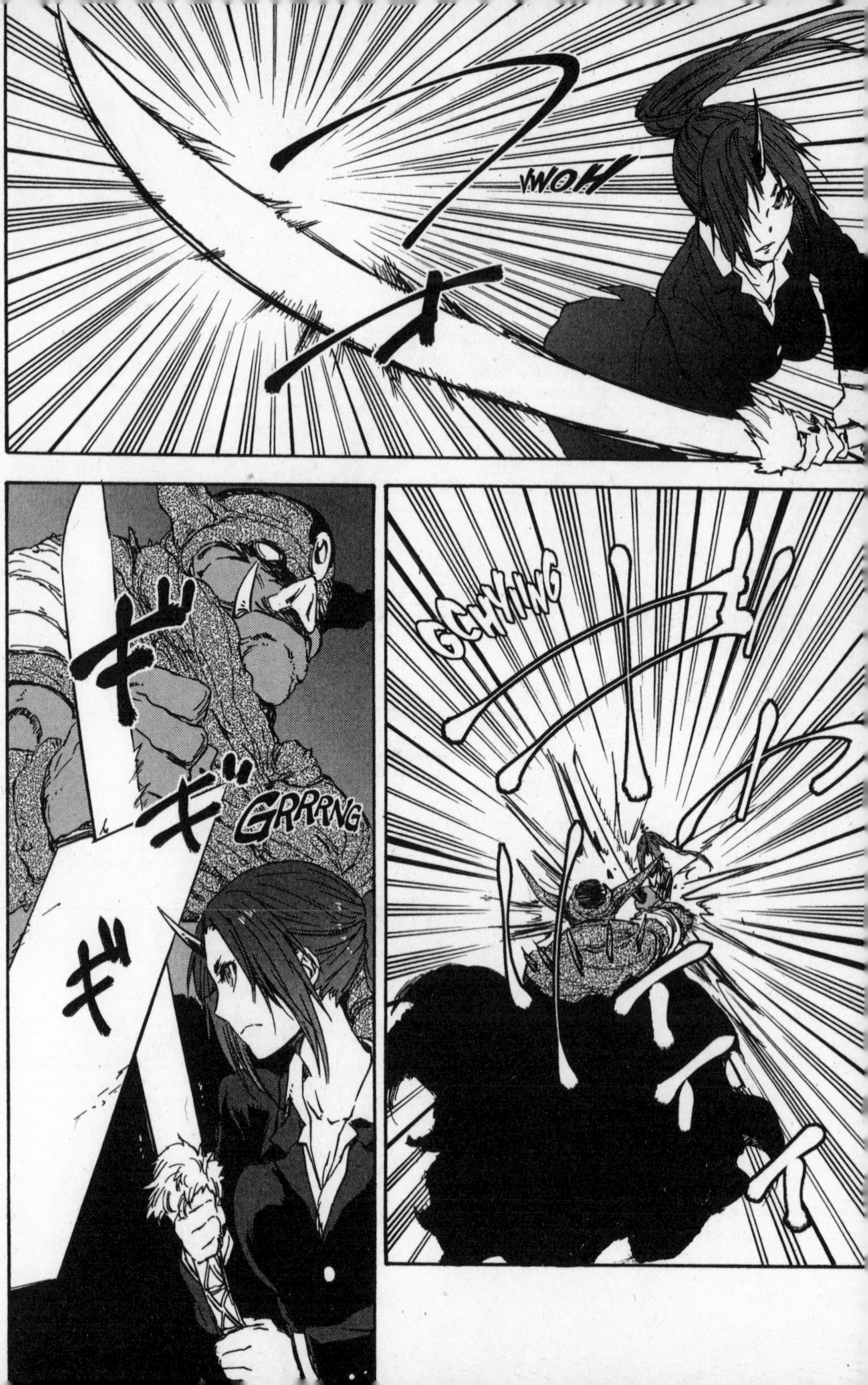
VWOH
GCHYING
GRRRNG

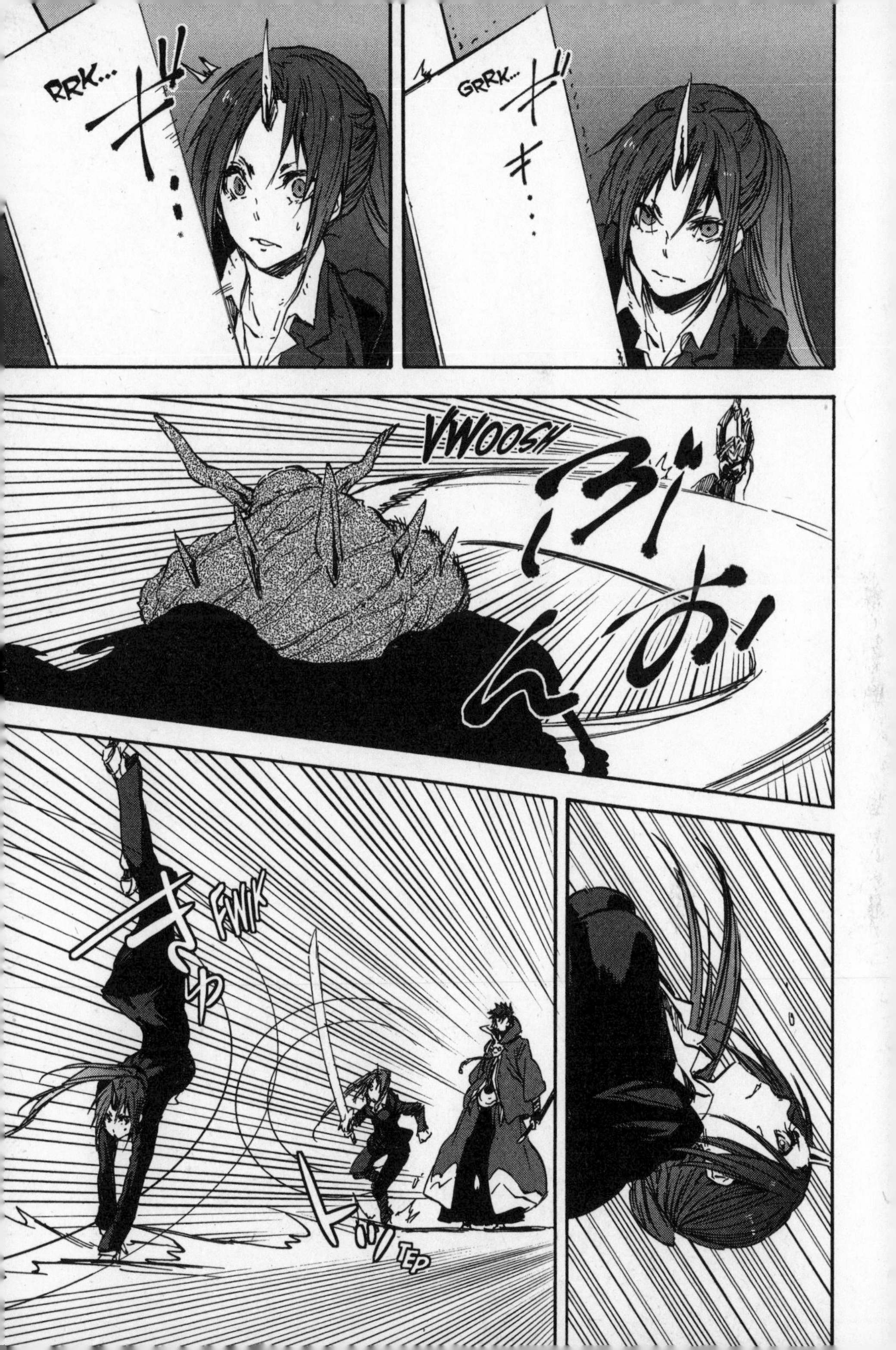
GRRK...
RRK...
VWOOSH
FWIK
TEP

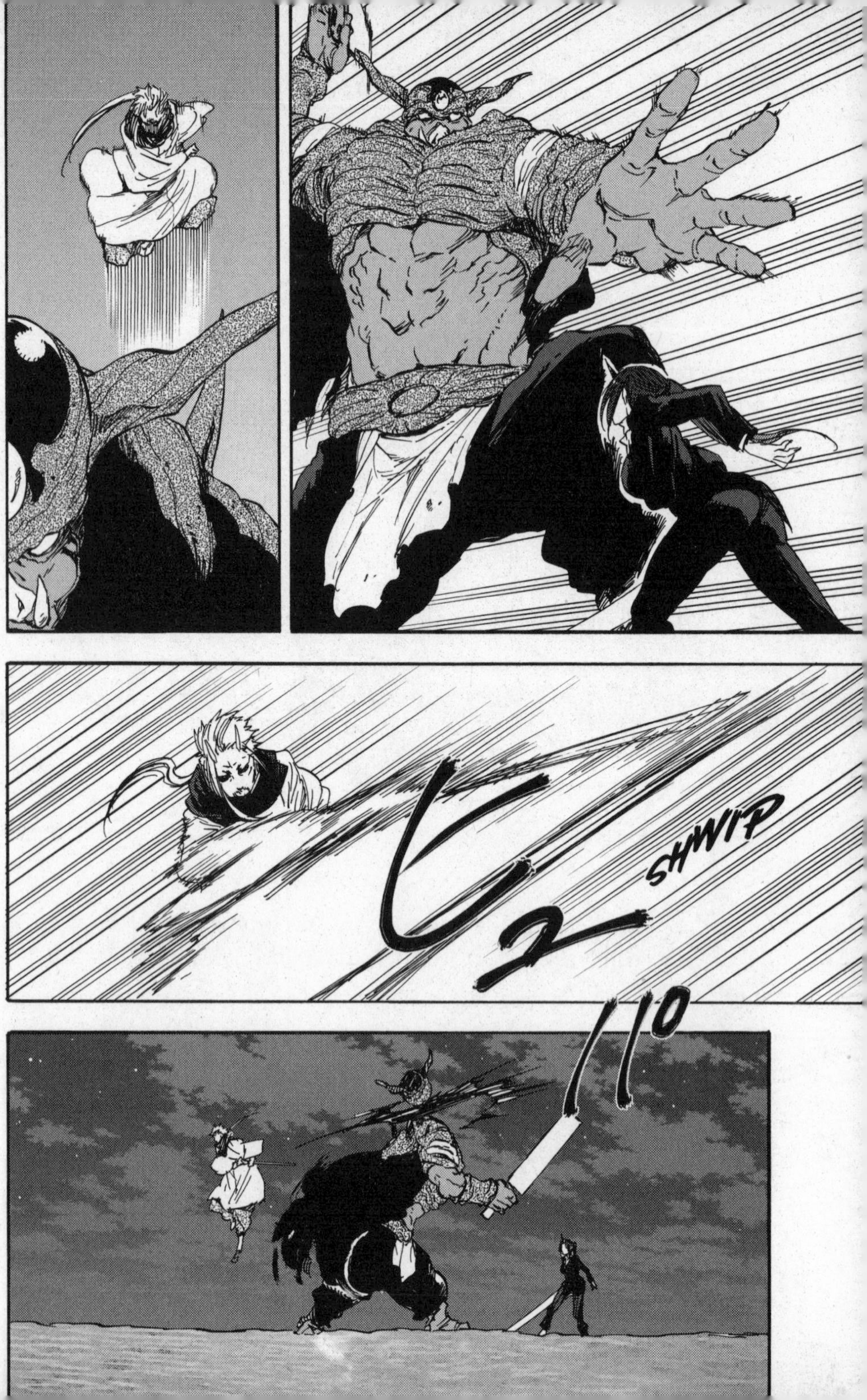
SHWIP

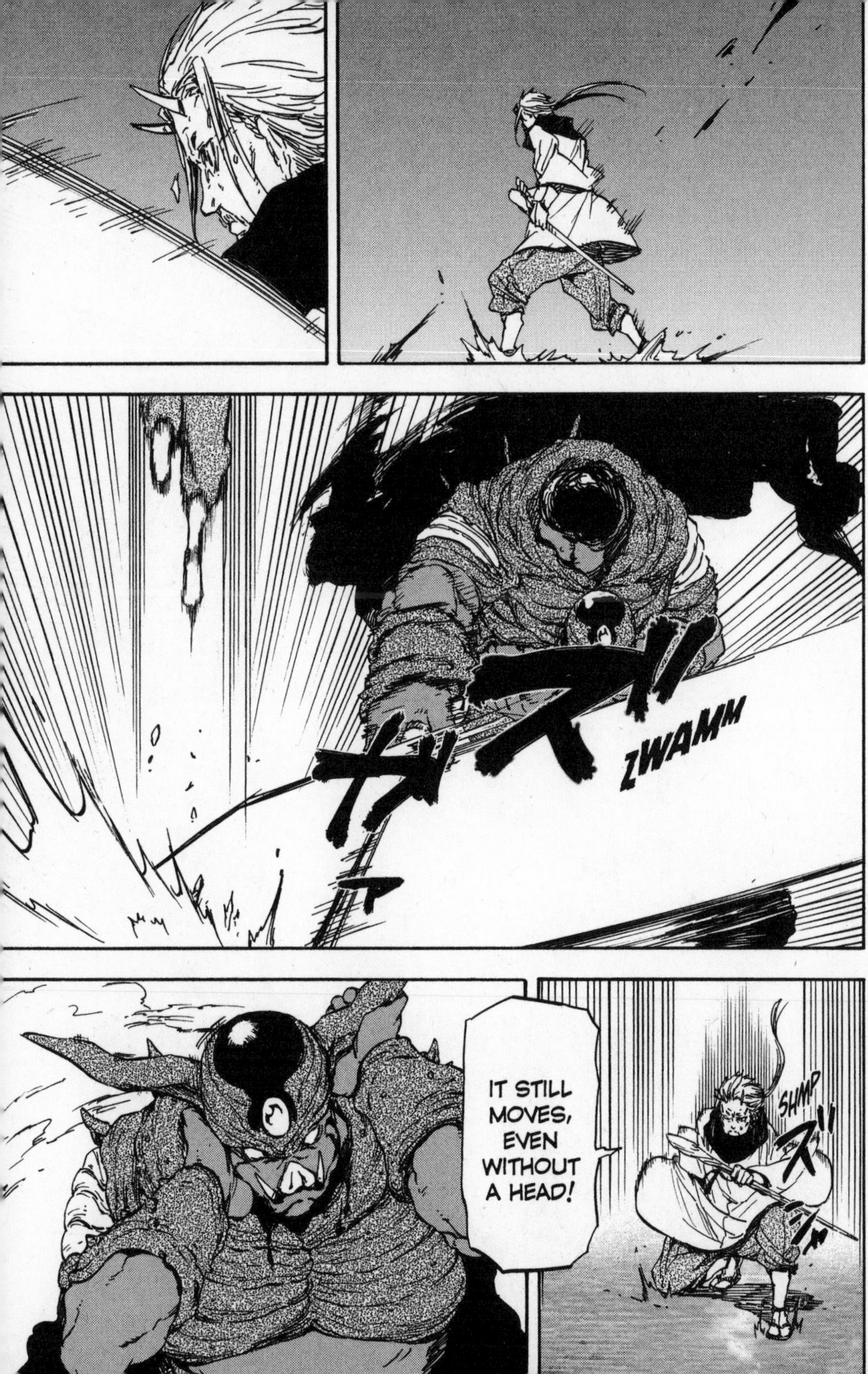
ZWAMM
SHMP
IT STILL MOVES, EVEN WITHOUT A HEAD!

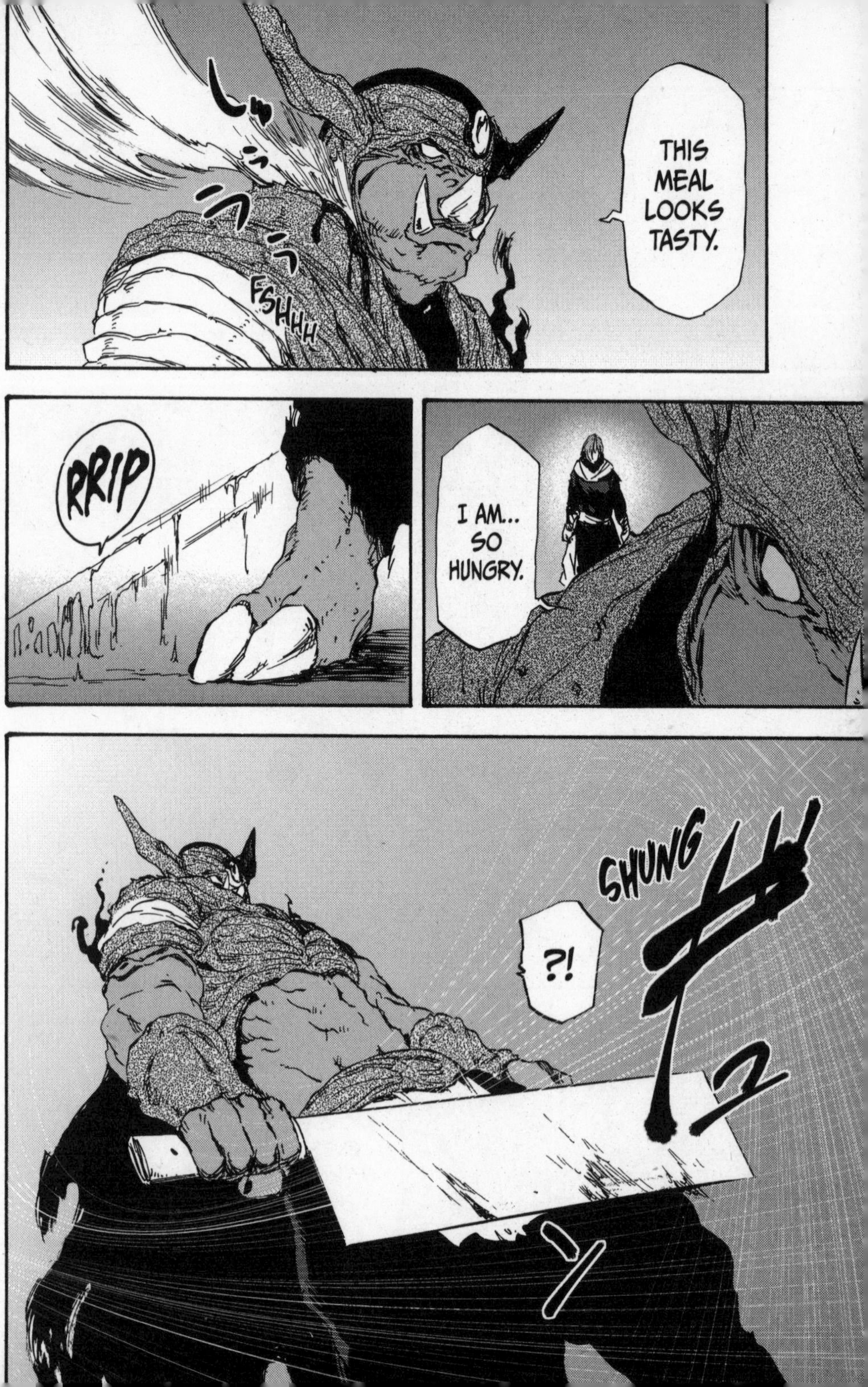
THIS MEAL LOOKS TASTY.
FSHHH
I AM... SO HUNGRY.
RRIP
SHUNG
?!

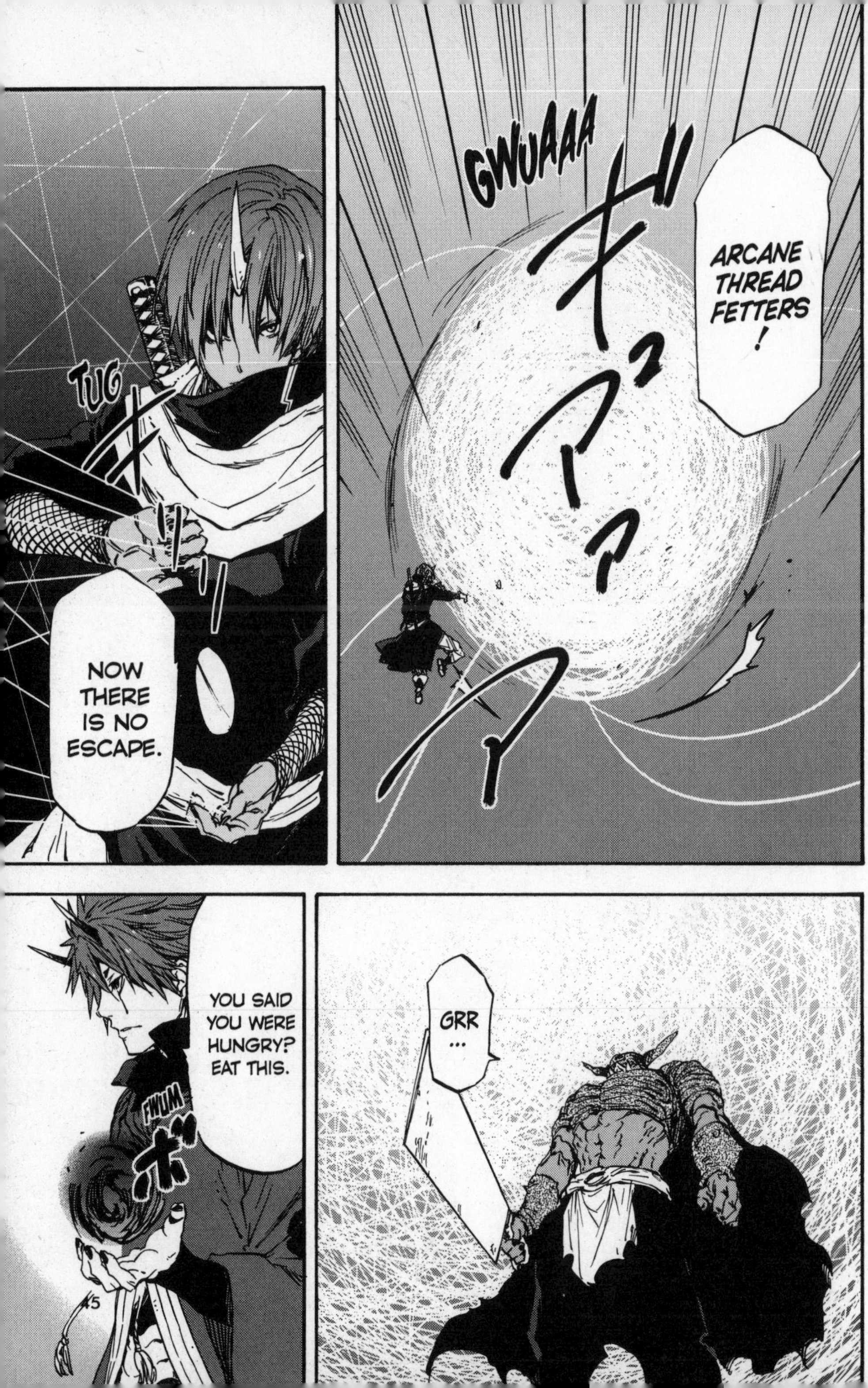
GWUAAA
ARCANE THREAD FETTERS!
TUG
NOW THERE IS NO ESCAPE.
GRR ...
YOU SAID YOU WERE HUNGRY? EAT THIS.
FWUM

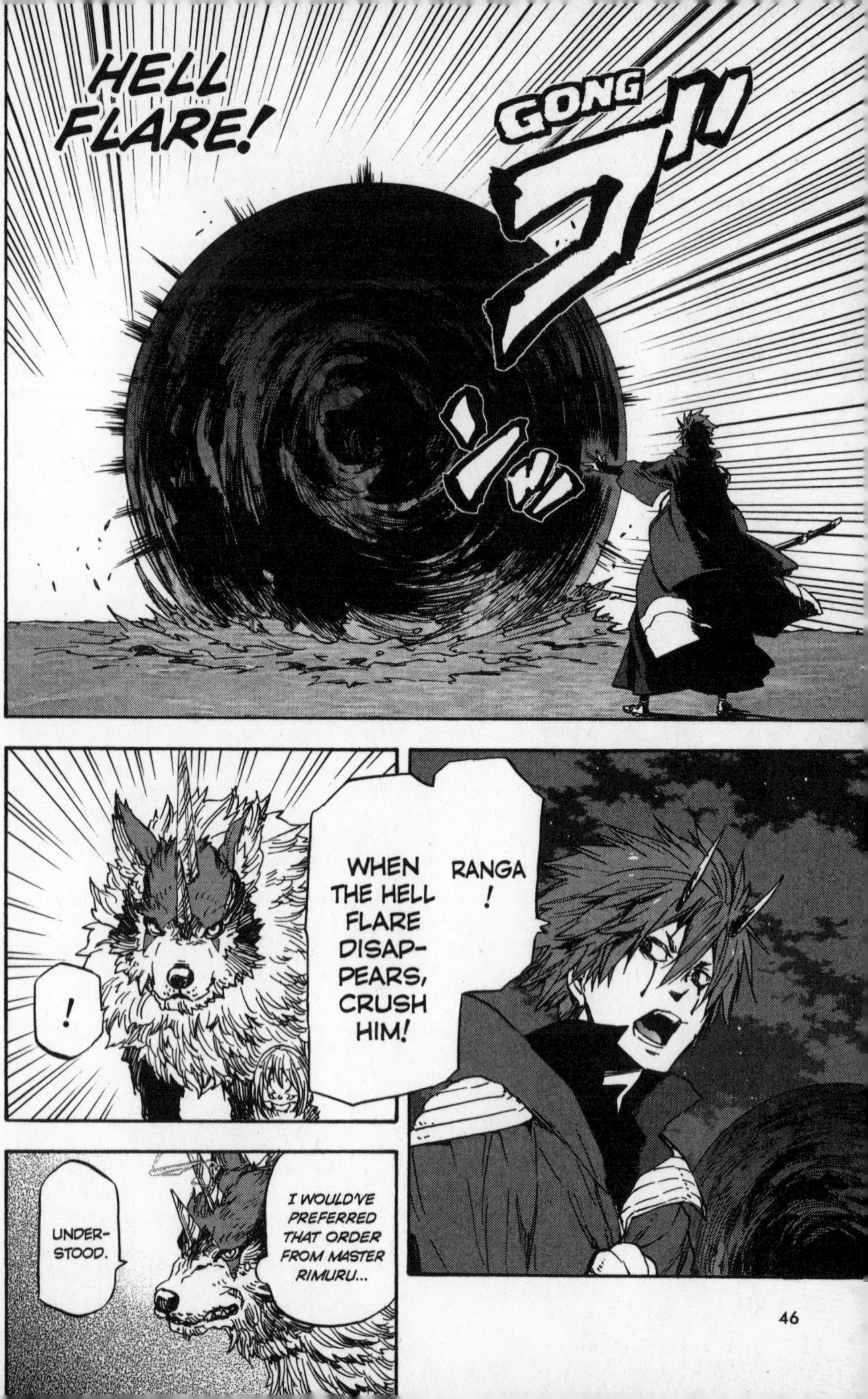
HELL FLARE!
GONG
RANGA!
WHEN THE HELL FLARE DISAPPEARS, CRUSH HIM!
!
I WOULD'VE PREFERRED THAT ORDER FROM MASTER RIMURU...
UNDER-STOOD.

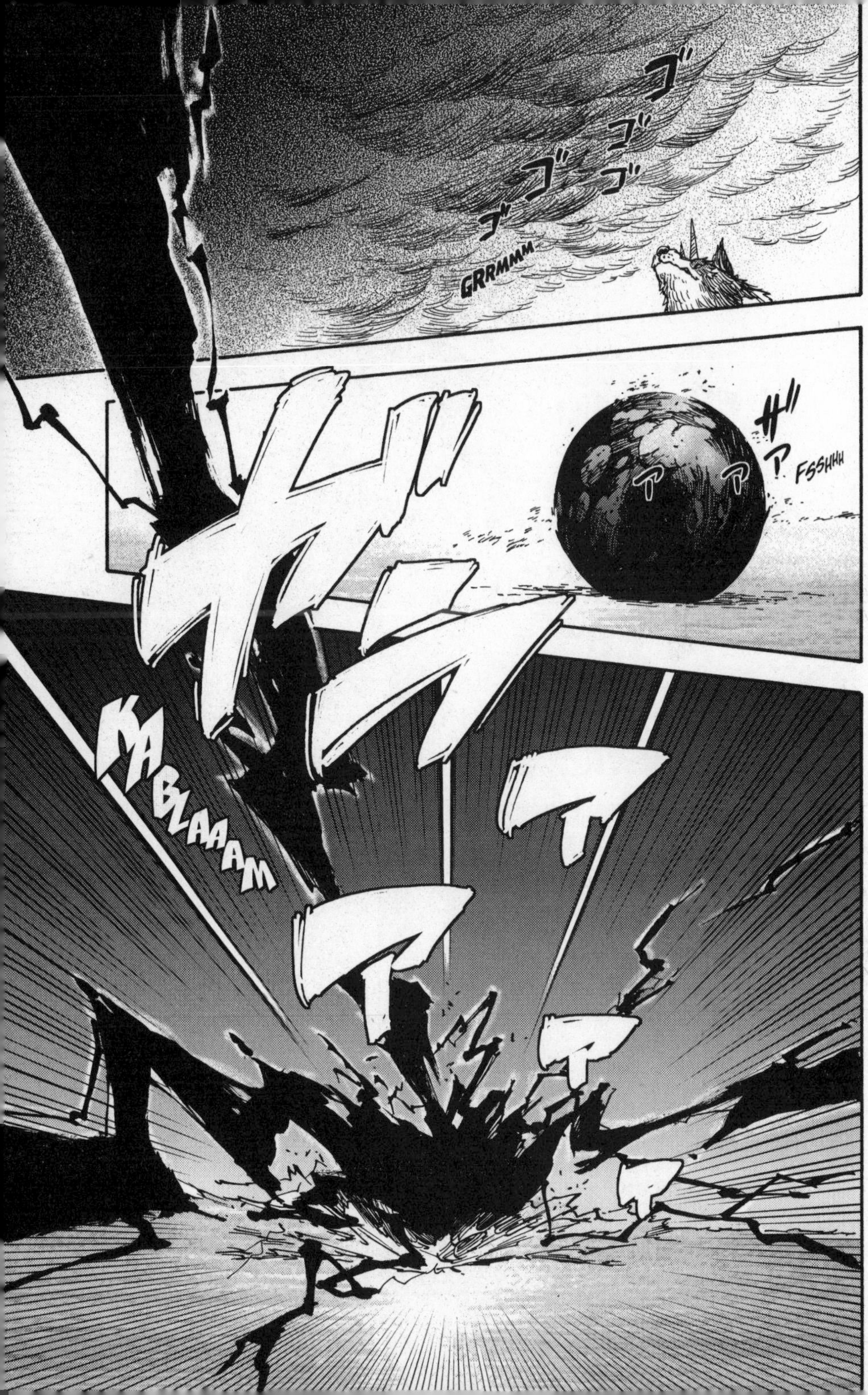
ゴゴゴゴゴ
GRRMMM
ザアア
FSSHHH
KABLAAAM

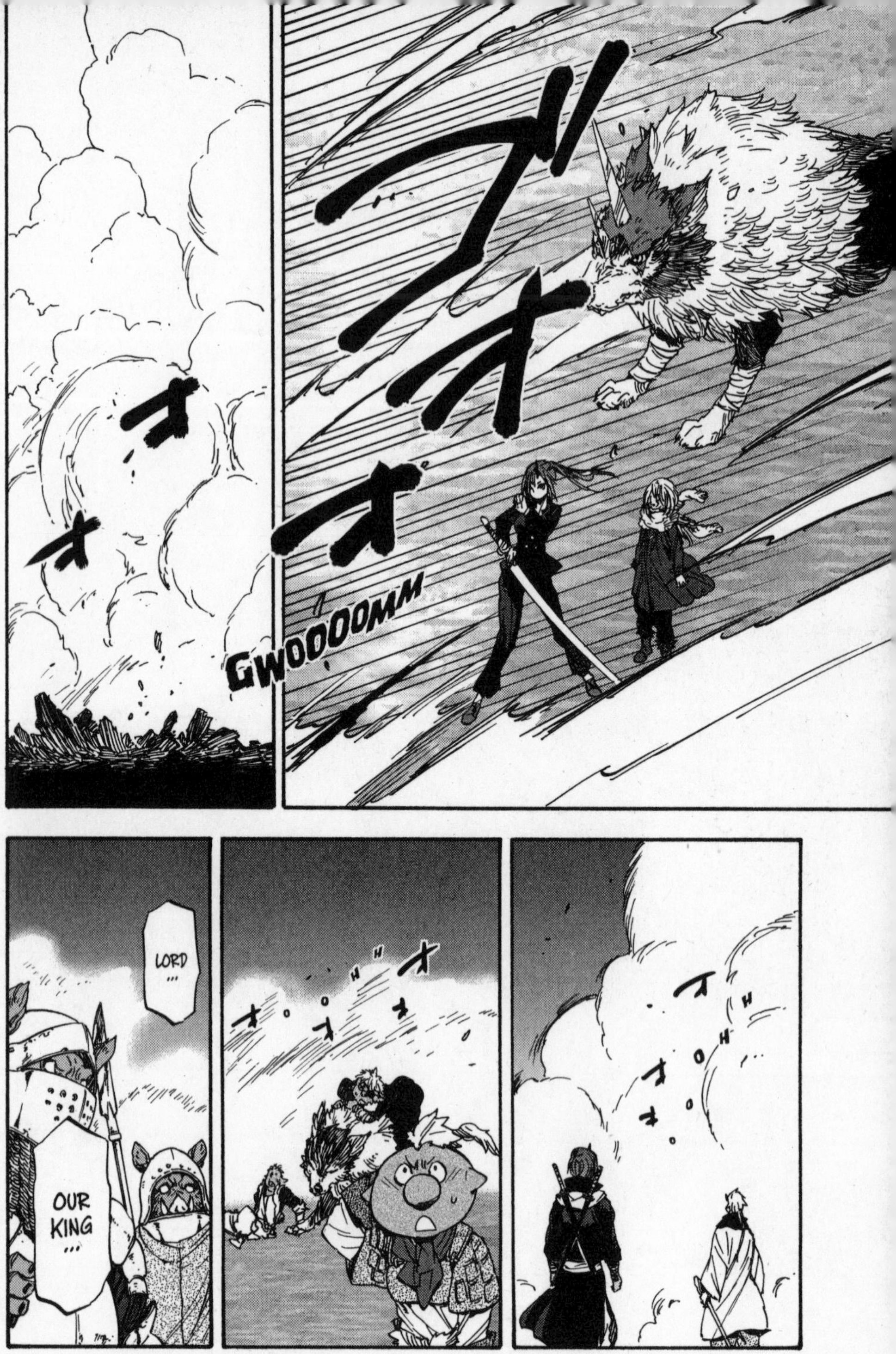
GWOOOOMM
OOHH...
OOHH
LORD...
OUR KING...

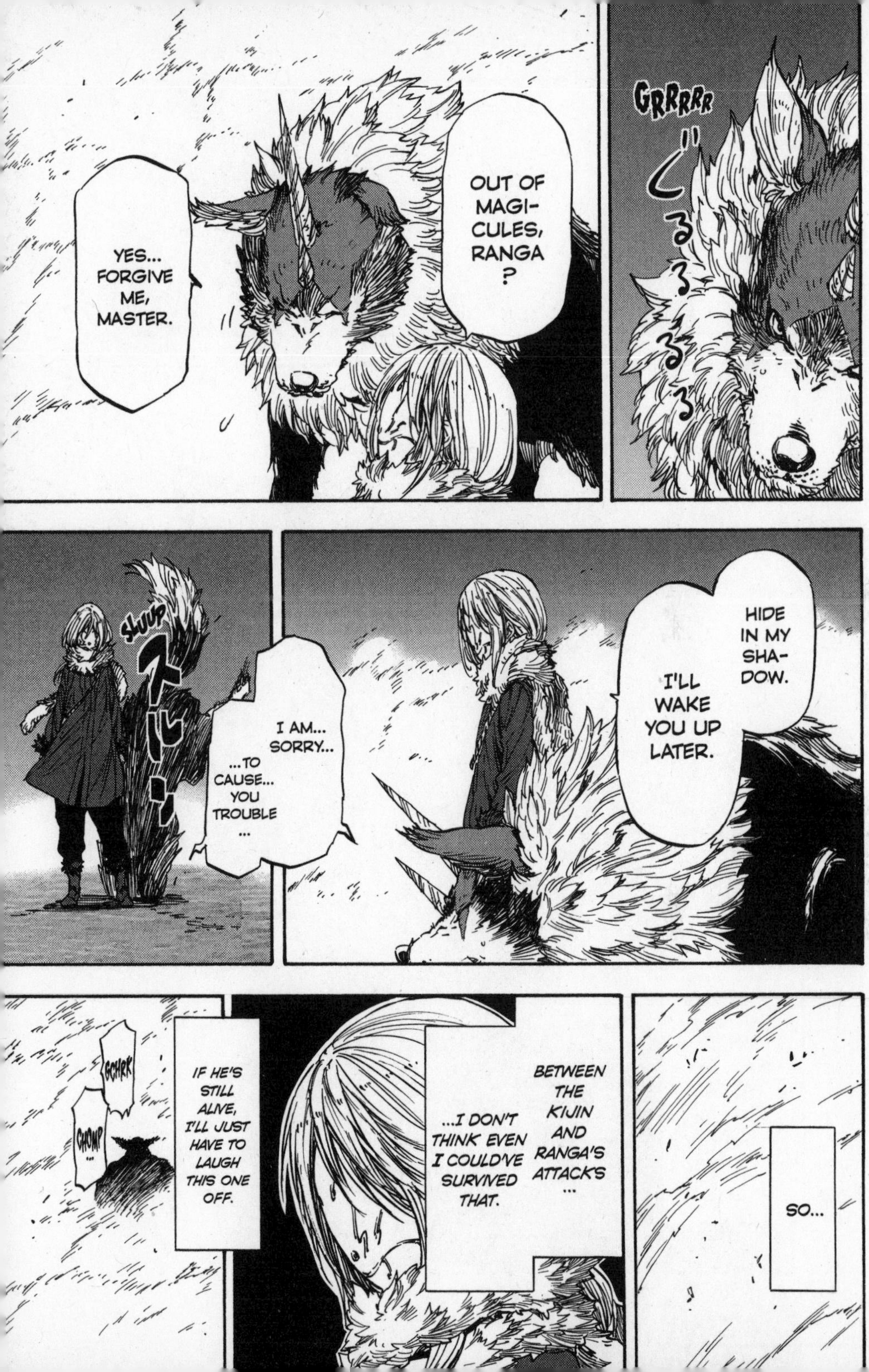
GRRRRR
ぐるるる
OUT OF MAGI-CULES, RANGA?
YES... FORGIVE ME, MASTER.
HIDE IN MY SHA-DOW.
I'LL WAKE YOU UP LATER.
SLUUP
I AM... SORRY...
...TO CAUSE... YOU TROUBLE ...
SO...
BETWEEN THE KIJIN AND RANGA'S ATTACKS ...
...I DON'T THINK EVEN I COULD'VE SURVIVED THAT.
IF HE'S STILL ALIVE, I'LL JUST HAVE TO LAUGH THIS ONE OFF.
GCHRK
CHOMP ...

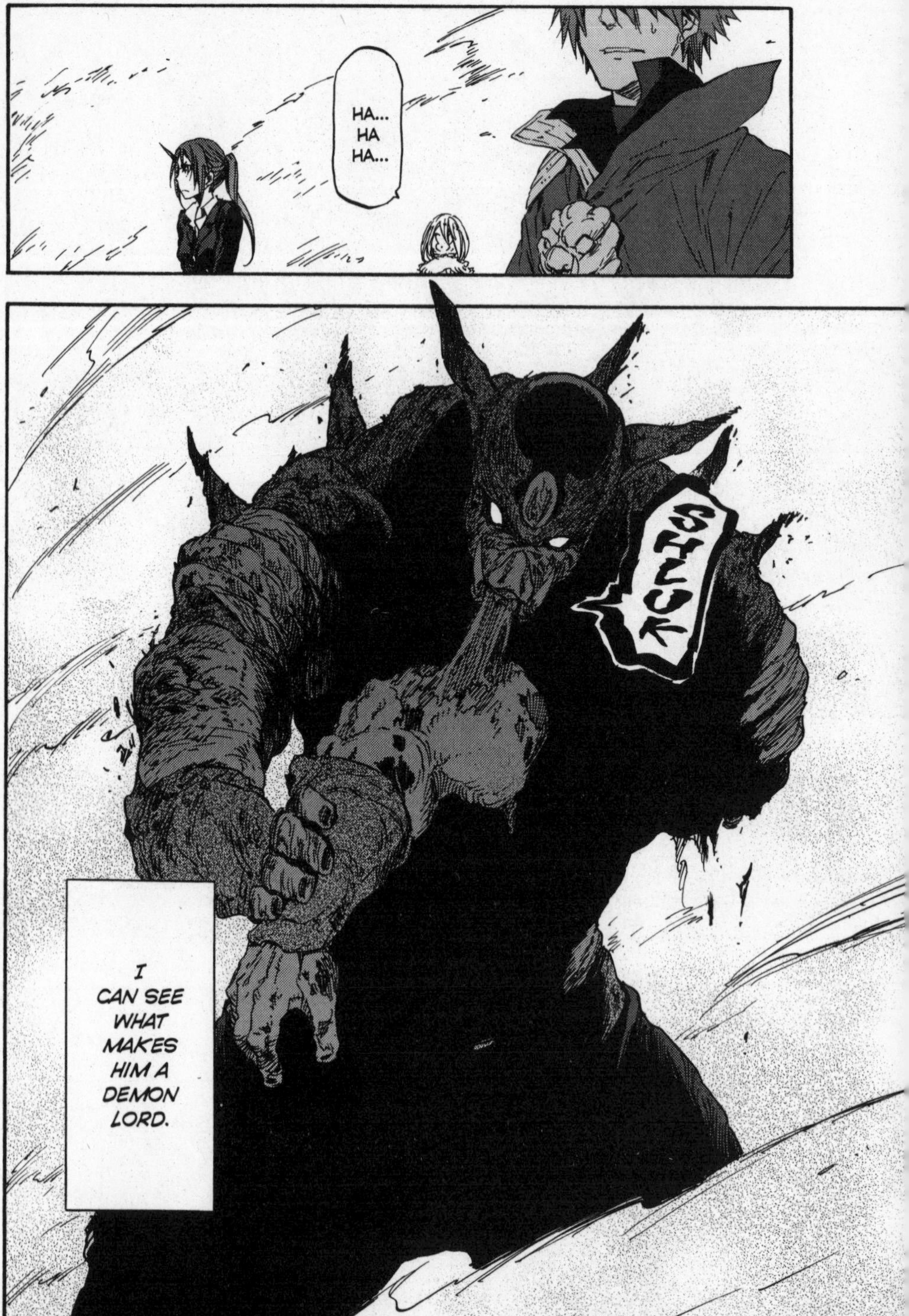
HA... HA HA...
SHLUK
I CAN SEE WHAT MAKES HIM A DEMON LORD.

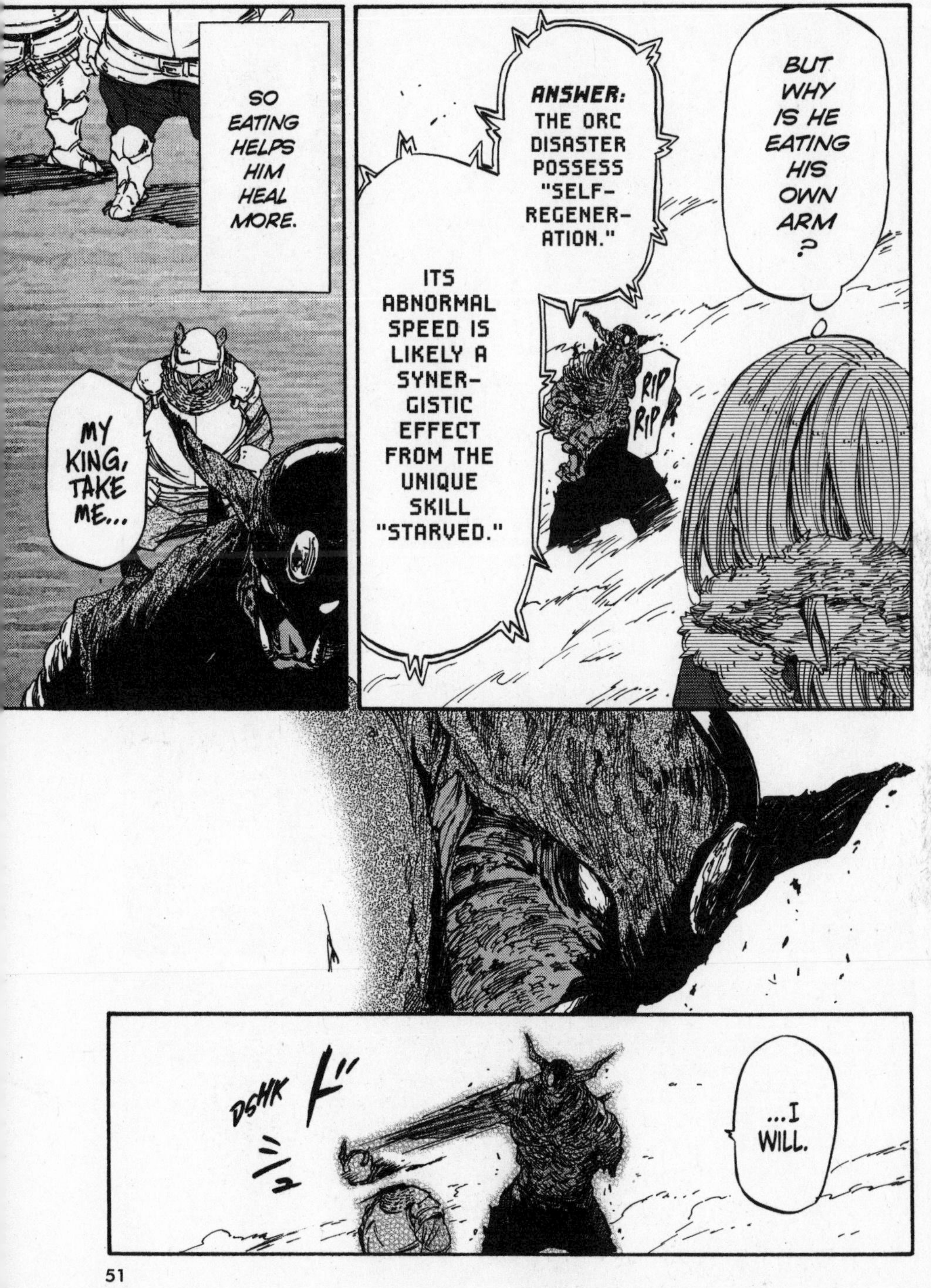

BUT WHY IS HE EATING HIS OWN ARM ?
ANSWER: THE ORC DISASTER POSSESS "SELF-REGENERATION."
RIP RIP
ITS ABNORMAL SPEED IS LIKELY A SYNERGISTIC EFFECT FROM THE UNIQUE SKILL "STARVED."
SO EATING HELPS HIM HEAL MORE.
MY KING, TAKE ME...
...I WILL.
DSHK

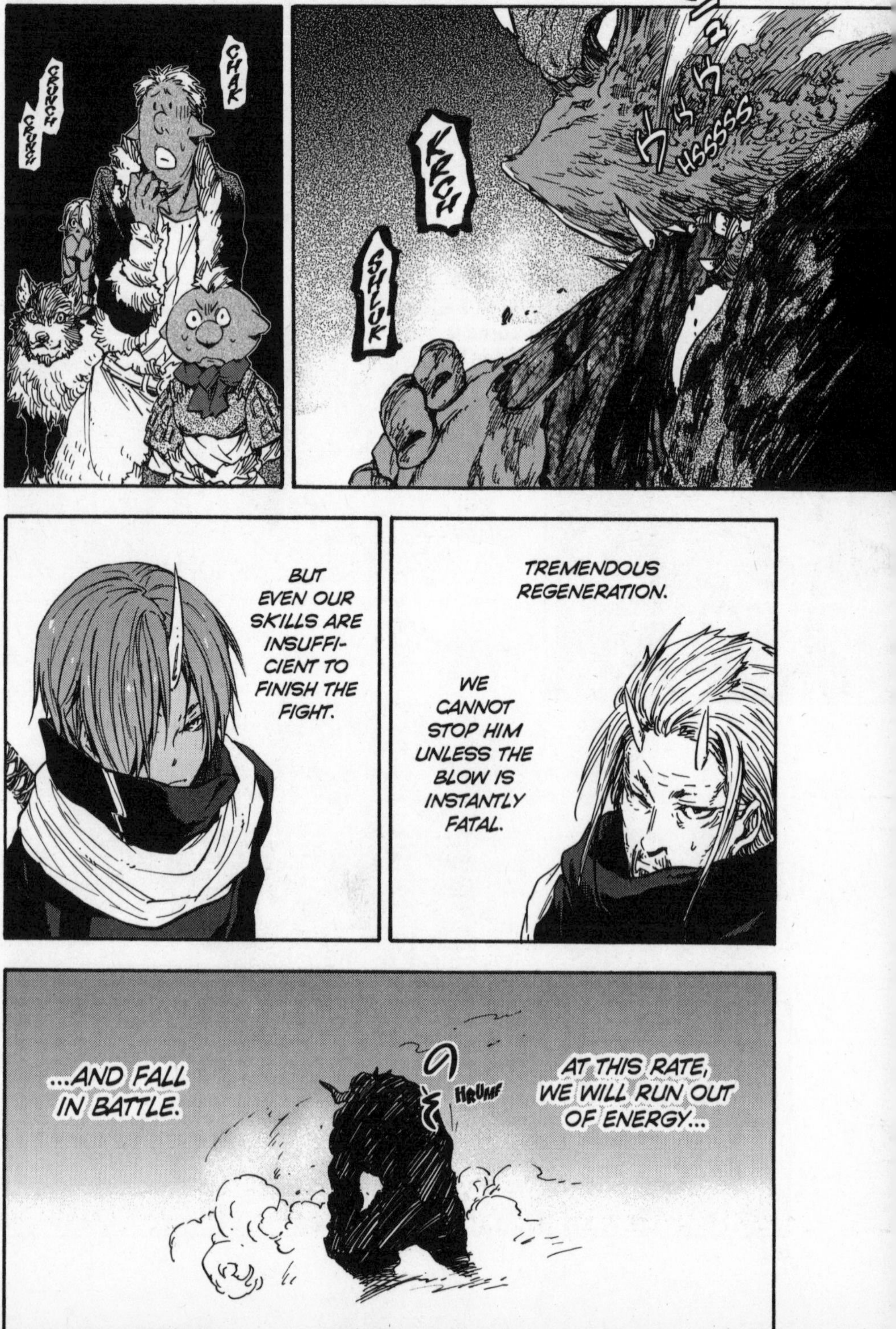
HSSSSS
KRCH
SHLUK
CHAK
CRUNCH
CRUNCH
TREMENDOUS REGENERATION.
WE CANNOT STOP HIM UNLESS THE BLOW IS INSTANTLY FATAL.
BUT EVEN OUR SKILLS ARE INSUFFI-CIENT TO FINISH THE FIGHT.
AT THIS RATE, WE WILL RUN OUT OF ENERGY...
HRUMF
...AND FALL IN BATTLE.

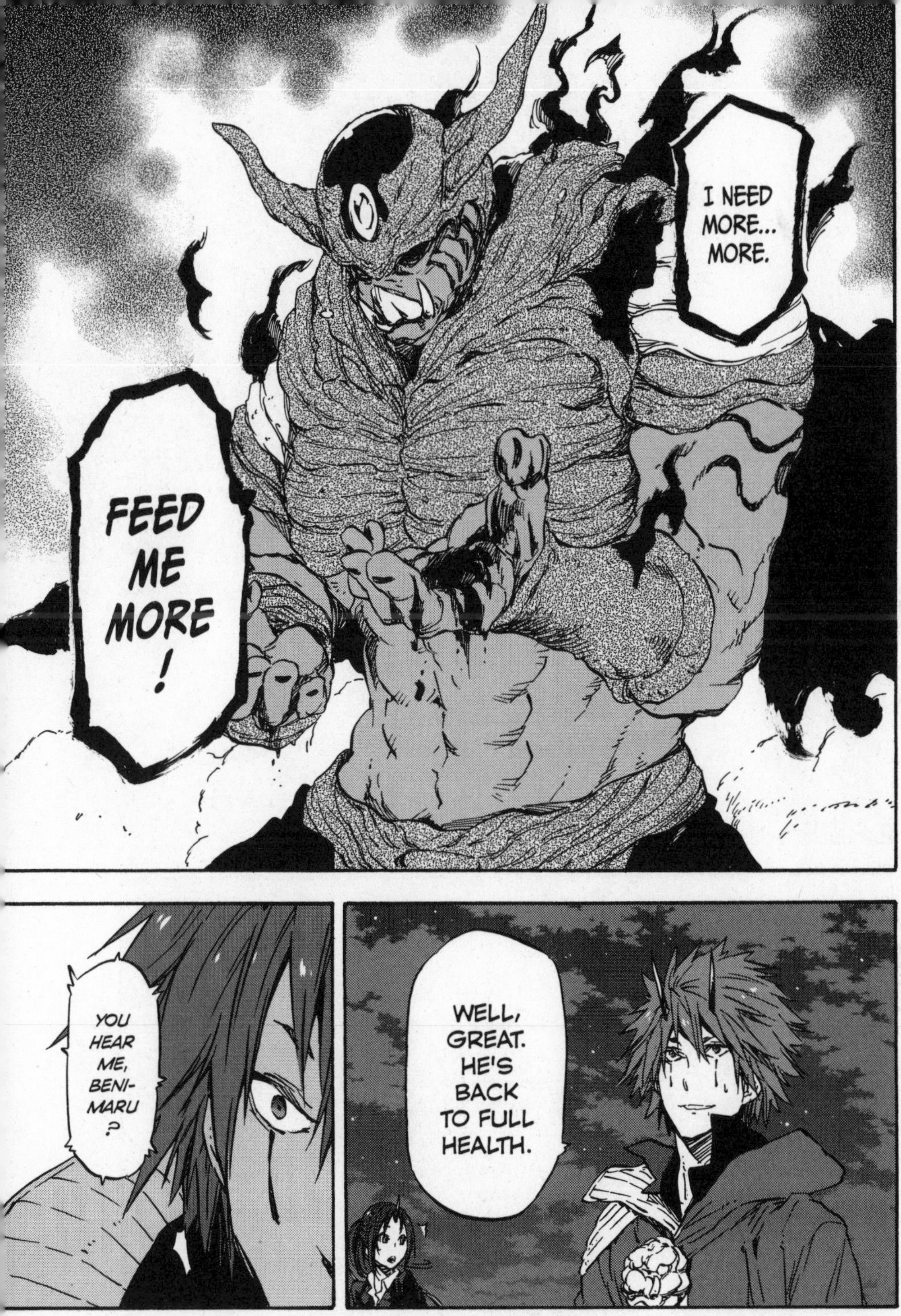
I NEED MORE... MORE.
FEED ME MORE!
WELL, GREAT. HE'S BACK TO FULL HEALTH.
YOU HEAR ME, BENIMARU?

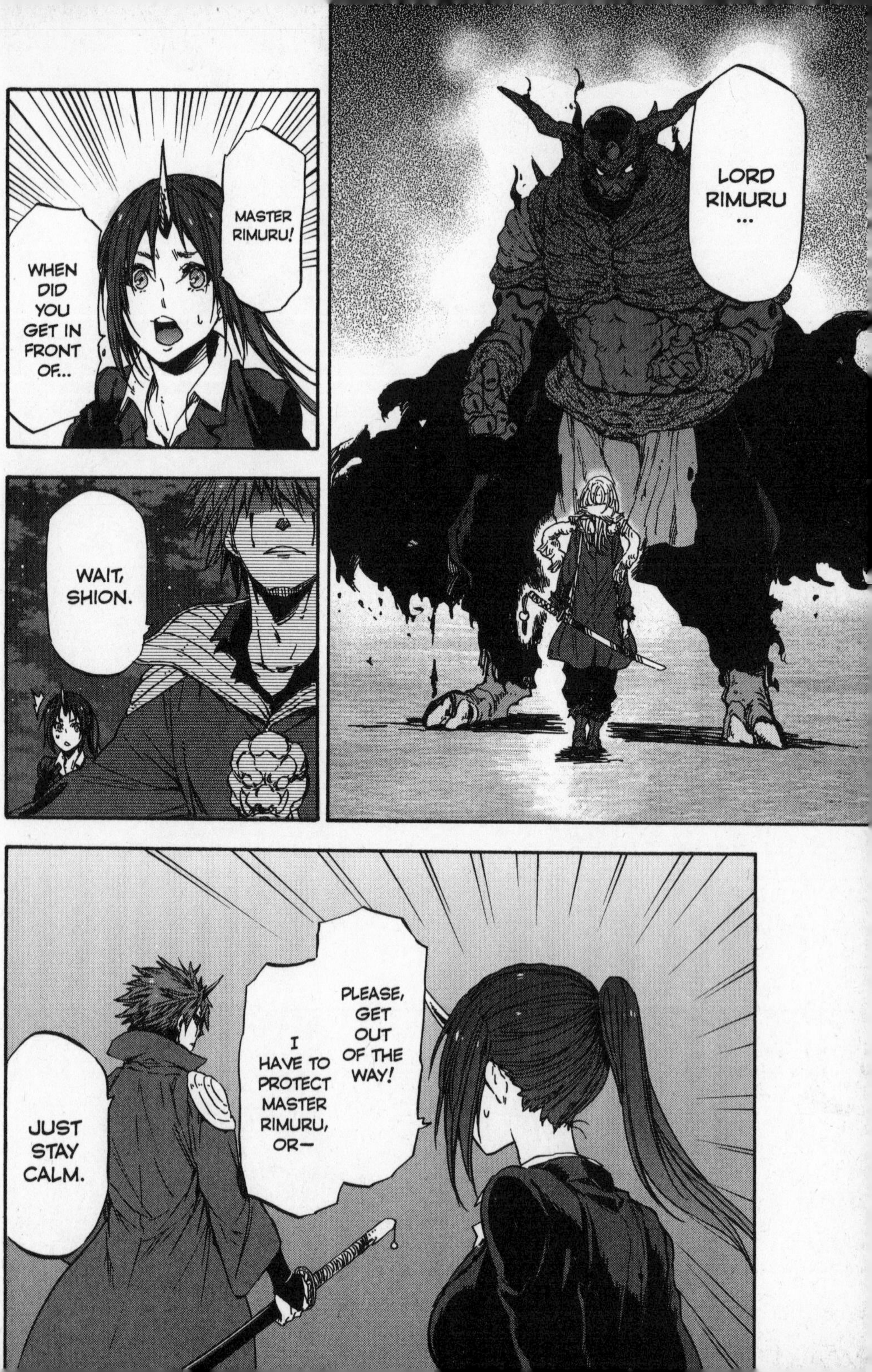
LORD RIMURU ...
MASTER RIMURU!
WHEN DID YOU GET IN FRONT OF...
WAIT, SHION.
PLEASE, GET OUT OF THE WAY!
I HAVE TO PROTECT MASTER RIMURU, OR—
JUST STAY CALM.

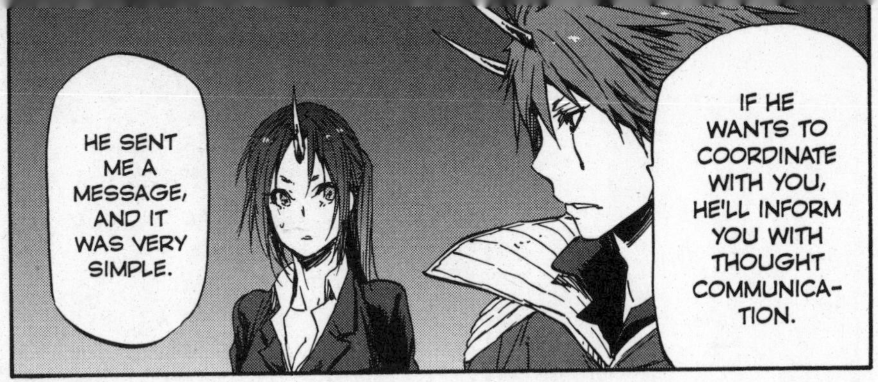
IF HE WANTS TO COORDINATE WITH YOU, HE'LL INFORM YOU WITH THOUGHT COMMUNICA-TION.
HE SENT ME A MESSAGE, AND IT WAS VERY SIMPLE.
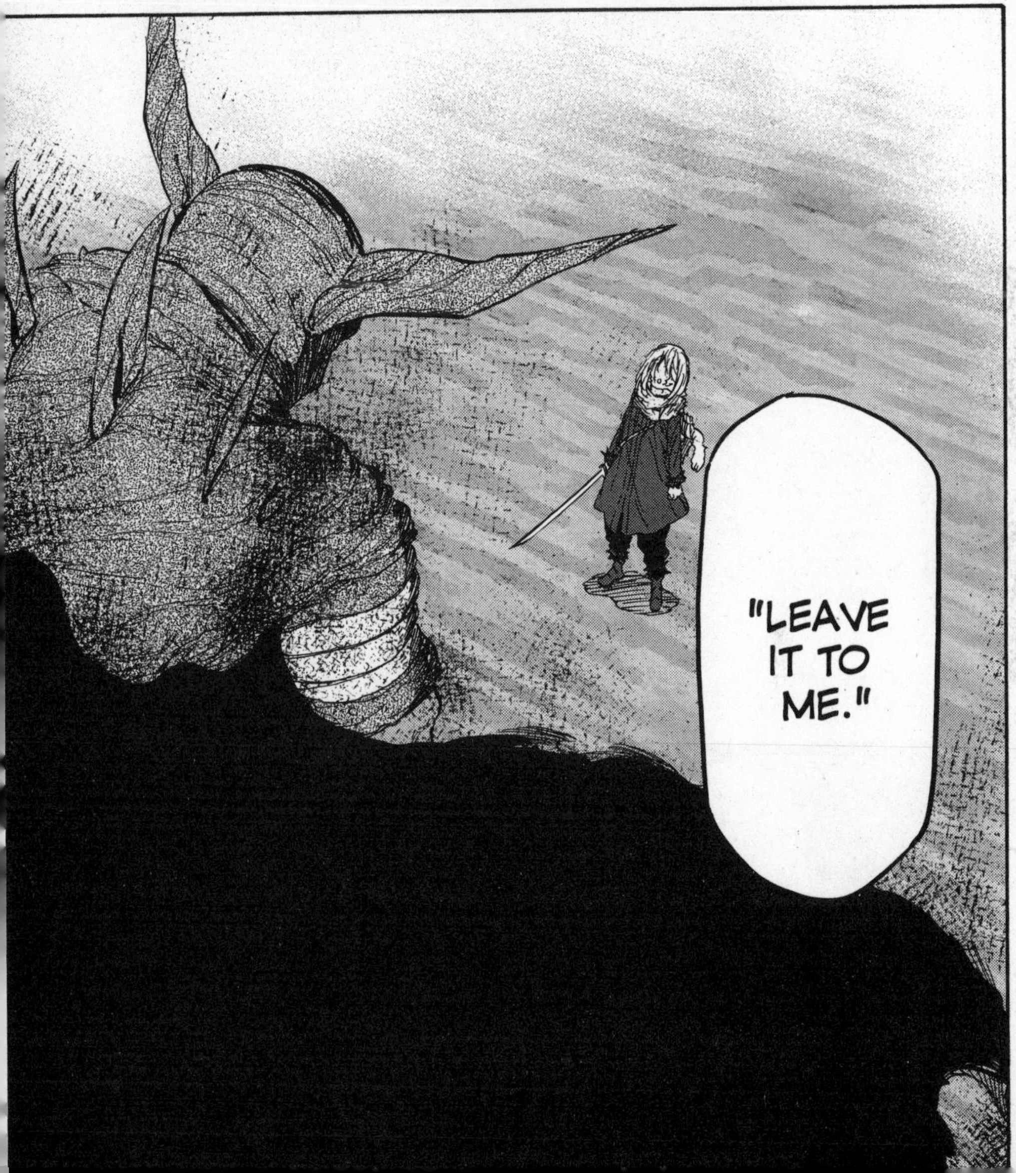
"LEAVE IT TO ME."

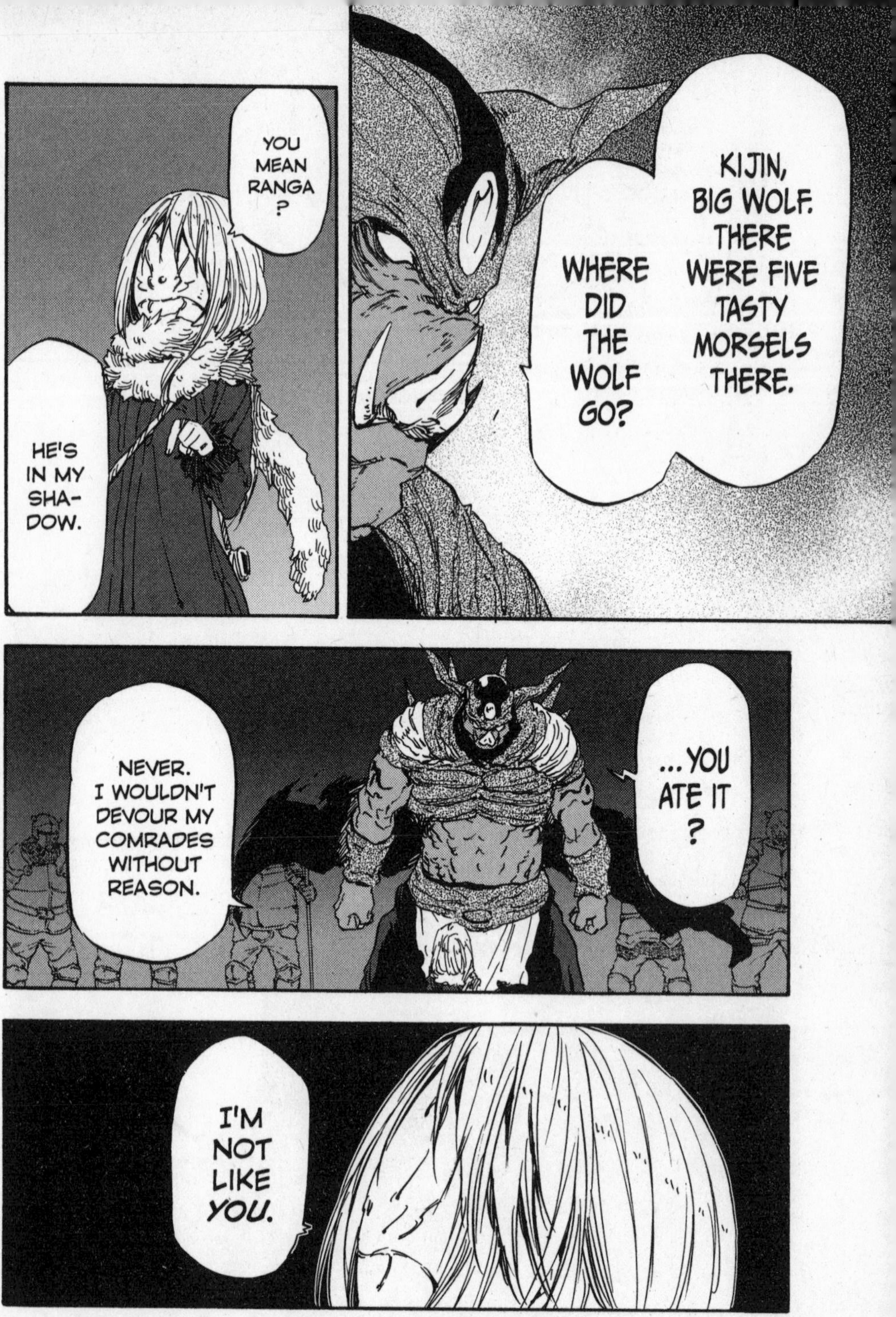
KIJIN, BIG WOLF. THERE WERE FIVE TASTY MORSELS THERE.
WHERE DID THE WOLF GO?
YOU MEAN RANGA?
HE'S IN MY SHADOW.
...YOU ATE IT?
NEVER. I WOULDN'T DEVOUR MY COMRADES WITHOUT REASON.
I'M NOT LIKE *YOU*.

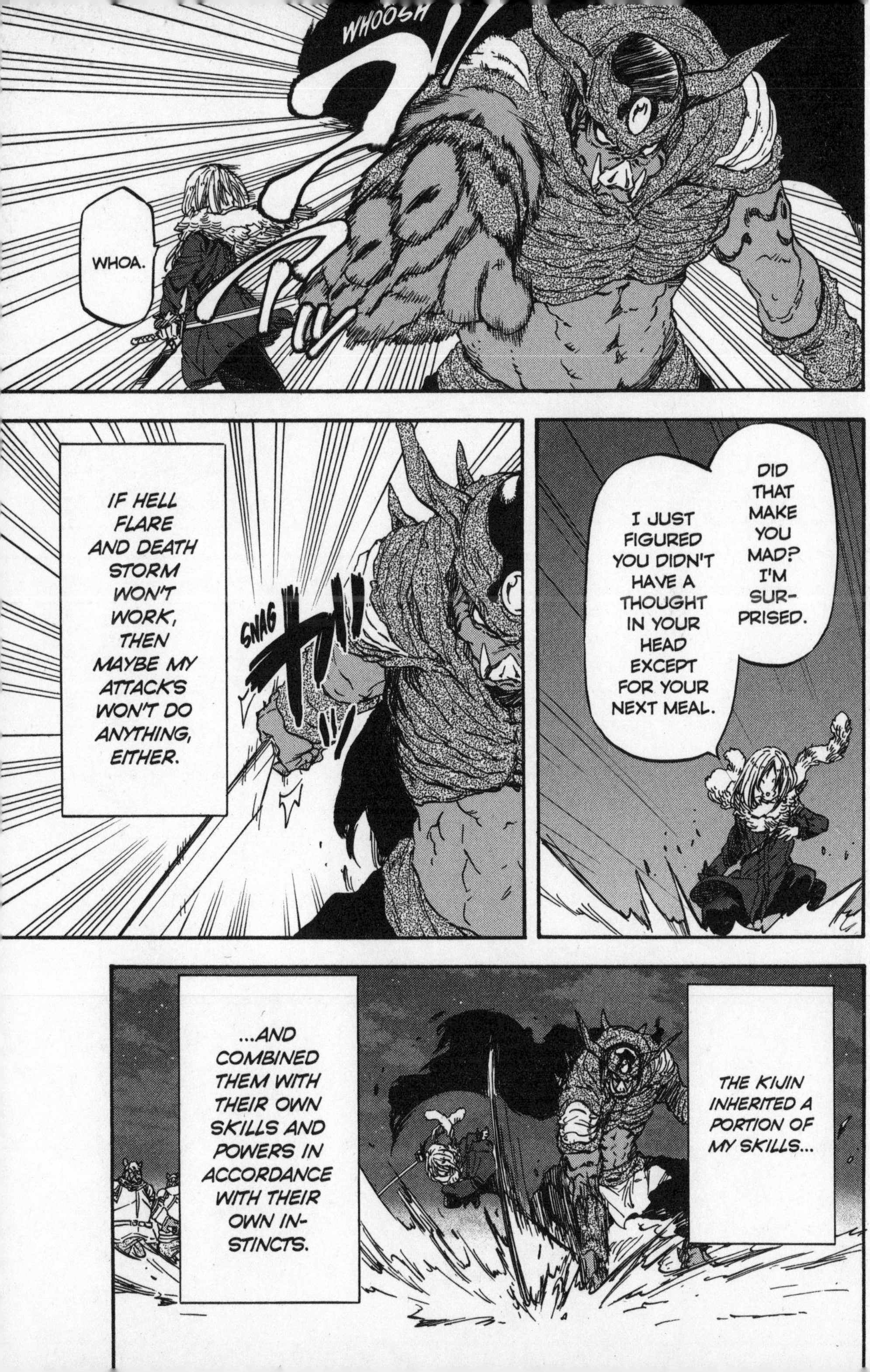
WHOOSH
WHOA.
DID THAT MAKE YOU MAD? I'M SURPRISED.
I JUST FIGURED YOU DIDN'T HAVE A THOUGHT IN YOUR HEAD EXCEPT FOR YOUR NEXT MEAL.
IF HELL FLARE AND DEATH STORM WON'T WORK, THEN MAYBE MY ATTACKS WON'T DO ANYTHING, EITHER.
SNAG
THE KIJIN INHERITED A PORTION OF MY SKILLS...
...AND COMBINED THEM WITH THEIR OWN SKILLS AND POWERS IN ACCORDANCE WITH THEIR OWN INSTINCTS.

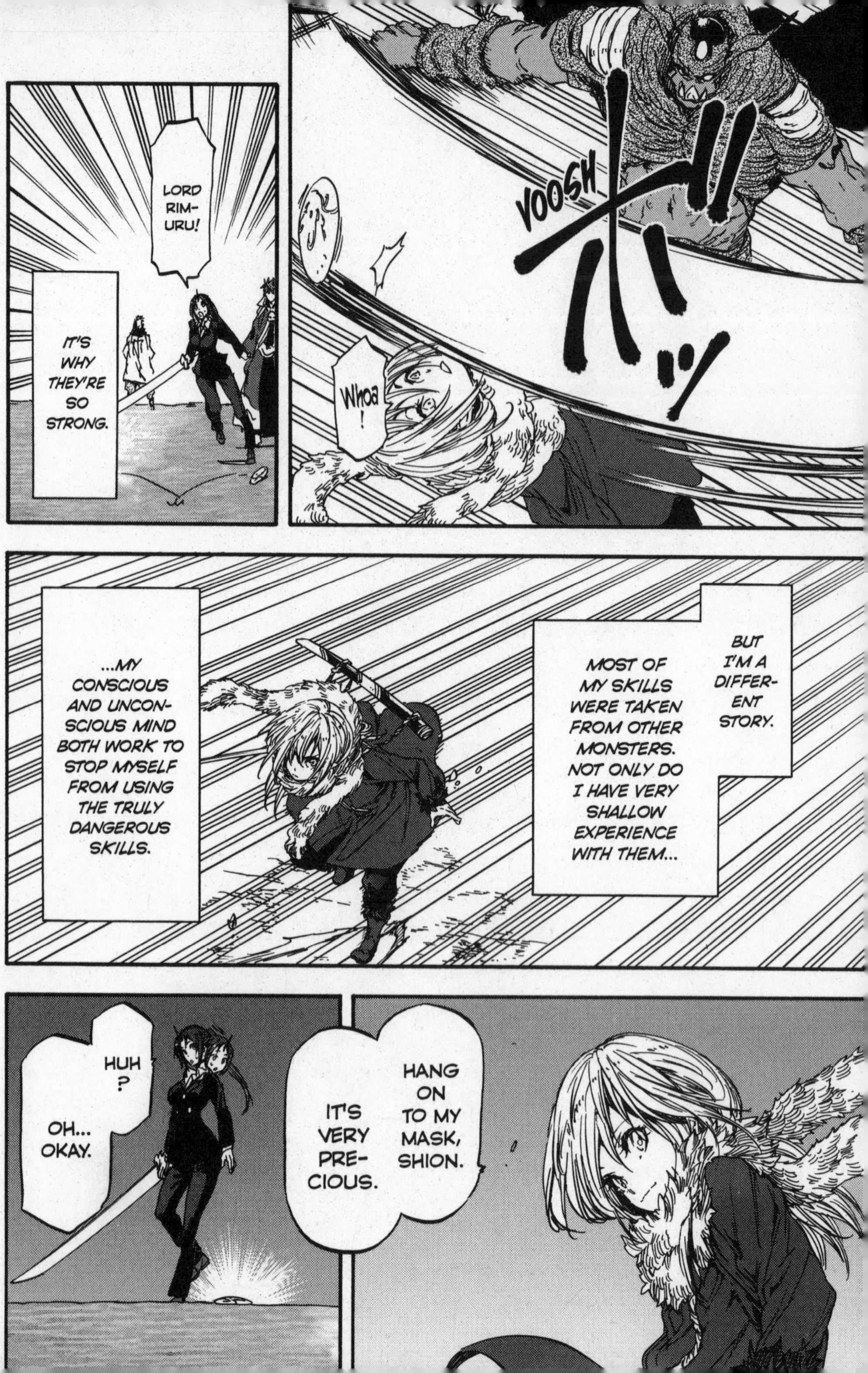
VOOSH
Whoa!
LORD RIM-URU!
IT'S WHY THEY'RE SO STRONG.
BUT I'M A DIFFER-ENT STORY.
MOST OF MY SKILLS WERE TAKEN FROM OTHER MONSTERS. NOT ONLY DO I HAVE VERY SHALLOW EXPERIENCE WITH THEM...
...MY CONSCIOUS AND UNCON-SCIOUS MIND BOTH WORK TO STOP MYSELF FROM USING THE TRULY DANGEROUS SKILLS.
HANG ON TO MY MASK, SHION.
IT'S VERY PRE-CIOUS.
HUH?
OH... OKAY.

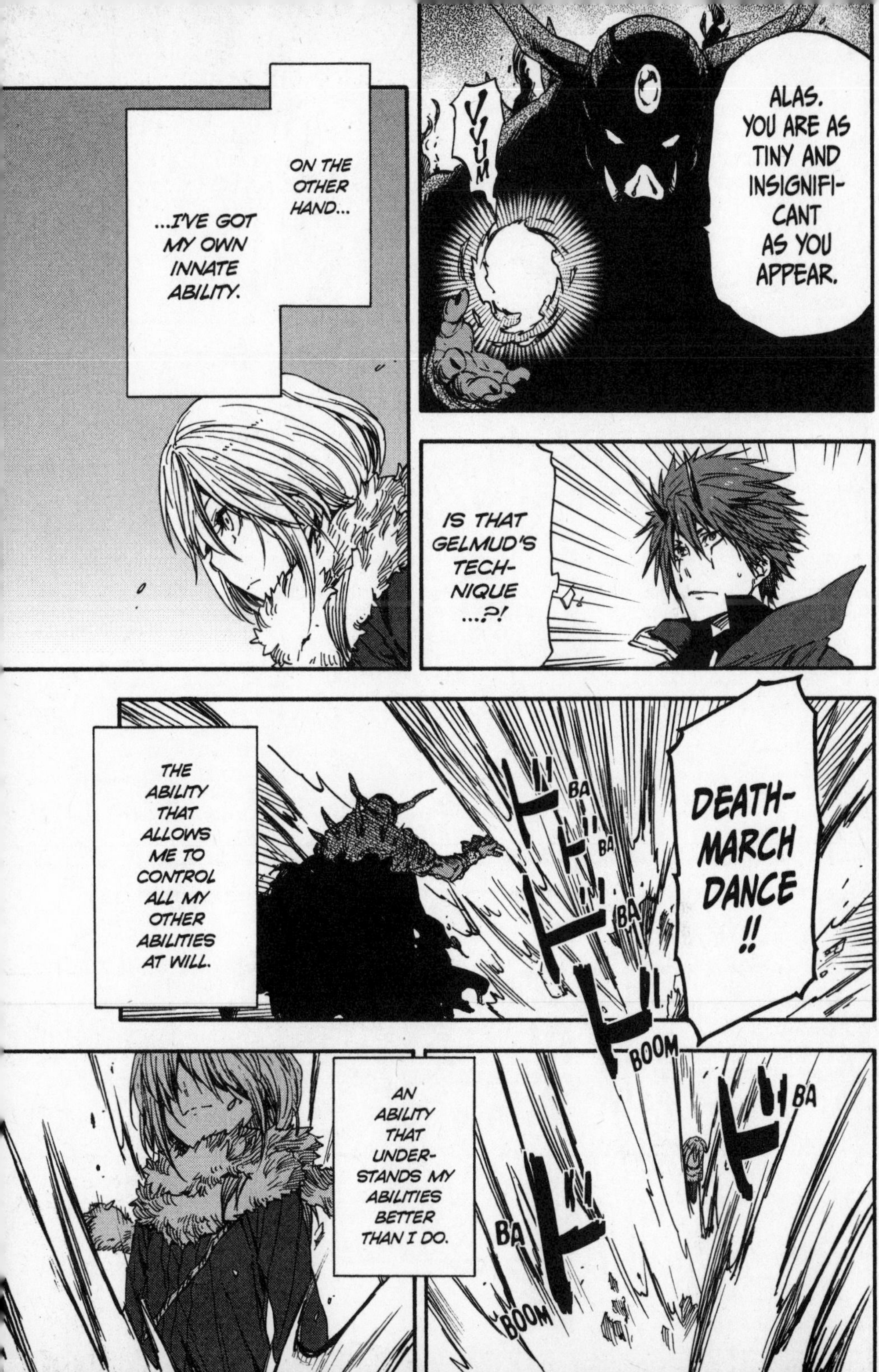
VVUM
ALAS. YOU ARE AS TINY AND INSIGNIFICANT AS YOU APPEAR.
IS THAT GELMUD'S TECHNIQUE ...?!
ON THE OTHER HAND...
...I'VE GOT MY OWN INNATE ABILITY.
DEATH-MARCH DANCE !!
BA
BA
BA
BOOM
THE ABILITY THAT ALLOWS ME TO CONTROL ALL MY OTHER ABILITIES AT WILL.
BA
BA
BOOM
AN ABILITY THAT UNDERSTANDS MY ABILITIES BETTER THAN I DO.

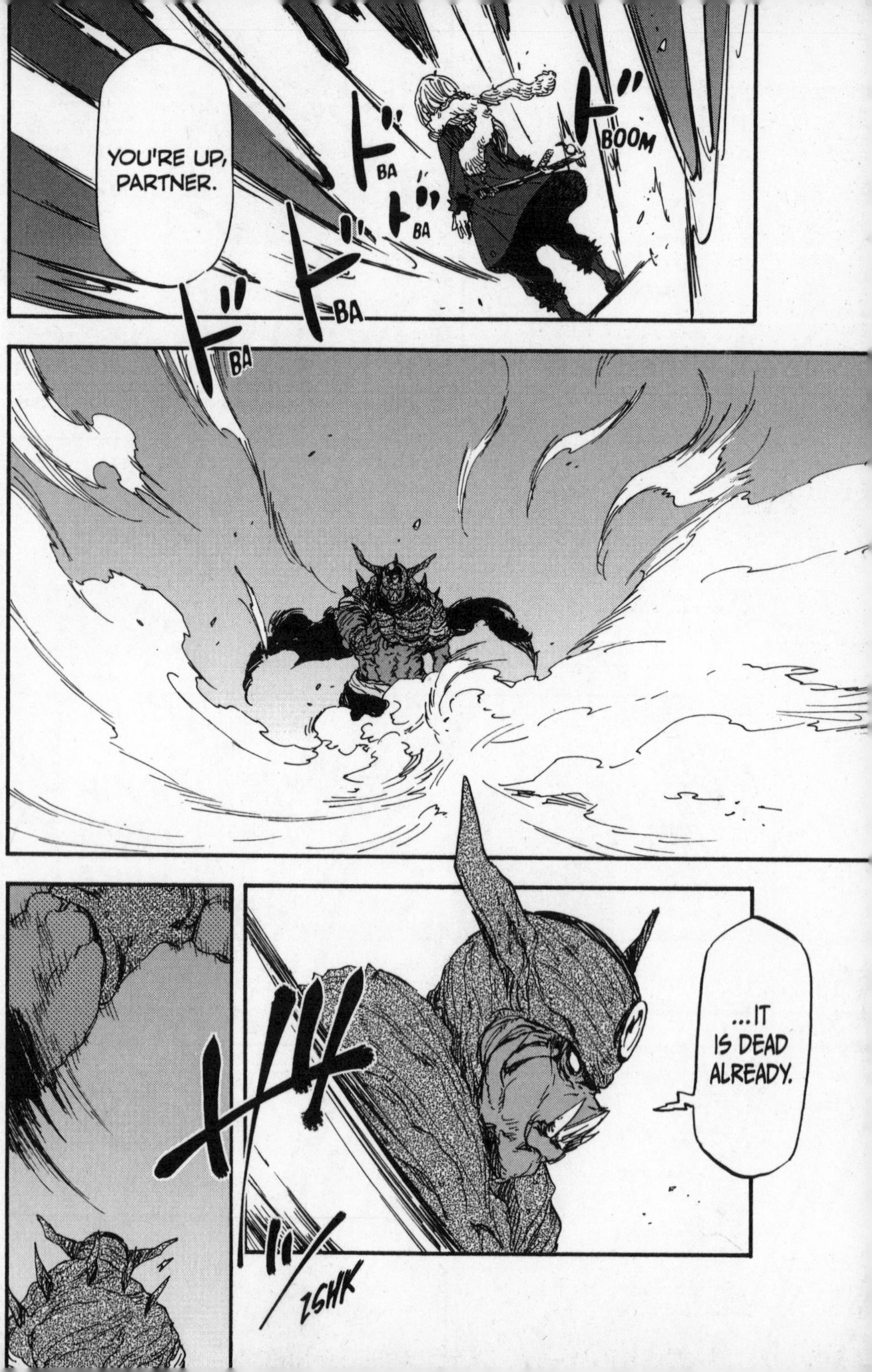
BOOM
BA
BA
YOU'RE UP, PARTNER.
BA
BA
...IT IS DEAD ALREADY.
ZSHK

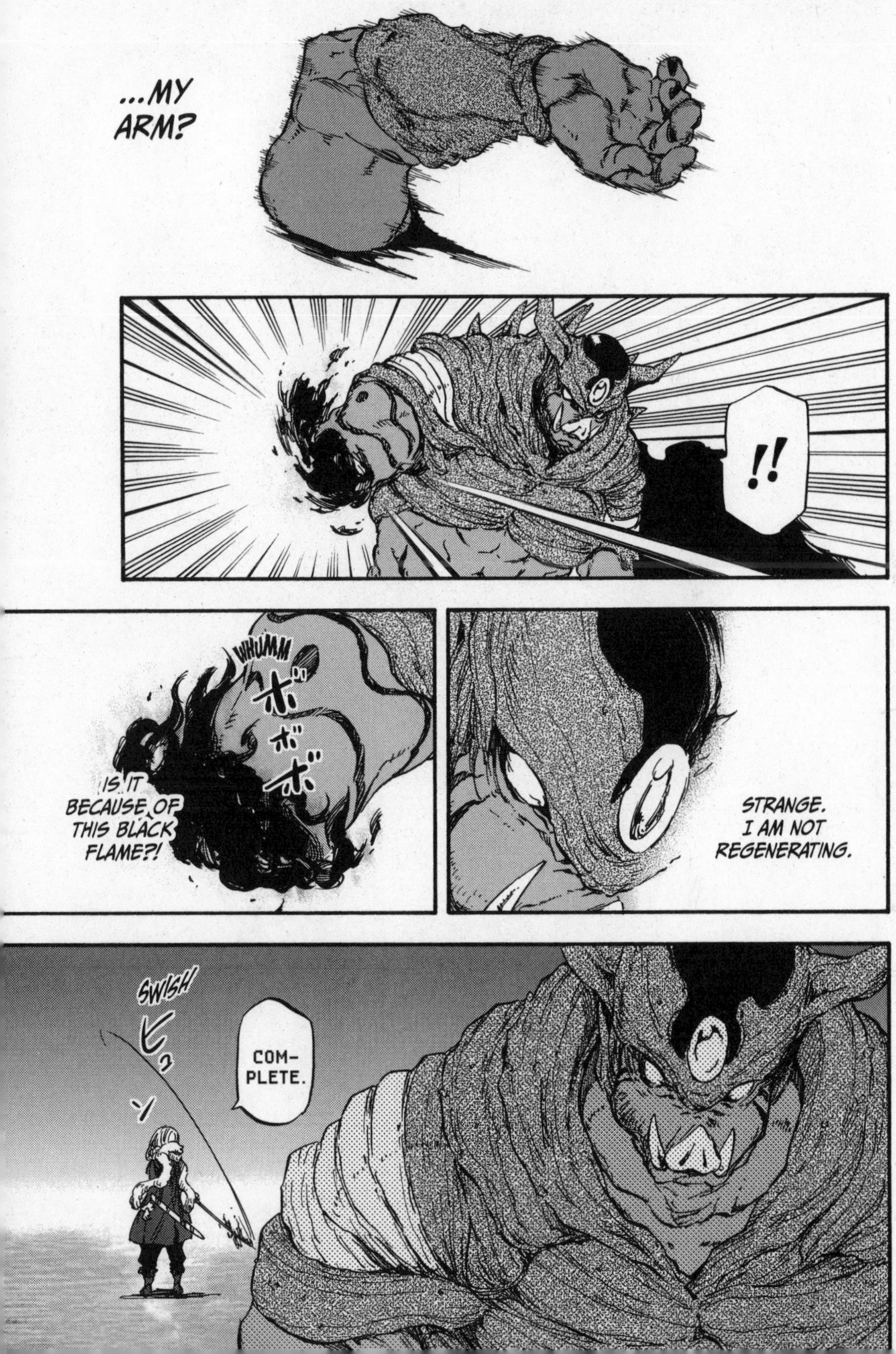
...MY ARM?
!!
STRANGE. I AM NOT REGENERATING.
WHUMM
ボボボ
IS IT BECAUSE OF THIS BLACK FLAME?!
COM-PLETE.
SWISH
ヒュン

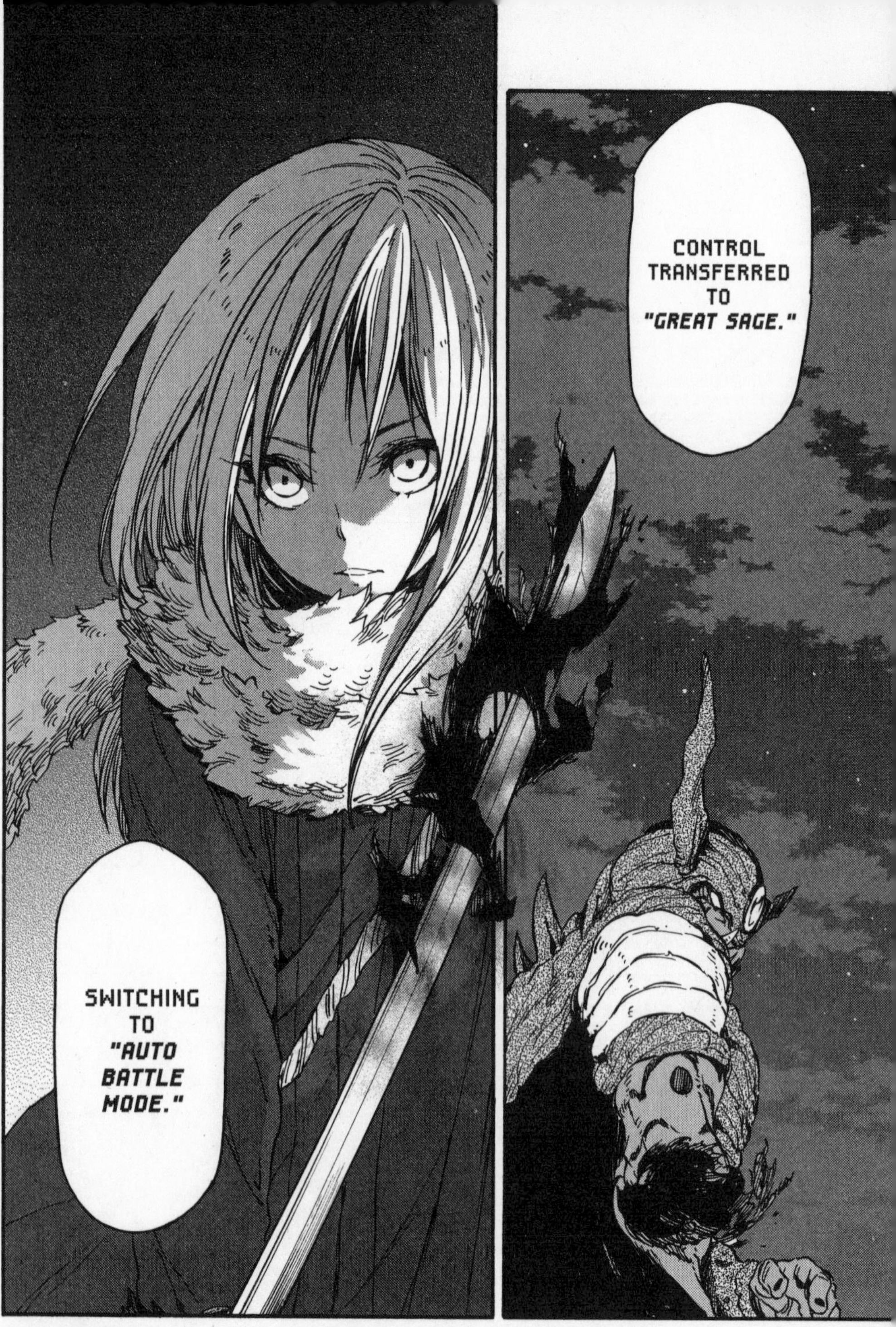
CONTROL TRANSFERRED TO *"GREAT SAGE."*
SWITCHING TO *"AUTO BATTLE MODE."*

GOBTA'S HENCHMEN

GOBTSU
& GOBTE

Twin brothers, apparently.

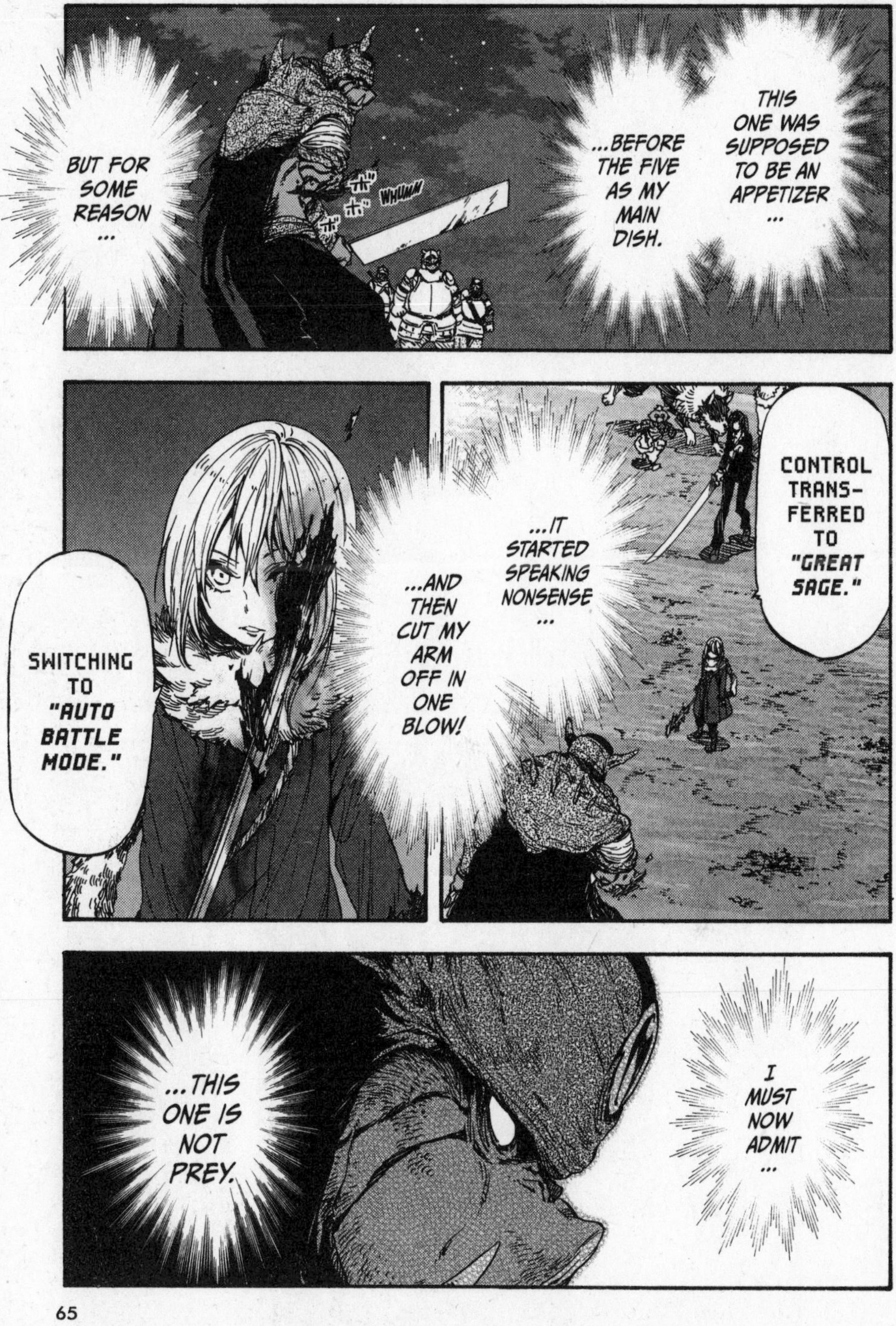
THIS ONE WAS SUPPOSED TO BE AN APPETIZER...
...BEFORE THE FIVE AS MY MAIN DISH.
BUT FOR SOME REASON...
WHUMM
CONTROL TRANS- FERRED TO "GREAT SAGE."
...IT STARTED SPEAKING NONSENSE...
...AND THEN CUT MY ARM OFF IN ONE BLOW!
SWITCHING TO "AUTO BATTLE MODE."
I MUST NOW ADMIT...
...THIS ONE IS NOT PREY.

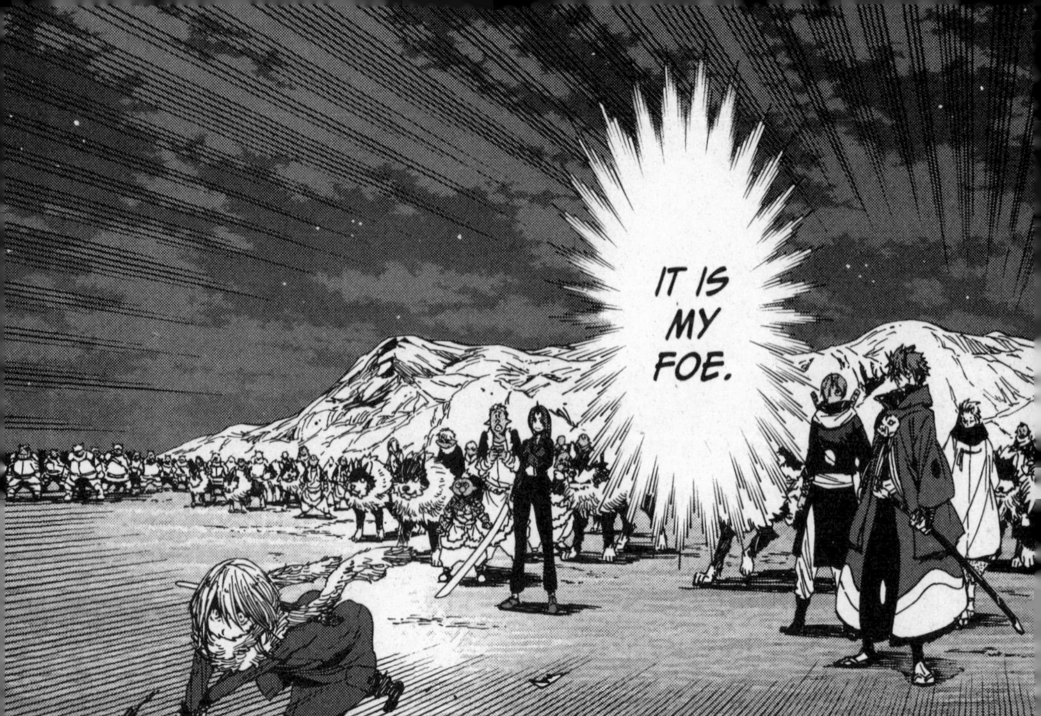
IT IS MY FOE.
CHAPTER 25 That Which Devours All

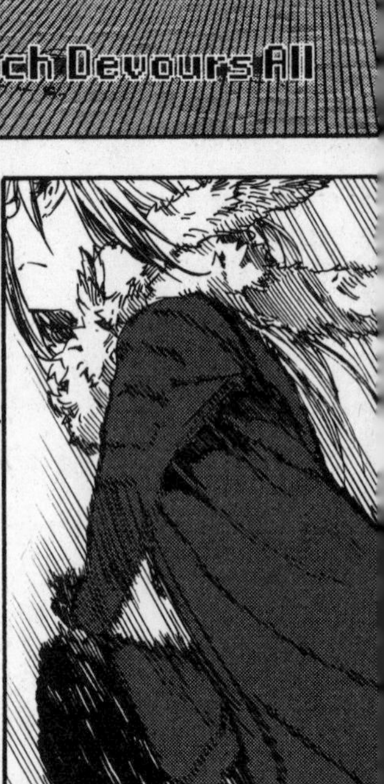

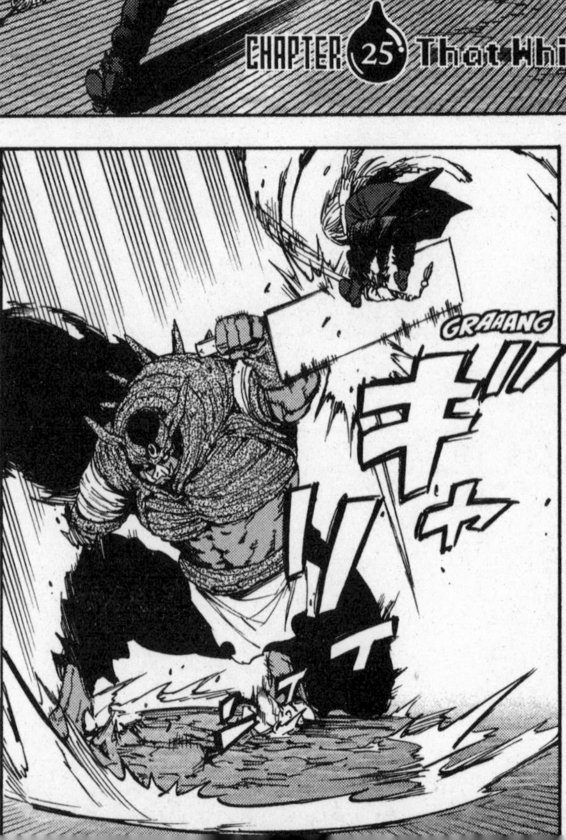
GRAAANG

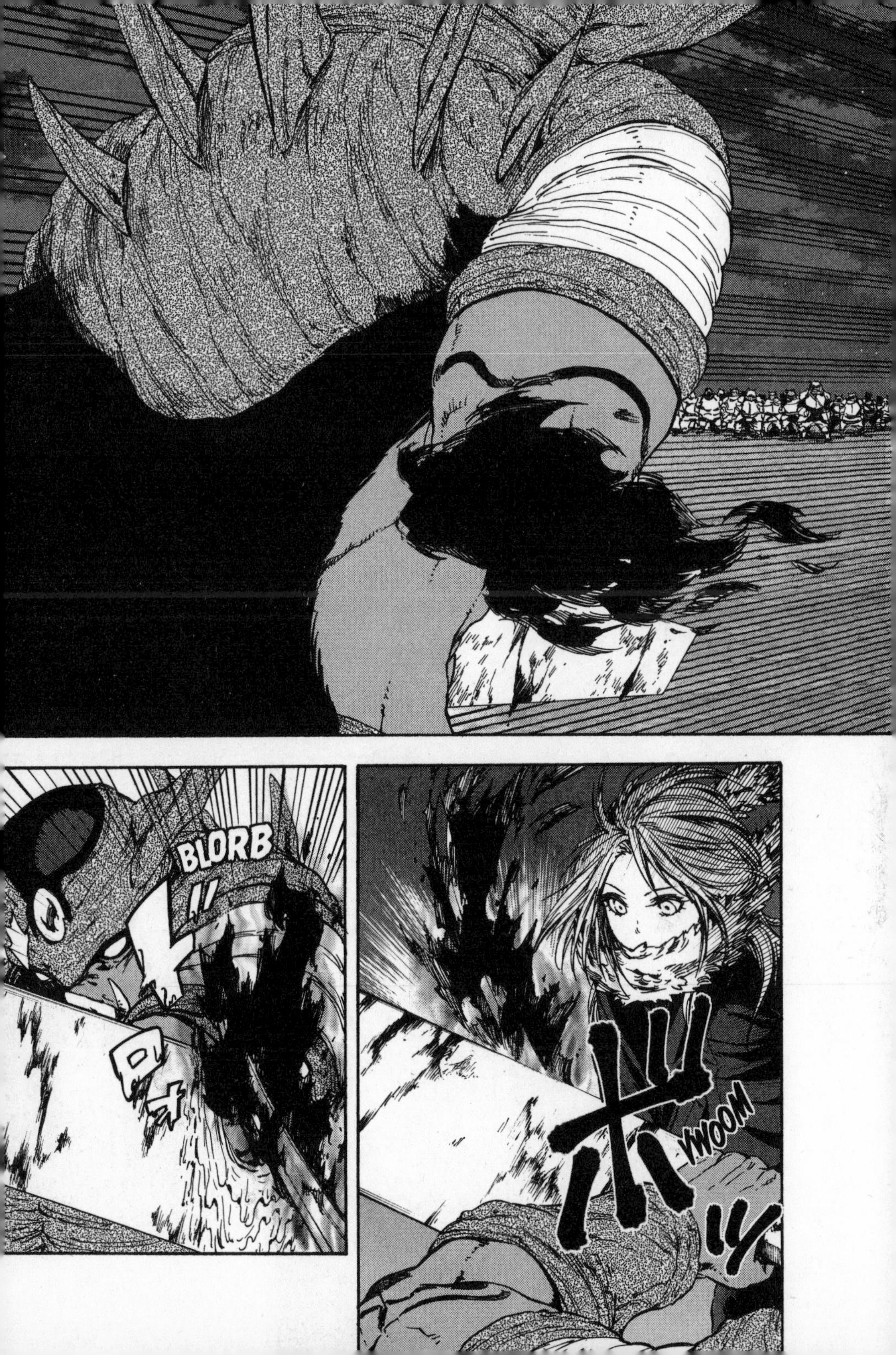
VWOOM
BLORB

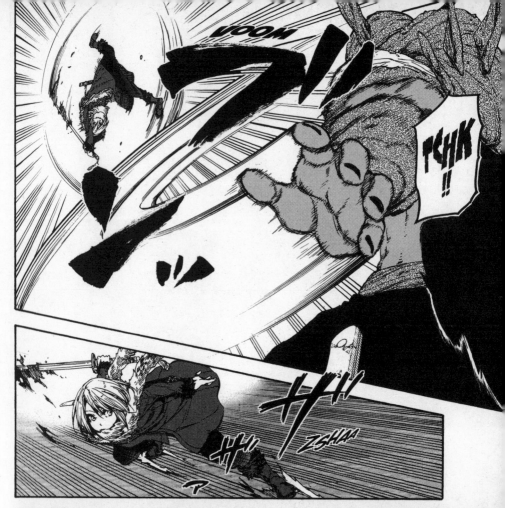

TCHK !!

VOOM

ZSHAA

WHY ISN'T THE ORC DISASTER'S ARM REGEN- ERATING ...?

CHAOS EATER!

WHOOSH

!

68

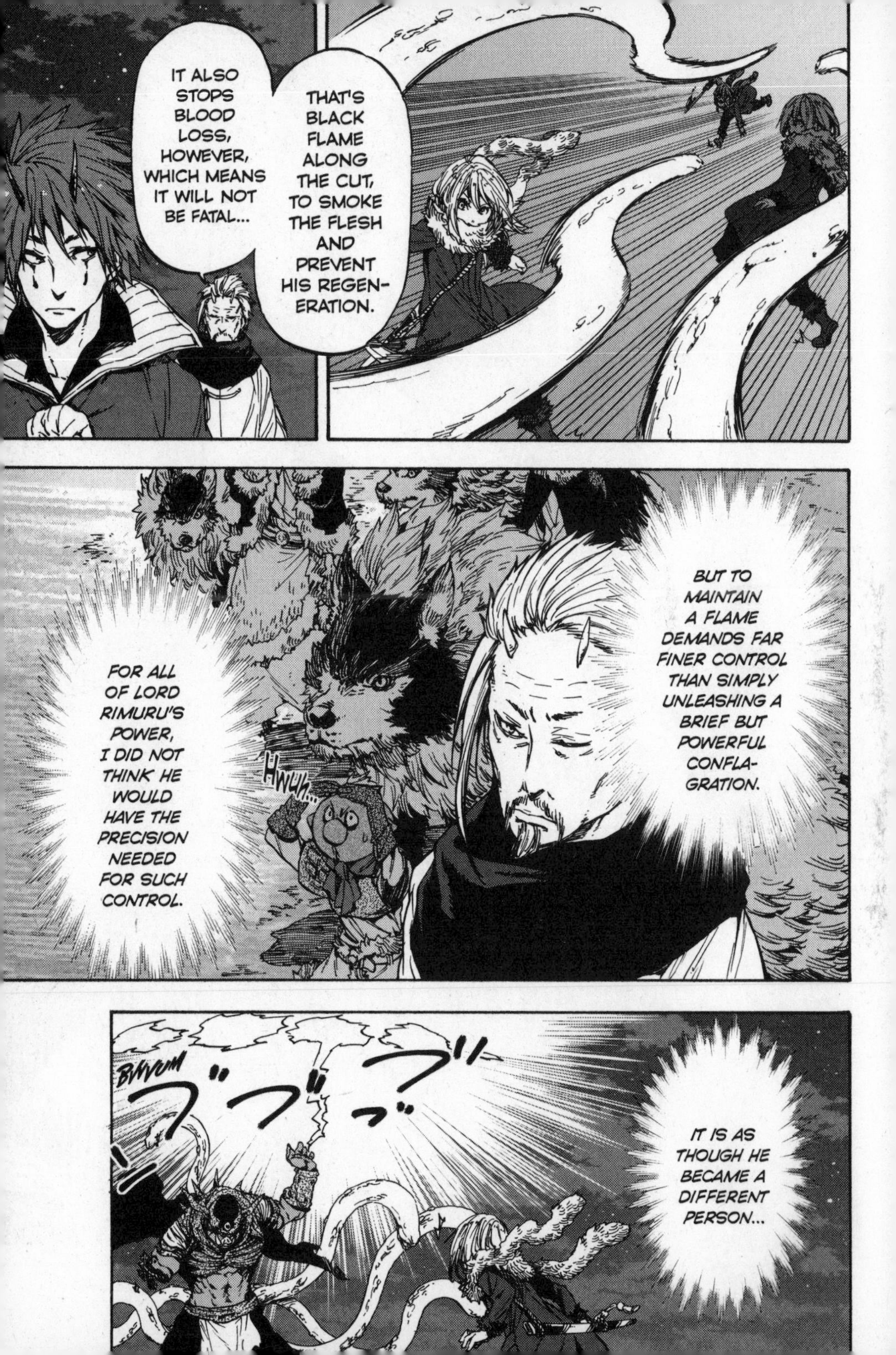
THAT'S BLACK FLAME ALONG THE CUT, TO SMOKE THE FLESH AND PREVENT HIS REGENERATION.
IT ALSO STOPS BLOOD LOSS, HOWEVER, WHICH MEANS IT WILL NOT BE FATAL...
BUT TO MAINTAIN A FLAME DEMANDS FAR FINER CONTROL THAN SIMPLY UNLEASHING A BRIEF BUT POWERFUL CONFLAGRATION.
HWUH...
FOR ALL OF LORD RIMURU'S POWER, I DID NOT THINK HE WOULD HAVE THE PRECISION NEEDED FOR SUCH CONTROL.
IT IS AS THOUGH HE BECAME A DIFFERENT PERSON...
BVVUM

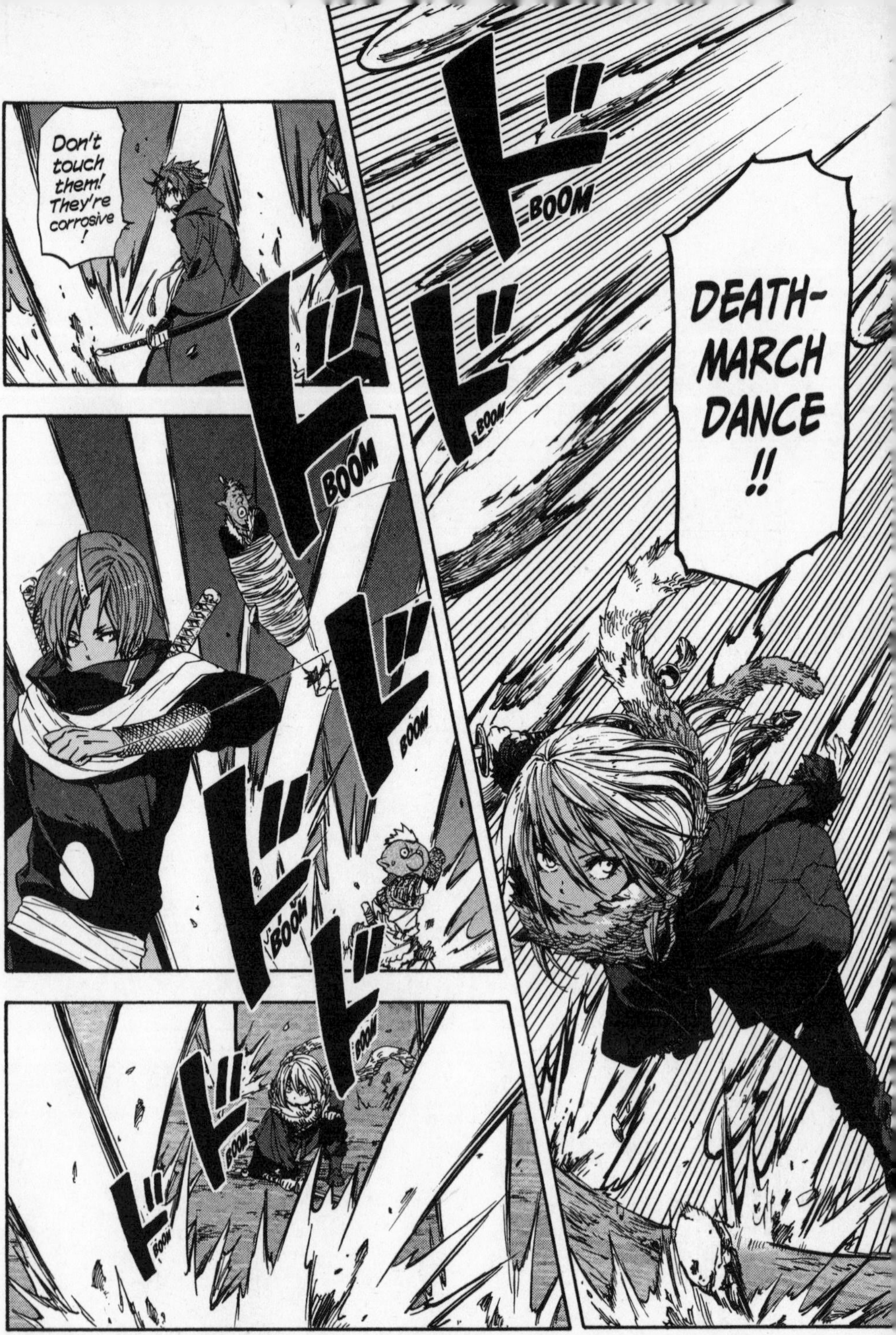
DEATH-MARCH DANCE!!
BOOM
BOOM
Don't touch them! They're corrosive!
BOOM
BOOM
BOOM
BOOM
BOOM
BOOM

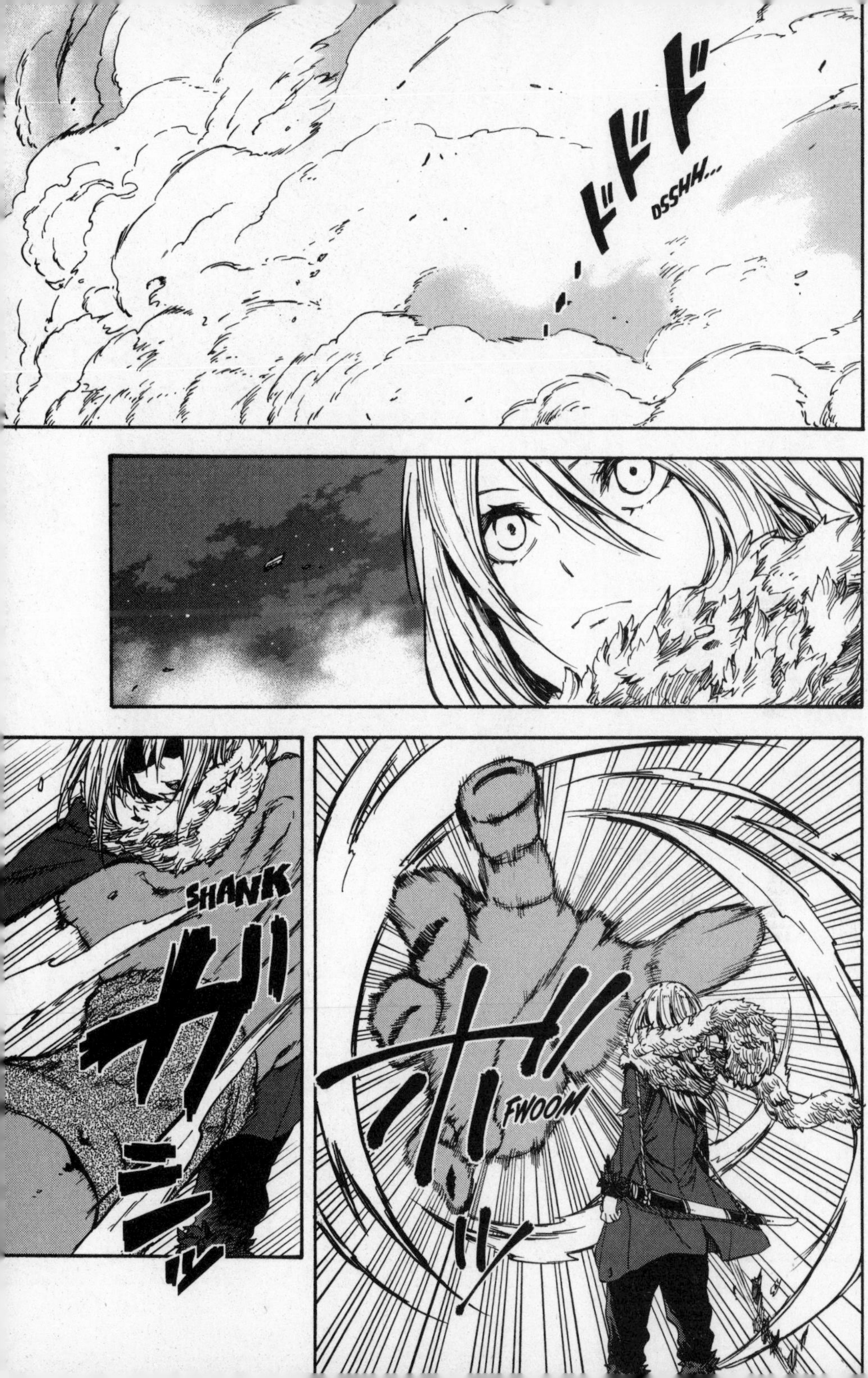
ドドド
DSSHH...
FWOOM
SHANK

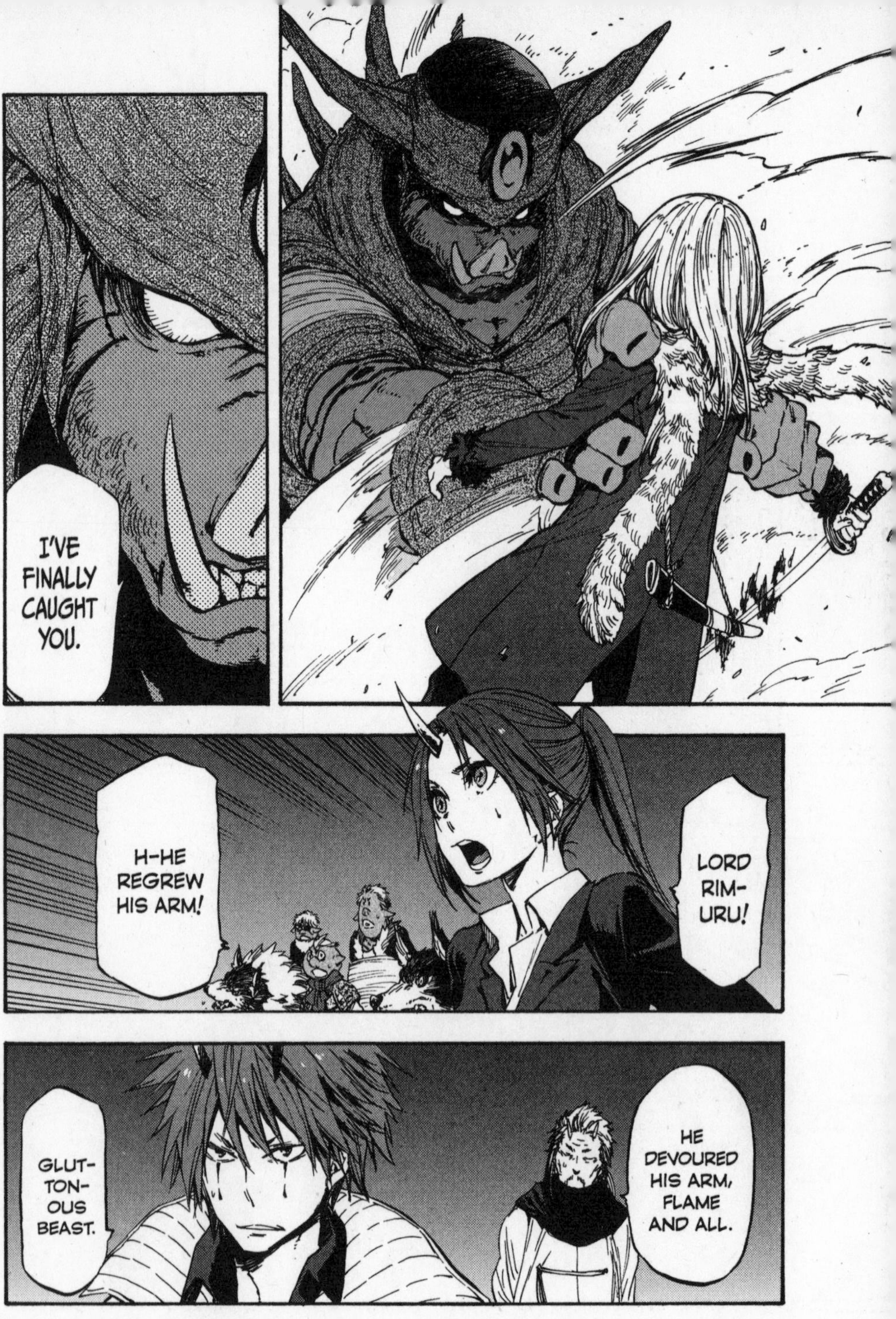
I'VE FINALLY CAUGHT YOU.
LORD RIM-URU!
H-HE REGREW HIS ARM!
HE DEVOURED HIS ARM, FLAME AND ALL.
GLUT-TON-OUS BEAST.

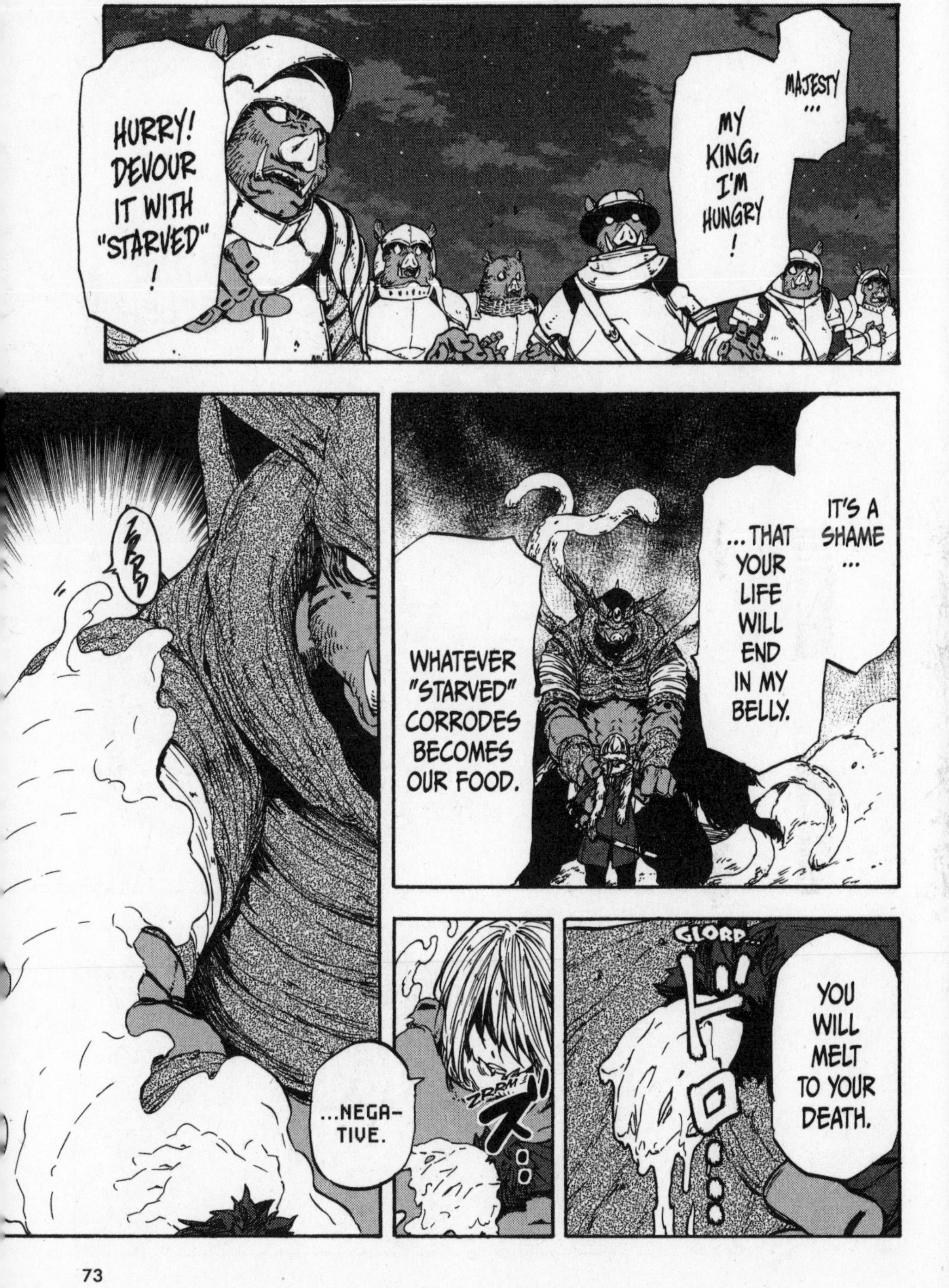
MAJESTY...
MY KING, I'M HUNGRY!
HURRY! DEVOUR IT WITH "STARVED"!
IT'S A SHAME...
...THAT YOUR LIFE WILL END IN MY BELLY.
WHATEVER "STARVED" CORRODES BECOMES OUR FOOD.
GLORP...
YOU WILL MELT TO YOUR DEATH.
ZRRM...
...NEGA-TIVE.
ZRRD

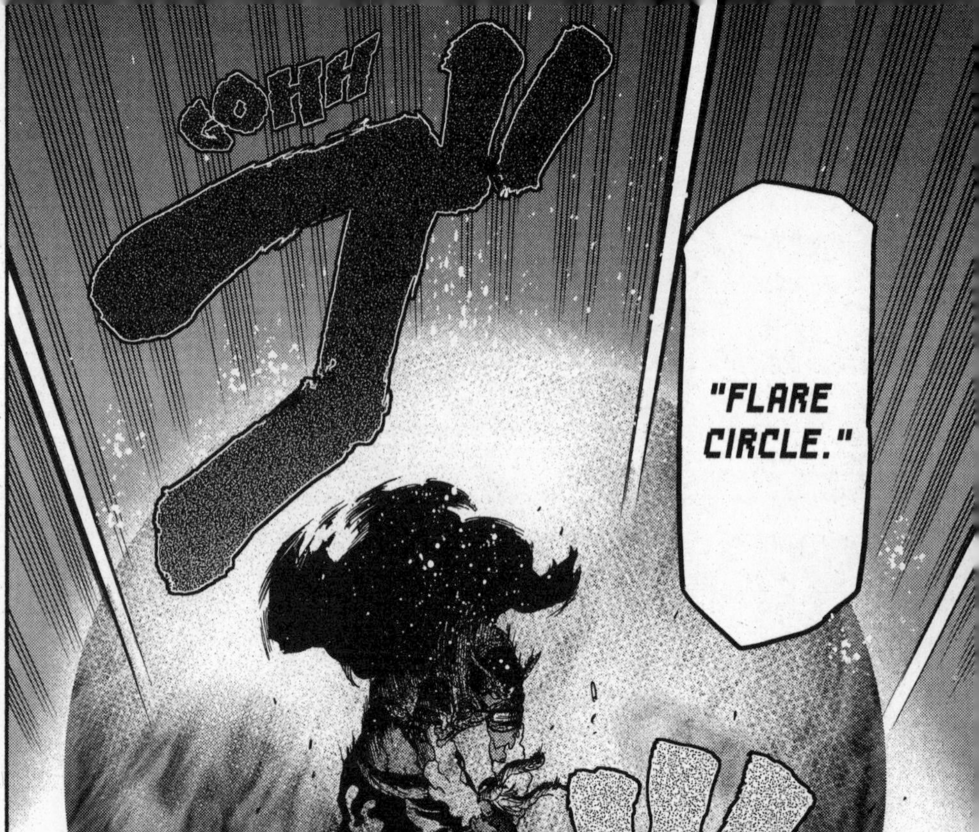
GOHH
"FLARE CIRCLE."
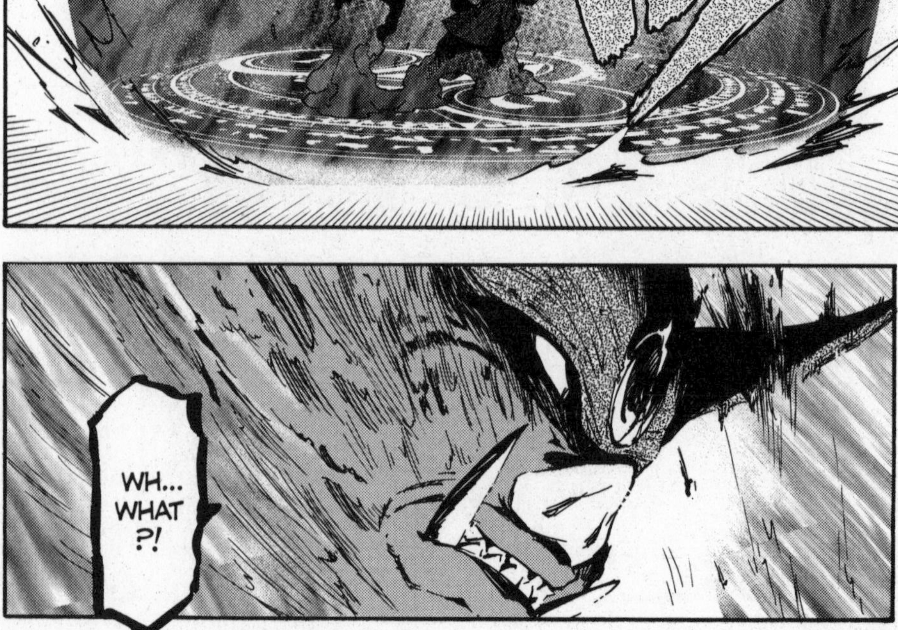
WH... WHAT ?!

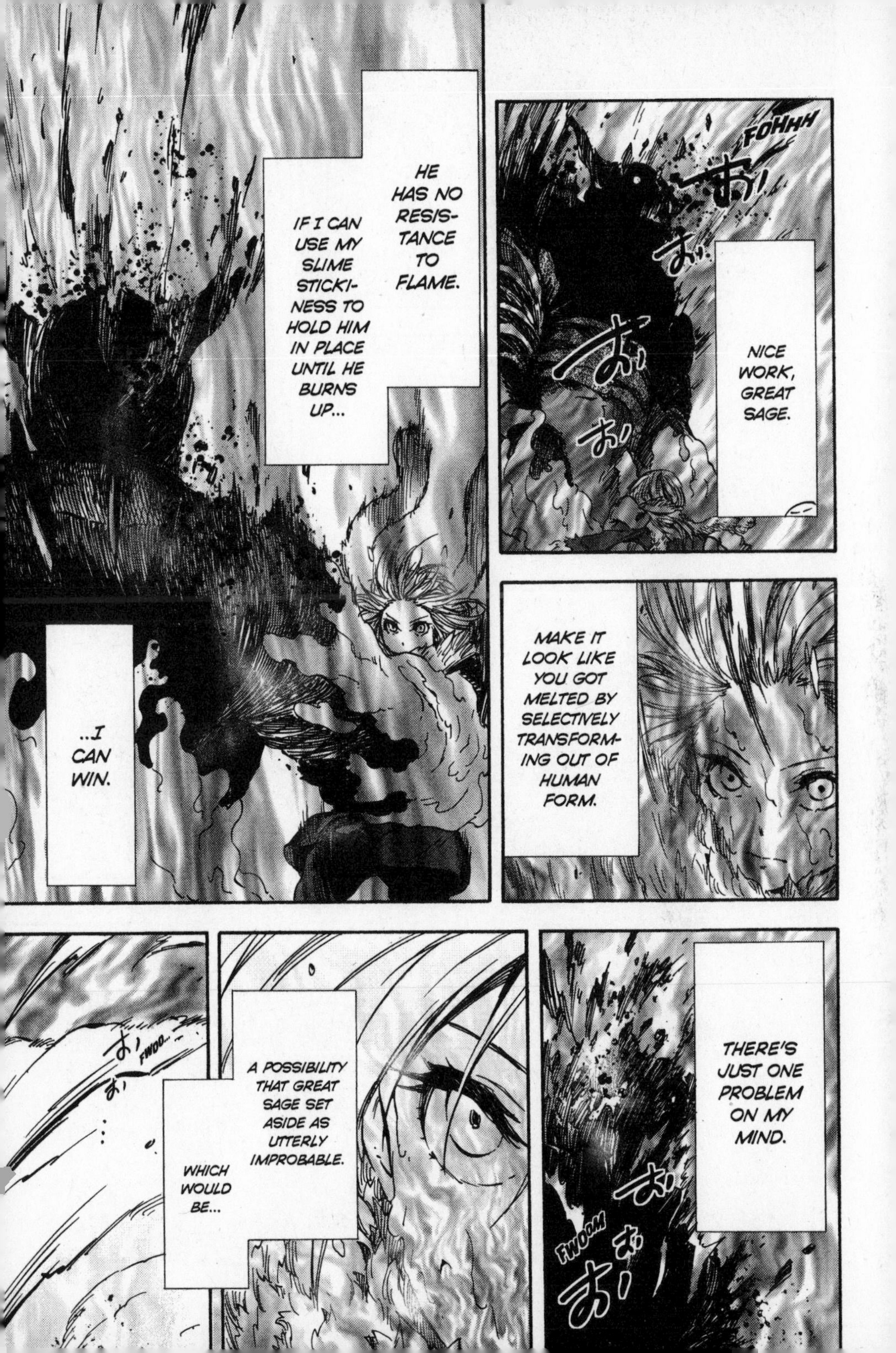
FOHHH
NICE WORK, GREAT SAGE.
MAKE IT LOOK LIKE YOU GOT MELTED BY SELECTIVELY TRANSFORMING OUT OF HUMAN FORM.
HE HAS NO RESISTANCE TO FLAME.
IF I CAN USE MY SLIME STICKINESS TO HOLD HIM IN PLACE UNTIL HE BURNS UP...
...I CAN WIN.
THERE'S JUST ONE PROBLEM ON MY MIND.
FWOOM
A POSSIBILITY THAT GREAT SAGE SET ASIDE AS UTTERLY IMPROBABLE.
WHICH WOULD BE...
FWOO...

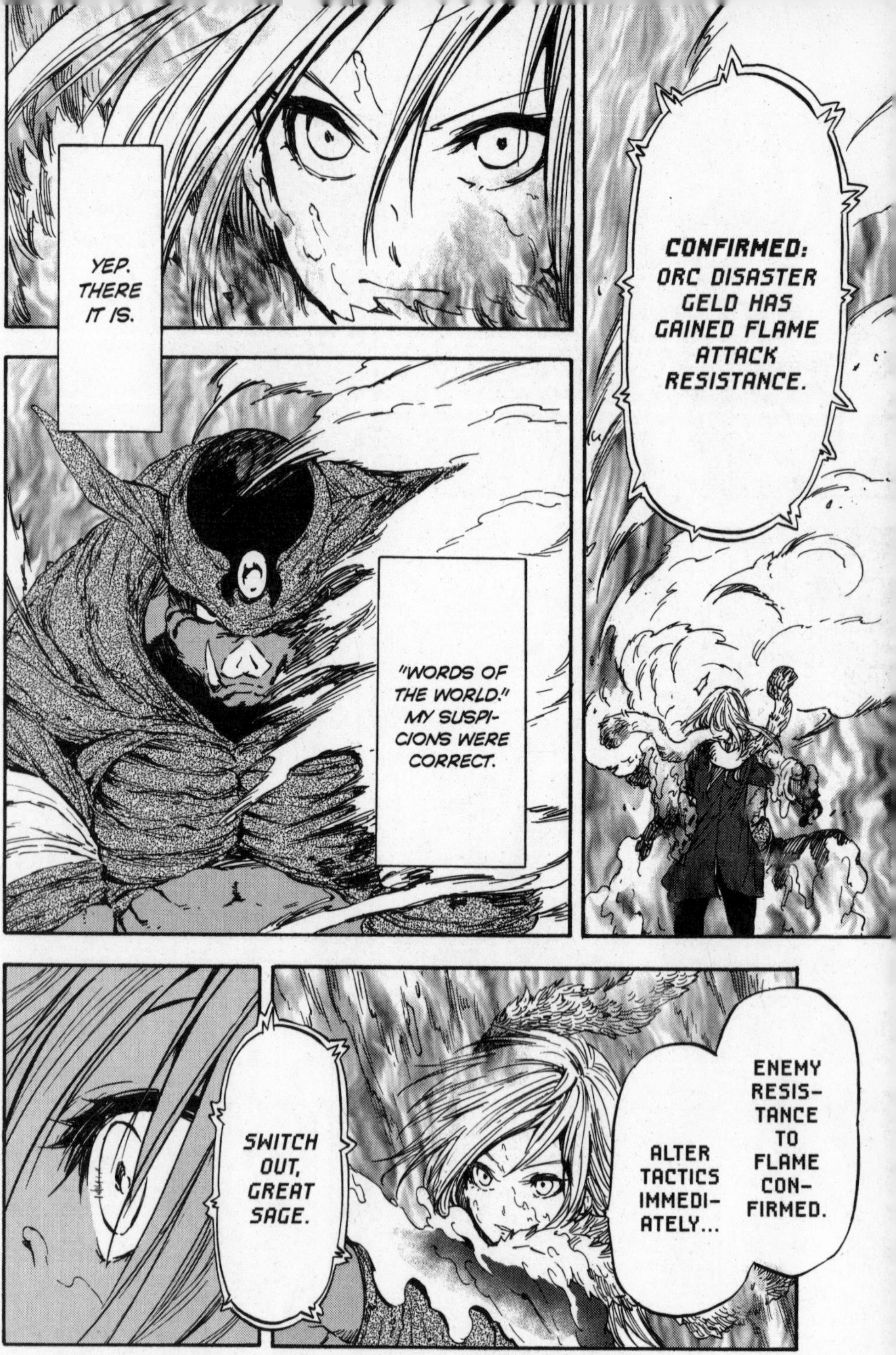
CONFIRMED: ORC DISASTER GELD HAS GAINED FLAME ATTACK RESISTANCE.
YEP. THERE IT IS.
"WORDS OF THE WORLD." MY SUSPICIONS WERE CORRECT.
ENEMY RESISTANCE TO FLAME CONFIRMED.
ALTER TACTICS IMMEDIATELY...
SWITCH OUT, GREAT SAGE.

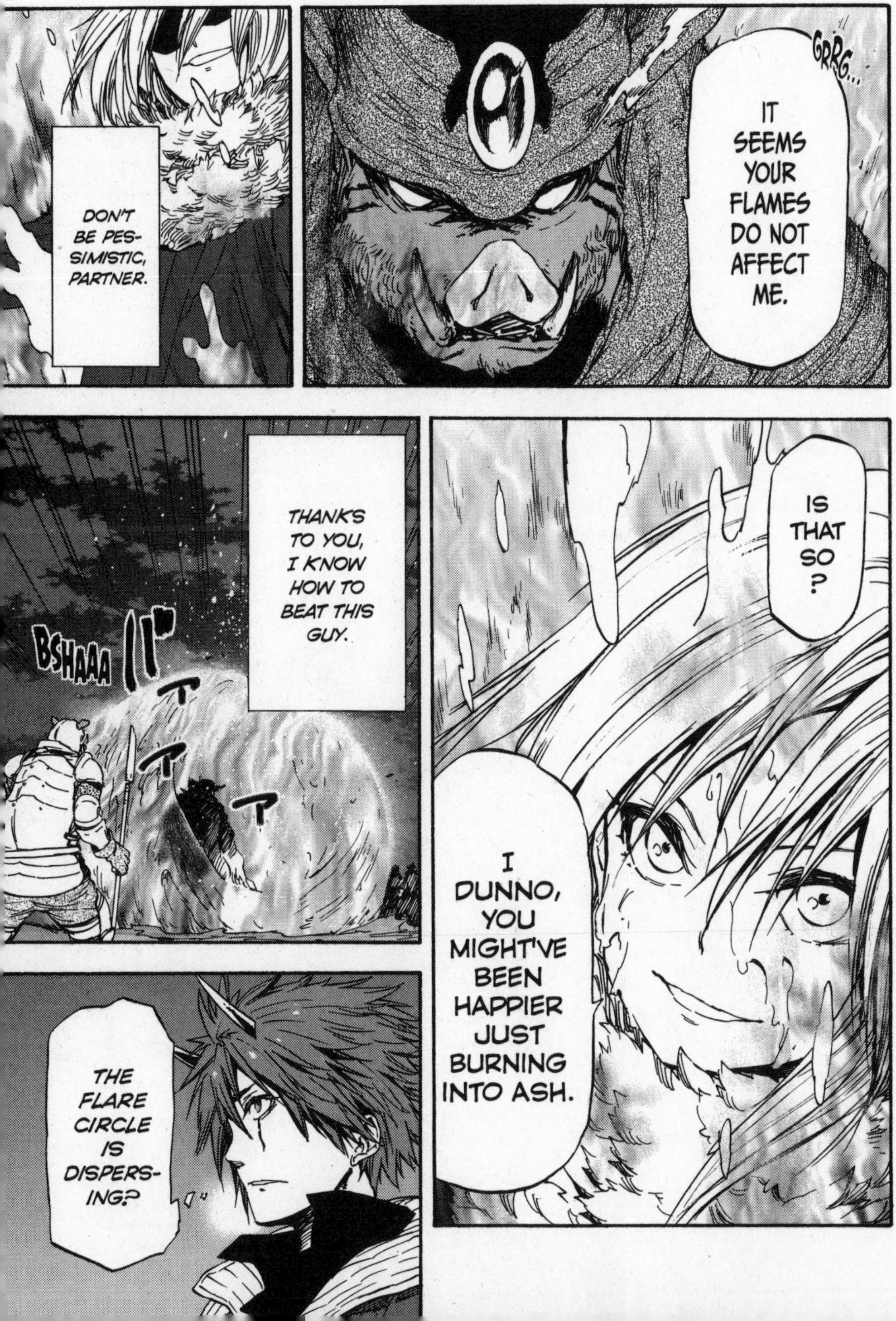
GRRG...
IT SEEMS YOUR FLAMES DO NOT AFFECT ME.
DON'T BE PES-SIMISTIC, PARTNER.
IS THAT SO?
I DUNNO, YOU MIGHT'VE BEEN HAPPIER JUST BURNING INTO ASH.
THANKS TO YOU, I KNOW HOW TO BEAT THIS GUY.
BSHAAA
THE FLARE CIRCLE IS DISPERSING?

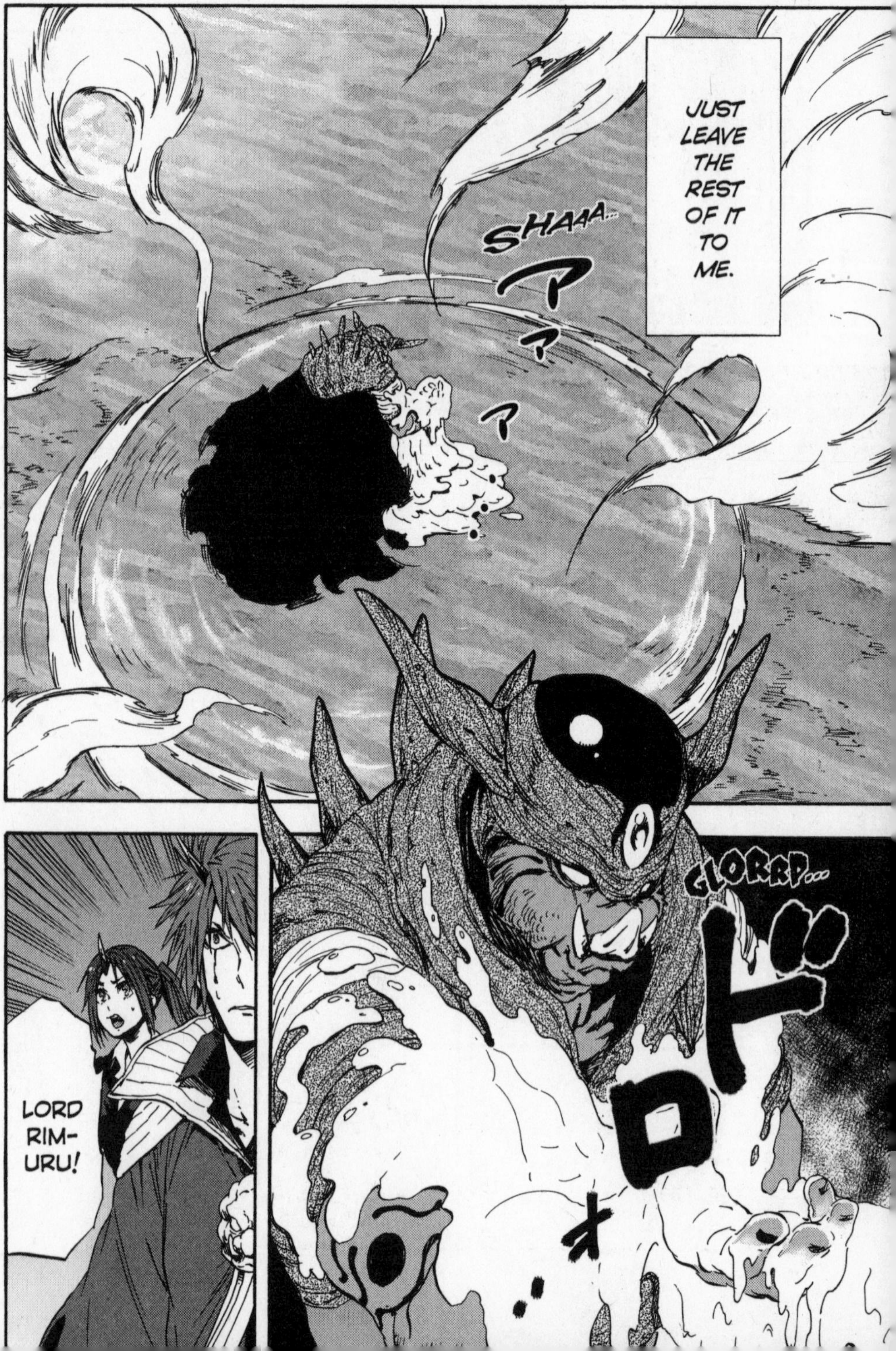
JUST LEAVE THE REST OF IT TO ME.
SHAAA...
アァア
GLORRP...
ドロォ
LORD RIM-URU!

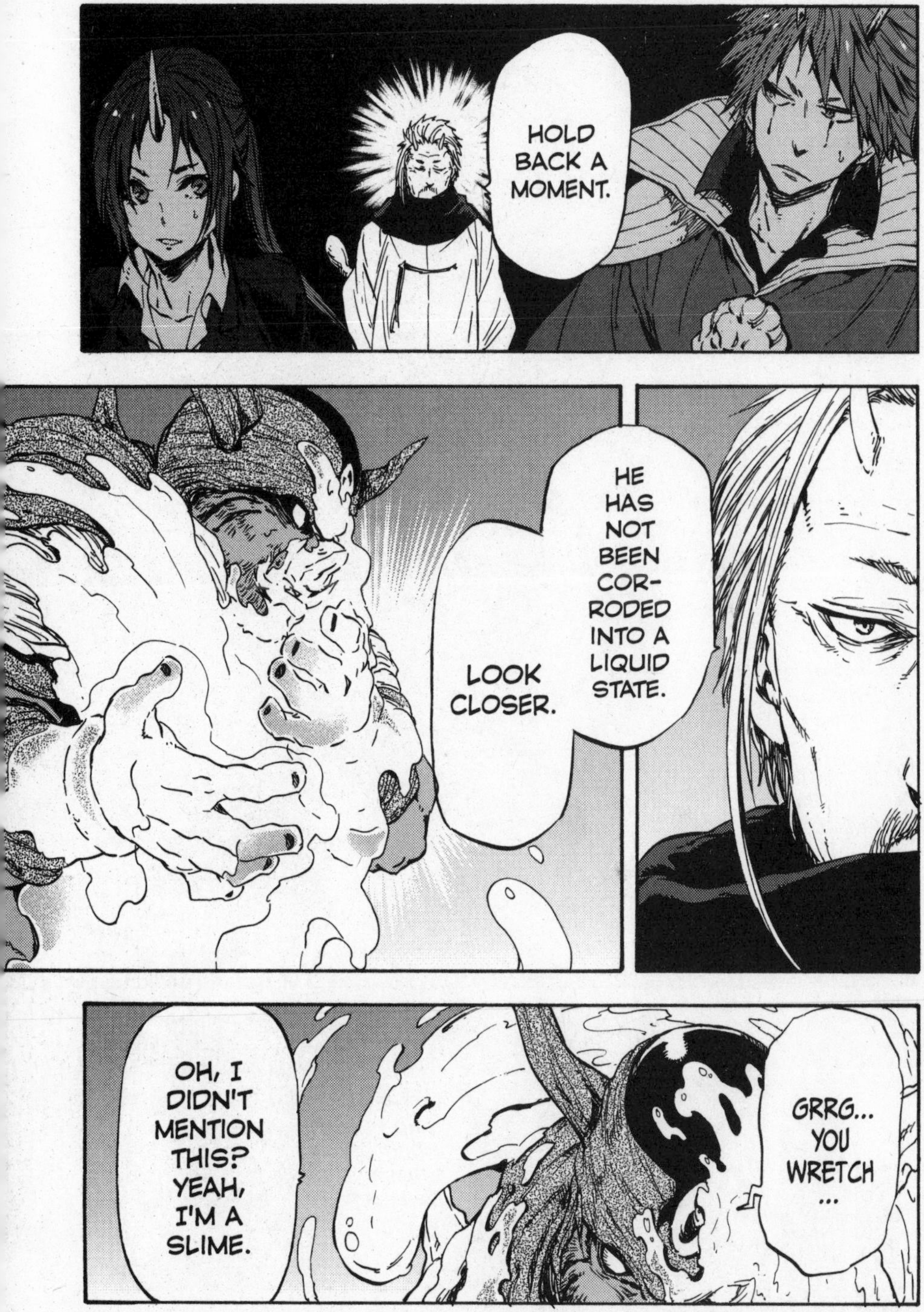
HOLD BACK A MOMENT.
HE HAS NOT BEEN COR-RODED INTO A LIQUID STATE.
LOOK CLOSER.
GRRG... YOU WRETCH...
OH, I DIDN'T MENTION THIS? YEAH, I'M A SLIME.

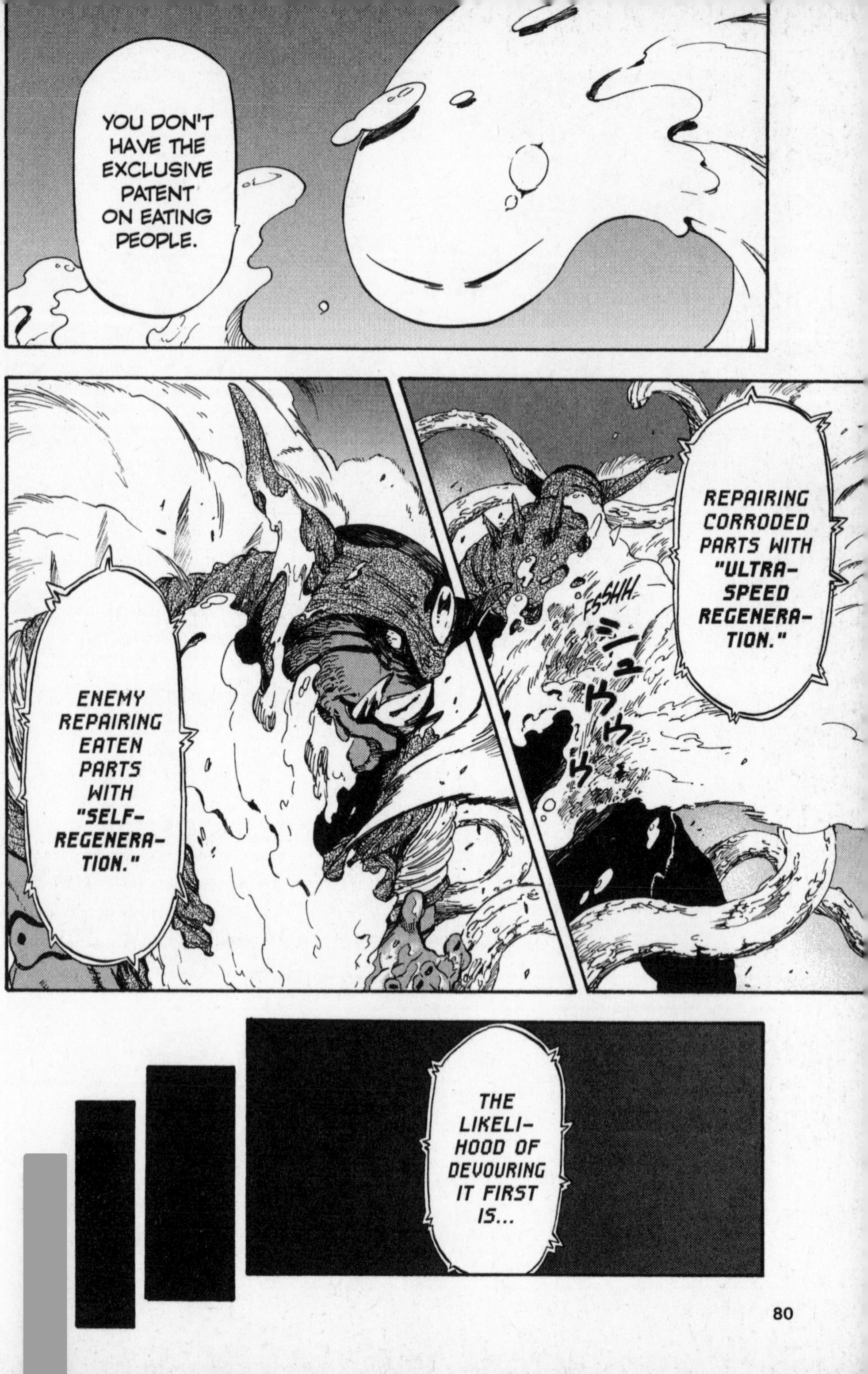
YOU DON'T HAVE THE EXCLUSIVE PATENT ON EATING PEOPLE.
REPAIRING CORRODED PARTS WITH "ULTRA-SPEED REGENERA-TION."
FSSHH
ENEMY REPAIRING EATEN PARTS WITH "SELF-REGENERA-TION."
THE LIKELI-HOOD OF DEVOURING IT FIRST IS...

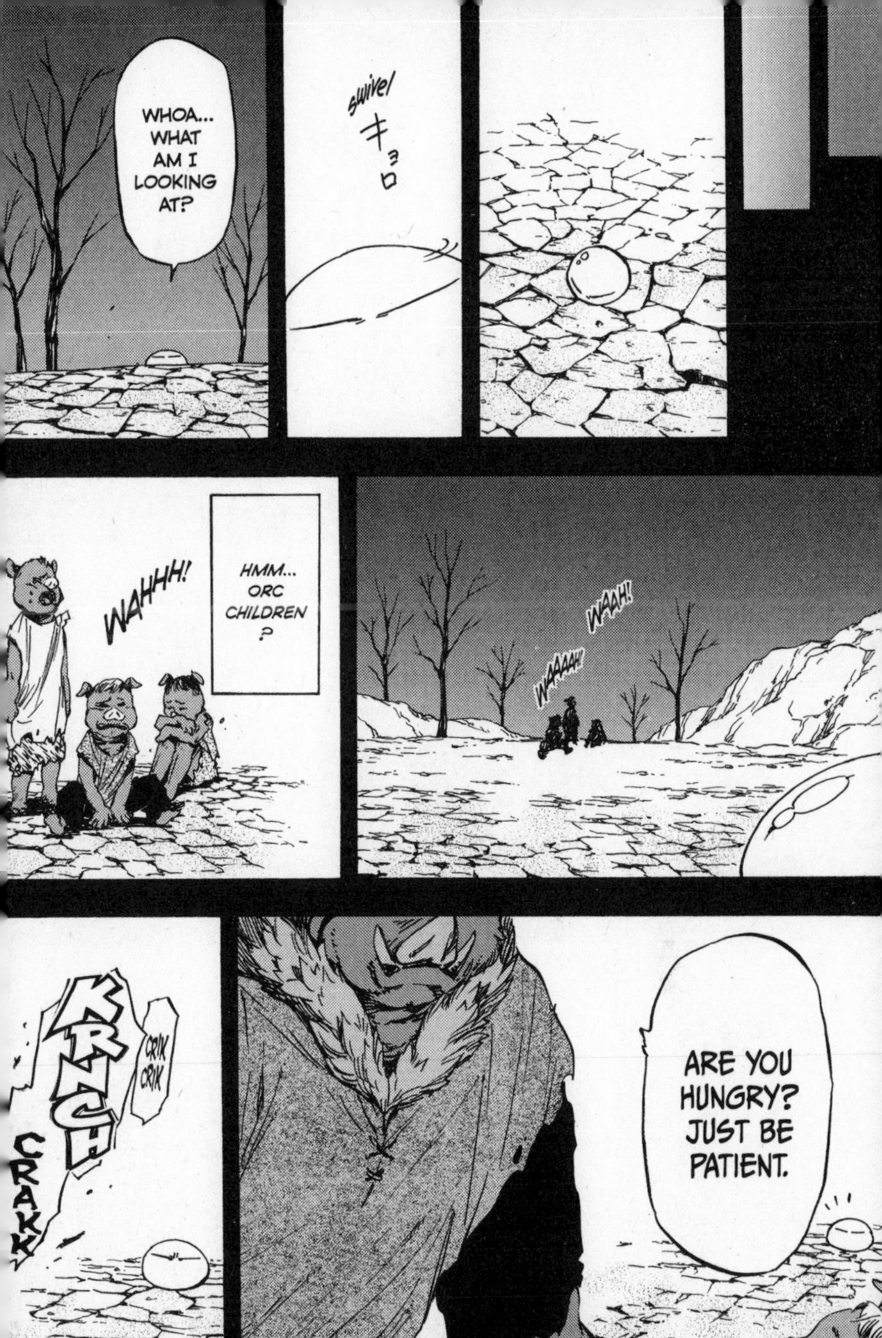
swivel
キョロ
WHOA... WHAT AM I LOOKING AT?
WAAH!
WAAAAH!
HMM... ORC CHILDREN ?
WAHHH!
ARE YOU HUNGRY? JUST BE PATIENT.
CRIK CRIK
KRNCH
CRAKK

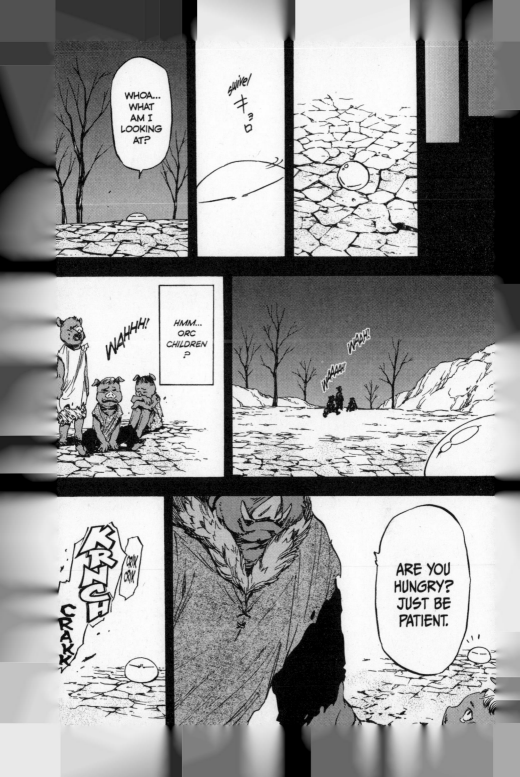

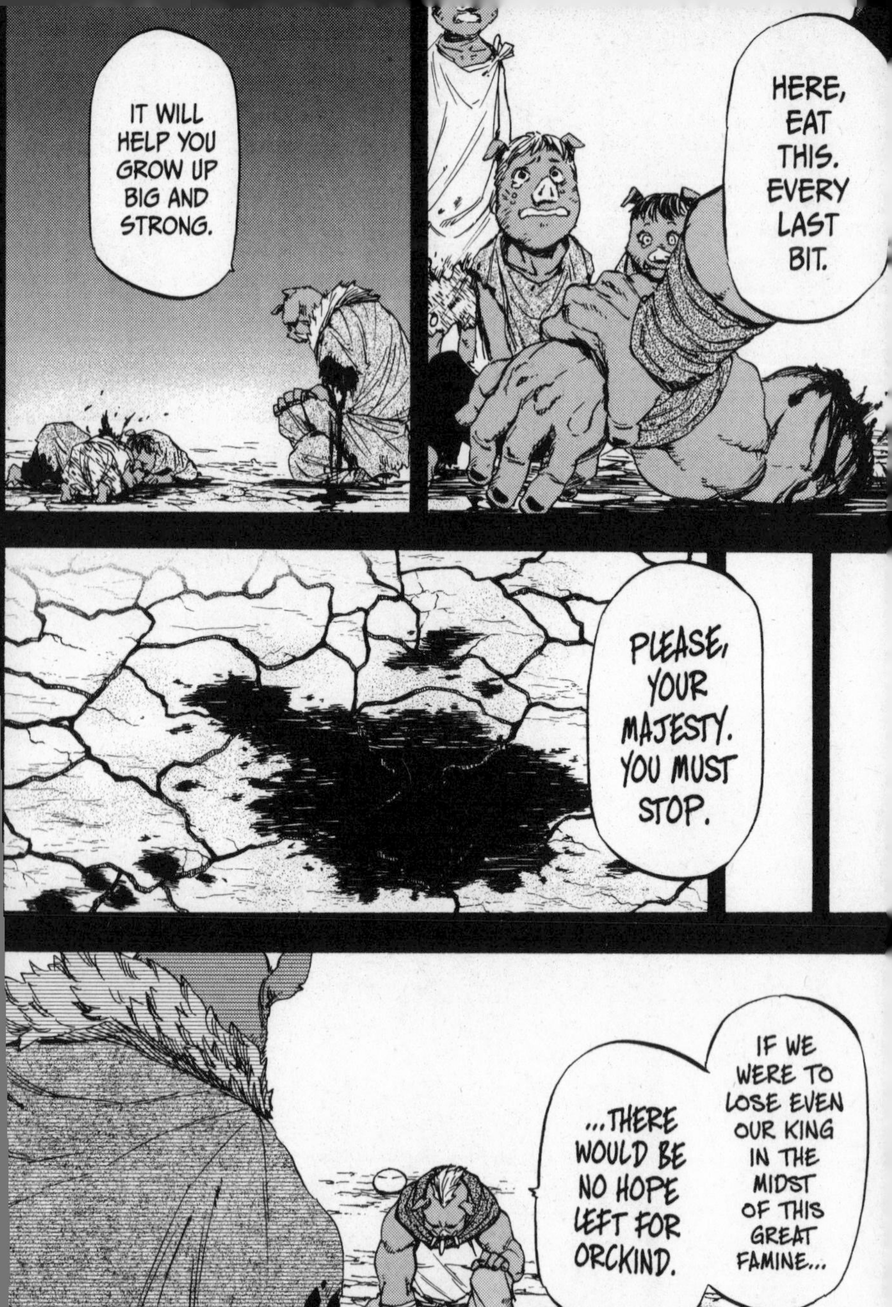
HERE, EAT THIS. EVERY LAST BIT.
IT WILL HELP YOU GROW UP BIG AND STRONG.
PLEASE, YOUR MAJESTY. YOU MUST STOP.
IF WE WERE TO LOSE EVEN OUR KING IN THE MIDST OF THIS GREAT FAMINE...
...THERE WOULD BE NO HOPE LEFT FOR ORCKIND.

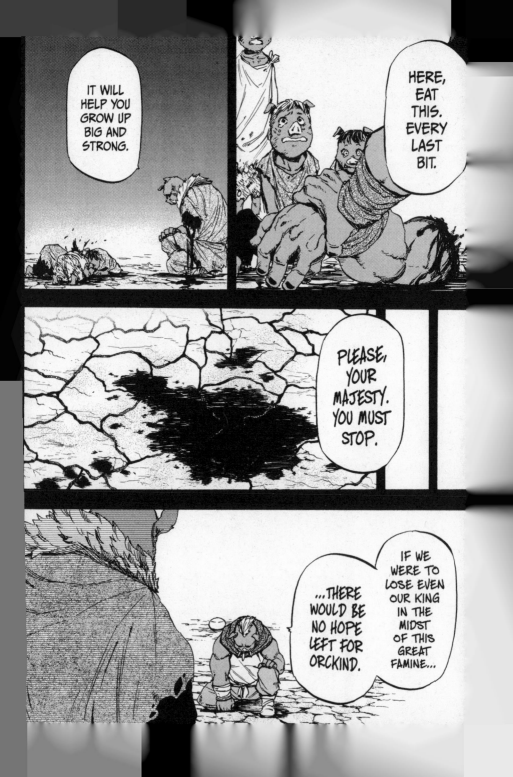

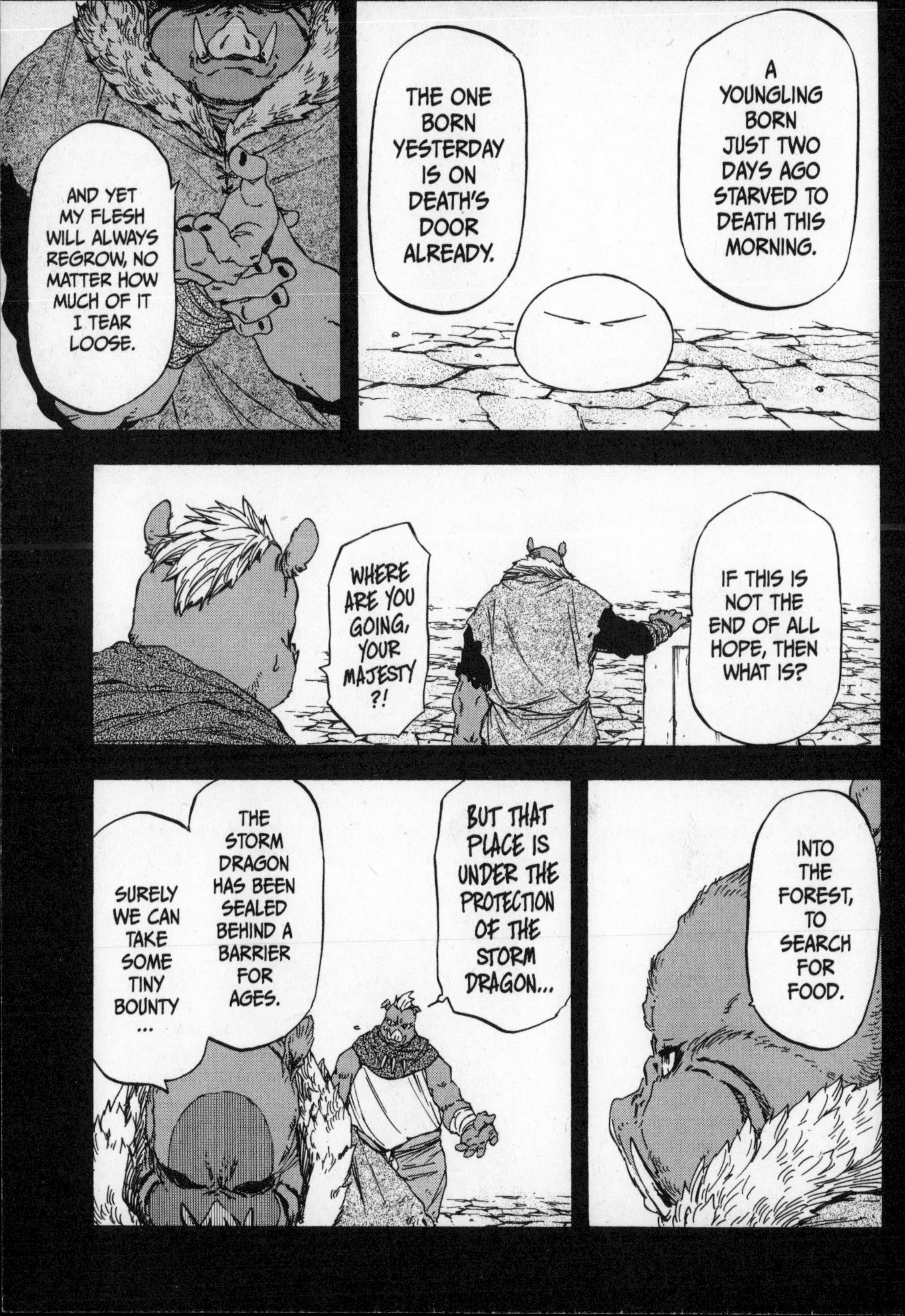
A YOUNGLING BORN JUST TWO DAYS AGO STARVED TO DEATH THIS MORNING.
THE ONE BORN YESTERDAY IS ON DEATH'S DOOR ALREADY.
AND YET MY FLESH WILL ALWAYS REGROW, NO MATTER HOW MUCH OF IT I TEAR LOOSE.
IF THIS IS NOT THE END OF ALL HOPE, THEN WHAT IS?
WHERE ARE YOU GOING, YOUR MAJESTY ?!
INTO THE FOREST, TO SEARCH FOR FOOD.
BUT THAT PLACE IS UNDER THE PROTECTION OF THE STORM DRAGON...
THE STORM DRAGON HAS BEEN SEALED BEHIND A BARRIER FOR AGES.
SURELY WE CAN TAKE SOME TINY BOUNTY ...

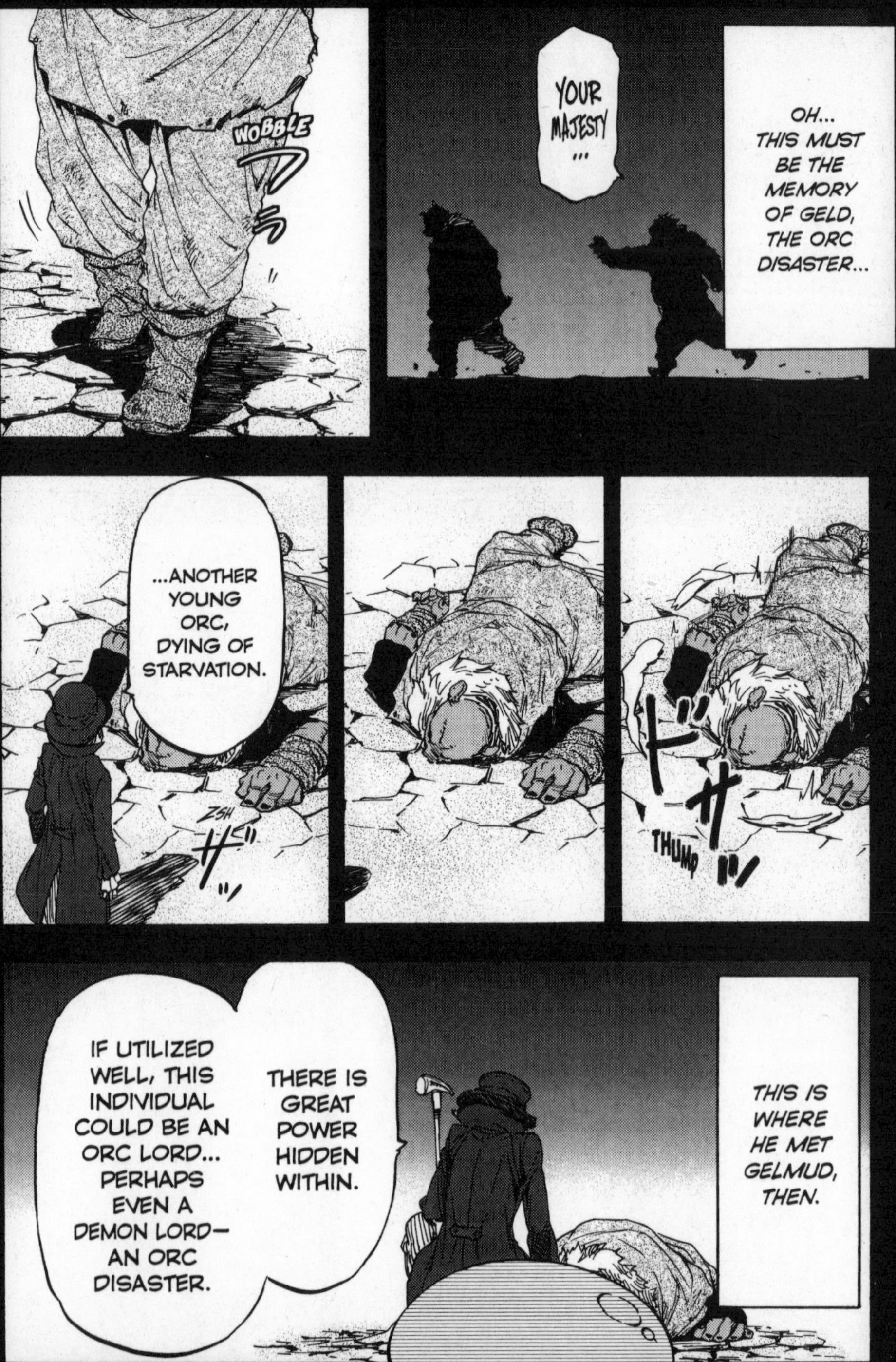
OH... THIS MUST BE THE MEMORY OF GELD, THE ORC DISASTER...
YOUR MAJESTY ...
WOBBLE
THUMP
...ANOTHER YOUNG ORC, DYING OF STARVATION.
ZSH
THIS IS WHERE HE MET GELMUD, THEN.
THERE IS GREAT POWER HIDDEN WITHIN.
IF UTILIZED WELL, THIS INDIVIDUAL COULD BE AN ORC LORD... PERHAPS EVEN A DEMON LORD— AN ORC DISASTER.

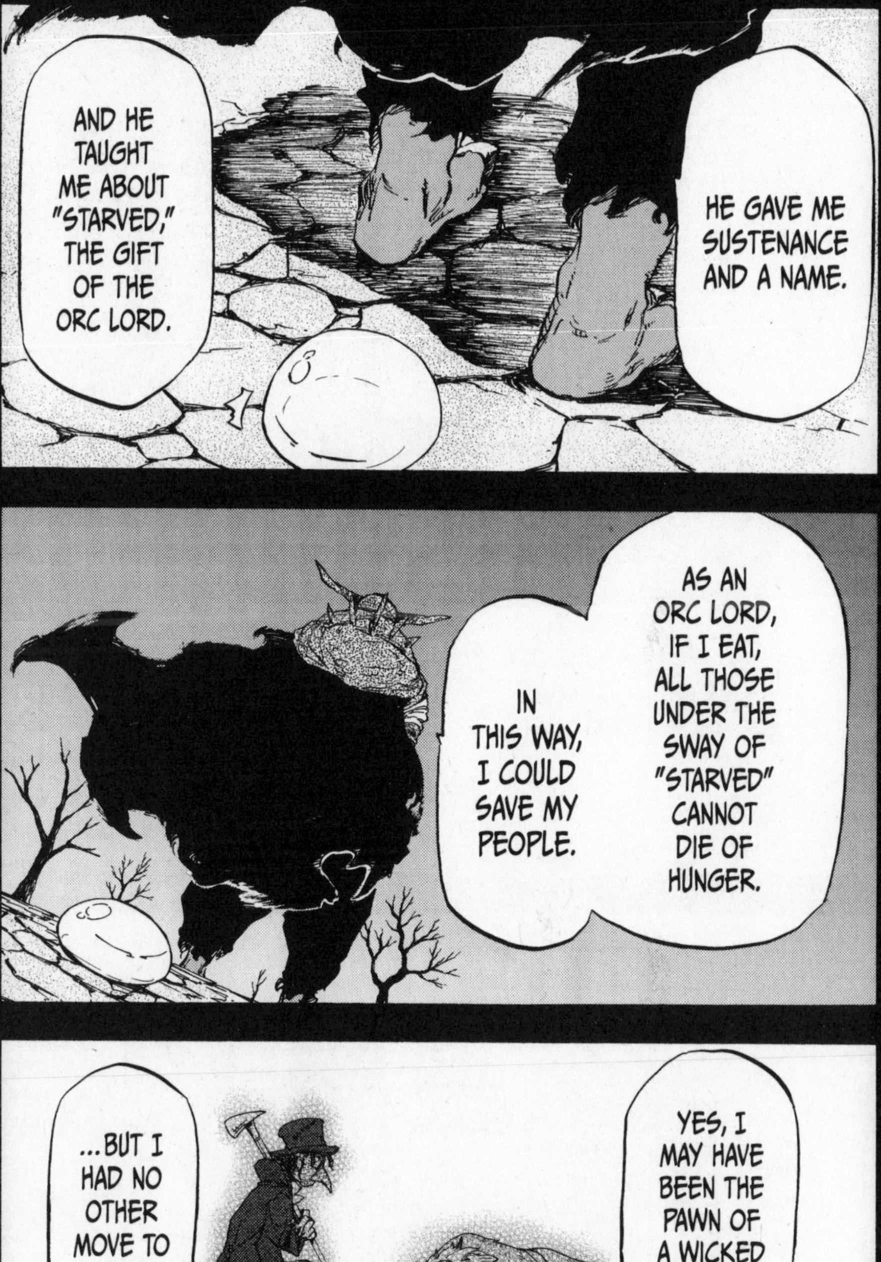
HE GAVE ME SUSTENANCE AND A NAME.
AND HE TAUGHT ME ABOUT "STARVED," THE GIFT OF THE ORC LORD.
AS AN ORC LORD, IF I EAT, ALL THOSE UNDER THE SWAY OF "STARVED" CANNOT DIE OF HUNGER.
IN THIS WAY, I COULD SAVE MY PEOPLE.
YES, I MAY HAVE BEEN THE PAWN OF A WICKED SCHEME...
...BUT I HAD NO OTHER MOVE TO PLAY.

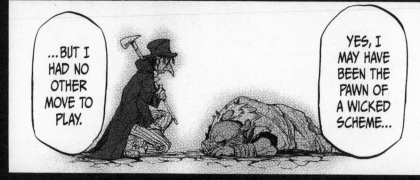

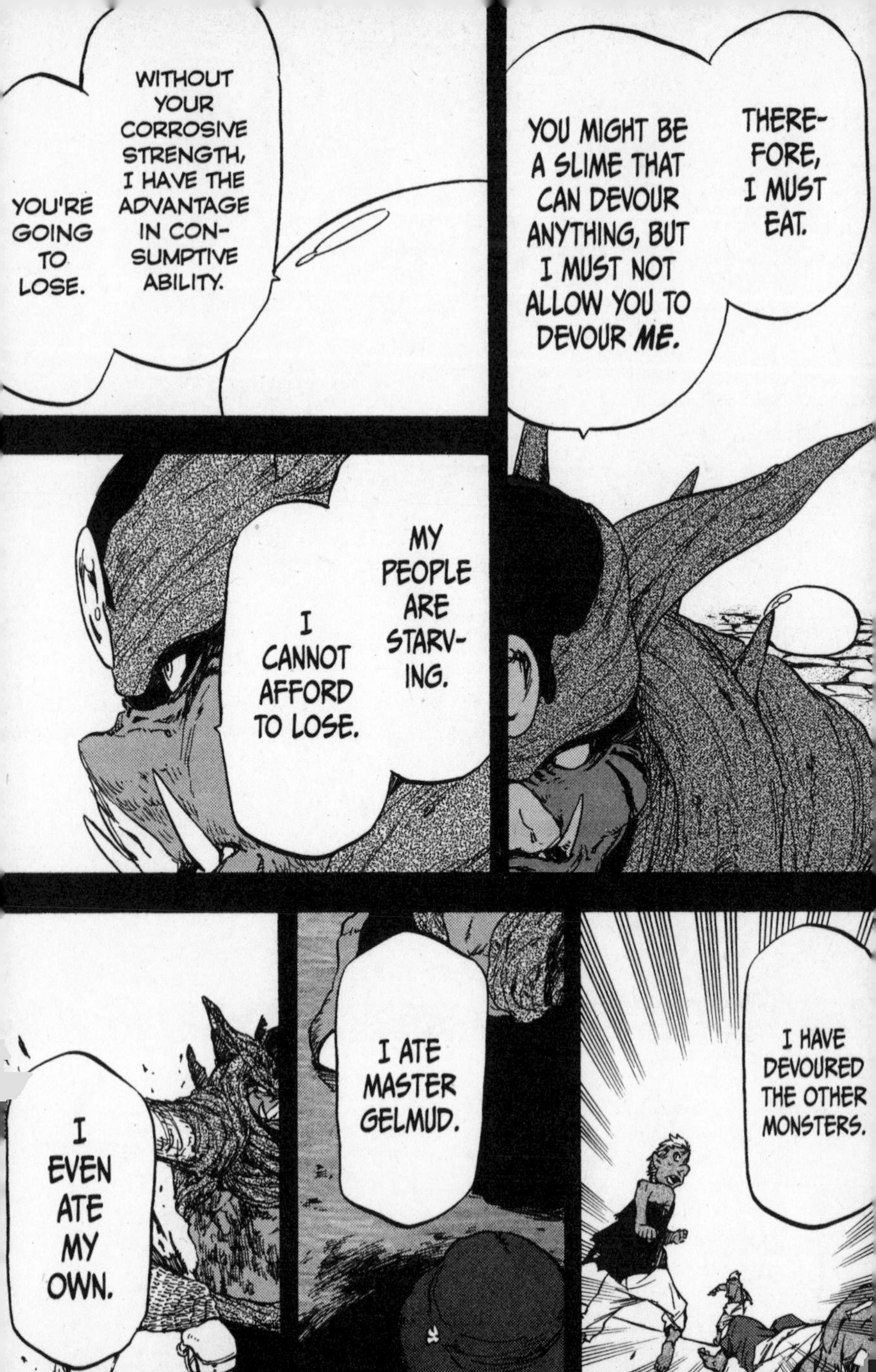
THERE-FORE, I MUST EAT.
YOU MIGHT BE A SLIME THAT CAN DEVOUR ANYTHING, BUT I MUST NOT ALLOW YOU TO DEVOUR *ME.*
WITHOUT YOUR CORROSIVE STRENGTH, I HAVE THE ADVANTAGE IN CON-SUMPTIVE ABILITY.
YOU'RE GOING TO LOSE.
MY PEOPLE ARE STARV-ING.
I CANNOT AFFORD TO LOSE.
I HAVE DEVOURED THE OTHER MONSTERS.
I ATE MASTER GELMUD.
I EVEN ATE MY OWN.

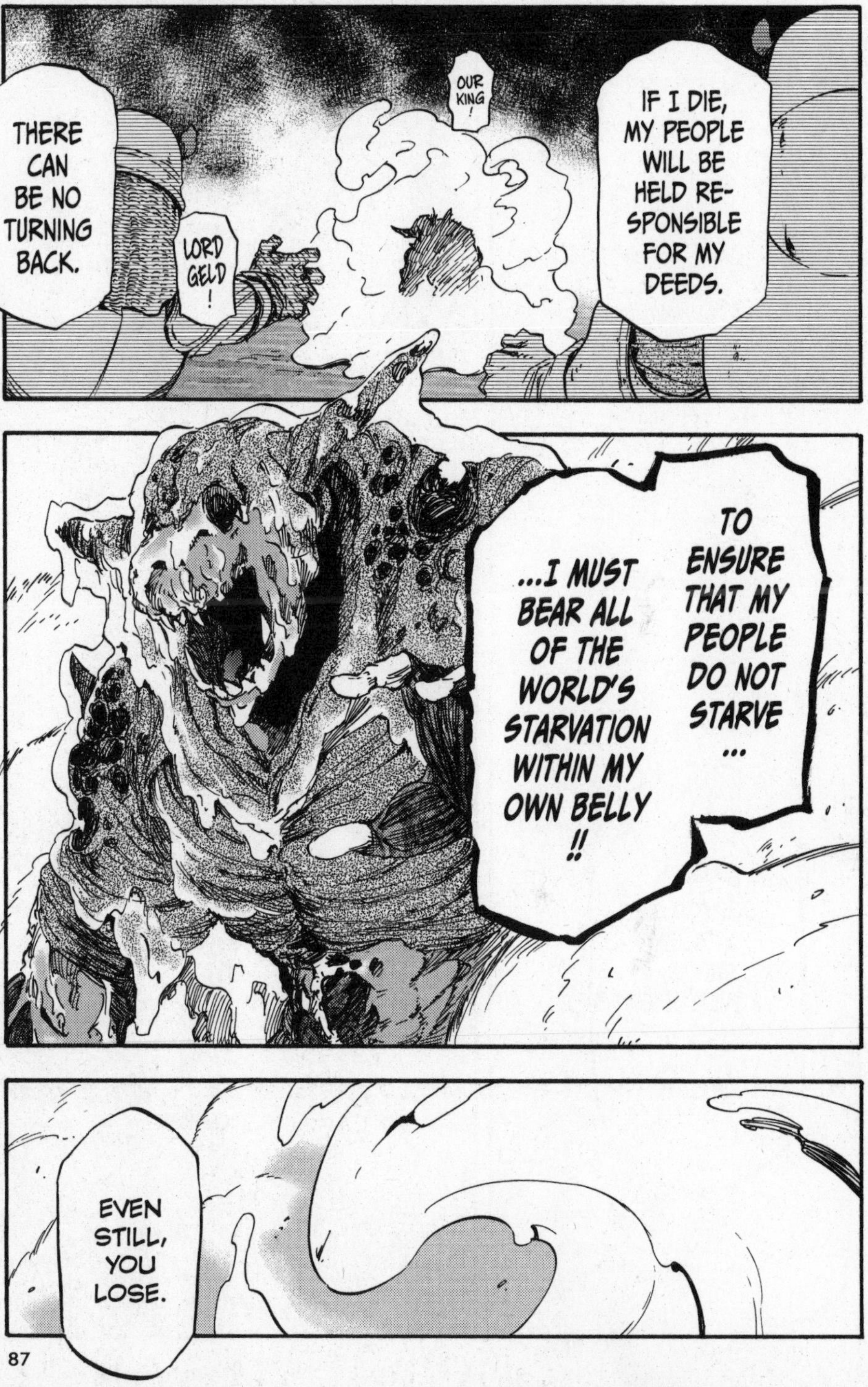
IF I DIE, MY PEOPLE WILL BE HELD RE-SPONSIBLE FOR MY DEEDS.
OUR KING!
LORD GELD!
THERE CAN BE NO TURNING BACK.
TO ENSURE THAT MY PEOPLE DO NOT STARVE...
...I MUST BEAR ALL OF THE WORLD'S STARVATION WITHIN MY OWN BELLY!!
EVEN STILL, YOU LOSE.

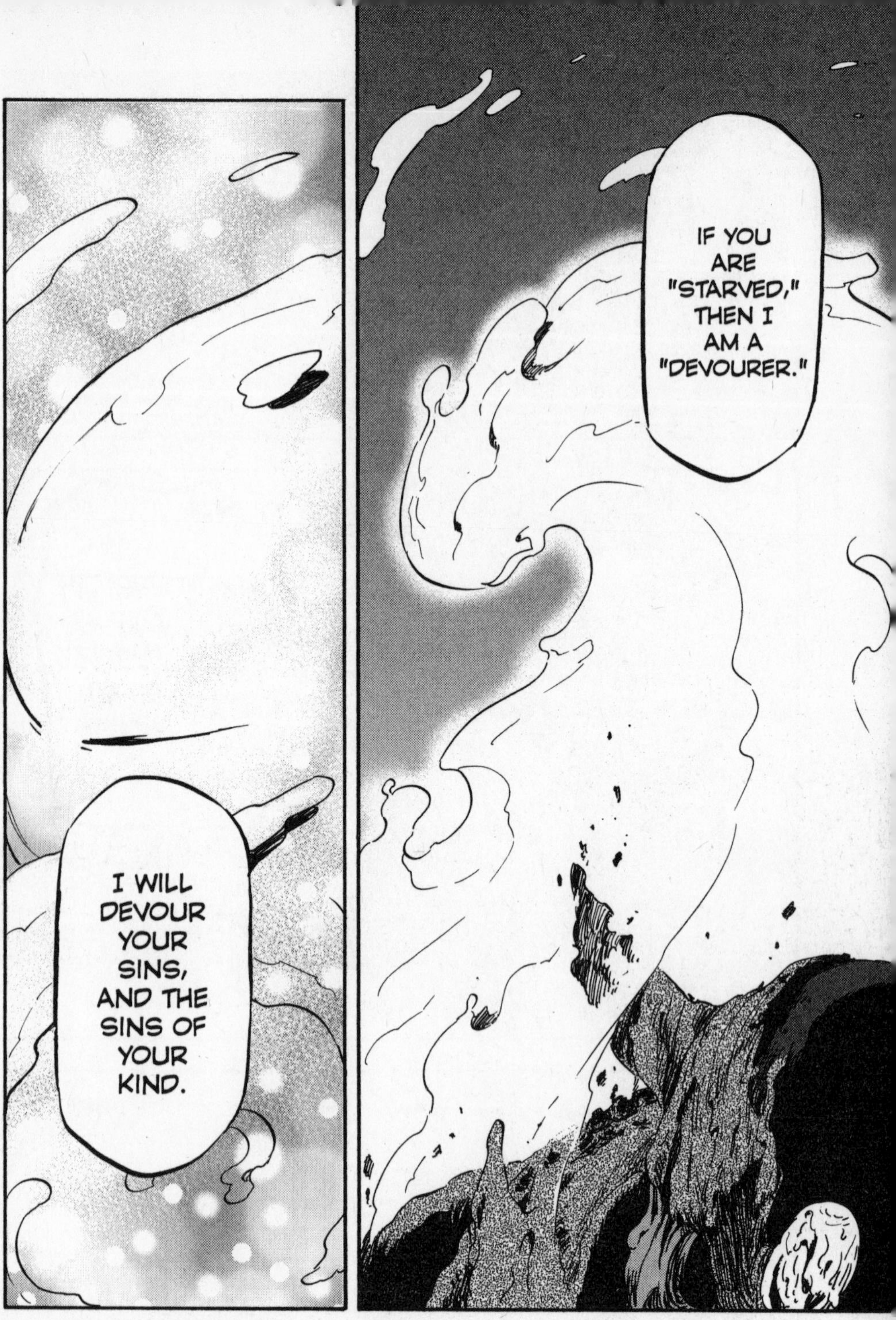
IF YOU ARE "STARVED," THEN I AM A "DEVOURER."
I WILL DEVOUR YOUR SINS, AND THE SINS OF YOUR KIND.

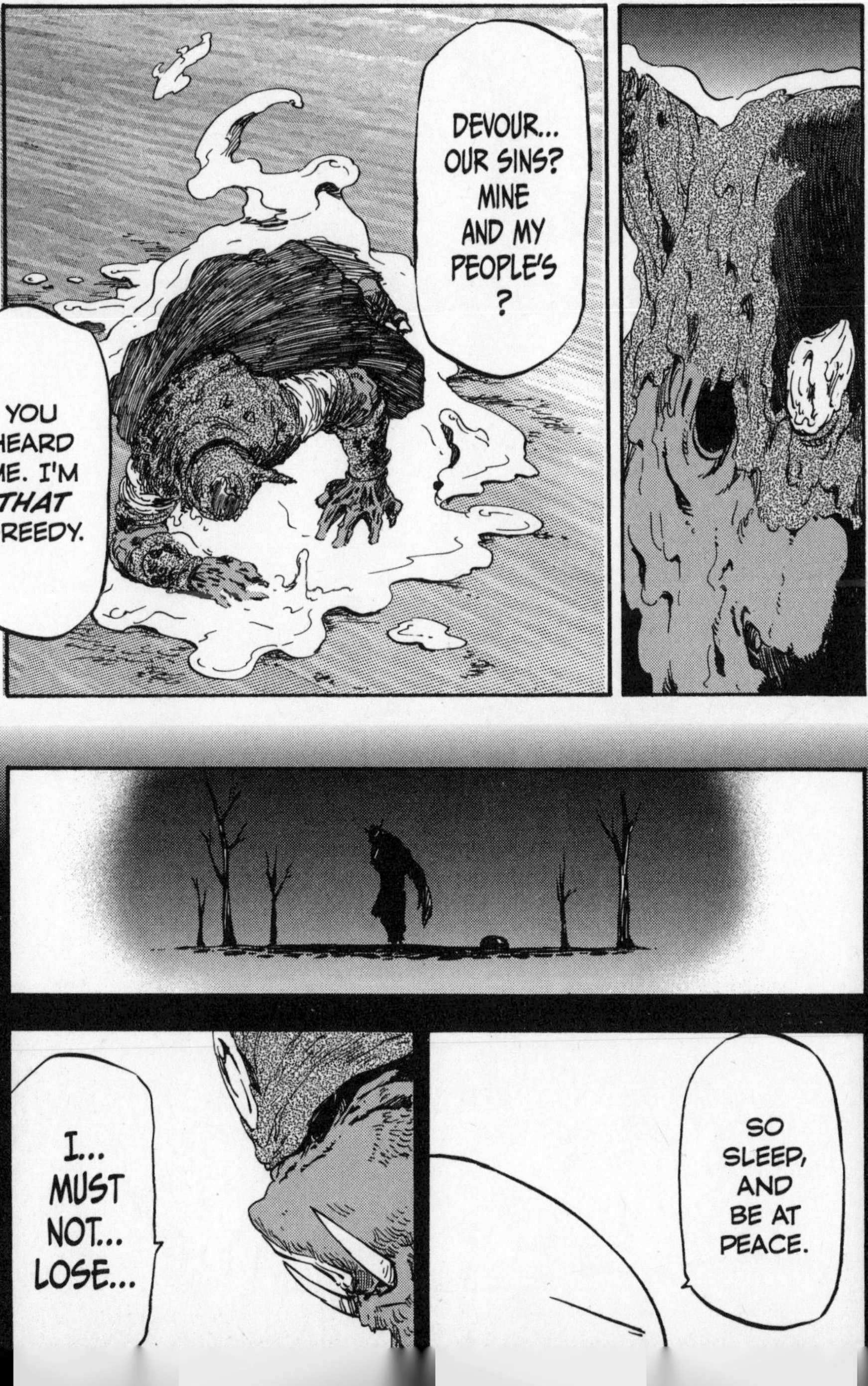
DEVOUR... OUR SINS? MINE AND MY PEOPLE'S ?
YOU HEARD ME. I'M *THAT* GREEDY.
SO SLEEP, AND BE AT PEACE.
I... MUST NOT... LOSE...

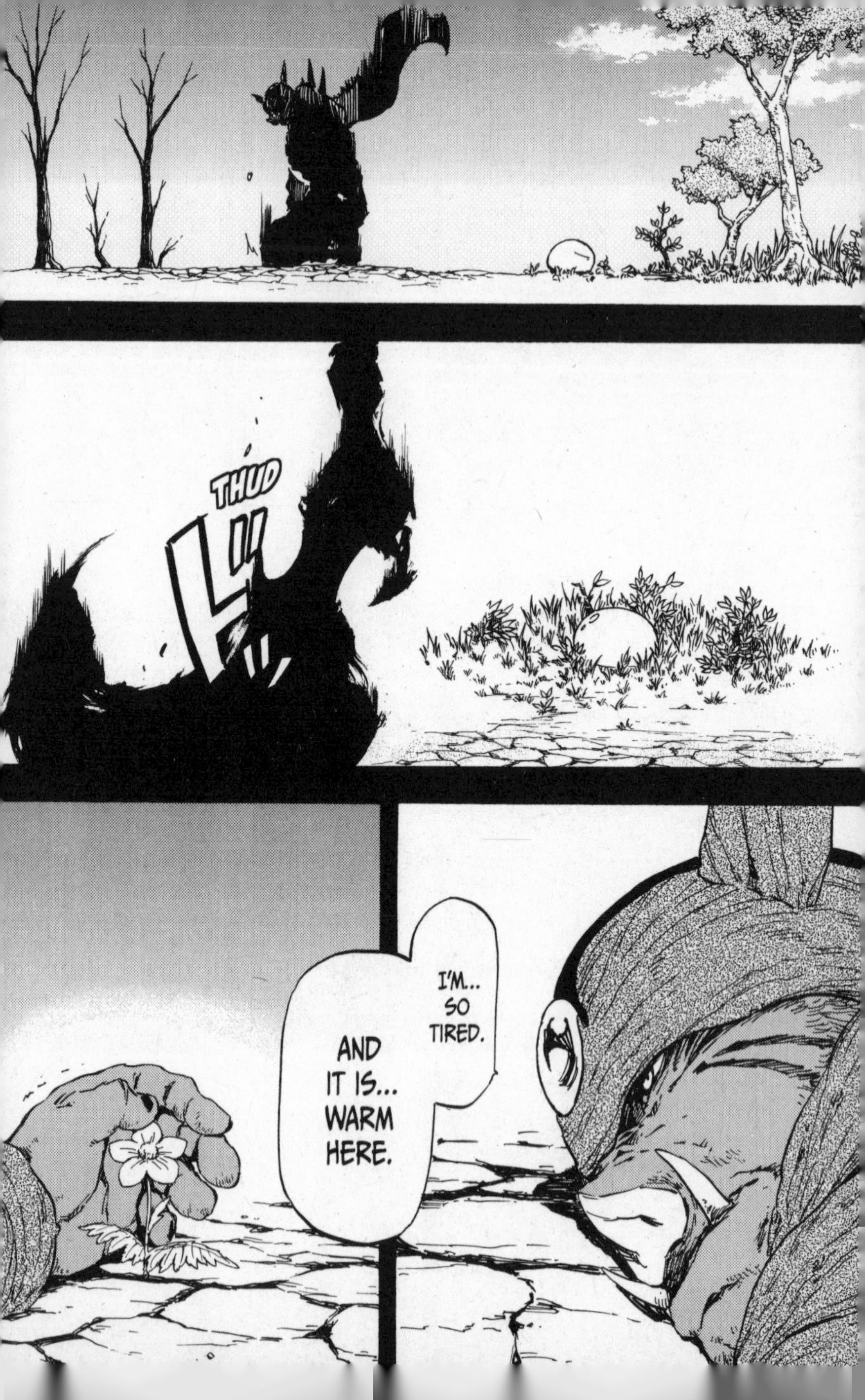
THUD
I'M... SO TIRED.
AND IT IS... WARM HERE.

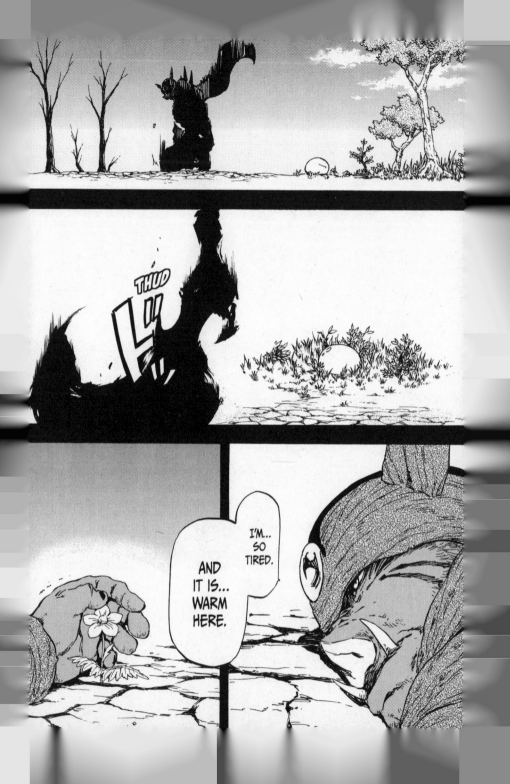

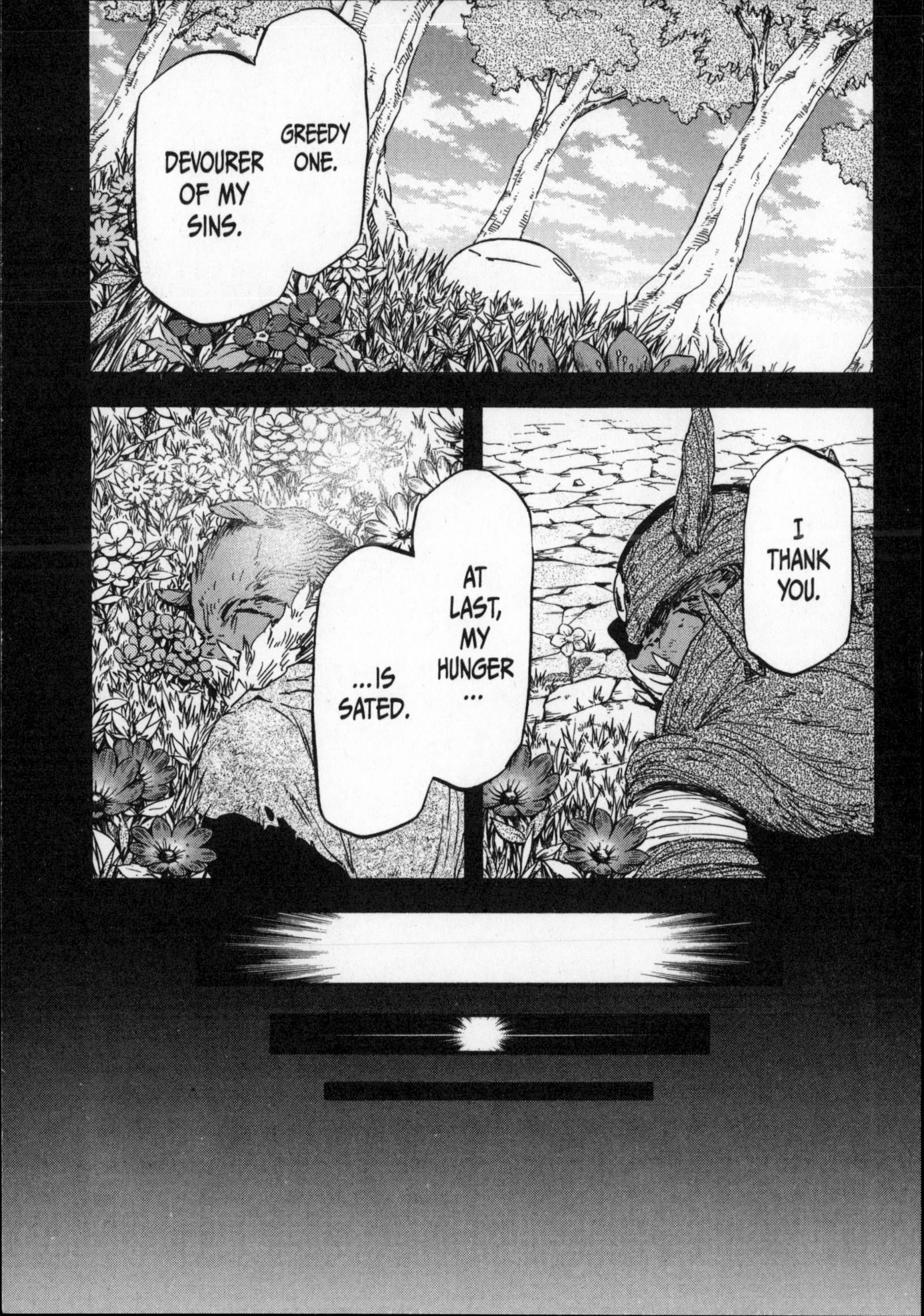
GREEDY ONE.
DEVOURER OF MY SINS.
I THANK YOU.
AT LAST, MY HUNGER ...
...IS SATED.

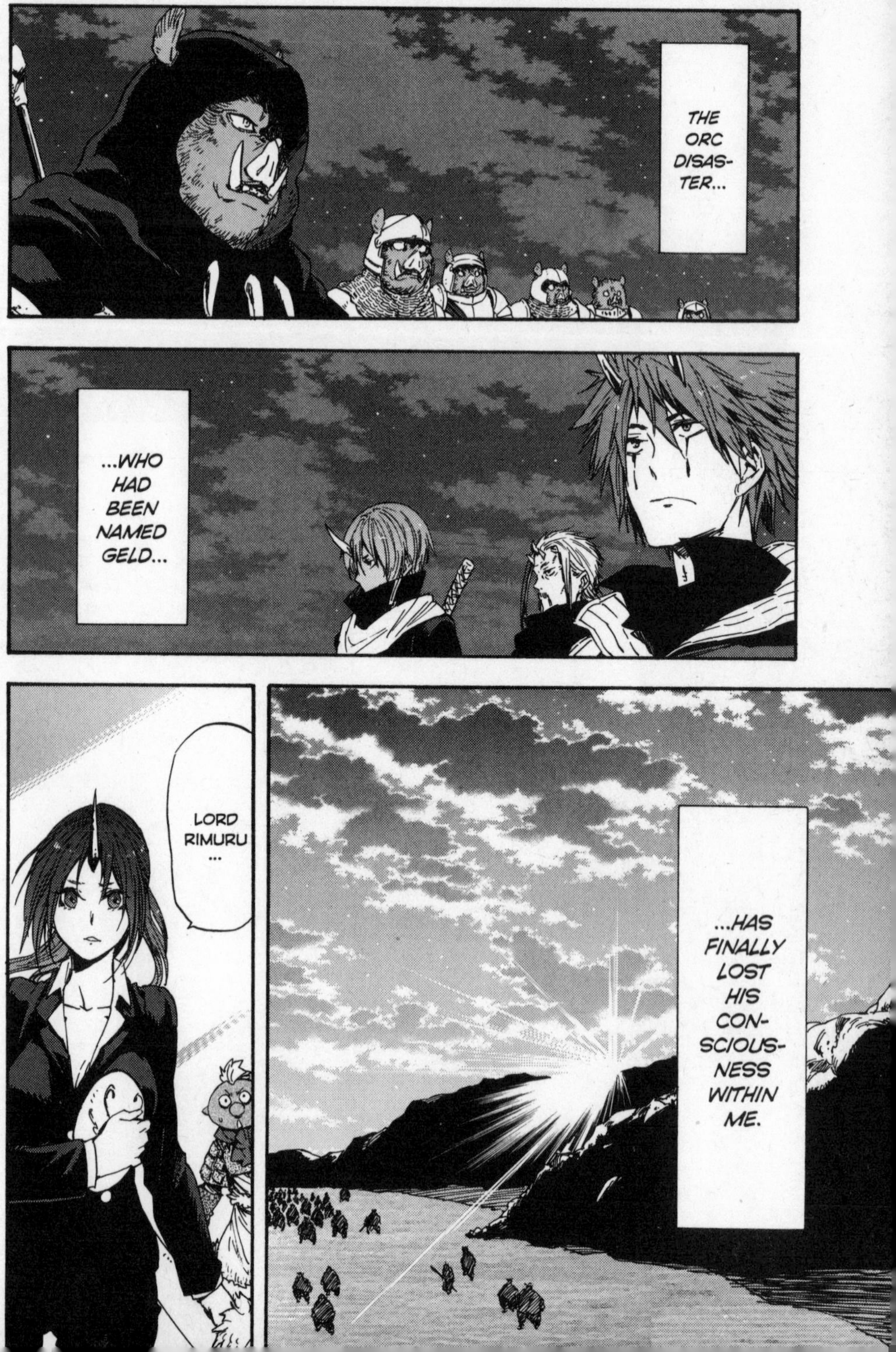
THE ORC DISASTER...
...WHO HAD BEEN NAMED GELD...
...HAS FINALLY LOST HIS CONSCIOUSNESS WITHIN ME.
LORD RIMURU...

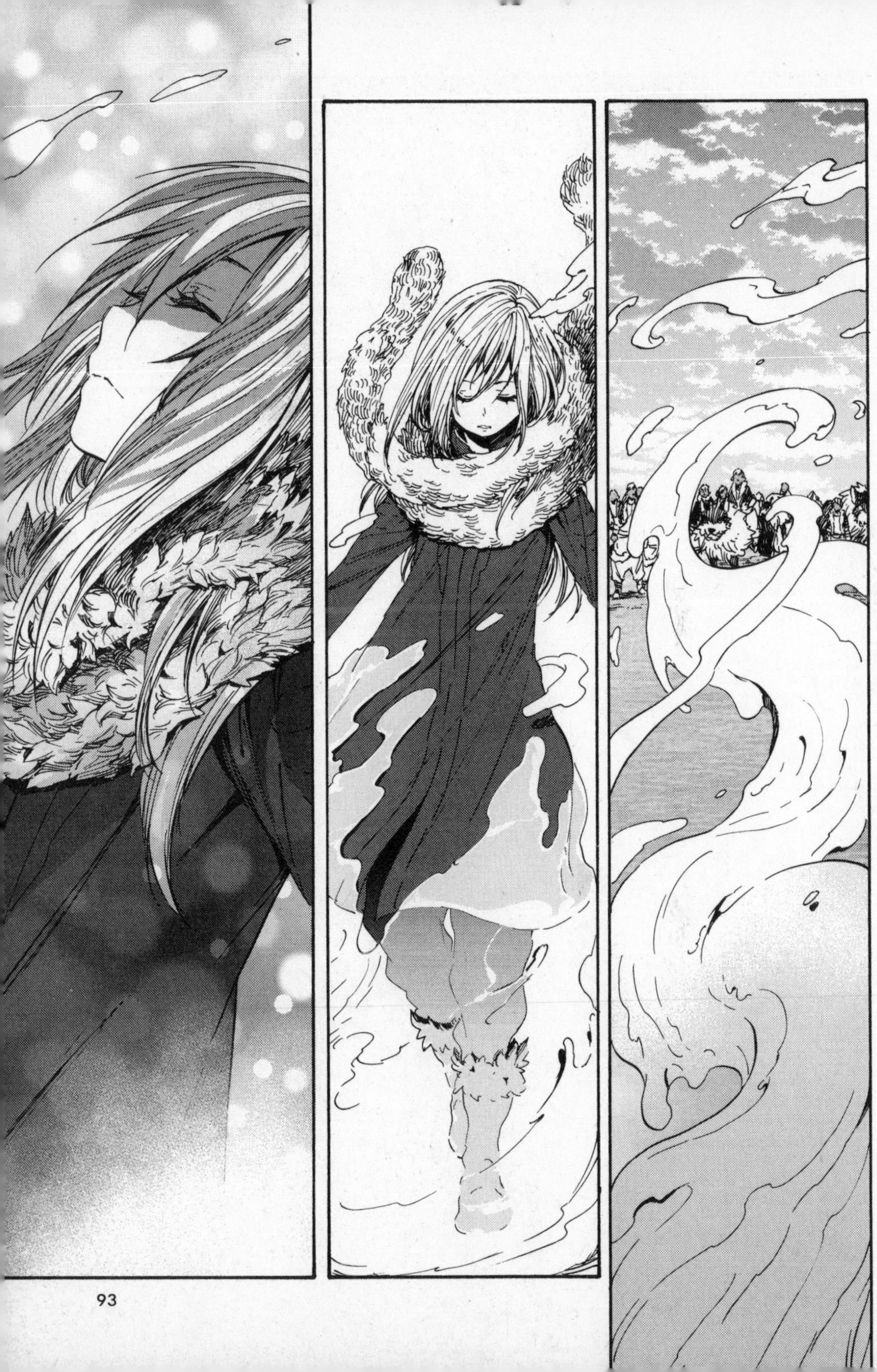

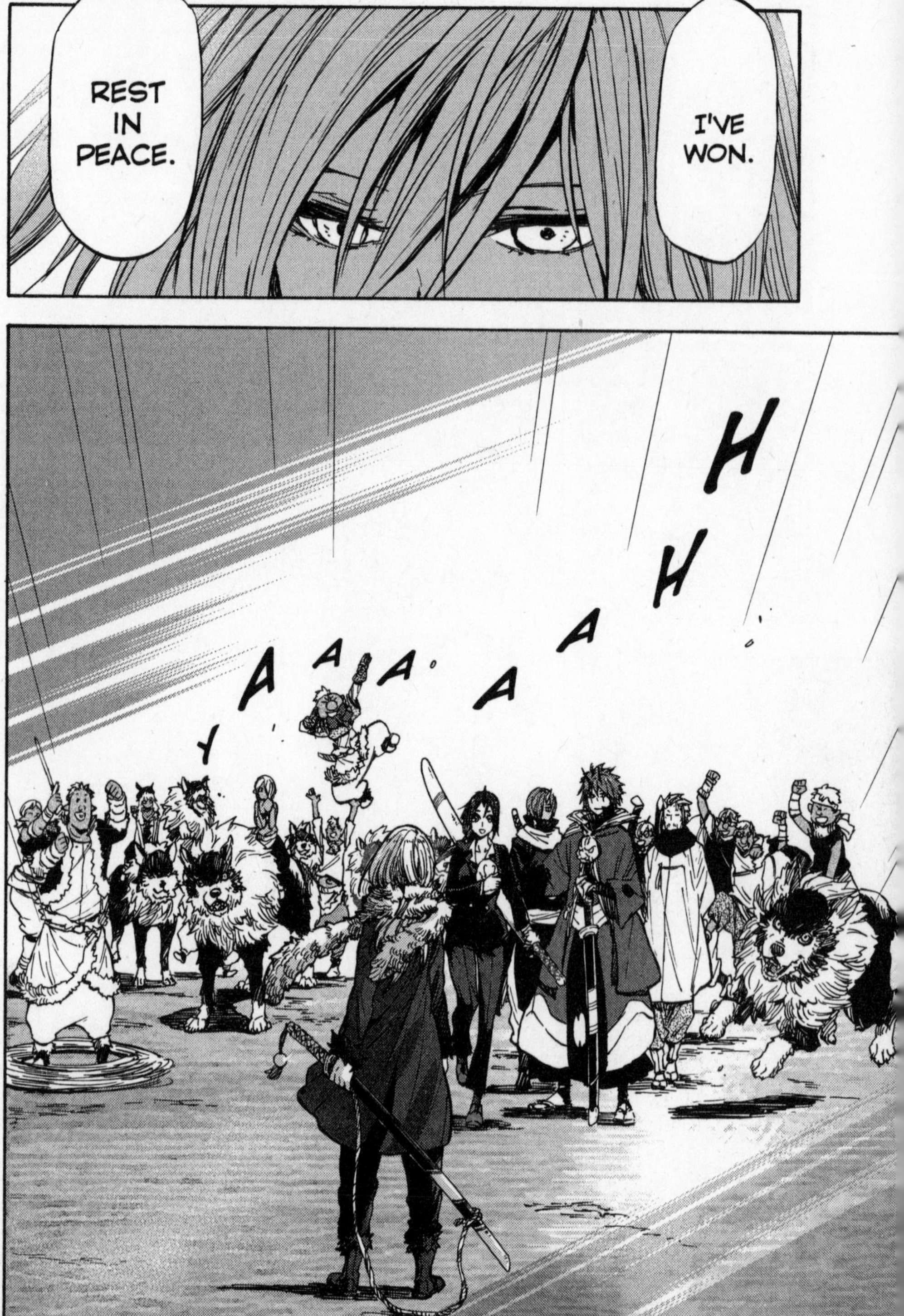
I'VE WON.
REST IN PEACE.
YAAAAAHH

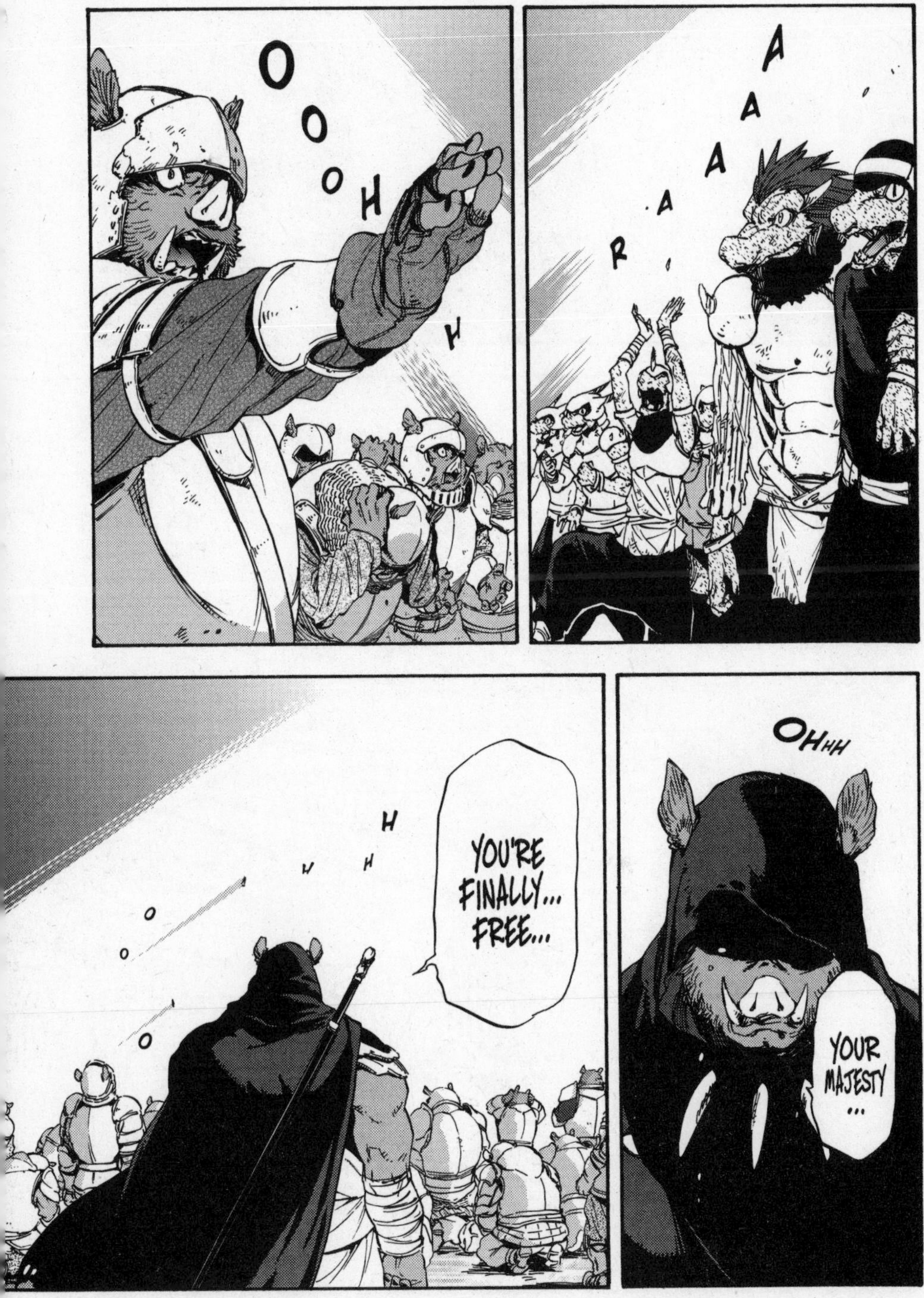
RAAAAA
OOOHH
OHHH
YOUR MAJESTY...
OOOHHH
YOU'RE FINALLY... FREE...

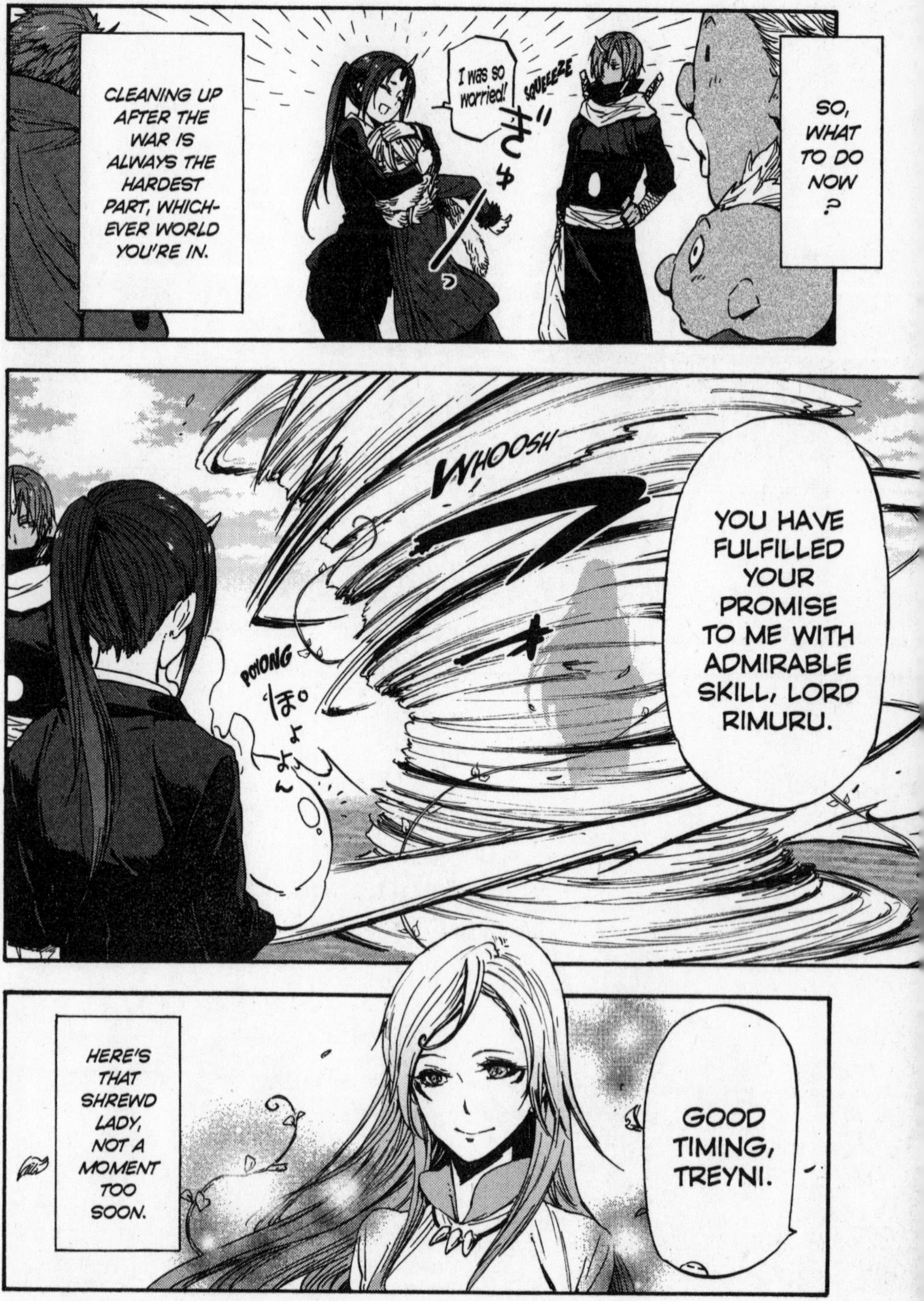
SO, WHAT TO DO NOW?
SQUEEEZE
I was so worried!
CLEANING UP AFTER THE WAR IS ALWAYS THE HARDEST PART, WHICHEVER WORLD YOU'RE IN.
YOU HAVE FULFILLED YOUR PROMISE TO ME WITH ADMIRABLE SKILL, LORD RIMURU.
WHOOSH
POYONG
GOOD TIMING, TREYNI.
HERE'S THAT SHREWD LADY, NOT A MOMENT TOO SOON.

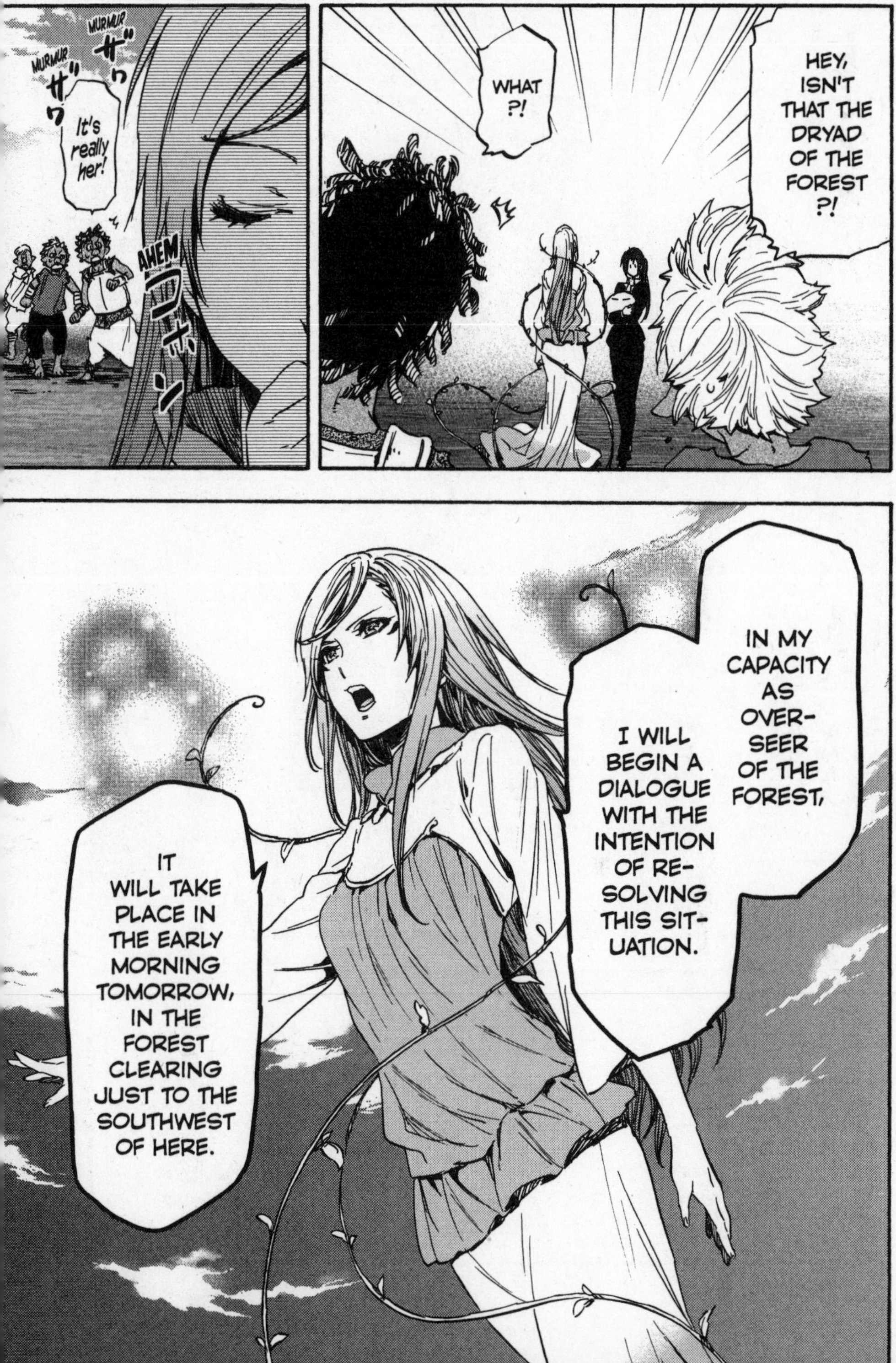
HEY, ISN'T THAT THE DRYAD OF THE FOREST ?!
WHAT ?!
MURMUR
ザワ
MURMUR
ザワ
It's really her!
AHEM
IN MY CAPACITY AS OVER-SEER OF THE FOREST,
I WILL BEGIN A DIALOGUE WITH THE INTENTION OF RE-SOLVING THIS SIT-UATION.
IT WILL TAKE PLACE IN THE EARLY MORNING TOMORROW, IN THE FOREST CLEARING JUST TO THE SOUTHWEST OF HERE.

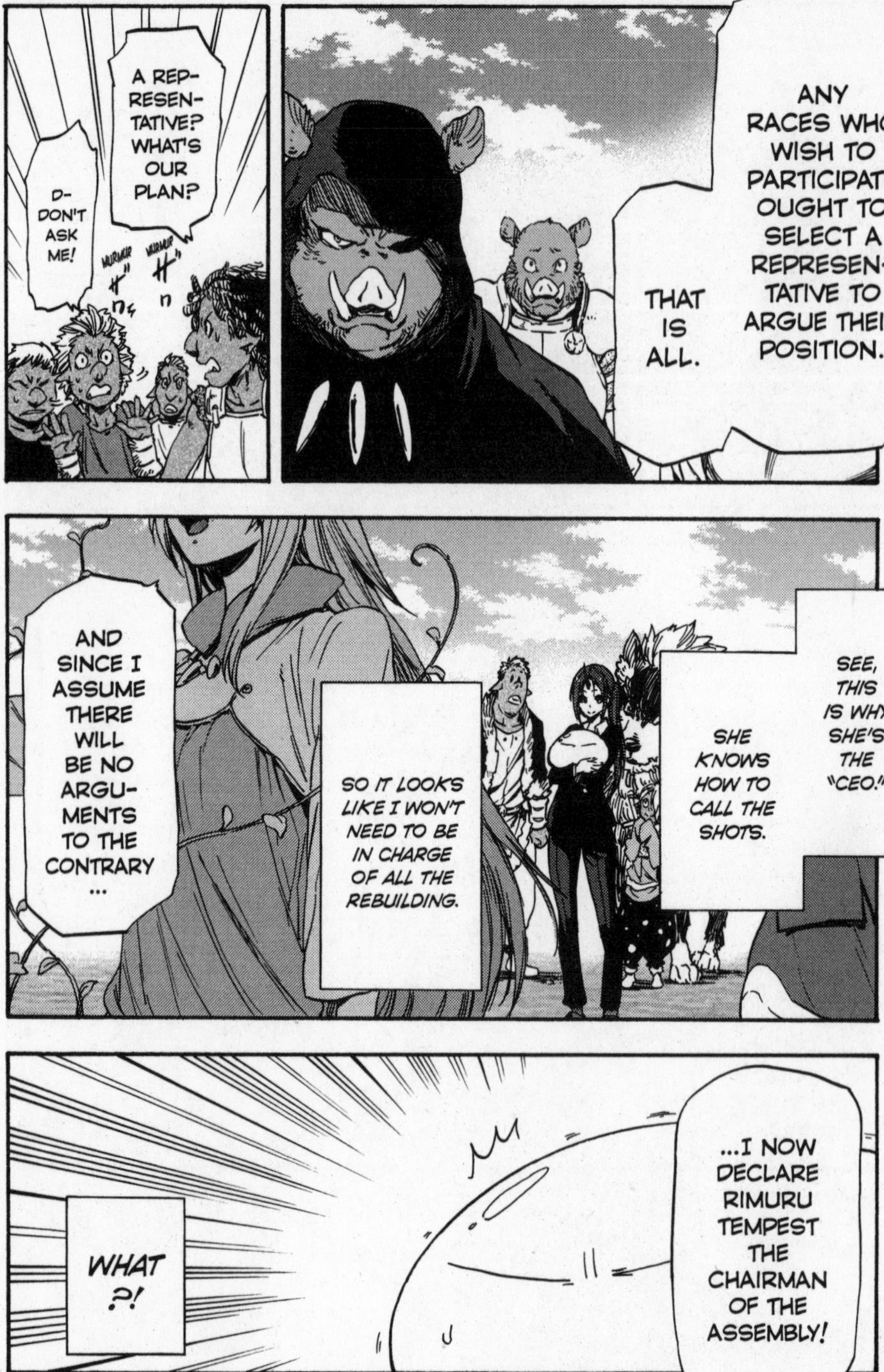
ANY RACES WHO WISH TO PARTICIPATE OUGHT TO SELECT A REPRESENTATIVE TO ARGUE THEIR POSITION.
THAT IS ALL.
A REPRESENTATIVE? WHAT'S OUR PLAN?
D-DON'T ASK ME!
MURMUR
MURMUR
SEE, THIS IS WHY SHE'S THE "CEO."
SHE KNOWS HOW TO CALL THE SHOTS.
SO IT LOOKS LIKE I WON'T NEED TO BE IN CHARGE OF ALL THE REBUILDING.
AND SINCE I ASSUME THERE WILL BE NO ARGUMENTS TO THE CONTRARY...
...I NOW DECLARE RIMURU TEMPEST THE CHAIRMAN OF THE ASSEMBLY!
WHAT?!

In
Memoriam.

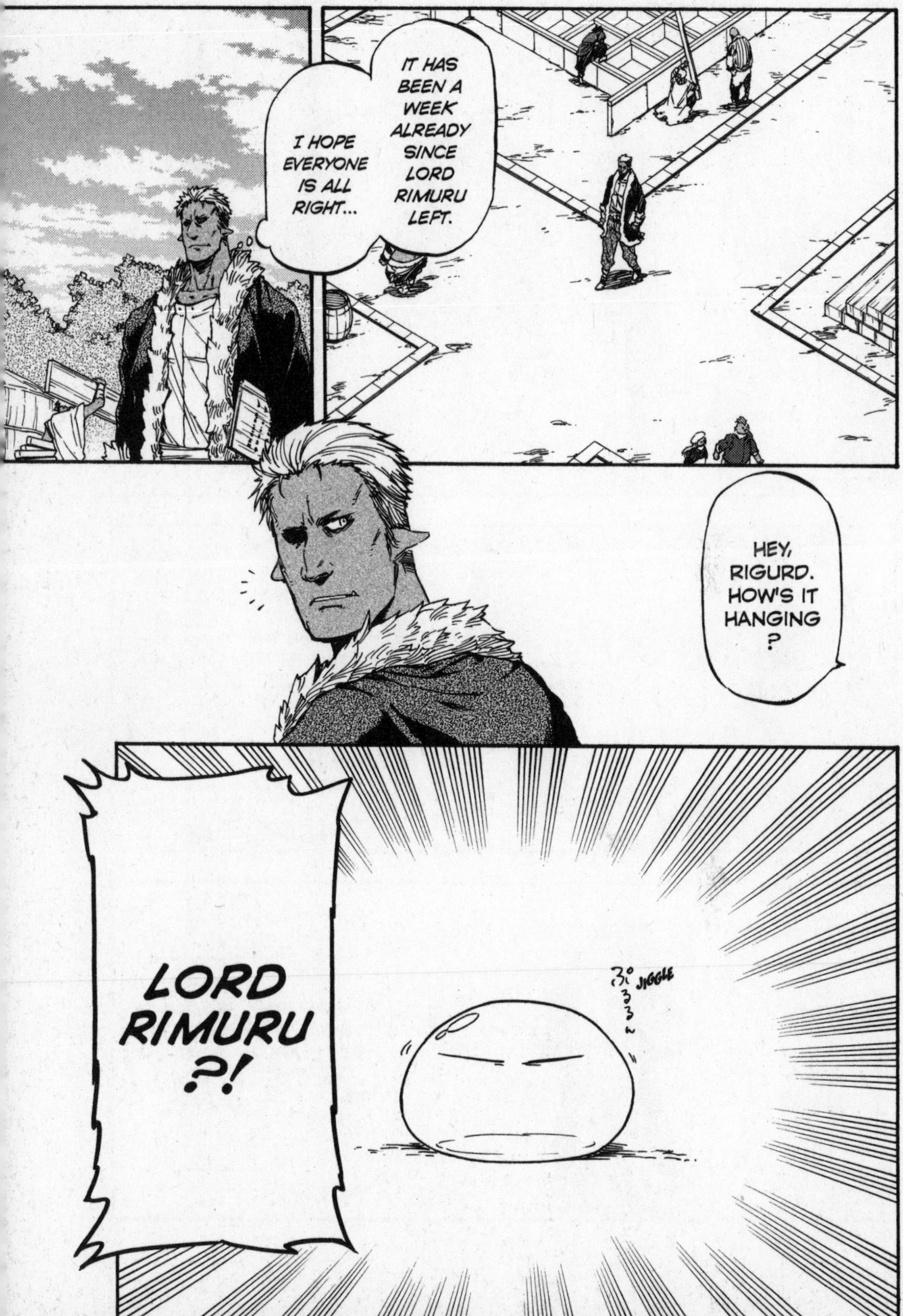
IT HAS BEEN A WEEK ALREADY SINCE LORD RIMURU LEFT.
I HOPE EVERYONE IS ALL RIGHT...
HEY, RIGURD. HOW'S IT HANGING?
ぷるるん JIGGLE
LORD RIMURU?!

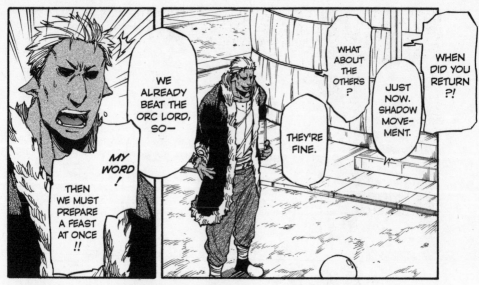

WHEN DID YOU RETURN?!
JUST NOW. SHADOW MOVEMENT.
WHAT ABOUT THE OTHERS?
THEY'RE FINE.
WE ALREADY BEAT THE ORC LORD, SO—
MY WORD!
THEN WE MUST PREPARE A FEAST AT ONCE!!
FIRST, CALM DOWN. WE CAN HOLD THAT IN A MONTH.
I ONLY CAME BACK TO DELIVER THE NEWS, SINCE I FIGURE YOU WERE WORRIED. I HAVE TO LEAVE AGAIN RIGHT AWAY.
MY WORD!!
PASS THE NEWS TO SHUNA, KUROBEI, AND KAIJIN'S BUNCH.
THINGS ARE ABOUT TO GET BUSY. ARE YOU READY FOR THAT?
OF COURSE!!
BUT SURELY YOU CAN REST BEFORE YOU GO...

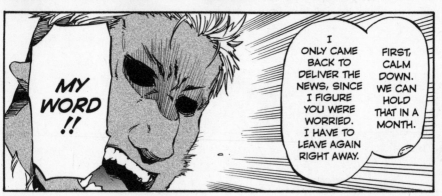

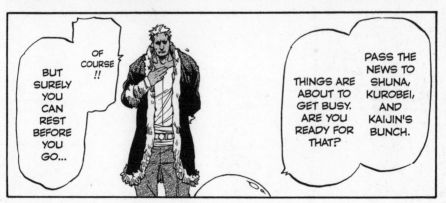

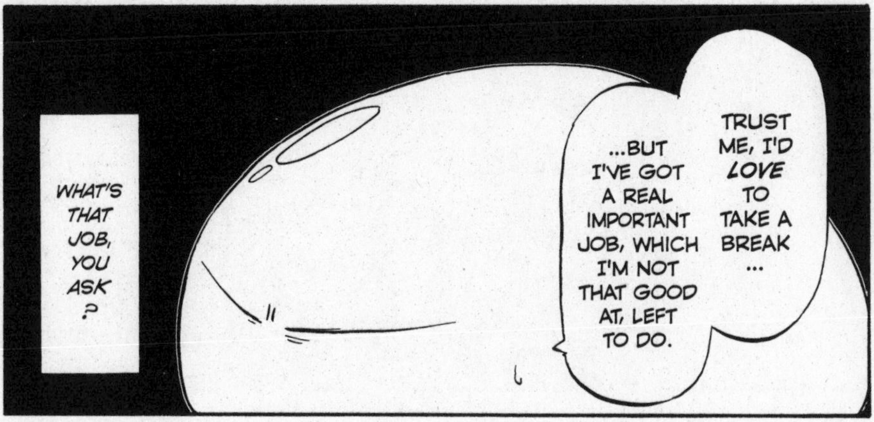
TRUST ME, I'D *LOVE* TO TAKE A BREAK ...
...BUT I'VE GOT A REAL IMPORTANT JOB, WHICH I'M NOT THAT GOOD AT, LEFT TO DO.
WHAT'S THAT JOB, YOU ASK?

CHAPTER 26 The Jura Forest Alliance

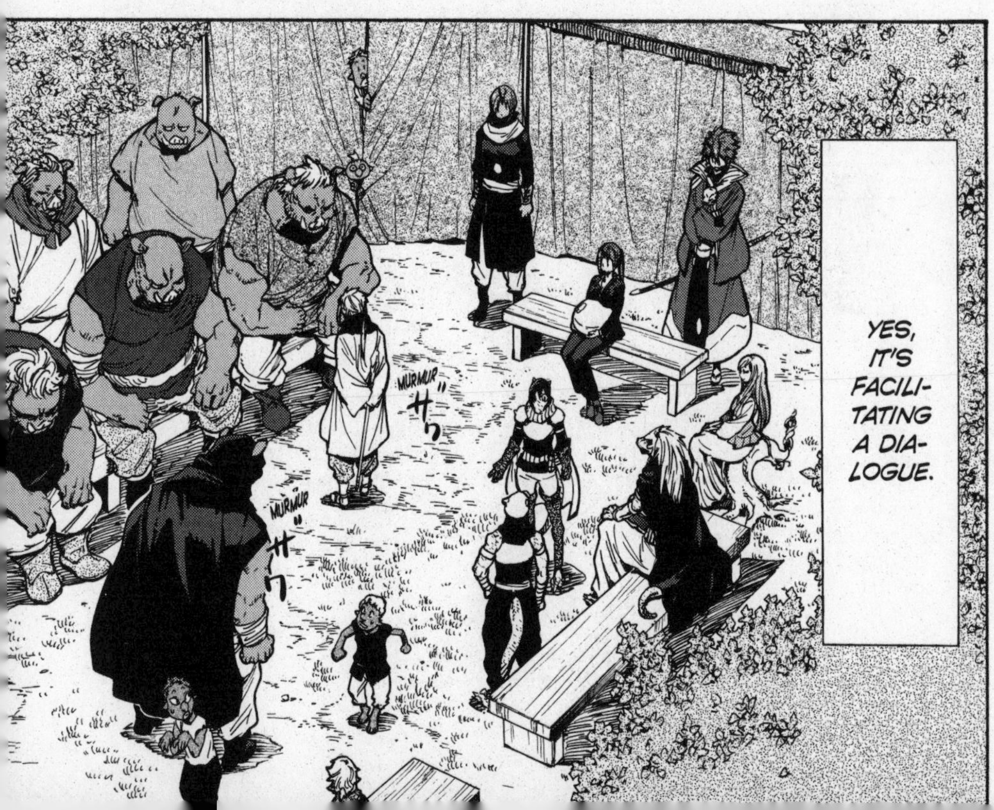
YES, IT'S FACILITATING A DIALOGUE.
MURMUR
MURMUR

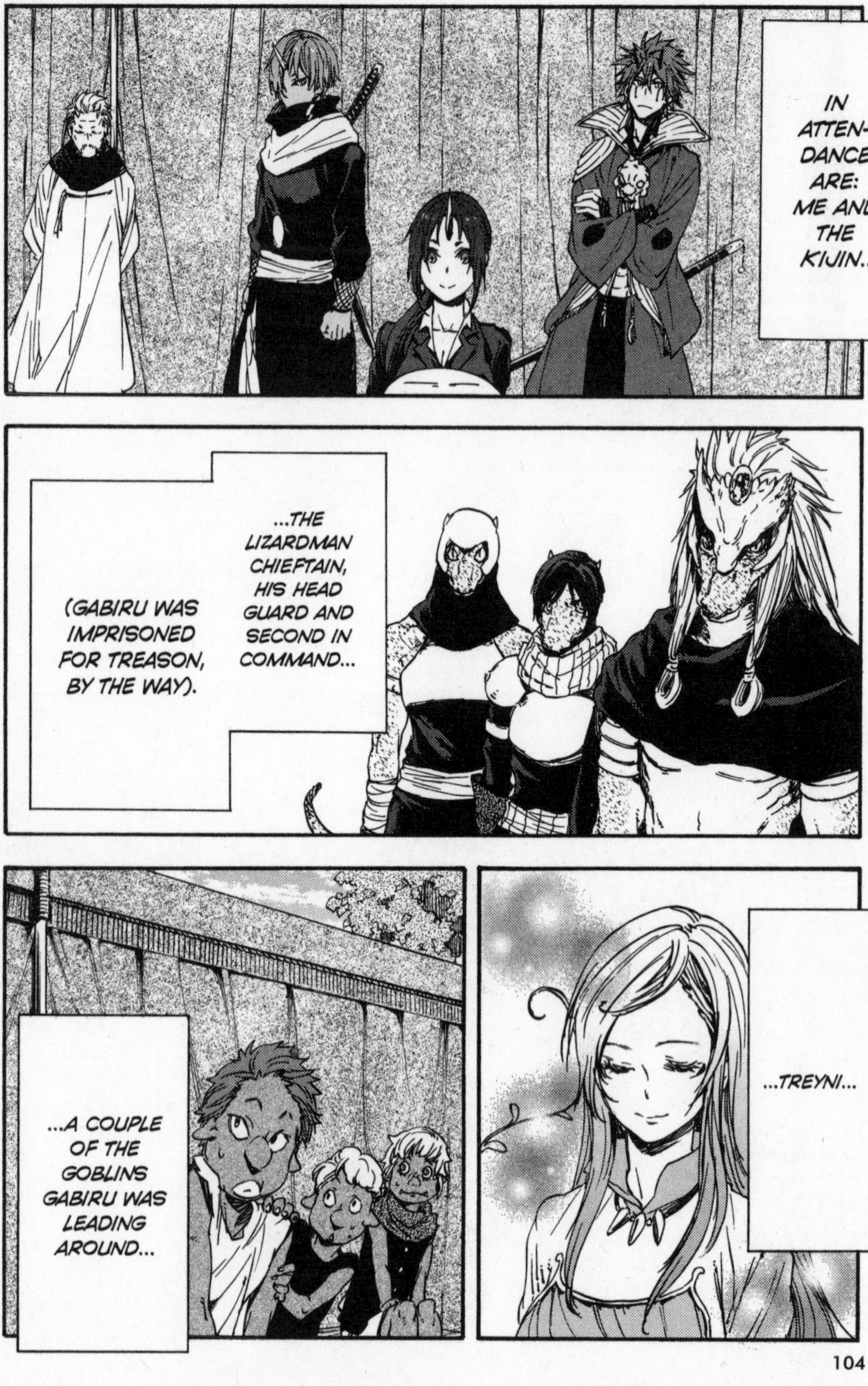
IN ATTEN-DANCE ARE: ME AND THE KIJIN...
...THE LIZARDMAN CHIEFTAIN, HIS HEAD GUARD AND SECOND IN COMMAND...
(GABIRU WAS IMPRISONED FOR TREASON, BY THE WAY).
...TREYNI...
...A COUPLE OF THE GOBLINS GABIRU WAS LEADING AROUND...

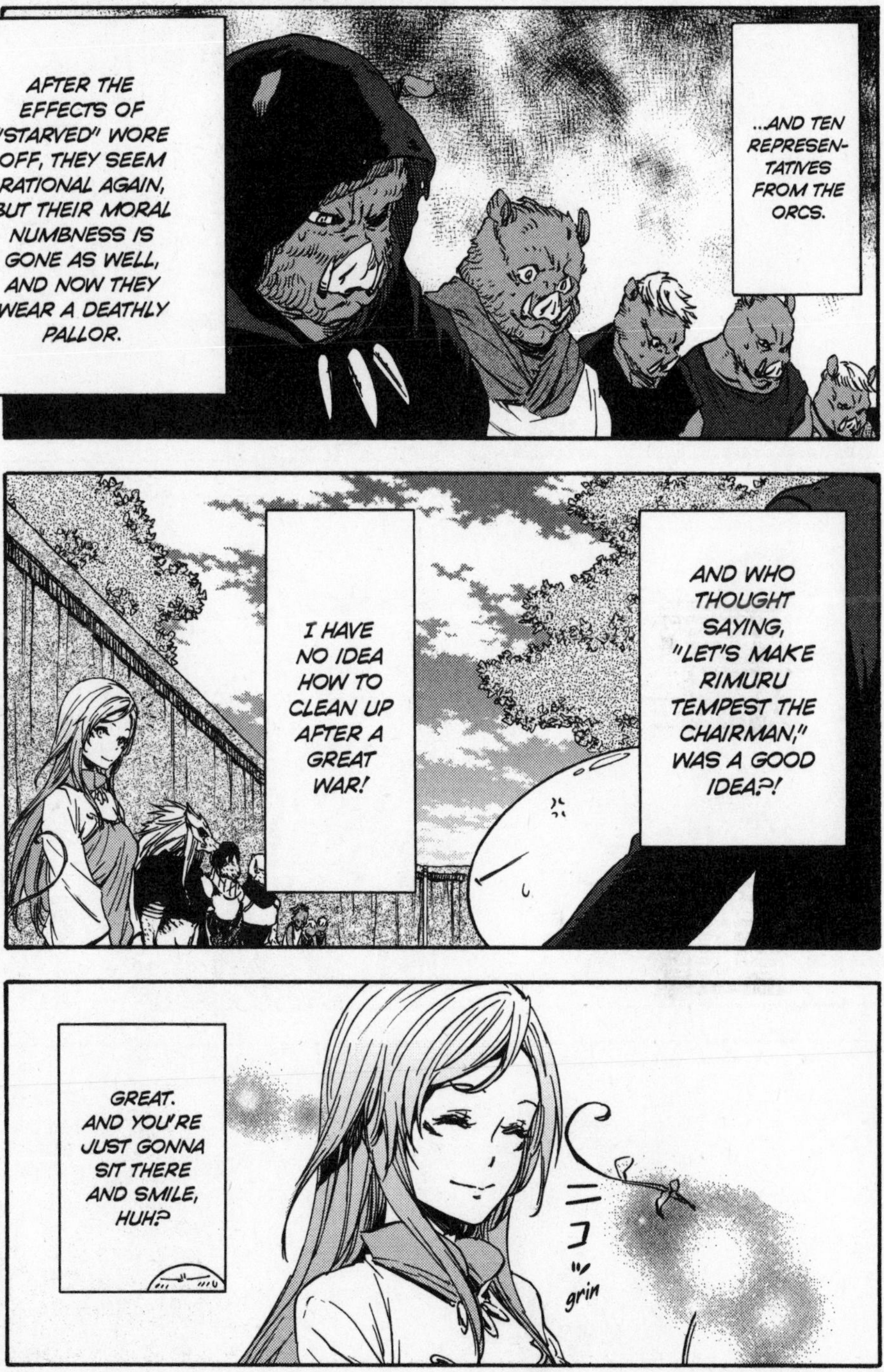
...AND TEN REPRESENTATIVES FROM THE ORCS.
AFTER THE EFFECTS OF "STARVED" WORE OFF, THEY SEEM RATIONAL AGAIN, BUT THEIR MORAL NUMBNESS IS GONE AS WELL, AND NOW THEY WEAR A DEATHLY PALLOR.
AND WHO THOUGHT SAYING, "LET'S MAKE RIMURU TEMPEST THE CHAIRMAN," WAS A GOOD IDEA?!
I HAVE NO IDEA HOW TO CLEAN UP AFTER A GREAT WAR!
GREAT. AND YOU'RE JUST GONNA SIT THERE AND SMILE, HUH?
grin

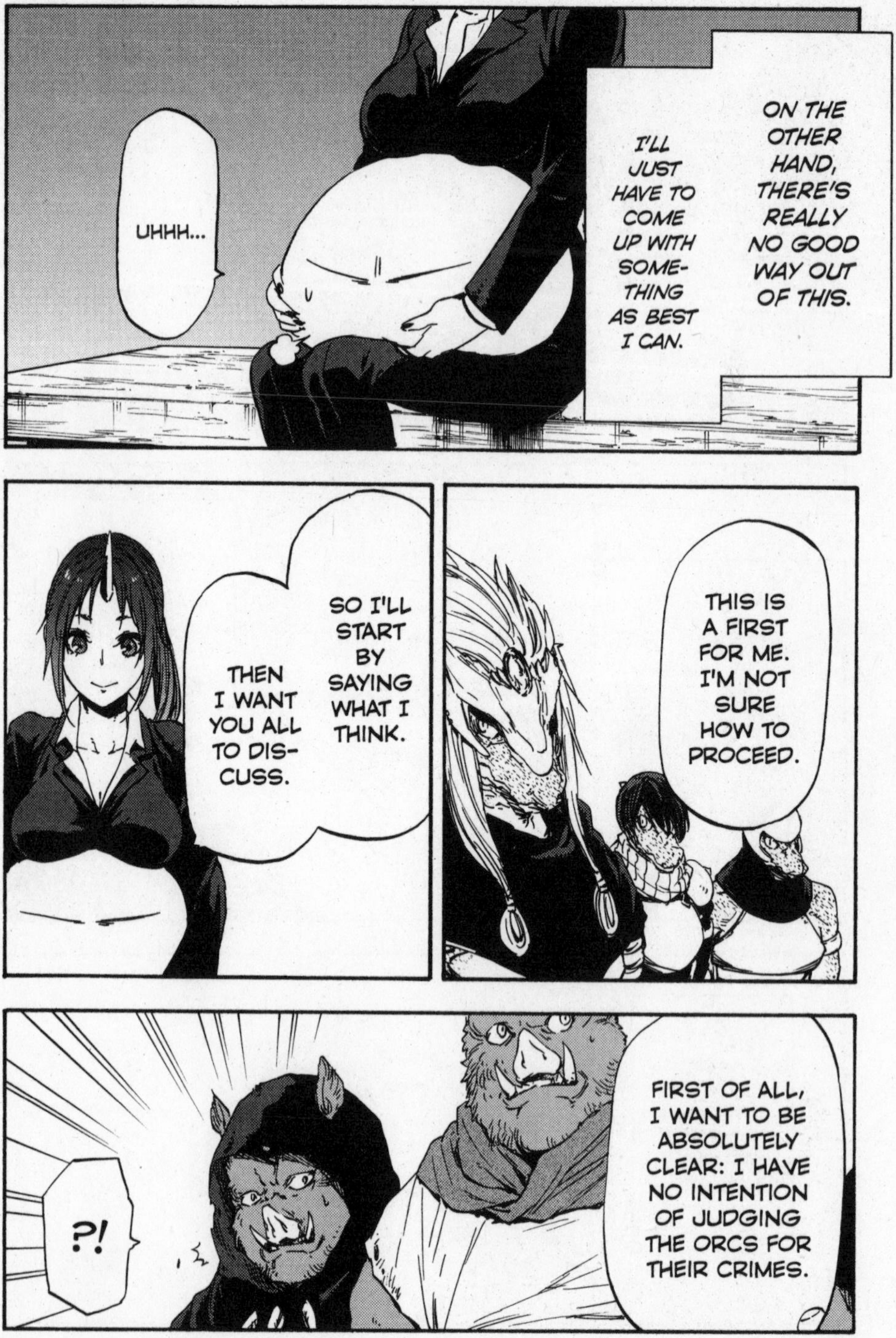
ON THE OTHER HAND, THERE'S REALLY NO GOOD WAY OUT OF THIS.
I'LL JUST HAVE TO COME UP WITH SOME-THING AS BEST I CAN.
UHHH...
THIS IS A FIRST FOR ME. I'M NOT SURE HOW TO PROCEED.
SO I'LL START BY SAYING WHAT I THINK.
THEN I WANT YOU ALL TO DIS-CUSS.
FIRST OF ALL, I WANT TO BE ABSOLUTELY CLEAR: I HAVE NO INTENTION OF JUDGING THE ORCS FOR THEIR CRIMES.
?!

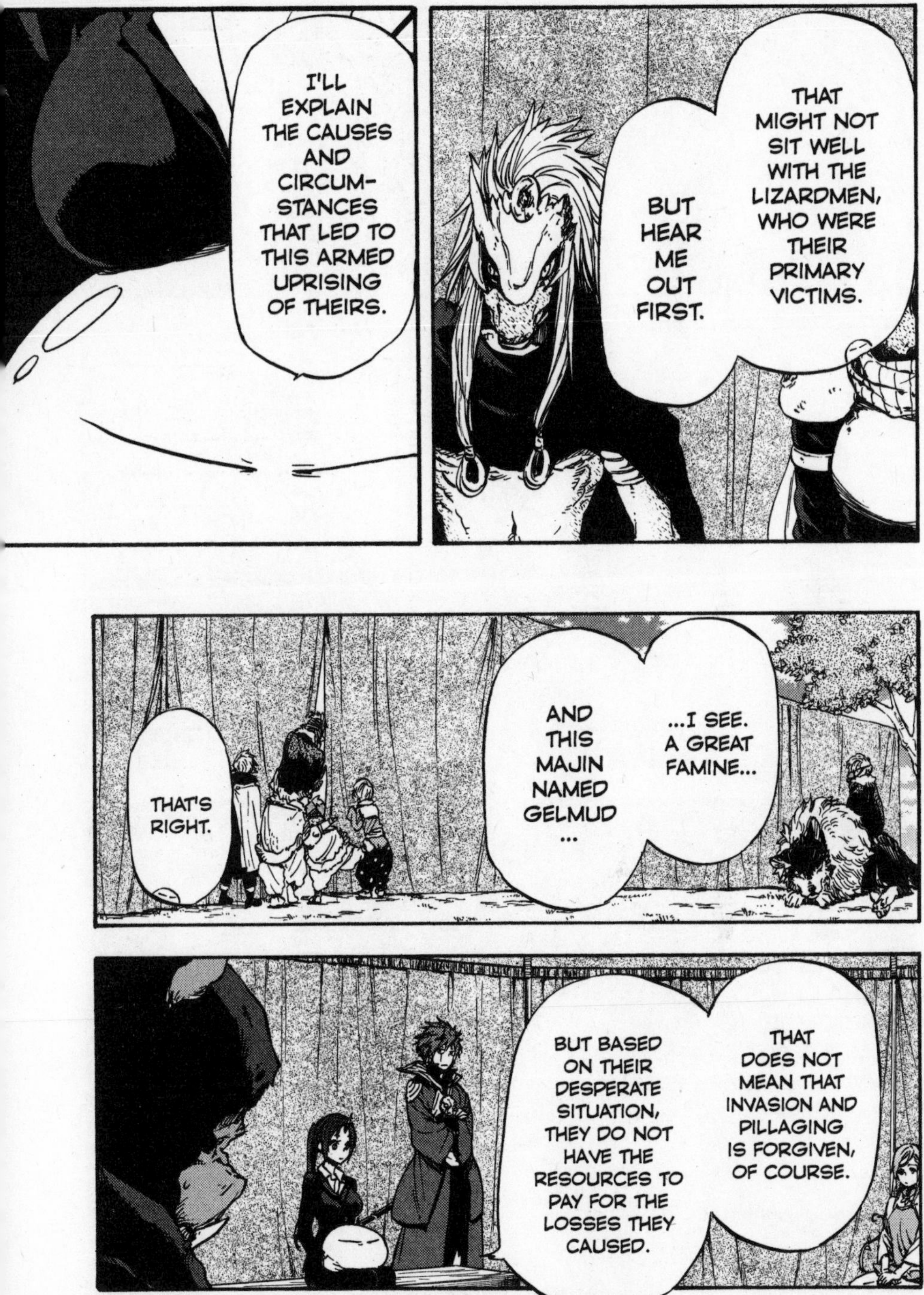
THAT MIGHT NOT SIT WELL WITH THE LIZARDMEN, WHO WERE THEIR PRIMARY VICTIMS.
BUT HEAR ME OUT FIRST.
I'LL EXPLAIN THE CAUSES AND CIRCUM-STANCES THAT LED TO THIS ARMED UPRISING OF THEIRS.
...I SEE. A GREAT FAMINE...
AND THIS MAJIN NAMED GELMUD ...
THAT'S RIGHT.
THAT DOES NOT MEAN THAT INVASION AND PILLAGING IS FORGIVEN, OF COURSE.
BUT BASED ON THEIR DESPERATE SITUATION, THEY DO NOT HAVE THE RESOURCES TO PAY FOR THE LOSSES THEY CAUSED.

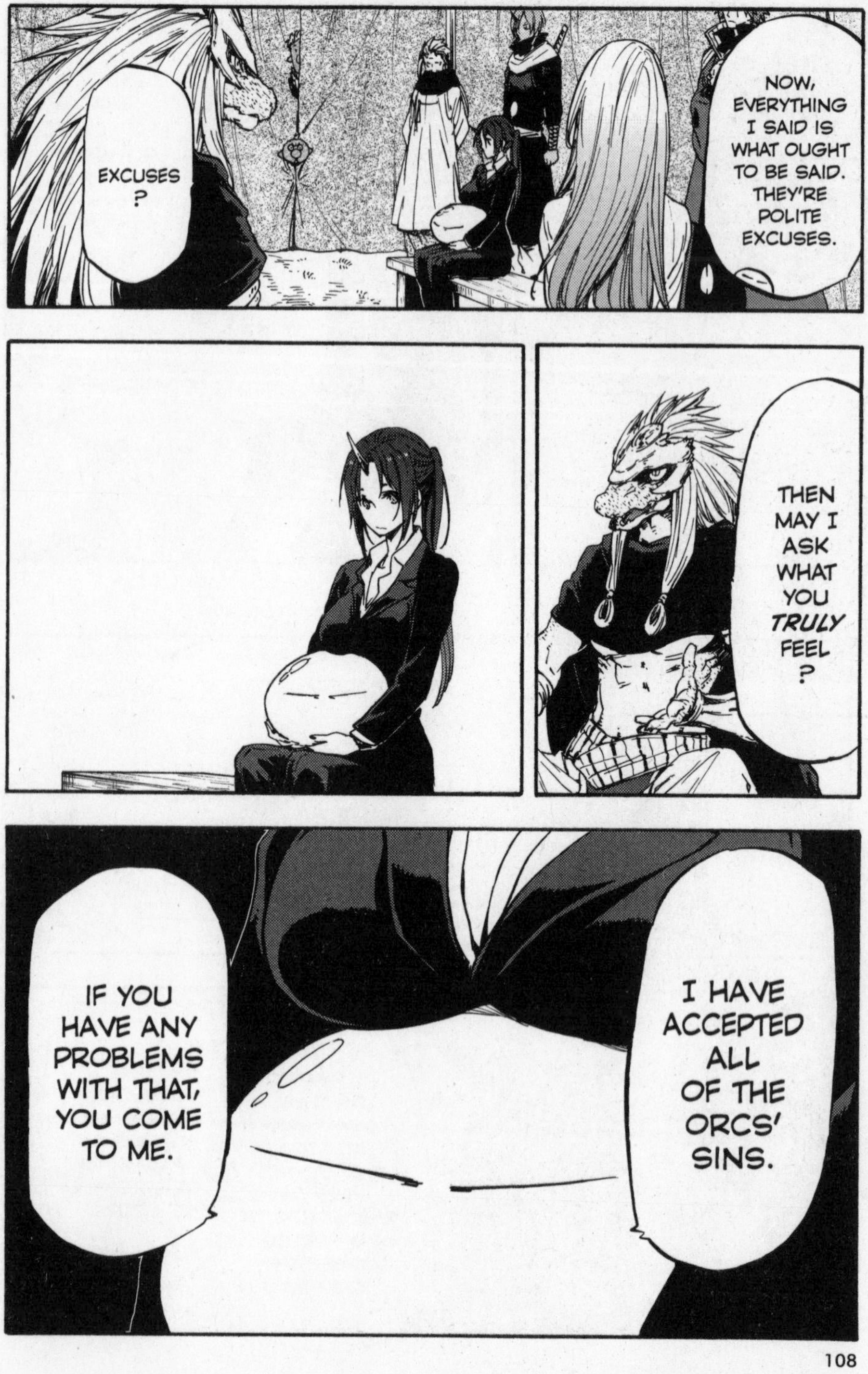
NOW, EVERYTHING I SAID IS WHAT OUGHT TO BE SAID. THEY'RE POLITE EXCUSES.
EXCUSES?
THEN MAY I ASK WHAT YOU *TRULY* FEEL?
I HAVE ACCEPTED ALL OF THE ORCS' SINS.
IF YOU HAVE ANY PROBLEMS WITH THAT, YOU COME TO ME.

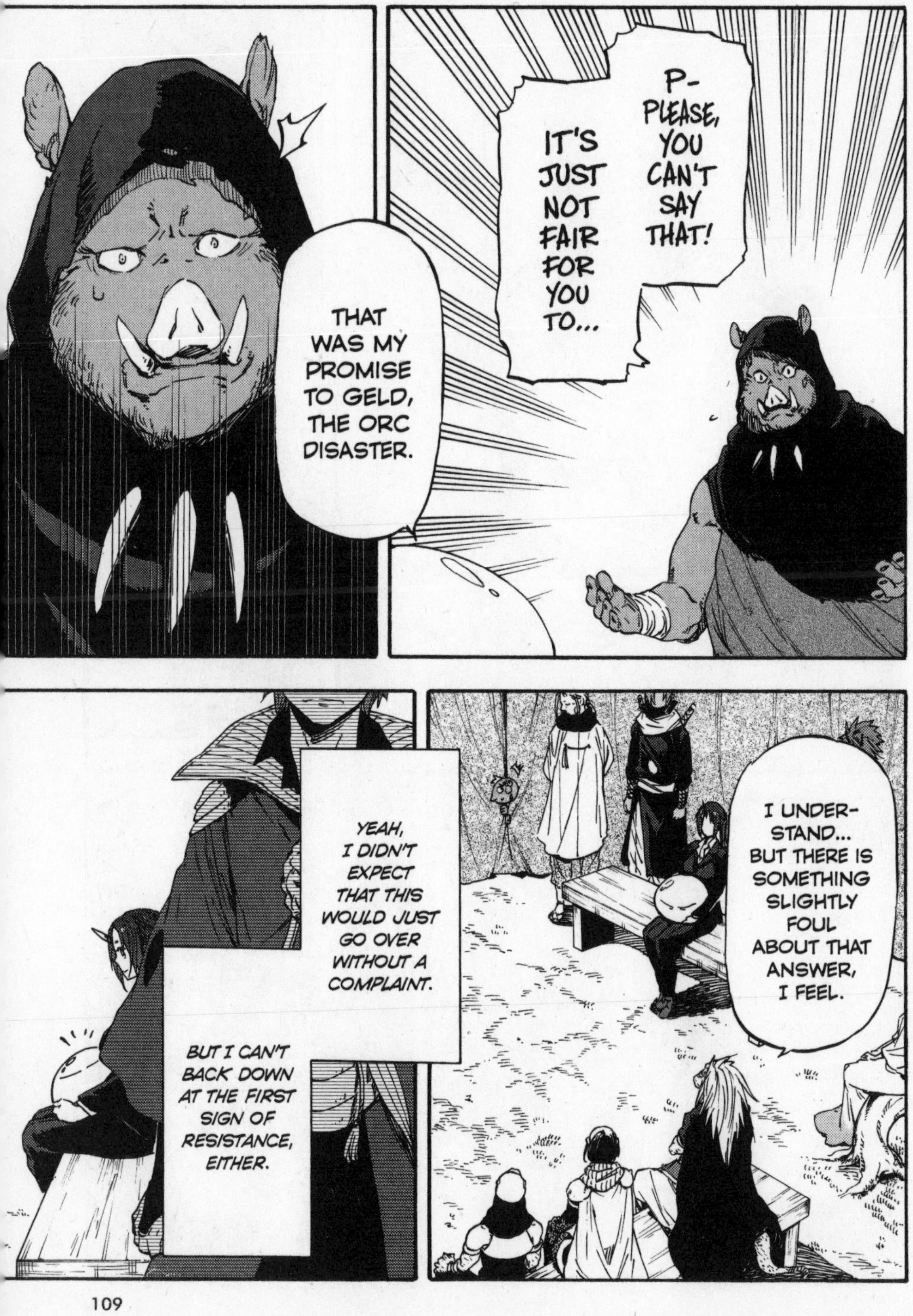
P-PLEASE, YOU CAN'T SAY THAT!
IT'S JUST NOT FAIR FOR YOU TO...
THAT WAS MY PROMISE TO GELD, THE ORC DISASTER.
I UNDERSTAND... BUT THERE IS SOMETHING SLIGHTLY FOUL ABOUT THAT ANSWER, I FEEL.
YEAH, I DIDN'T EXPECT THAT THIS WOULD JUST GO OVER WITHOUT A COMPLAINT.
BUT I CAN'T BACK DOWN AT THE FIRST SIGN OF RESISTANCE, EITHER.

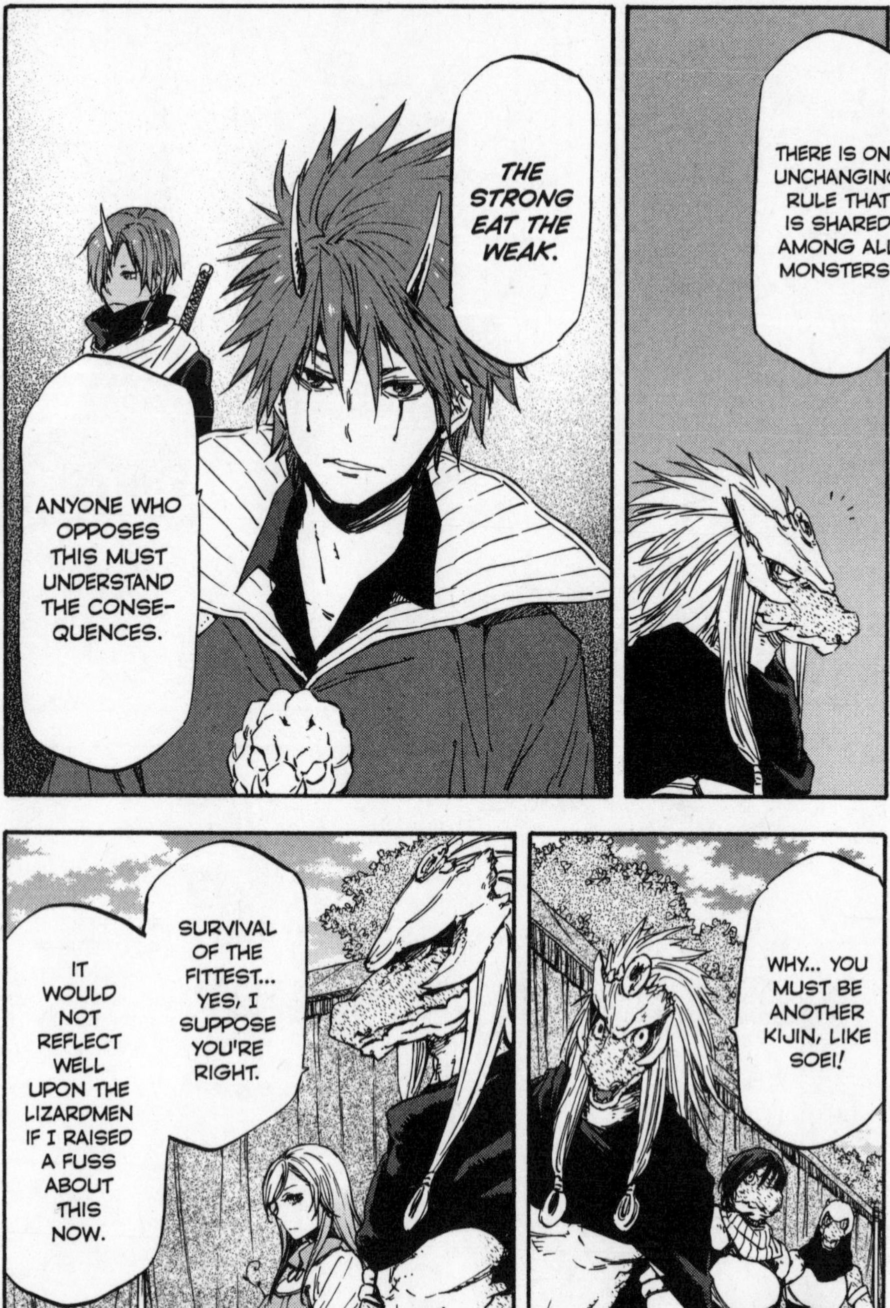
THERE IS ONE UNCHANGING RULE THAT IS SHARED AMONG ALL MONSTERS.
THE STRONG EAT THE WEAK.
ANYONE WHO OPPOSES THIS MUST UNDERSTAND THE CONSE-QUENCES.
WHY... YOU MUST BE ANOTHER KIJIN, LIKE SOEI!
SURVIVAL OF THE FITTEST... YES, I SUPPOSE YOU'RE RIGHT.
IT WOULD NOT REFLECT WELL UPON THE LIZARDMEN IF I RAISED A FUSS ABOUT THIS NOW.

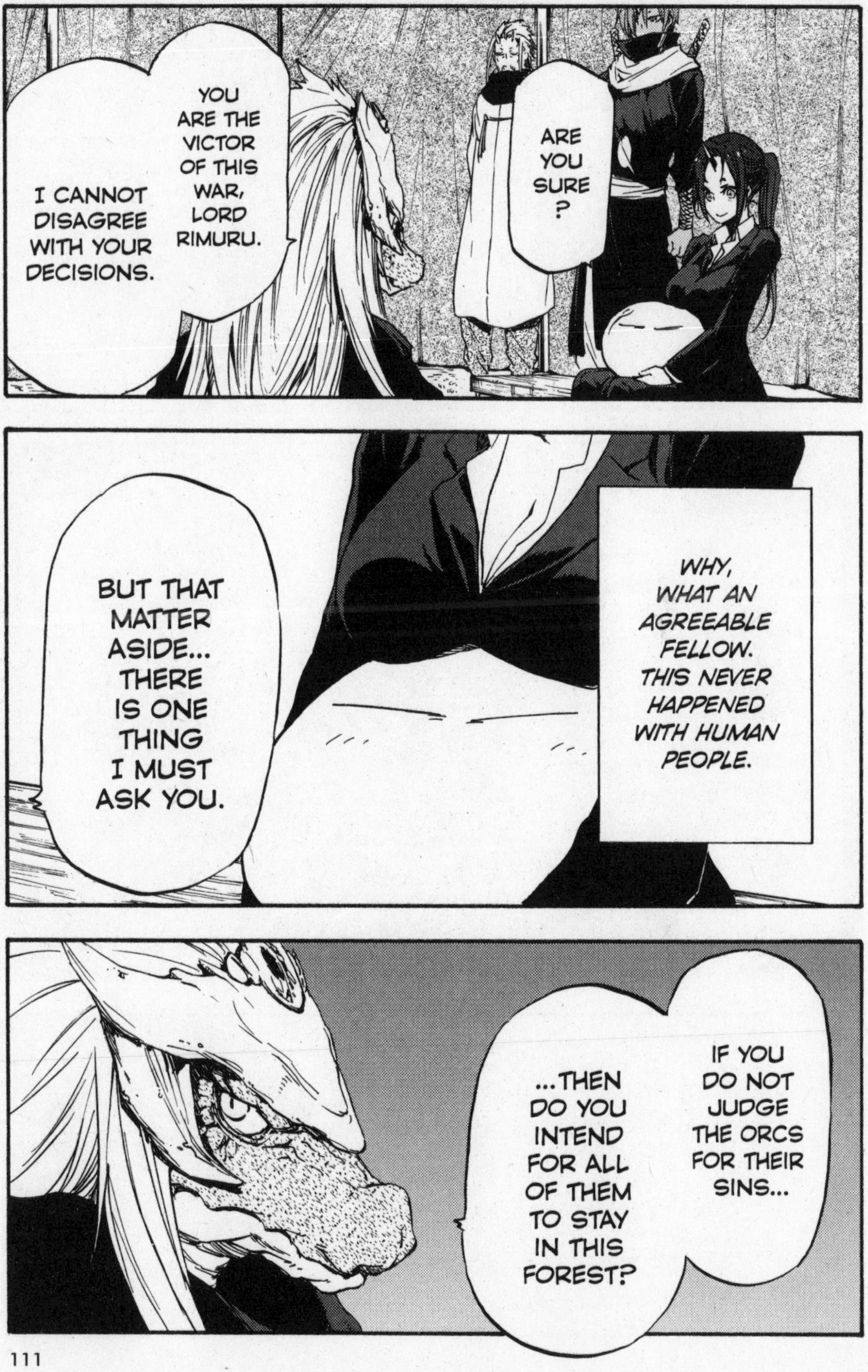
ARE YOU SURE?
YOU ARE THE VICTOR OF THIS WAR, LORD RIMURU.
I CANNOT DISAGREE WITH YOUR DECISIONS.
WHY, WHAT AN AGREEABLE FELLOW. THIS NEVER HAPPENED WITH HUMAN PEOPLE.
BUT THAT MATTER ASIDE... THERE IS ONE THING I MUST ASK YOU.
IF YOU DO NOT JUDGE THE ORCS FOR THEIR SINS...
...THEN DO YOU INTEND FOR ALL OF THEM TO STAY IN THIS FOREST?

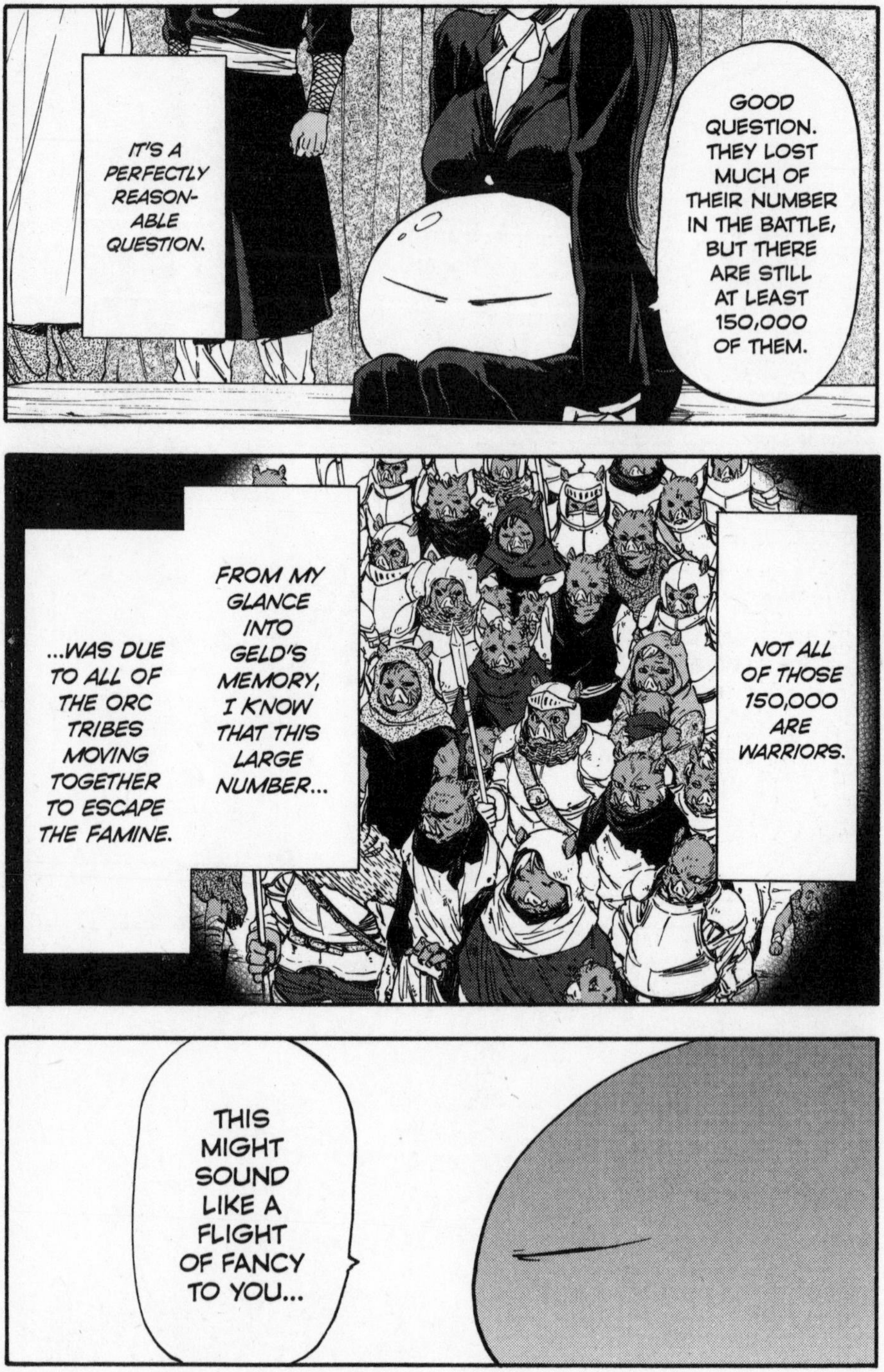
GOOD QUESTION. THEY LOST MUCH OF THEIR NUMBER IN THE BATTLE, BUT THERE ARE STILL AT LEAST 150,000 OF THEM.
IT'S A PERFECTLY REASON-ABLE QUESTION.
NOT ALL OF THOSE 150,000 ARE WARRIORS.
FROM MY GLANCE INTO GELD'S MEMORY, I KNOW THAT THIS LARGE NUMBER...
...WAS DUE TO ALL OF THE ORC TRIBES MOVING TOGETHER TO ESCAPE THE FAMINE.
THIS MIGHT SOUND LIKE A FLIGHT OF FANCY TO YOU...

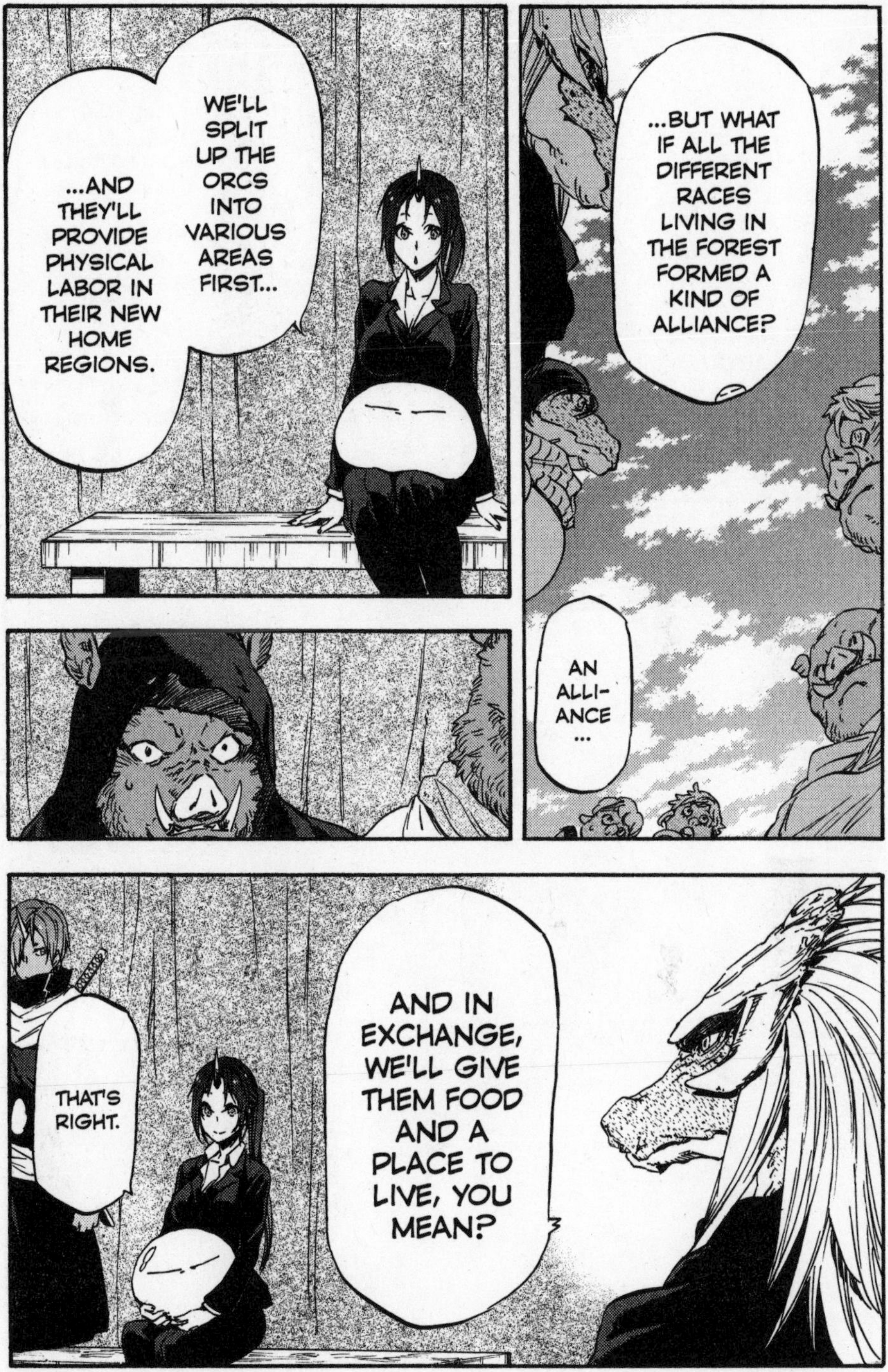
...BUT WHAT IF ALL THE DIFFERENT RACES LIVING IN THE FOREST FORMED A KIND OF ALLIANCE?
AN ALLI-ANCE...
WE'LL SPLIT UP THE ORCS INTO VARIOUS AREAS FIRST...
...AND THEY'LL PROVIDE PHYSICAL LABOR IN THEIR NEW HOME REGIONS.
AND IN EXCHANGE, WE'LL GIVE THEM FOOD AND A PLACE TO LIVE, YOU MEAN?
THAT'S RIGHT.

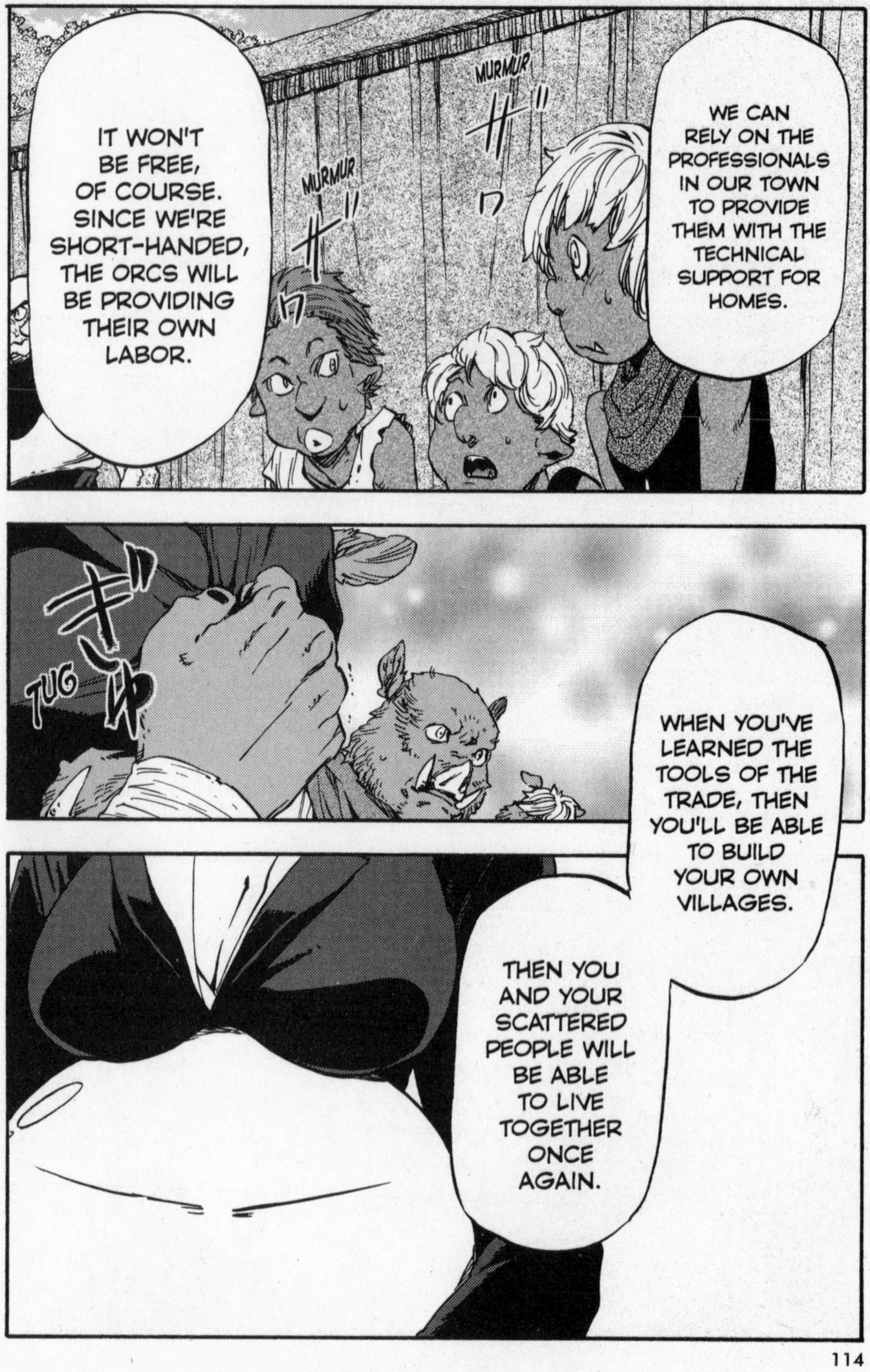
WE CAN RELY ON THE PROFESSIONALS IN OUR TOWN TO PROVIDE THEM WITH THE TECHNICAL SUPPORT FOR HOMES.
MURMUR
MURMUR
IT WON'T BE FREE, OF COURSE. SINCE WE'RE SHORT-HANDED, THE ORCS WILL BE PROVIDING THEIR OWN LABOR.
TUG
WHEN YOU'VE LEARNED THE TOOLS OF THE TRADE, THEN YOU'LL BE ABLE TO BUILD YOUR OWN VILLAGES.
THEN YOU AND YOUR SCATTERED PEOPLE WILL BE ABLE TO LIVE TOGETHER ONCE AGAIN.

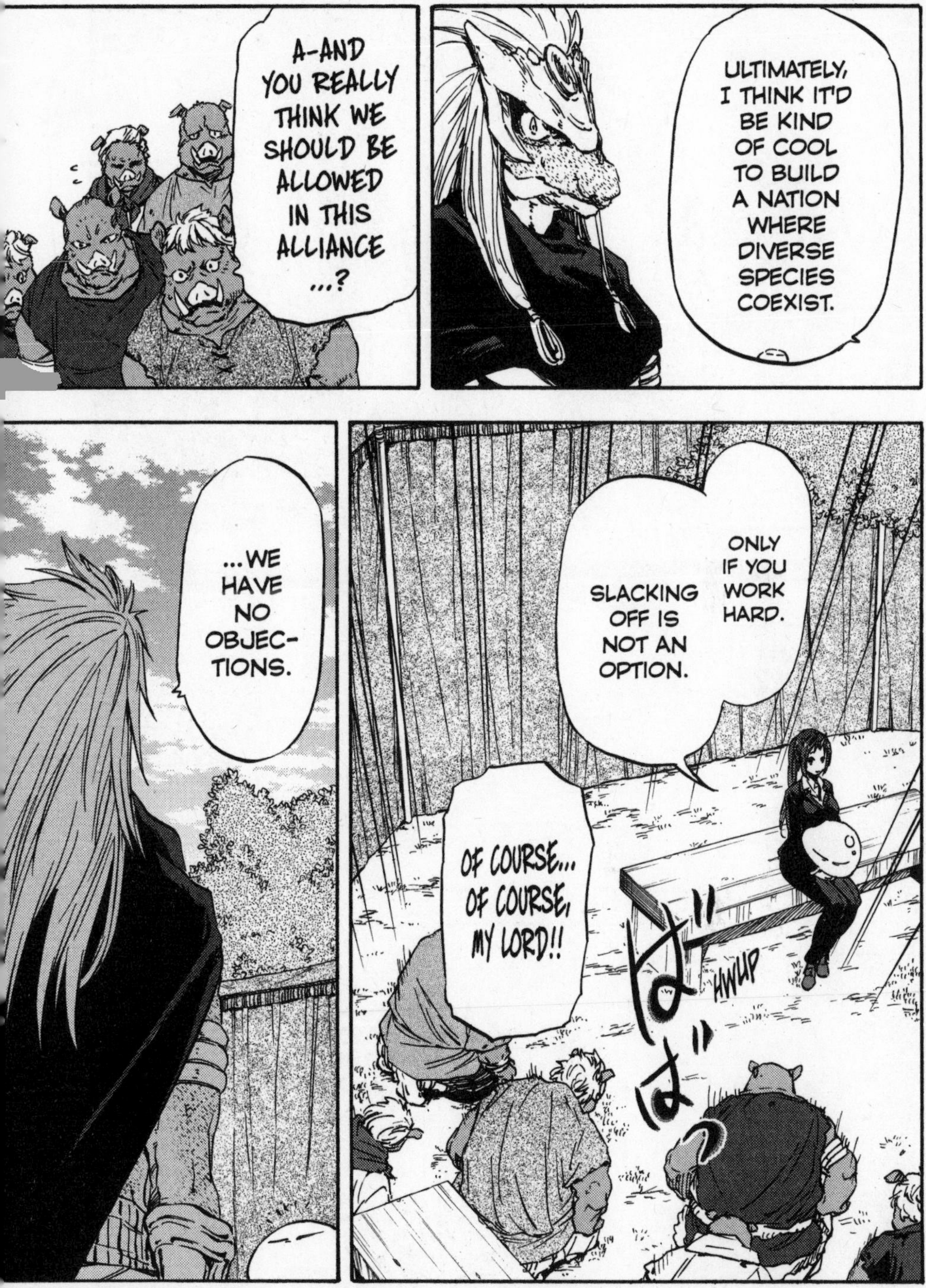
ULTIMATELY, I THINK IT'D BE KIND OF COOL TO BUILD A NATION WHERE DIVERSE SPECIES COEXIST.
A-AND YOU REALLY THINK WE SHOULD BE ALLOWED IN THIS ALLIANCE ...?
ONLY IF YOU WORK HARD.
SLACKING OFF IS NOT AN OPTION.
OF COURSE... OF COURSE, MY LORD!!
HWUP
...WE HAVE NO OBJECTIONS.

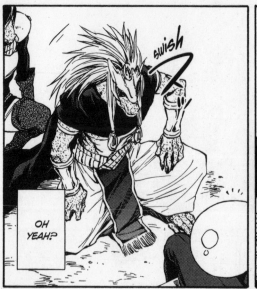

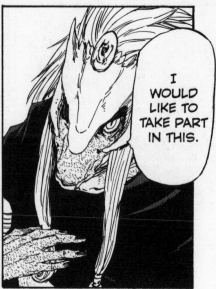

I WOULD LIKE TO TAKE PART IN THIS.
swish
OH YEAH?
WHAT ARE THEY DOING? IS THIS SOME KIND OF CUSTOM THAT GOES ALONG WITH FORMING AN ALLIANCE?
SOMETIMES I STILL DON'T GET HOW THESE MONSTERS THINK.
WHAT ARE YOU TRYING TO DO?
Then I guess I'll...
HUH? ISN'T THIS SOME KIND OF... RITUAL THING?

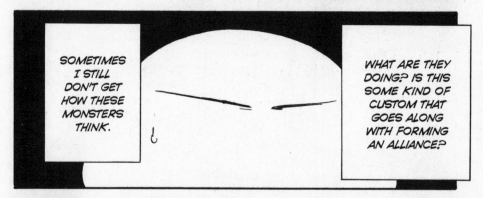

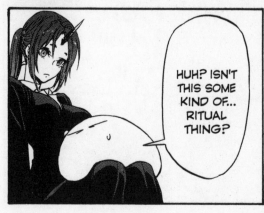

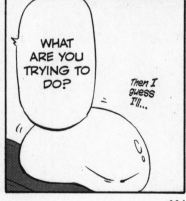

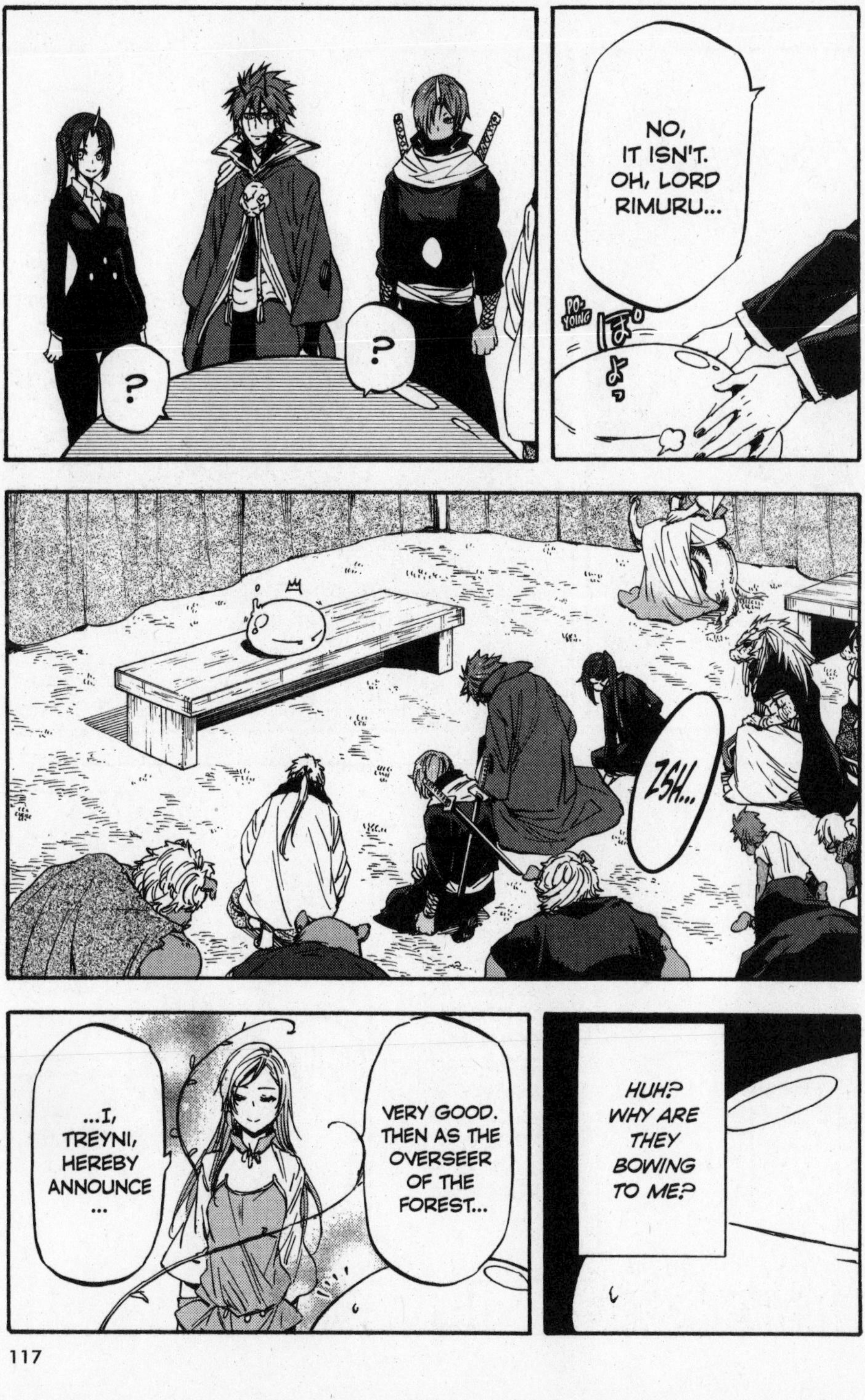
NO, IT ISN'T. OH, LORD RIMURU...
PO-YOING
ぽよっ
?
?
ZSH...
HUH? WHY ARE THEY BOWING TO ME?
VERY GOOD. THEN AS THE OVERSEER OF THE FOREST...
...I, TREYNI, HEREBY ANNOUNCE...

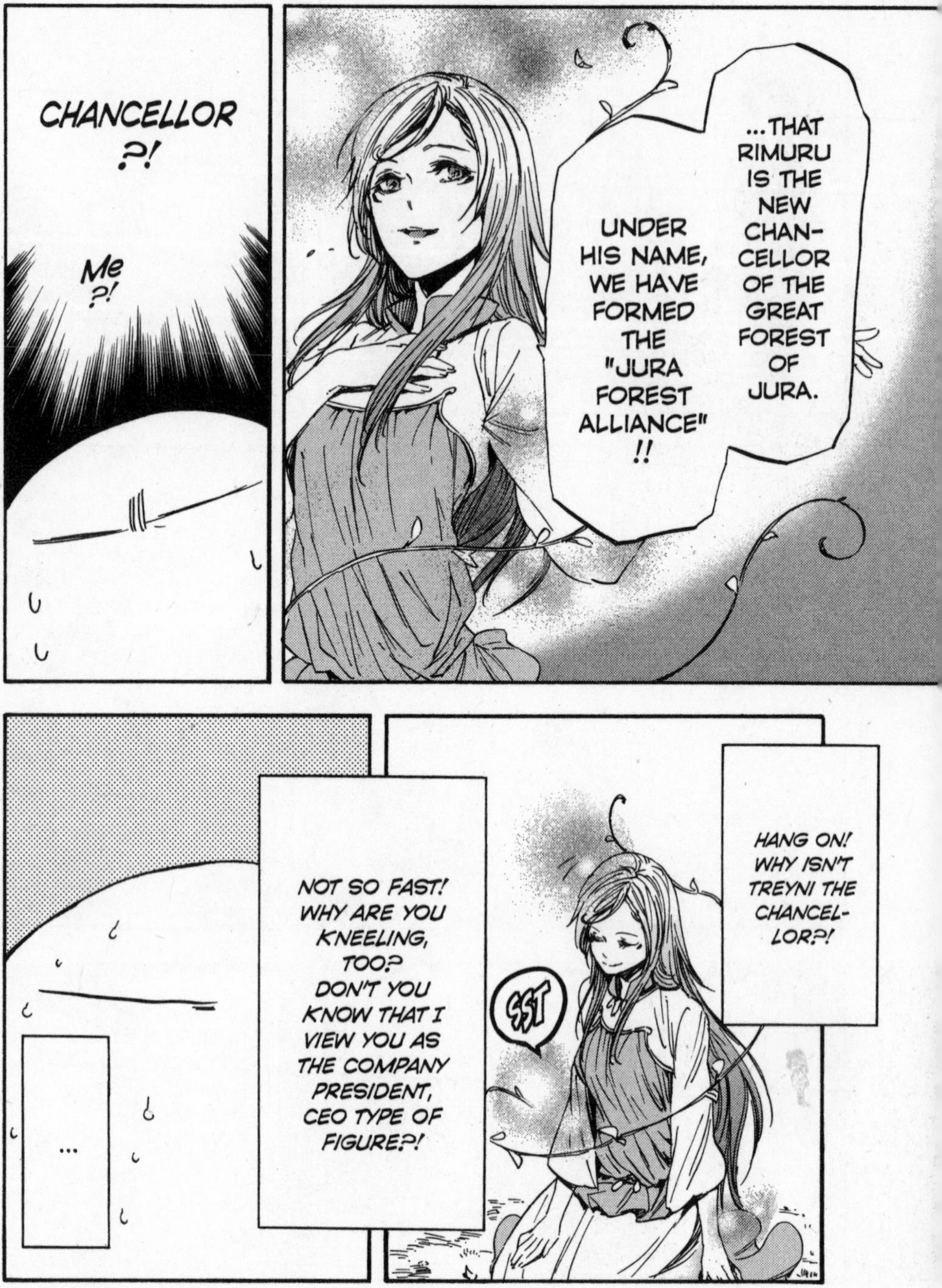
...THAT RIMURU IS THE NEW CHANCELLOR OF THE GREAT FOREST OF JURA.
UNDER HIS NAME, WE HAVE FORMED THE "JURA FOREST ALLIANCE" !!
CHANCELLOR ?!
Me ?!
HANG ON! WHY ISN'T TREYNI THE CHANCELLOR?!
SST
NOT SO FAST! WHY ARE YOU KNEELING, TOO? DON'T YOU KNOW THAT I VIEW YOU AS THE COMPANY PRESIDENT, CEO TYPE OF FIGURE?!
...

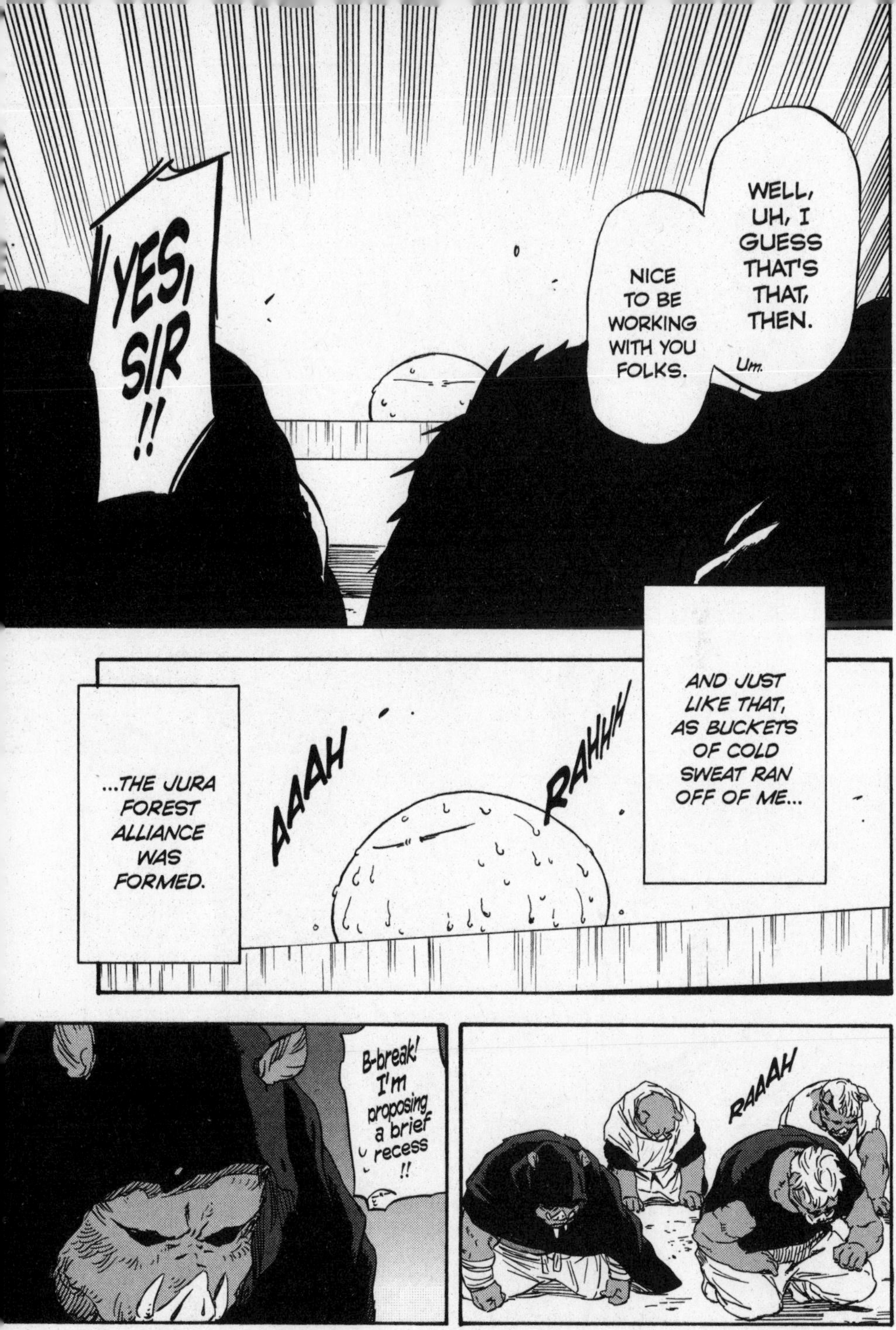
WELL, UH, I GUESS THAT'S THAT, THEN.
Um.
NICE TO BE WORKING WITH YOU FOLKS.
YES, SIR !!
AND JUST LIKE THAT, AS BUCKETS OF COLD SWEAT RAN OFF OF ME...
RAHHH
AAAH
...THE JURA FOREST ALLIANCE WAS FORMED.
RAAAH
B-break! I'm proposing a brief recess !!

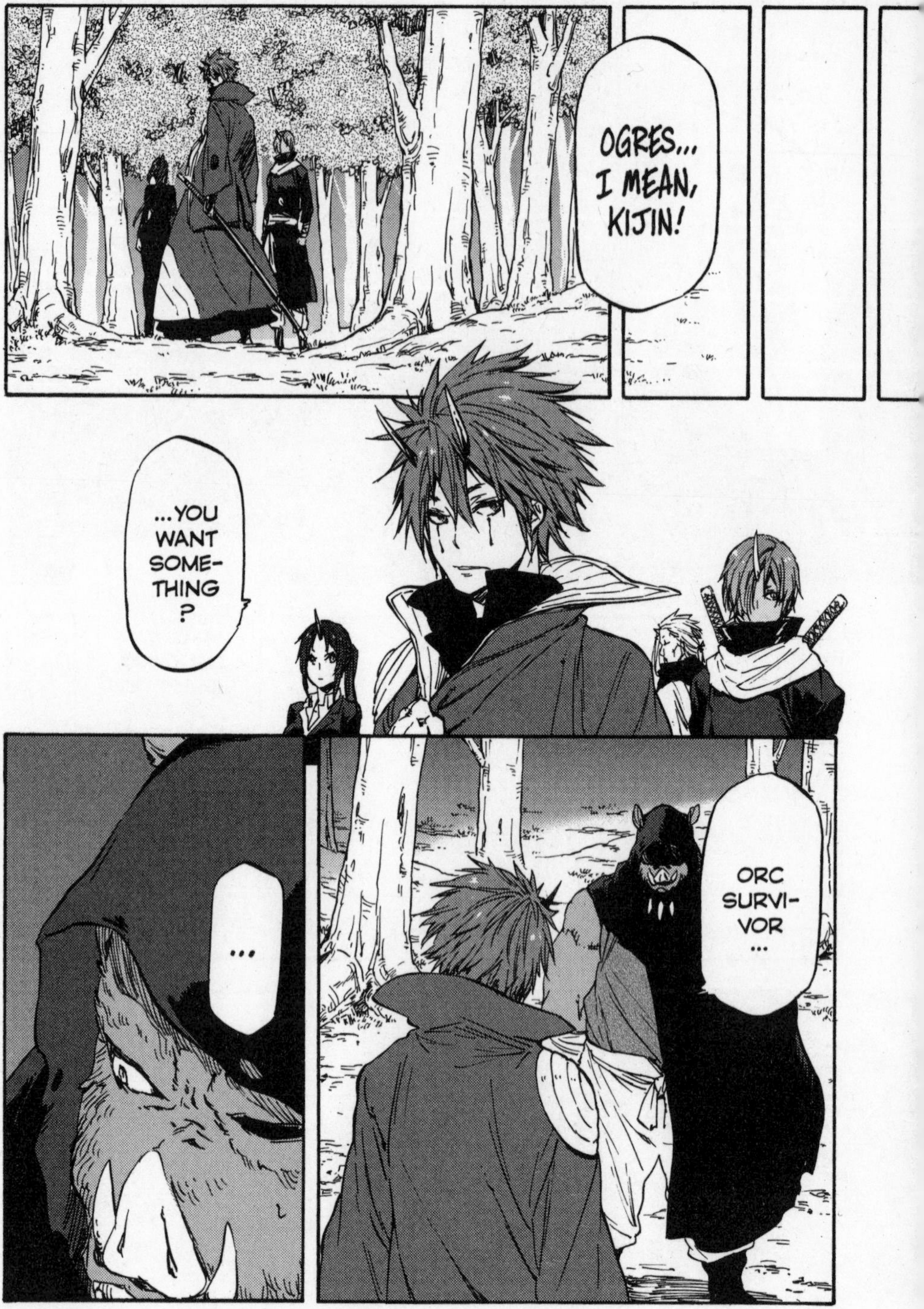
OGRES... I MEAN, KIJIN!
...YOU WANT SOME-THING?
ORC SURVI-VOR...
...

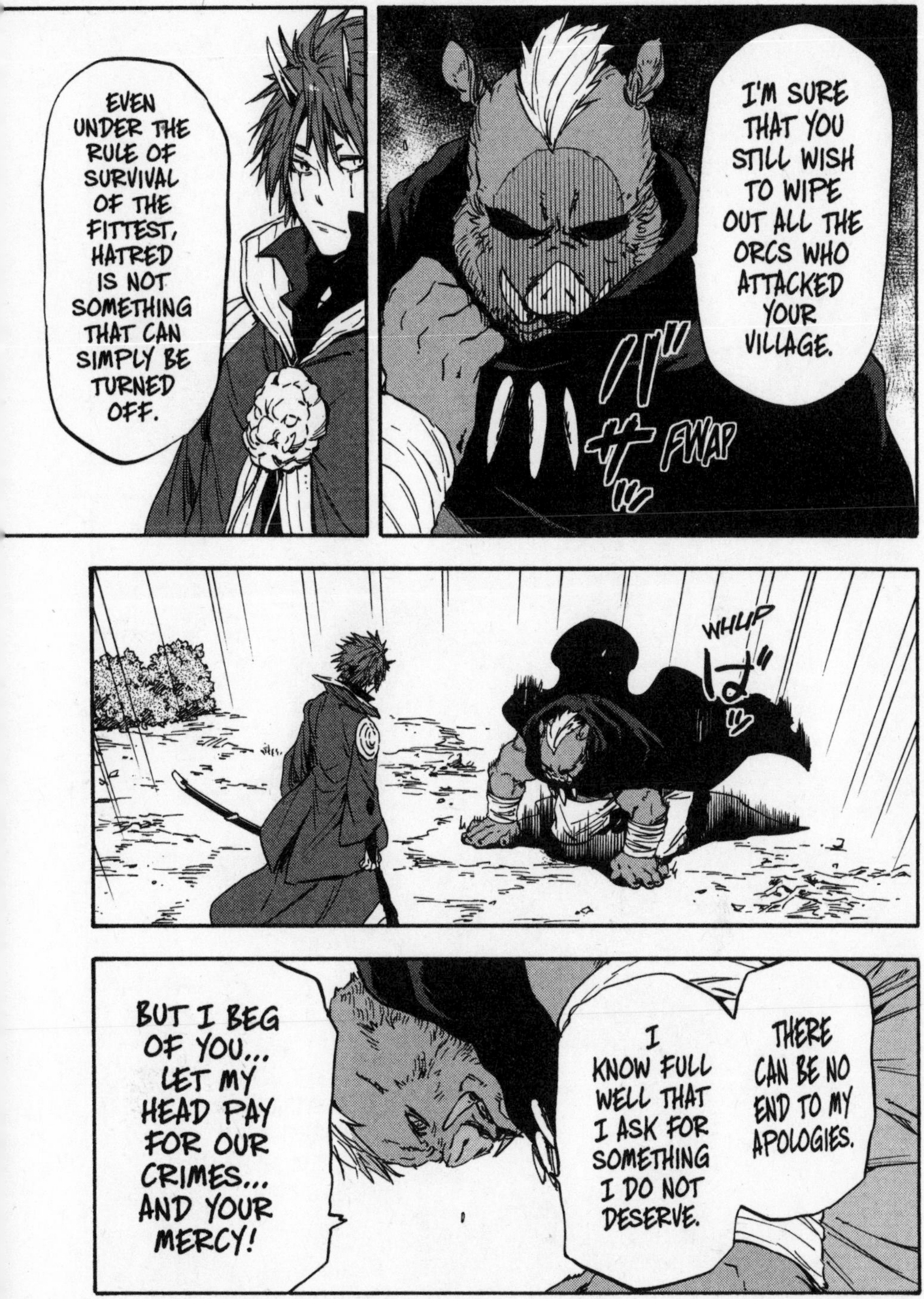
I'M SURE THAT YOU STILL WISH TO WIPE OUT ALL THE ORCS WHO ATTACKED YOUR VILLAGE.
FWAP
EVEN UNDER THE RULE OF SURVIVAL OF THE FITTEST, HATRED IS NOT SOMETHING THAT CAN SIMPLY BE TURNED OFF.
WHUP
THERE CAN BE NO END TO MY APOLOGIES.
I KNOW FULL WELL THAT I ASK FOR SOMETHING I DO NOT DESERVE.
BUT I BEG OF YOU... LET MY HEAD PAY FOR OUR CRIMES... AND YOUR MERCY!

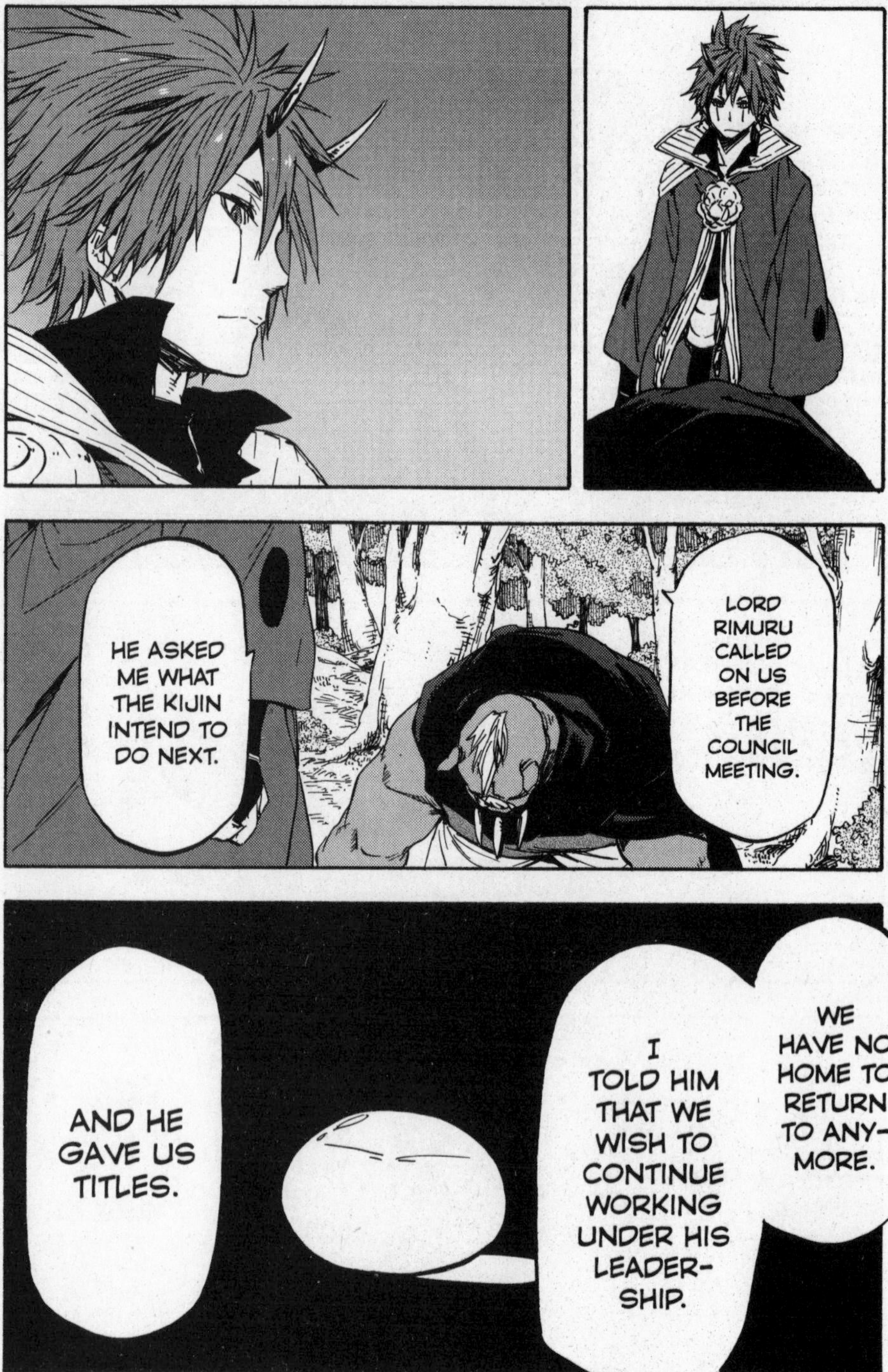
LORD RIMURU CALLED ON US BEFORE THE COUNCIL MEETING.
HE ASKED ME WHAT THE KIJIN INTEND TO DO NEXT.
WE HAVE NO HOME TO RETURN TO ANY-MORE.
I TOLD HIM THAT WE WISH TO CONTINUE WORKING UNDER HIS LEADER-SHIP.
AND HE GAVE US TITLES.

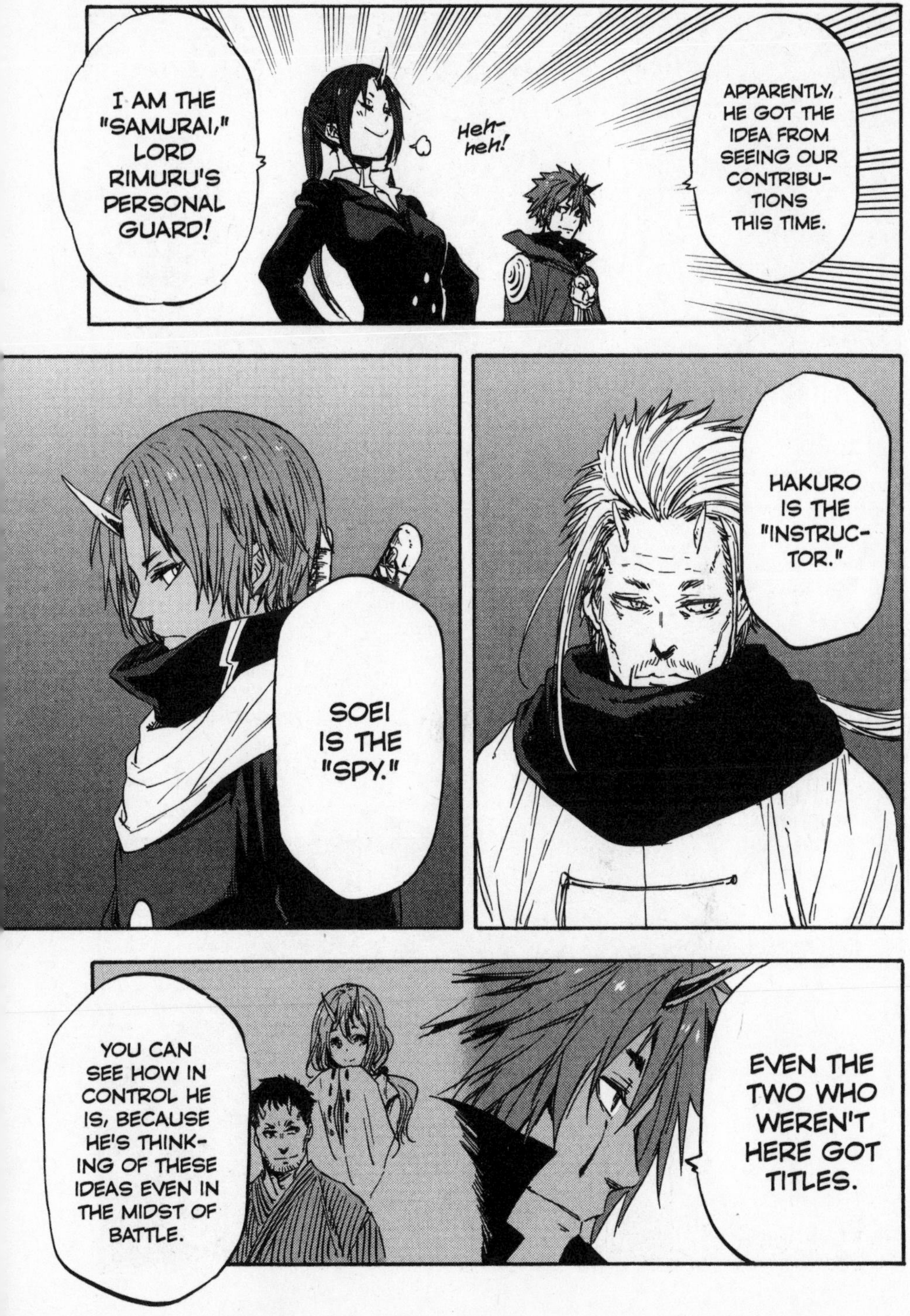
APPARENTLY, HE GOT THE IDEA FROM SEEING OUR CONTRIBU-TIONS THIS TIME.
Heh-heh!
I AM THE "SAMURAI," LORD RIMURU'S PERSONAL GUARD!
HAKURO IS THE "INSTRUC-TOR."
SOEI IS THE "SPY."
EVEN THE TWO WHO WEREN'T HERE GOT TITLES.
YOU CAN SEE HOW IN CONTROL HE IS, BECAUSE HE'S THINK-ING OF THESE IDEAS EVEN IN THE MIDST OF BATTLE.

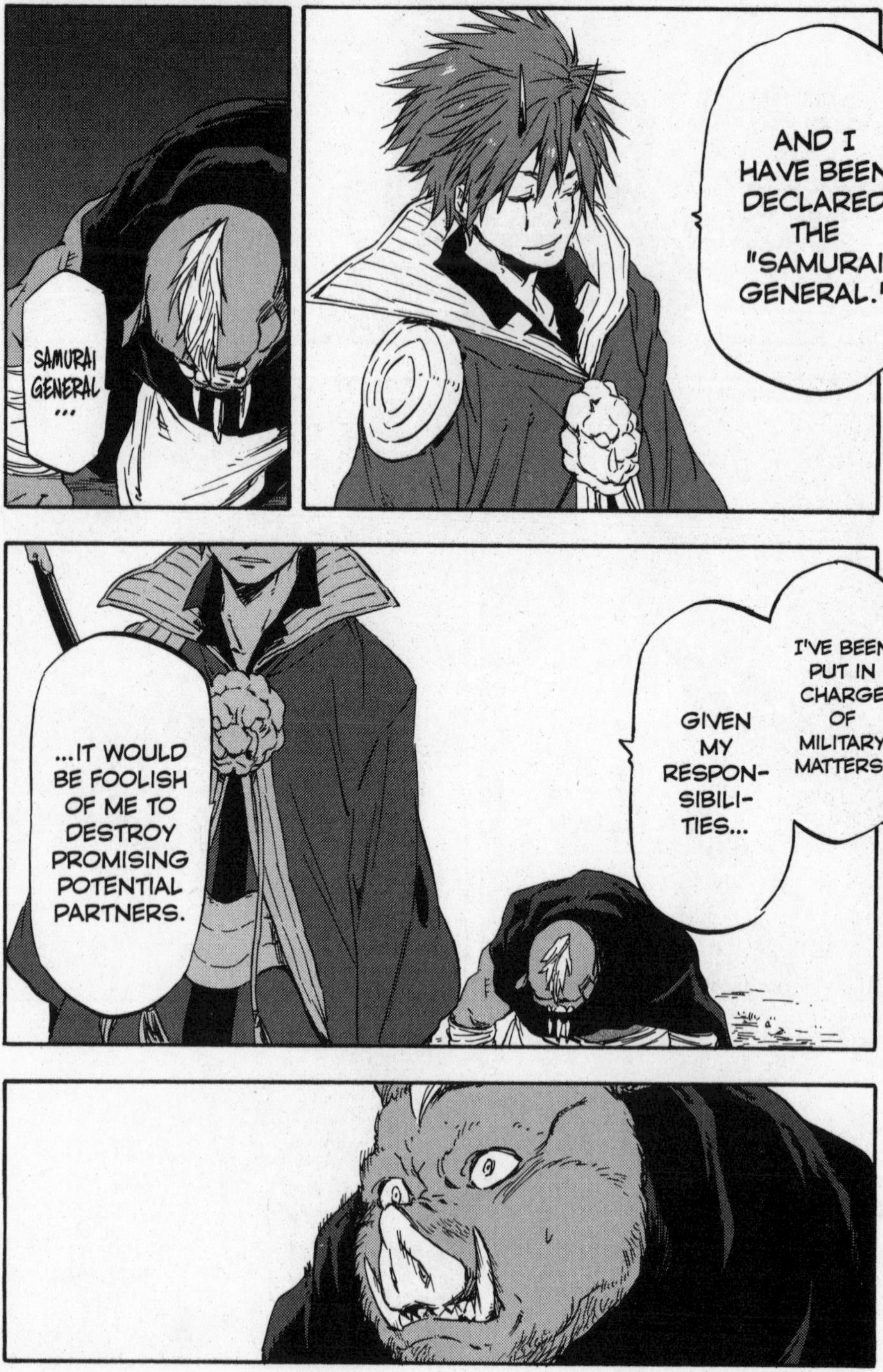
AND I HAVE BEEN DECLARED THE "SAMURAI GENERAL."
SAMURAI GENERAL...
I'VE BEEN PUT IN CHARGE OF MILITARY MATTERS.
GIVEN MY RESPONSIBILITIES...
...IT WOULD BE FOOLISH OF ME TO DESTROY PROMISING POTENTIAL PARTNERS.

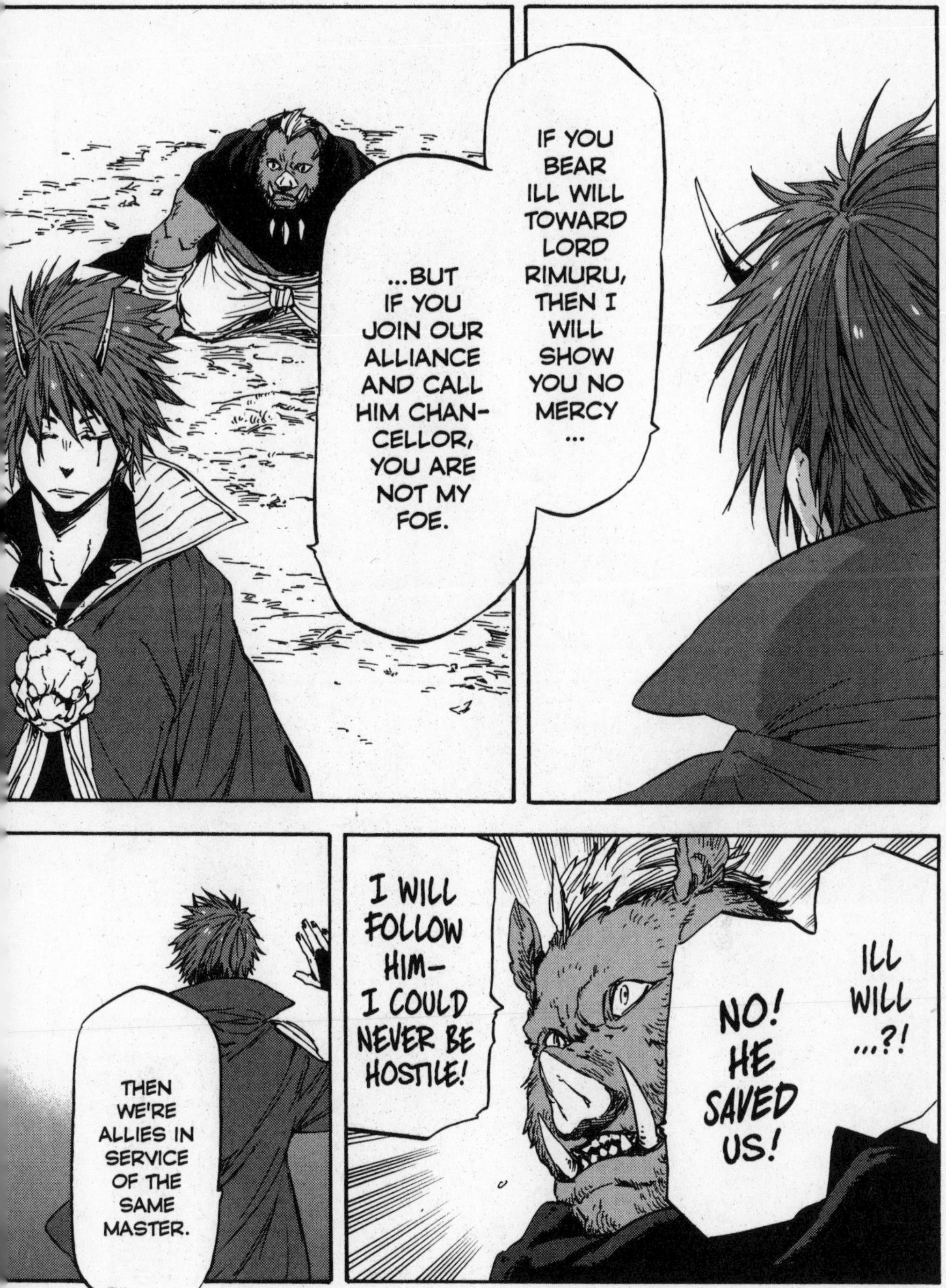
IF YOU BEAR ILL WILL TOWARD LORD RIMURU, THEN I WILL SHOW YOU NO MERCY...
...BUT IF YOU JOIN OUR ALLIANCE AND CALL HIM CHANCELLOR, YOU ARE NOT MY FOE.
ILL WILL...?!
NO! HE SAVED US!
I WILL FOLLOW HIM— I COULD NEVER BE HOSTILE!
THEN WE'RE ALLIES IN SERVICE OF THE SAME MASTER.

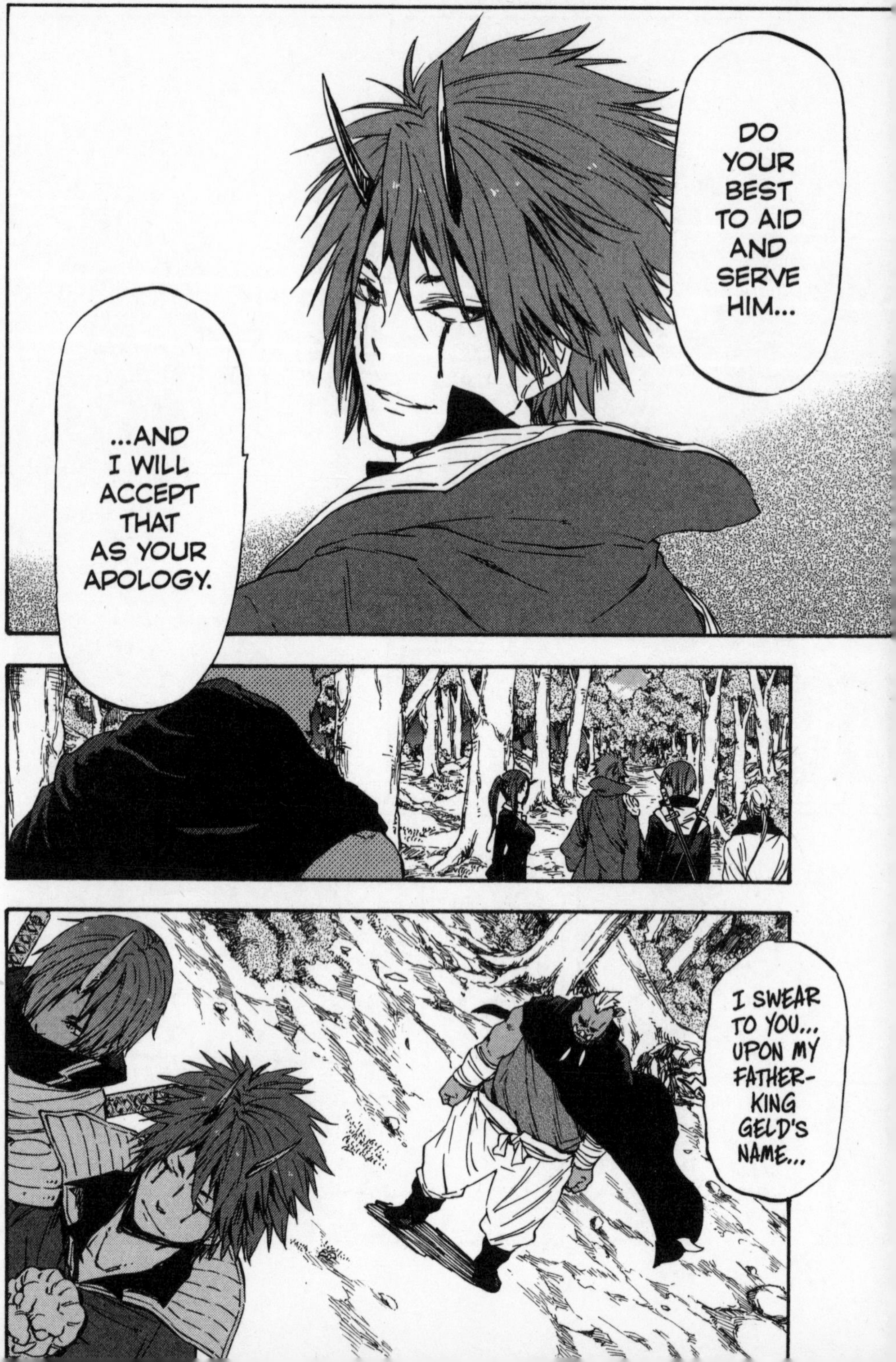
DO YOUR BEST TO AID AND SERVE HIM...
...AND I WILL ACCEPT THAT AS YOUR APOLOGY.
I SWEAR TO YOU... UPON MY FATHER-KING GELD'S NAME...

I just want
to turn into
cold sweat
and evaporate
into nothing.

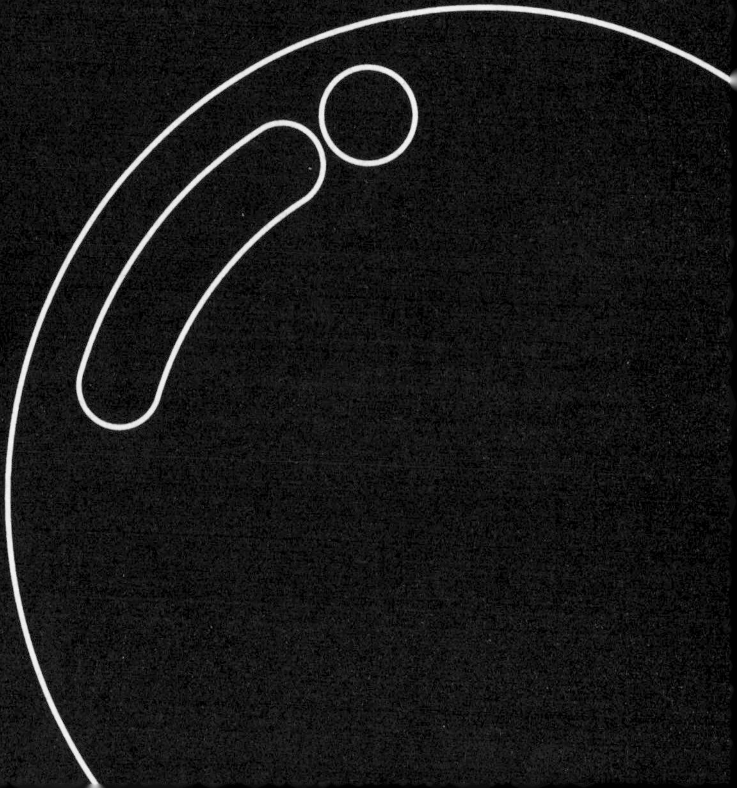

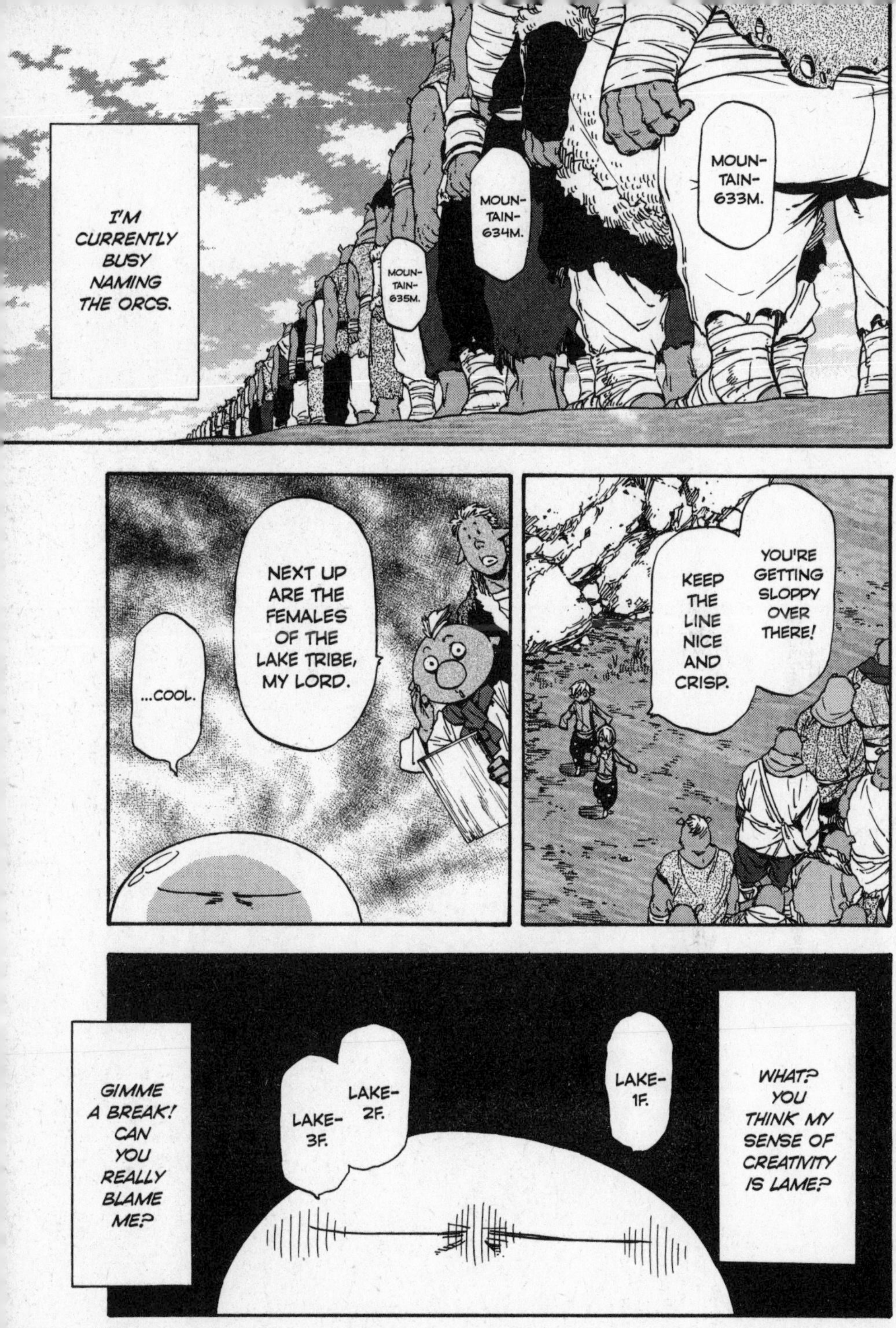
MOUNTAIN-633M.
MOUNTAIN-634M.
MOUNTAIN-635M.
I'M CURRENTLY BUSY NAMING THE ORCS.
YOU'RE GETTING SLOPPY OVER THERE!
KEEP THE LINE NICE AND CRISP.
NEXT UP ARE THE FEMALES OF THE LAKE TRIBE, MY LORD.
...COOL.
WHAT? YOU THINK MY SENSE OF CREATIVITY IS LAME?
LAKE-1F.
LAKE-2F.
LAKE-3F.
GIMME A BREAK! CAN YOU REALLY BLAME ME?

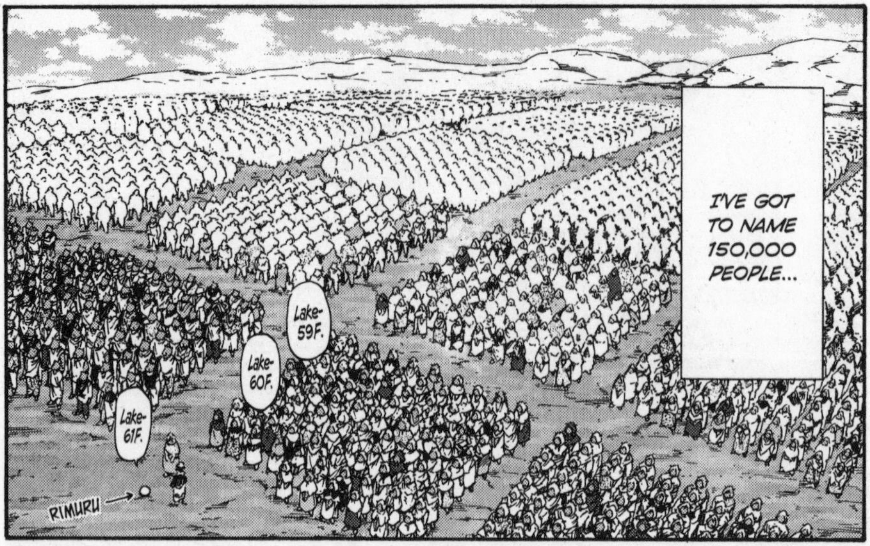
I'VE GOT TO NAME 150,000 PEOPLE...
Lake-59F.
Lake-60F.
Lake-61F.
RIMURU

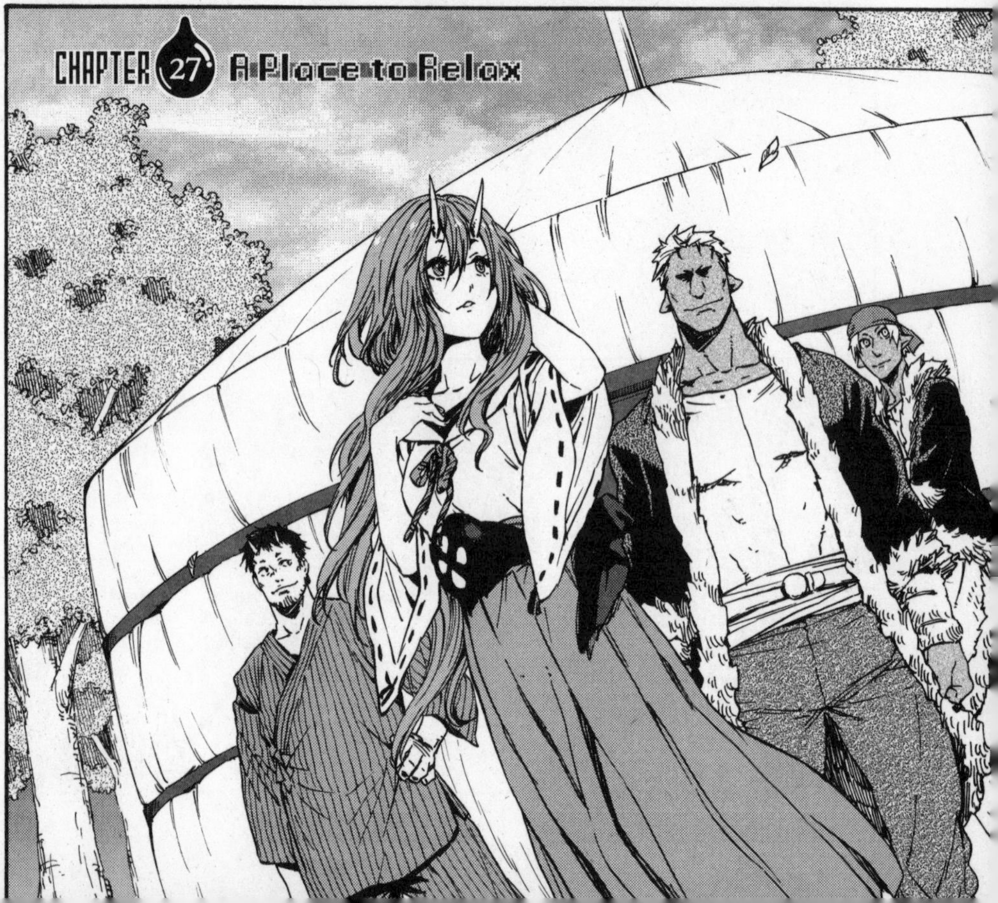
CHAPTER 27 A Place to Relax

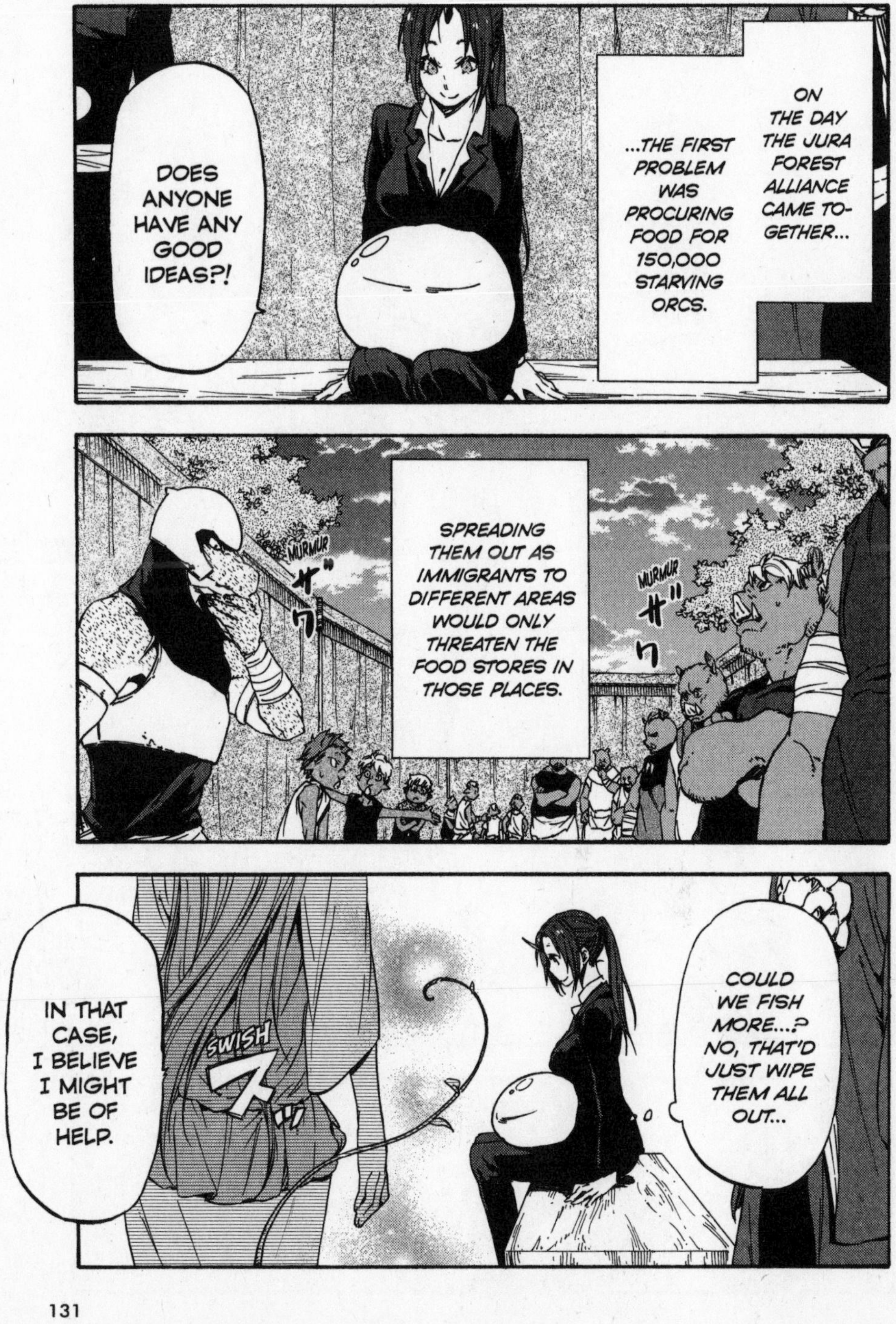
ON THE DAY THE JURA FOREST ALLIANCE CAME TOGETHER...
...THE FIRST PROBLEM WAS PROCURING FOOD FOR 150,000 STARVING ORCS.
DOES ANYONE HAVE ANY GOOD IDEAS?!
MURMUR
SPREADING THEM OUT AS IMMIGRANTS TO DIFFERENT AREAS WOULD ONLY THREATEN THE FOOD STORES IN THOSE PLACES.
MURMUR
COULD WE FISH MORE...? NO, THAT'D JUST WIPE THEM ALL OUT...
SWISH
IN THAT CASE, I BELIEVE I MIGHT BE OF HELP.

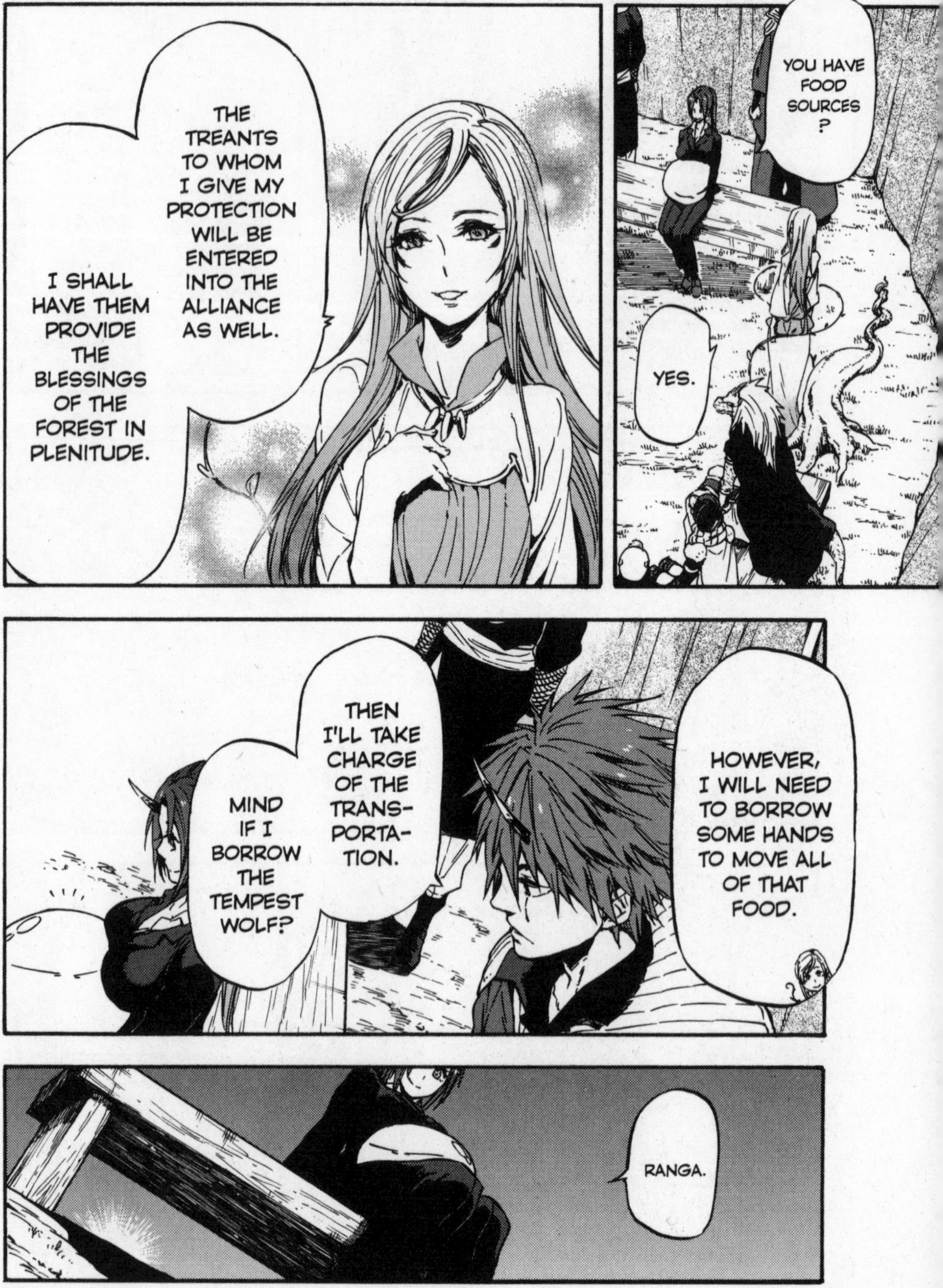
YOU HAVE FOOD SOURCES?
YES.
THE TREANTS TO WHOM I GIVE MY PROTECTION WILL BE ENTERED INTO THE ALLIANCE AS WELL.
I SHALL HAVE THEM PROVIDE THE BLESSINGS OF THE FOREST IN PLENITUDE.
HOWEVER, I WILL NEED TO BORROW SOME HANDS TO MOVE ALL OF THAT FOOD.
THEN I'LL TAKE CHARGE OF THE TRANS-PORTA-TION.
MIND IF I BORROW THE TEMPEST WOLF?
RANGA.

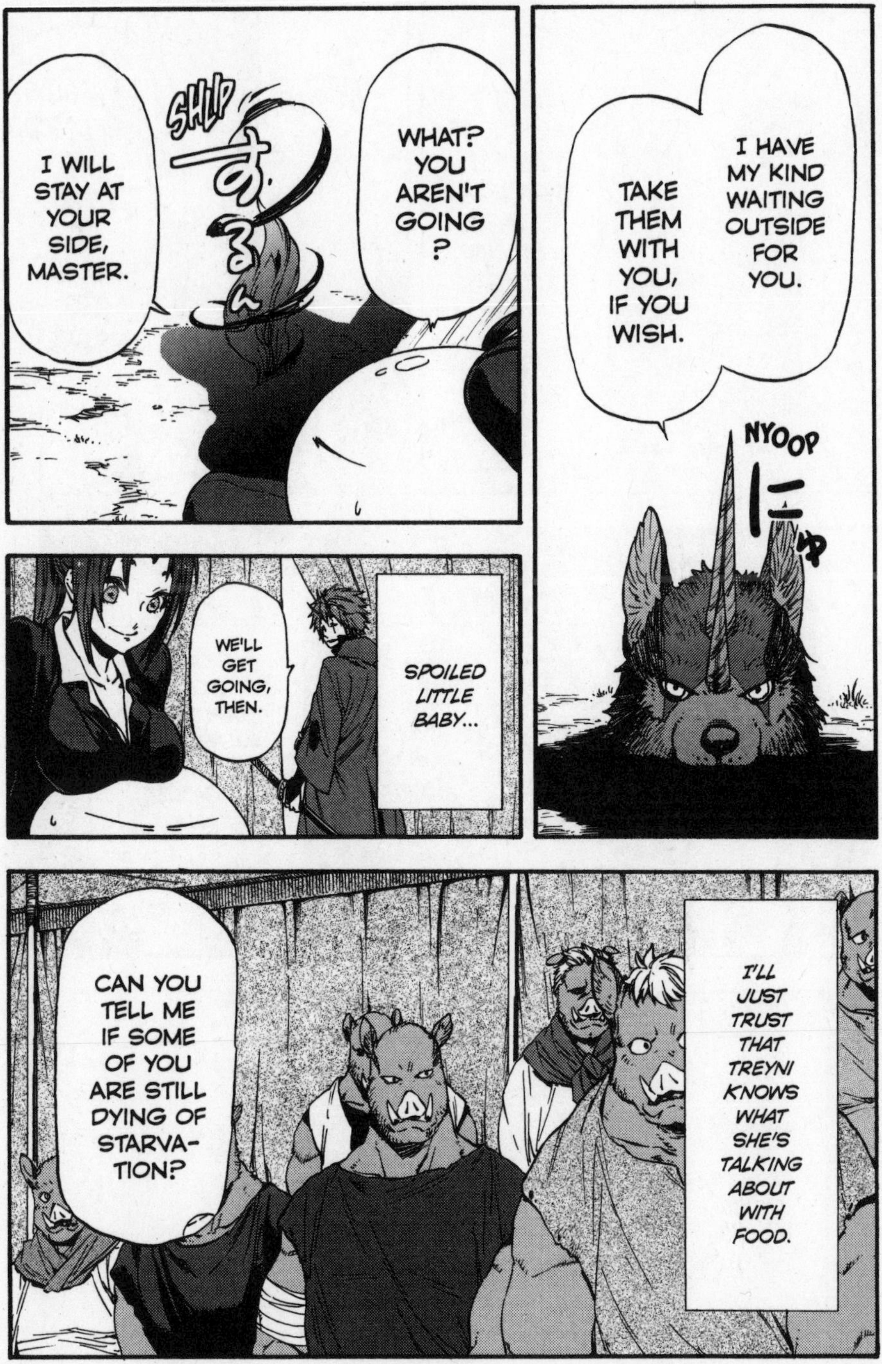

I HAVE MY KIND WAITING OUTSIDE FOR YOU.
TAKE THEM WITH YOU, IF YOU WISH.
NYOOP
にゅ
WHAT? YOU AREN'T GOING?
SHLIP
するん
I WILL STAY AT YOUR SIDE, MASTER.
SPOILED LITTLE BABY...
WE'LL GET GOING, THEN.
I'LL JUST TRUST THAT TREYNI KNOWS WHAT SHE'S TALKING ABOUT WITH FOOD.
CAN YOU TELL ME IF SOME OF YOU ARE STILL DYING OF STARVATION?

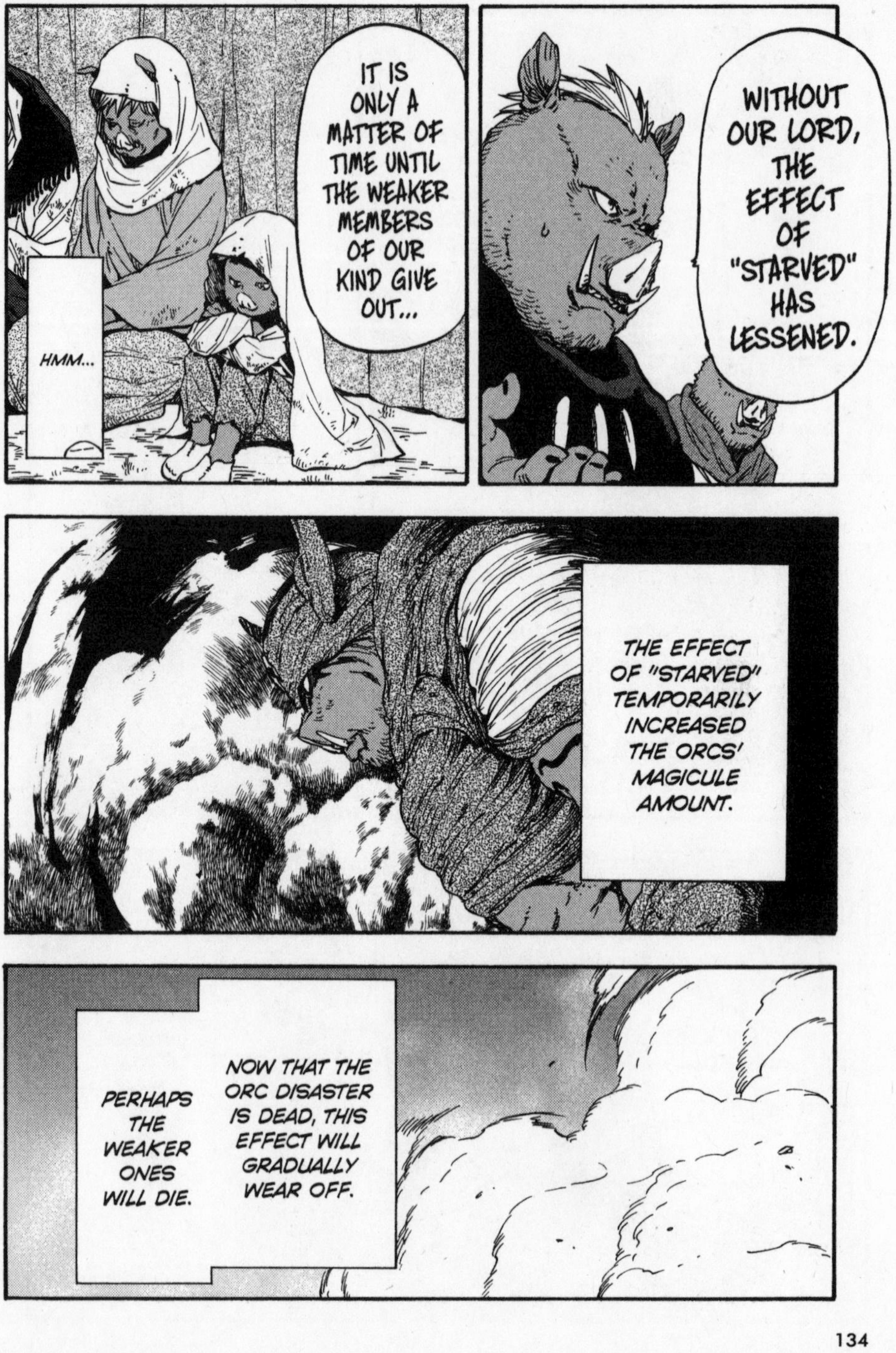
WITHOUT OUR LORD, THE EFFECT OF "STARVED" HAS LESSENED.
IT IS ONLY A MATTER OF TIME UNTIL THE WEAKER MEMBERS OF OUR KIND GIVE OUT...
HMM...
THE EFFECT OF "STARVED" TEMPORARILY INCREASED THE ORCS' MAGICULE AMOUNT.
NOW THAT THE ORC DISASTER IS DEAD, THIS EFFECT WILL GRADUALLY WEAR OFF.
PERHAPS THE WEAKER ONES WILL DIE.

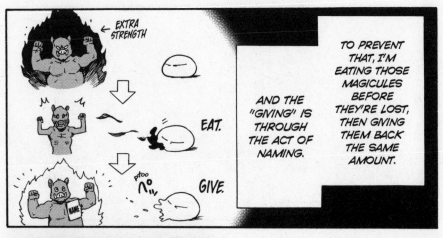

TO PREVENT THAT, I'M EATING THOSE MAGICULES BEFORE THEY'RE LOST, THEN GIVING THEM BACK THE SAME AMOUNT.
AND THE "GIVING" IS THROUGH THE ACT OF NAMING.
← EXTRA STRENGTH
EAT.
ptoo
GIVE.
NAME
... NAMES.
NAMES, HUH.
AND THAT LED TO THIS NAME-GIVING HELL.
NEXT GROUP IS THE LAST ONE, LORD RIMURU.
Deathmarch Dance is starting to work...

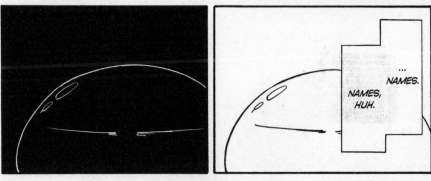

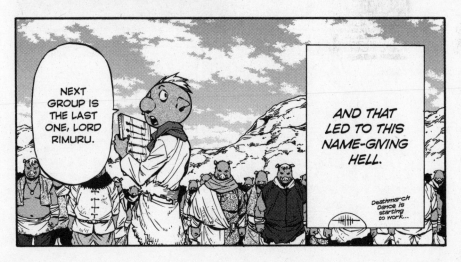

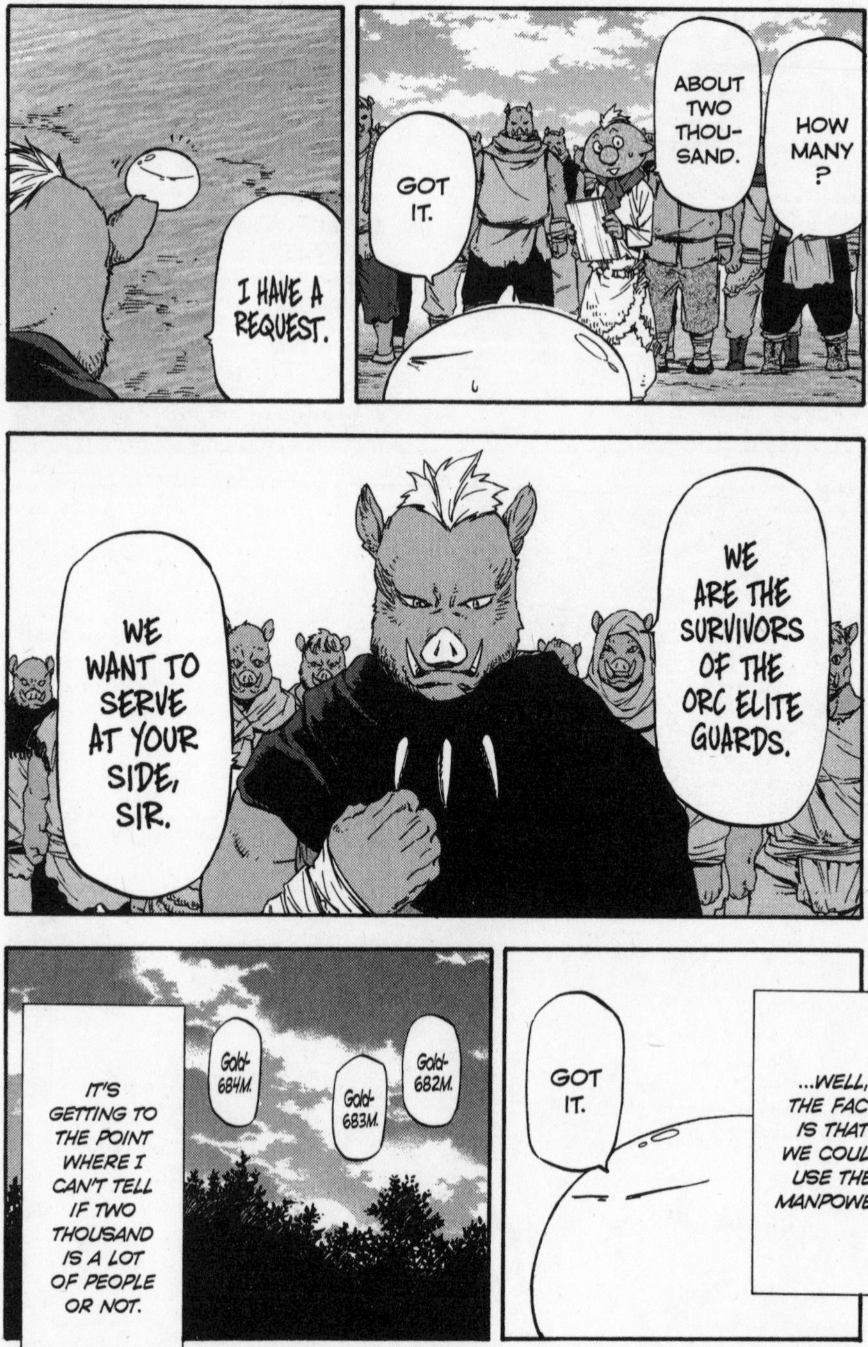
HOW MANY ?
ABOUT TWO THOUSAND.
GOT IT.
I HAVE A REQUEST.
WE ARE THE SURVIVORS OF THE ORC ELITE GUARDS.
WE WANT TO SERVE AT YOUR SIDE, SIR.
...WELL, THE FACT IS THAT WE COULD USE THE MANPOWER.
GOT IT.
Gold-682M.
Gold-683M.
Gold-684M.
IT'S GETTING TO THE POINT WHERE I CAN'T TELL IF TWO THOUSAND IS A LOT OF PEOPLE OR NOT.

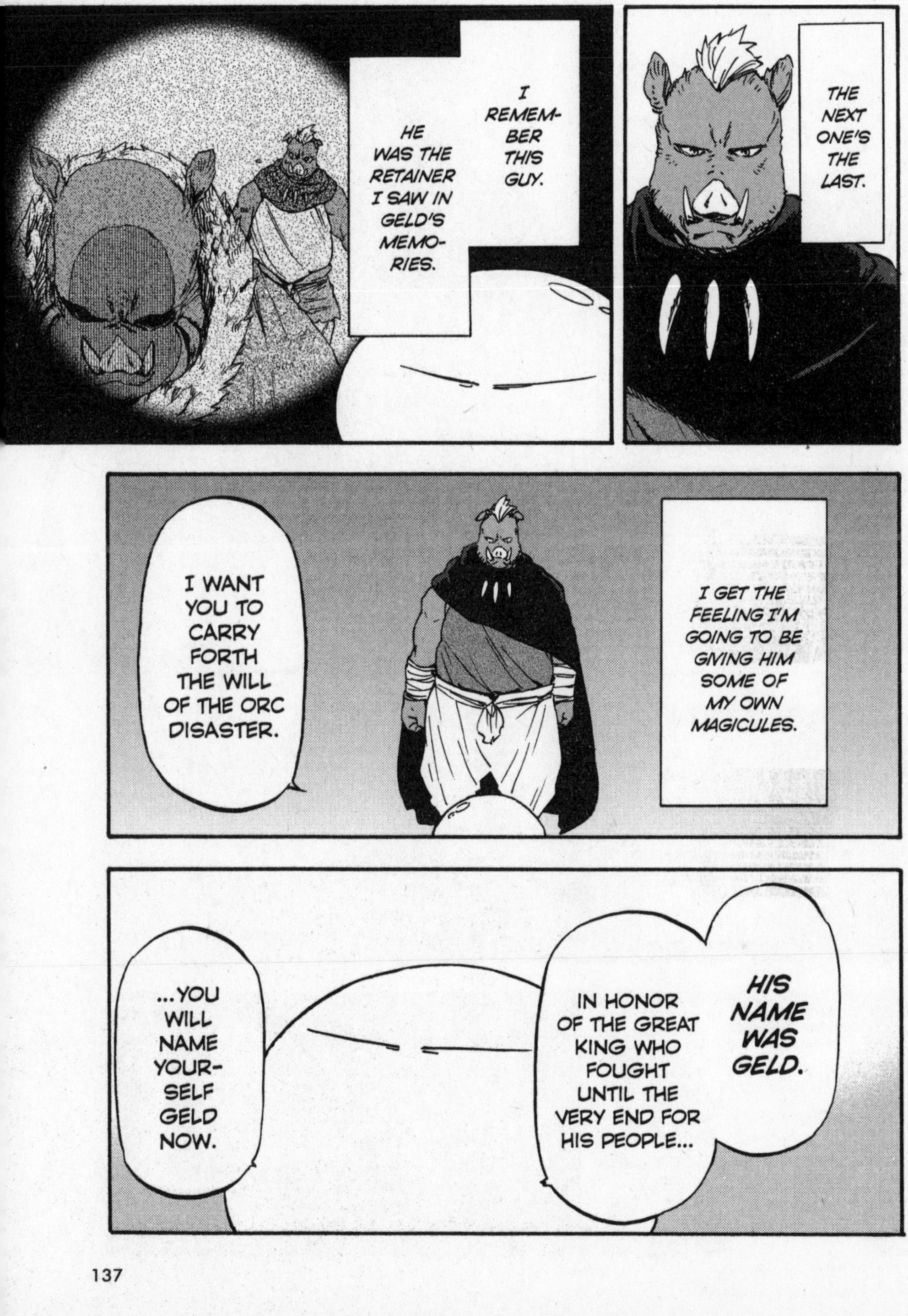
THE NEXT ONE'S THE LAST.
I REMEMBER THIS GUY.
HE WAS THE RETAINER I SAW IN GELD'S MEMORIES.
I GET THE FEELING I'M GOING TO BE GIVING HIM SOME OF MY OWN MAGICULES.
I WANT YOU TO CARRY FORTH THE WILL OF THE ORC DISASTER.
HIS NAME WAS GELD.
IN HONOR OF THE GREAT KING WHO FOUGHT UNTIL THE VERY END FOR HIS PEOPLE...
...YOU WILL NAME YOURSELF GELD NOW.

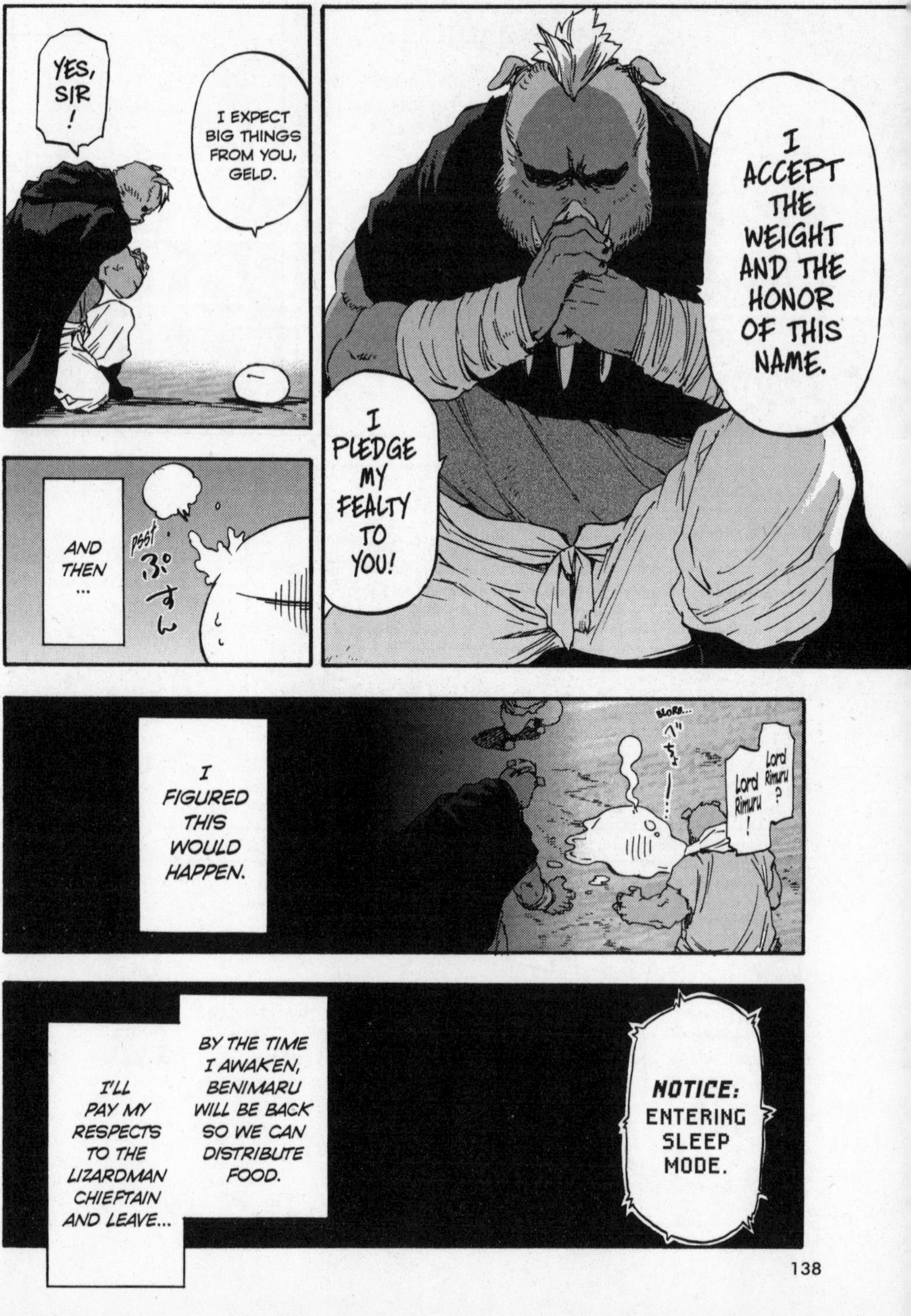
I ACCEPT THE WEIGHT AND THE HONOR OF THIS NAME.
I PLEDGE MY FEALTY TO YOU!
I EXPECT BIG THINGS FROM YOU, GELD.
YES, SIR!
pssst
ぷすん
AND THEN...
Lord Rimuru?
Lord Rimuru!
BLORB...
べちょ———...
I FIGURED THIS WOULD HAPPEN.
NOTICE: ENTERING SLEEP MODE.
BY THE TIME I AWAKEN, BENIMARU WILL BE BACK SO WE CAN DISTRIBUTE FOOD.
I'LL PAY MY RESPECTS TO THE LIZARDMAN CHIEFTAIN AND LEAVE...

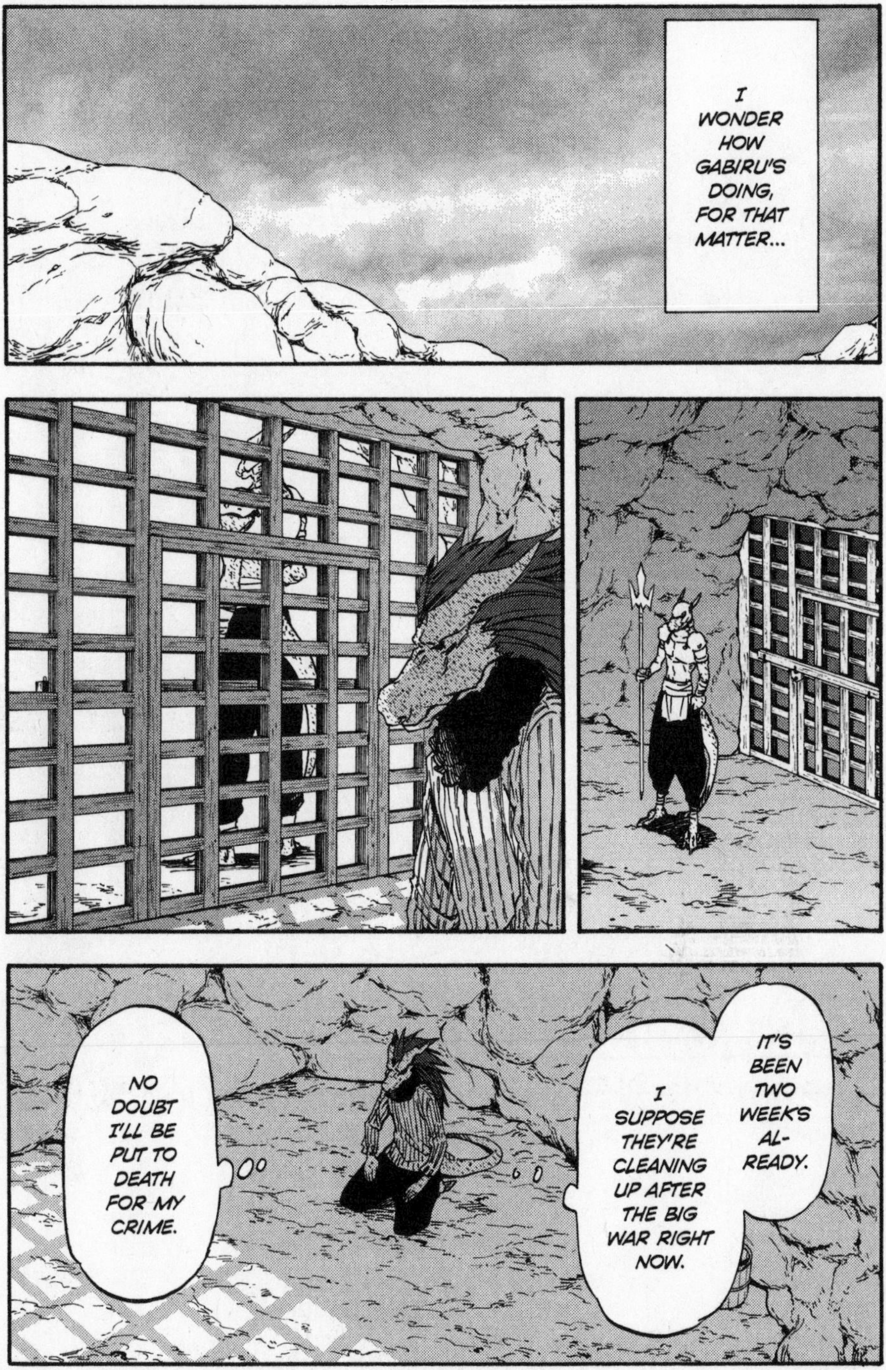
I WONDER HOW GABIRU'S DOING, FOR THAT MATTER...
IT'S BEEN TWO WEEKS AL- READY.
I SUPPOSE THEY'RE CLEANING UP AFTER THE BIG WAR RIGHT NOW.
NO DOUBT I'LL BE PUT TO DEATH FOR MY CRIME.

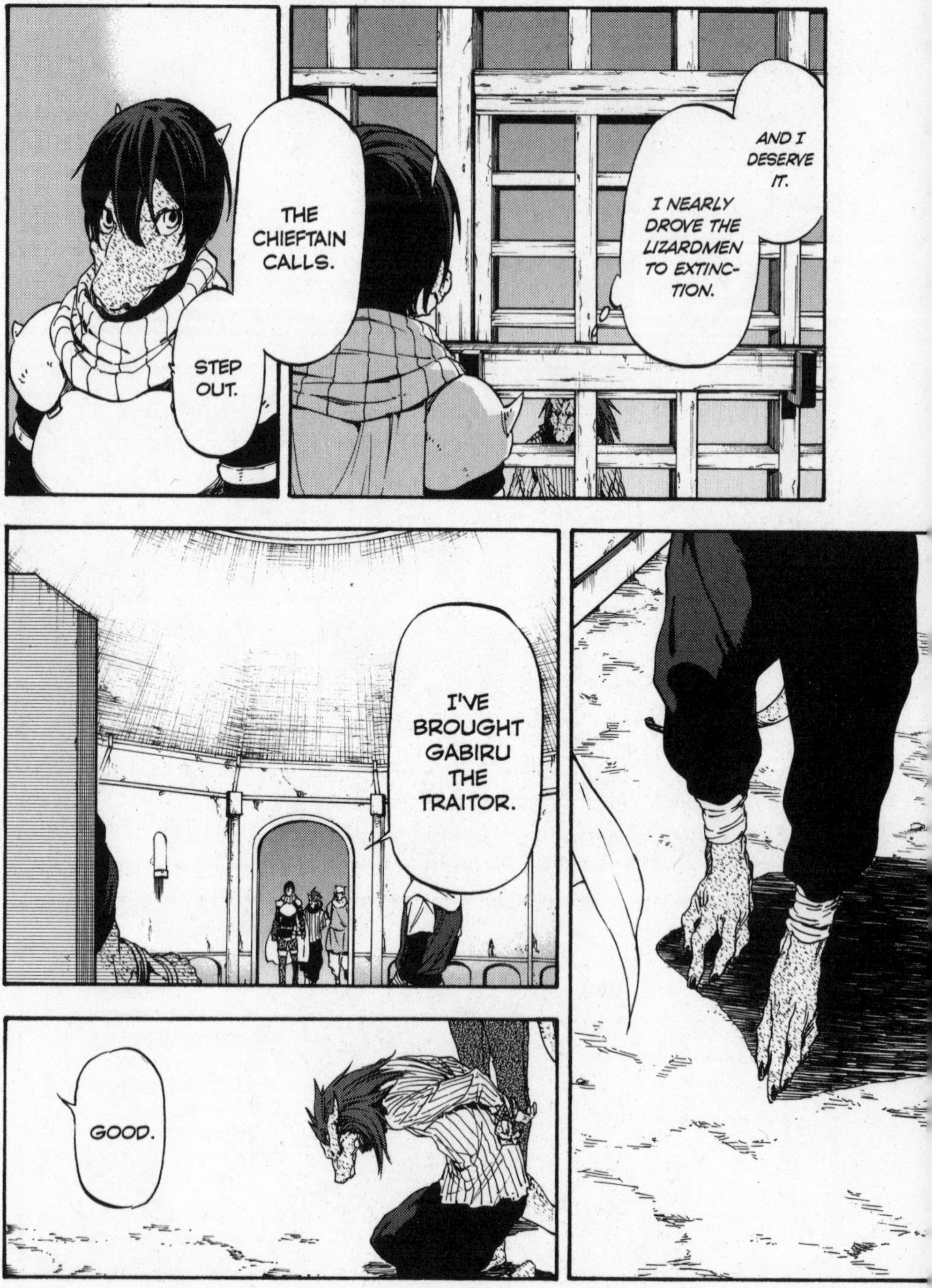
I NEARLY DROVE THE LIZARDMEN TO EXTINCTION.
AND I DESERVE IT.
THE CHIEFTAIN CALLS.
STEP OUT.
I'VE BROUGHT GABIRU THE TRAITOR.
GOOD.

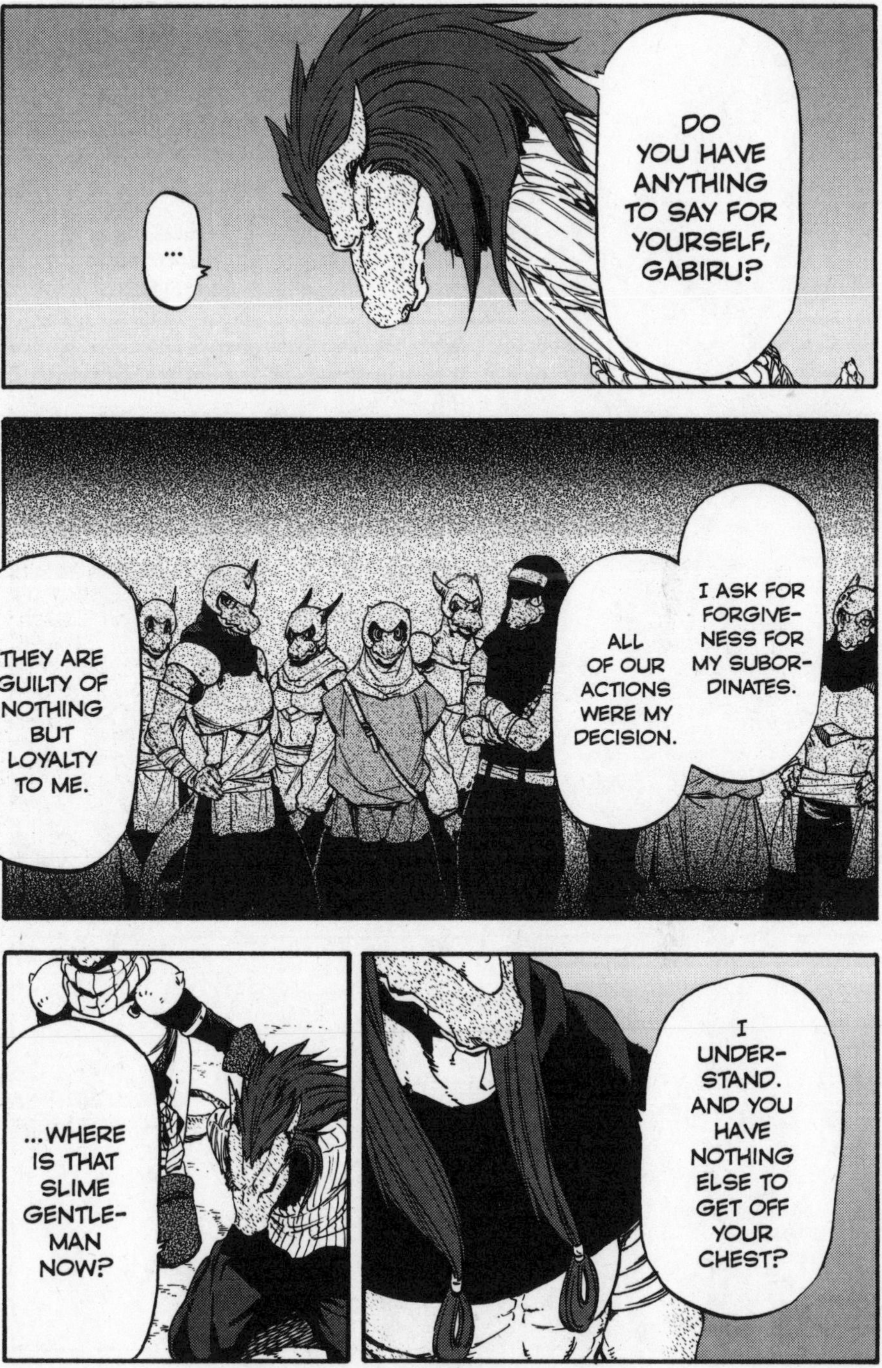
DO YOU HAVE ANYTHING TO SAY FOR YOURSELF, GABIRU?
...
I ASK FOR FORGIVENESS FOR MY SUBORDINATES.
ALL OF OUR ACTIONS WERE MY DECISION.
THEY ARE GUILTY OF NOTHING BUT LOYALTY TO ME.
I UNDERSTAND. AND YOU HAVE NOTHING ELSE TO GET OFF YOUR CHEST?
...WHERE IS THAT SLIME GENTLEMAN NOW?

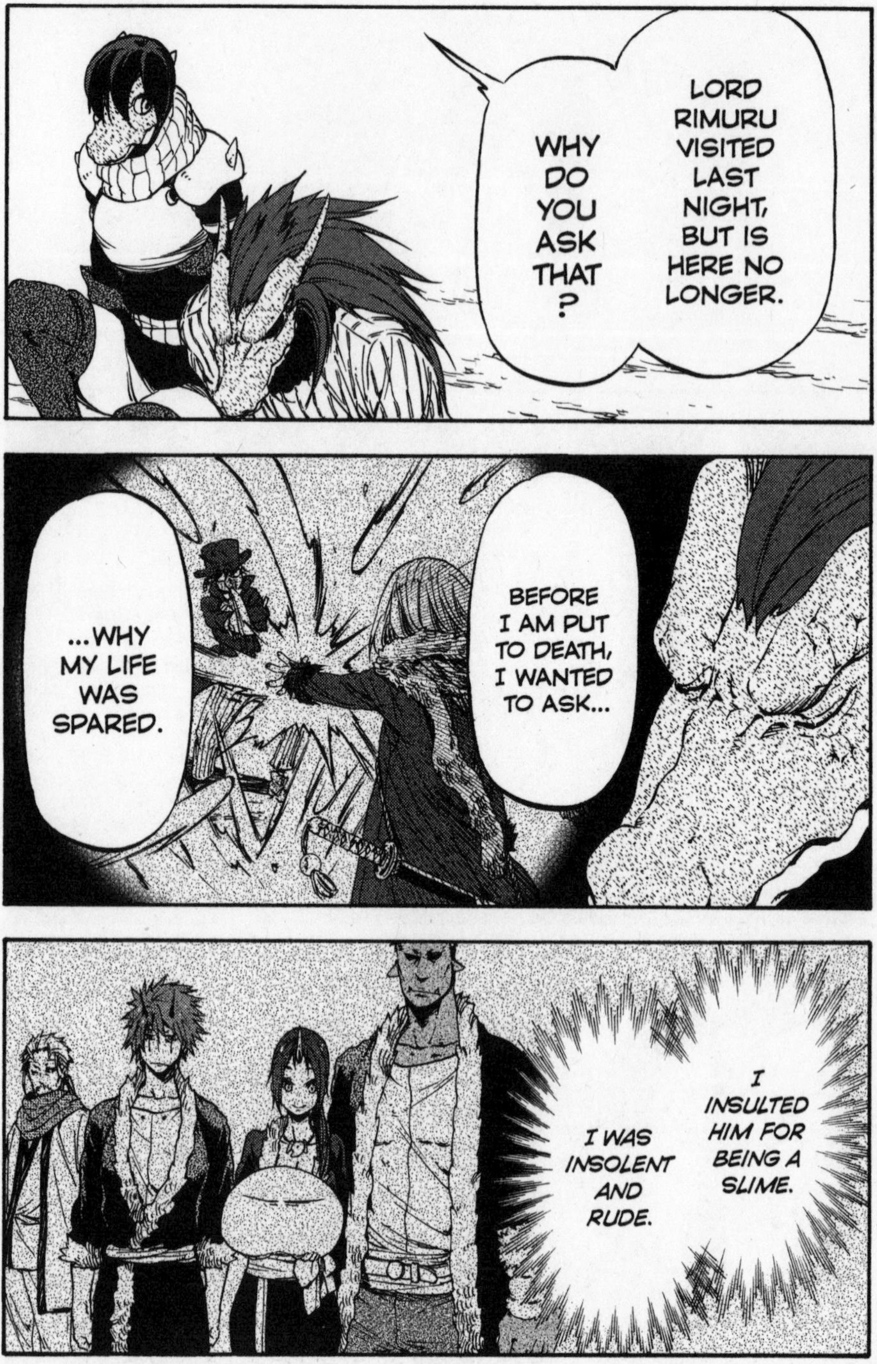
LORD RIMURU VISITED LAST NIGHT, BUT IS HERE NO LONGER.
WHY DO YOU ASK THAT?
BEFORE I AM PUT TO DEATH, I WANTED TO ASK...
...WHY MY LIFE WAS SPARED.
I INSULTED HIM FOR BEING A SLIME.
I WAS INSOLENT AND RUDE.

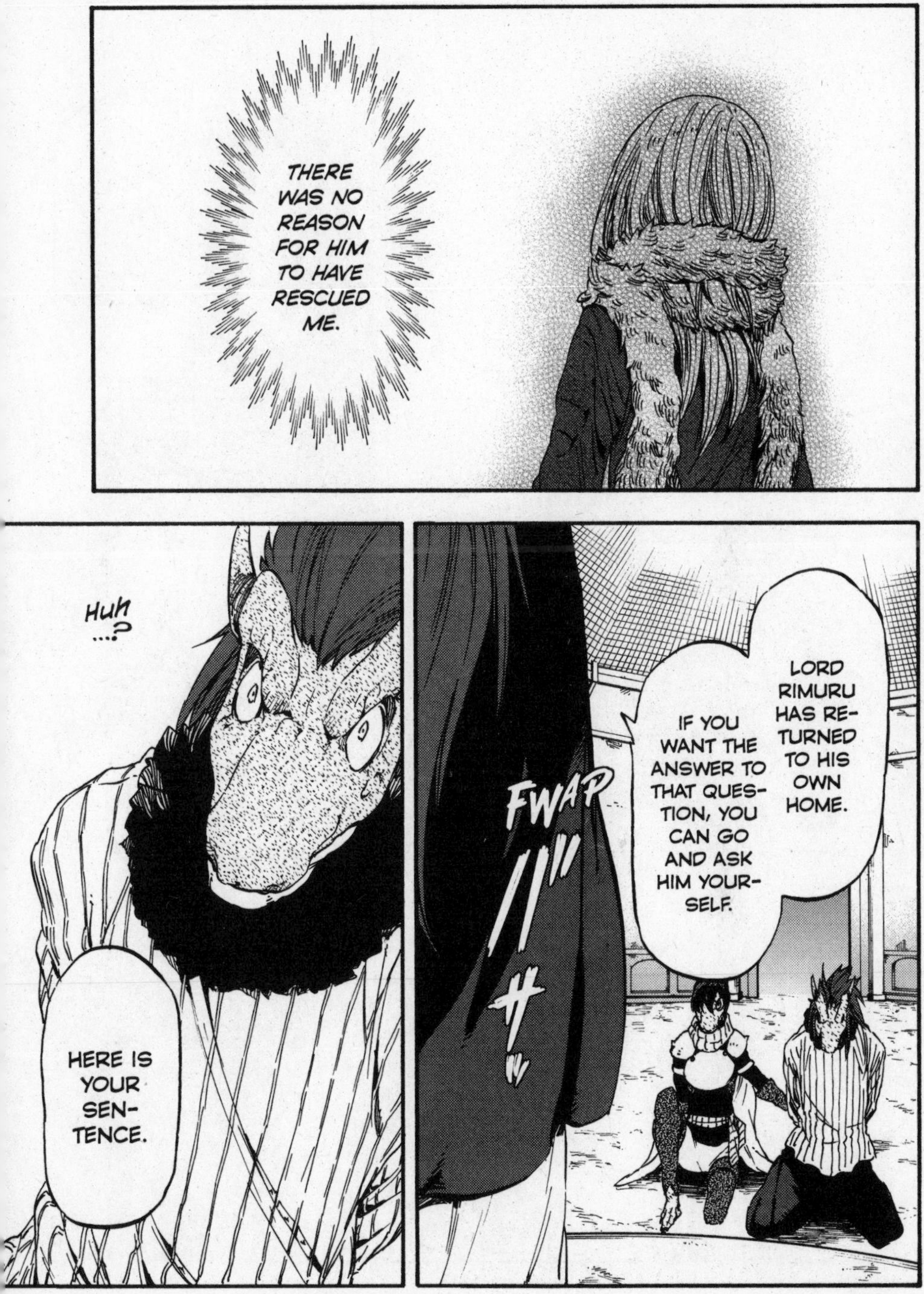
THERE WAS NO REASON FOR HIM TO HAVE RESCUED ME.
LORD RIMURU HAS RE-TURNED TO HIS OWN HOME.
IF YOU WANT THE ANSWER TO THAT QUES-TION, YOU CAN GO AND ASK HIM YOUR-SELF.
FWAP
Huh ...?
HERE IS YOUR SEN-TENCE.

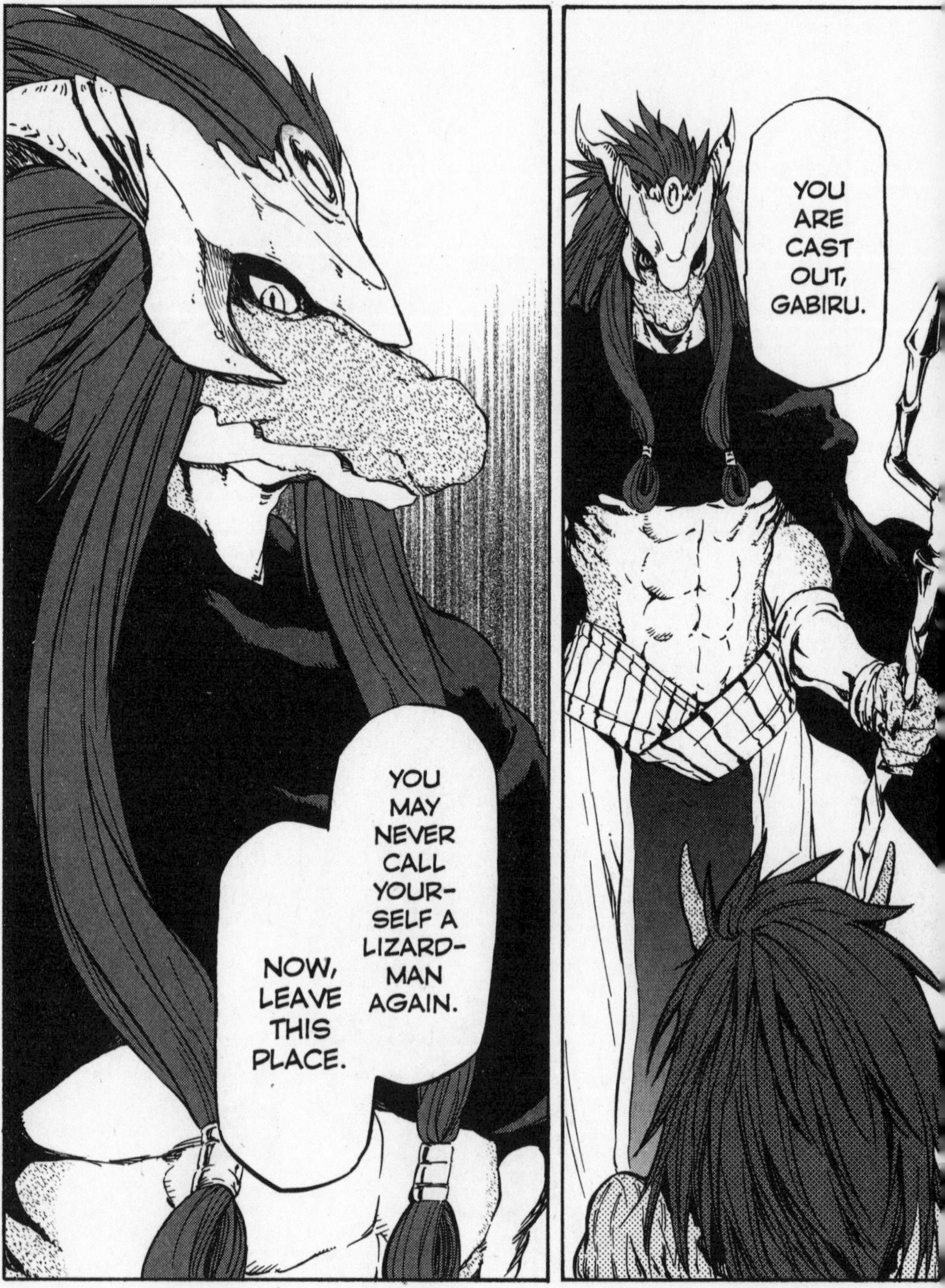
YOU ARE CAST OUT, GABIRU.
YOU MAY NEVER CALL YOUR-SELF A LIZARD-MAN AGAIN.
NOW, LEAVE THIS PLACE.

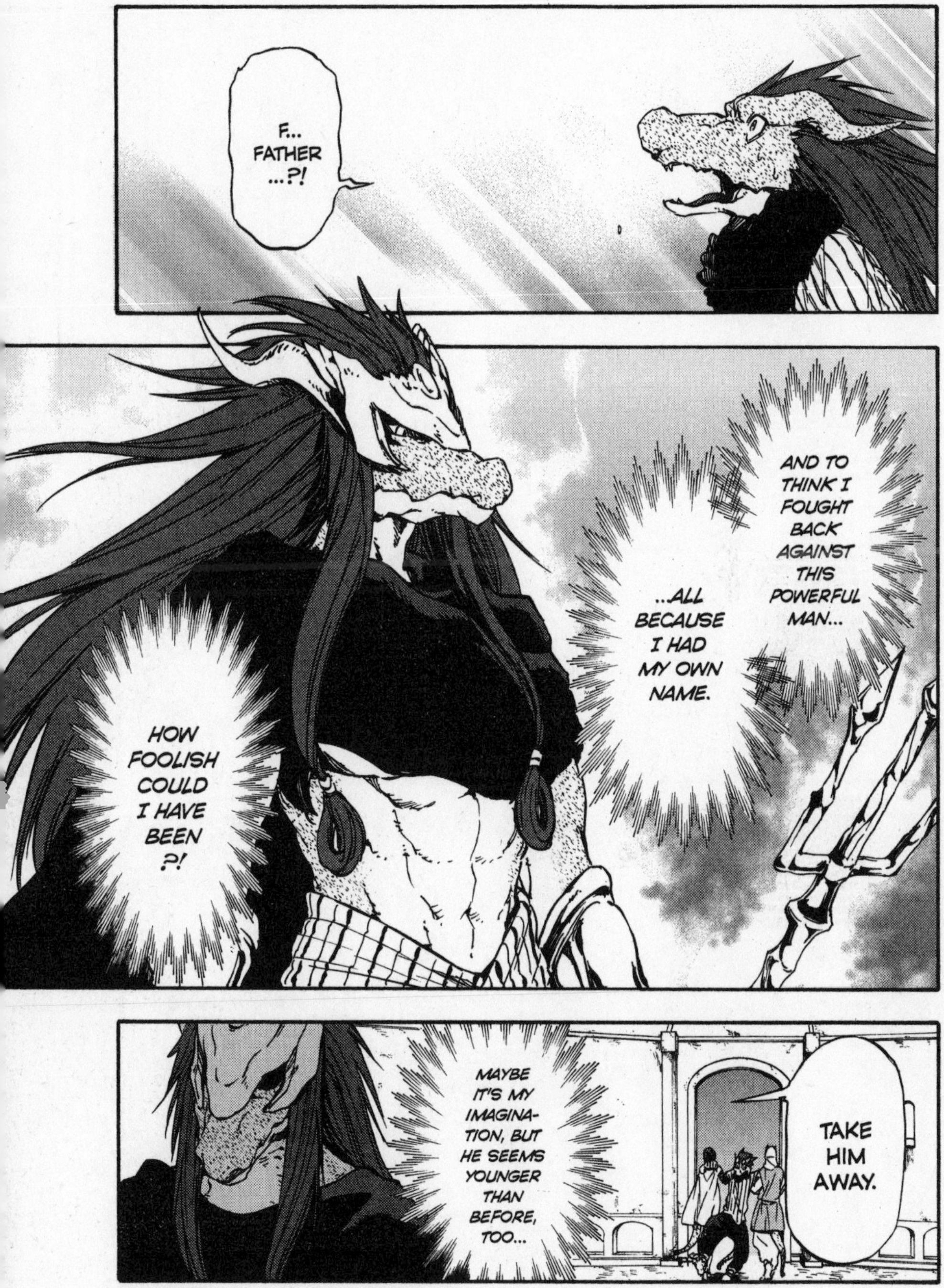
F... FATHER ...?!
AND TO THINK I FOUGHT BACK AGAINST THIS POWERFUL MAN...
...ALL BECAUSE I HAD MY OWN NAME.
HOW FOOLISH COULD I HAVE BEEN ?!
TAKE HIM AWAY.
MAYBE IT'S MY IMAGINATION, BUT HE SEEMS YOUNGER THAN BEFORE, TOO...

HEY. YOU FORGOT SOMETHING.

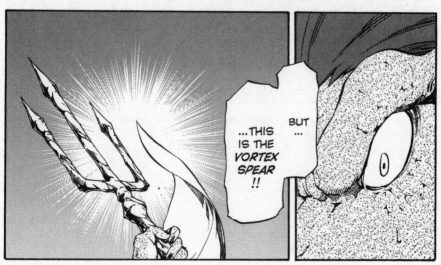

BUT...

...THIS IS THE *VORTEX SPEAR* !!

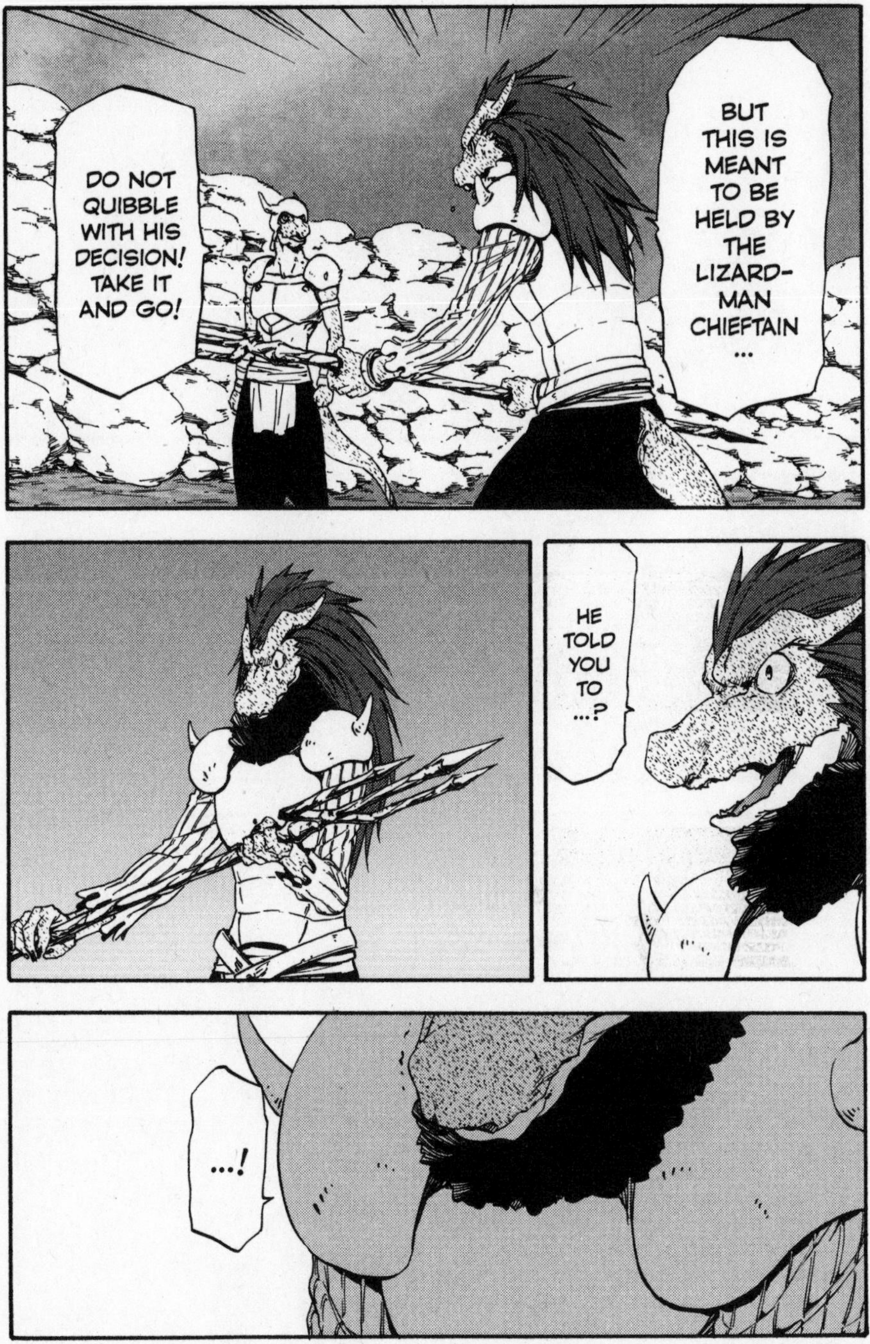
BUT THIS IS MEANT TO BE HELD BY THE LIZARD-MAN CHIEFTAIN ...
DO NOT QUIBBLE WITH HIS DECISION! TAKE IT AND GO!
HE TOLD YOU TO ...?
...!

AS LONG AS I AM ALIVE AND WELL, WITH THE NAME OF "ABIRU" GRANTED TO ME BY LORD RIMURU, THE LIZARDMEN WILL BE SECURE.

GABIRU, MY SON...

YOU OUGHT TO LIVE AS YOU SEE FIT.

BUT DO NOT TRAFFIC IN HALF-MEASURES AND IDLE WHIMS.

TAKE THIS ADVICE TO HEART.

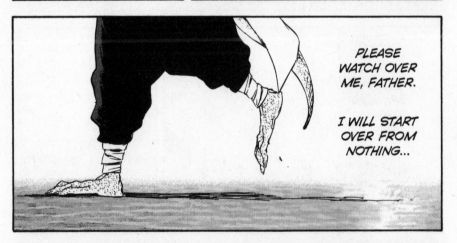

PLEASE WATCH OVER ME, FATHER.

I WILL START OVER FROM NOTHING...

...IN ORDER TO BE A MAN WORTHY OF THIS SPEAR.

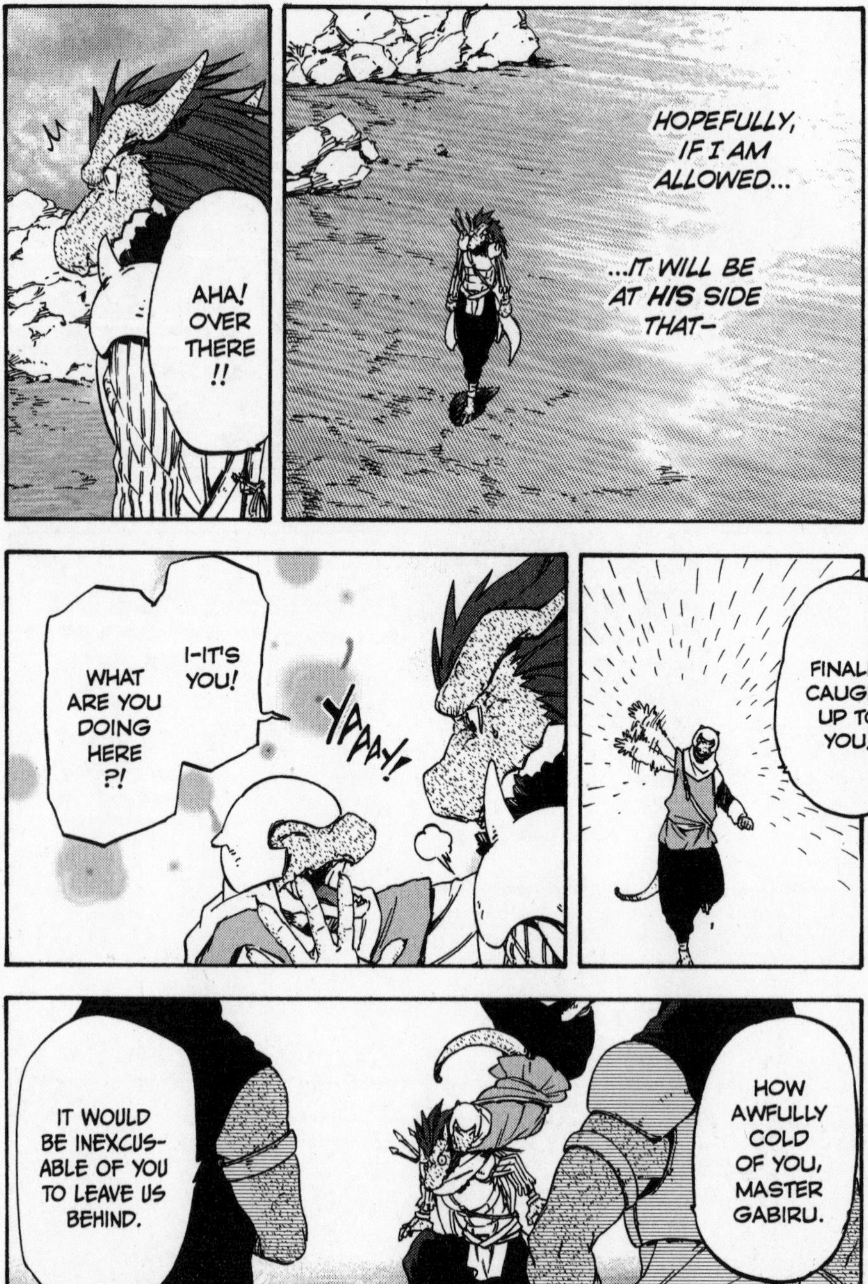
HOPEFULLY, IF I AM ALLOWED...
...IT WILL BE AT HIS SIDE THAT-
AHA! OVER THERE !!
FINALLY CAUGHT UP TO YOU!
I-IT'S YOU!
WHAT ARE YOU DOING HERE ?!
HOW AWFULLY COLD OF YOU, MASTER GABIRU.
IT WOULD BE INEXCUS-ABLE OF YOU TO LEAVE US BEHIND.

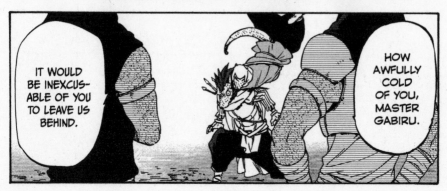

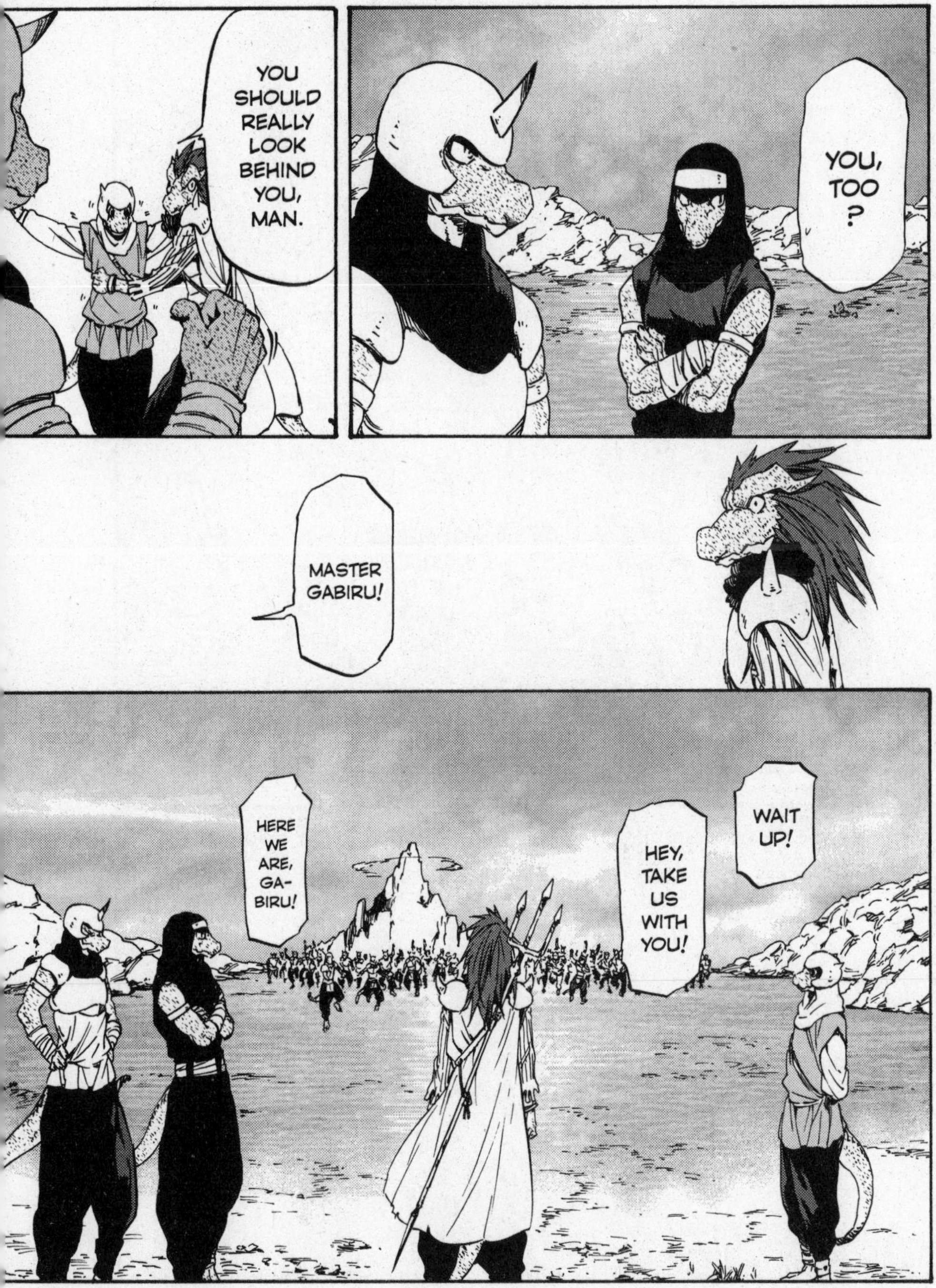
YOU, TOO?
YOU SHOULD REALLY LOOK BEHIND YOU, MAN.
MASTER GABIRU!
WAIT UP!
HEY, TAKE US WITH YOU!
HERE WE ARE, GA-BIRU!

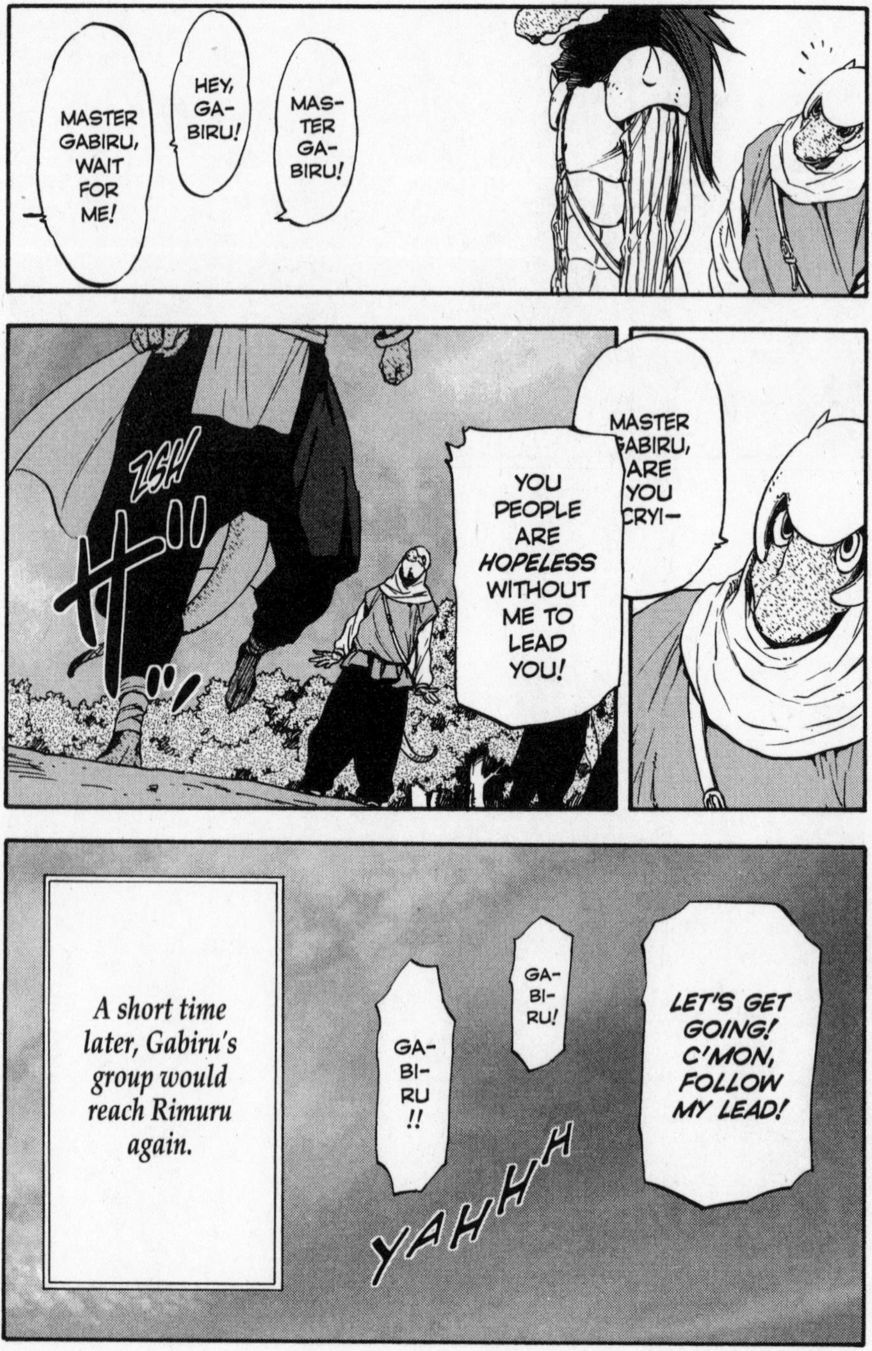
MAS-TER GA-BIRU!
HEY, GA-BIRU!
MASTER GABIRU, WAIT FOR ME!
MASTER GABIRU, ARE YOU CRYI—
YOU PEOPLE ARE *HOPELESS* WITHOUT ME TO LEAD YOU!
ZSH
LET'S GET GOING! C'MON, FOLLOW MY LEAD!
GA-BI-RU!
GA-BI-RU!!
YAHHHH
A short time later, Gabiru's group would reach Rimuru again.

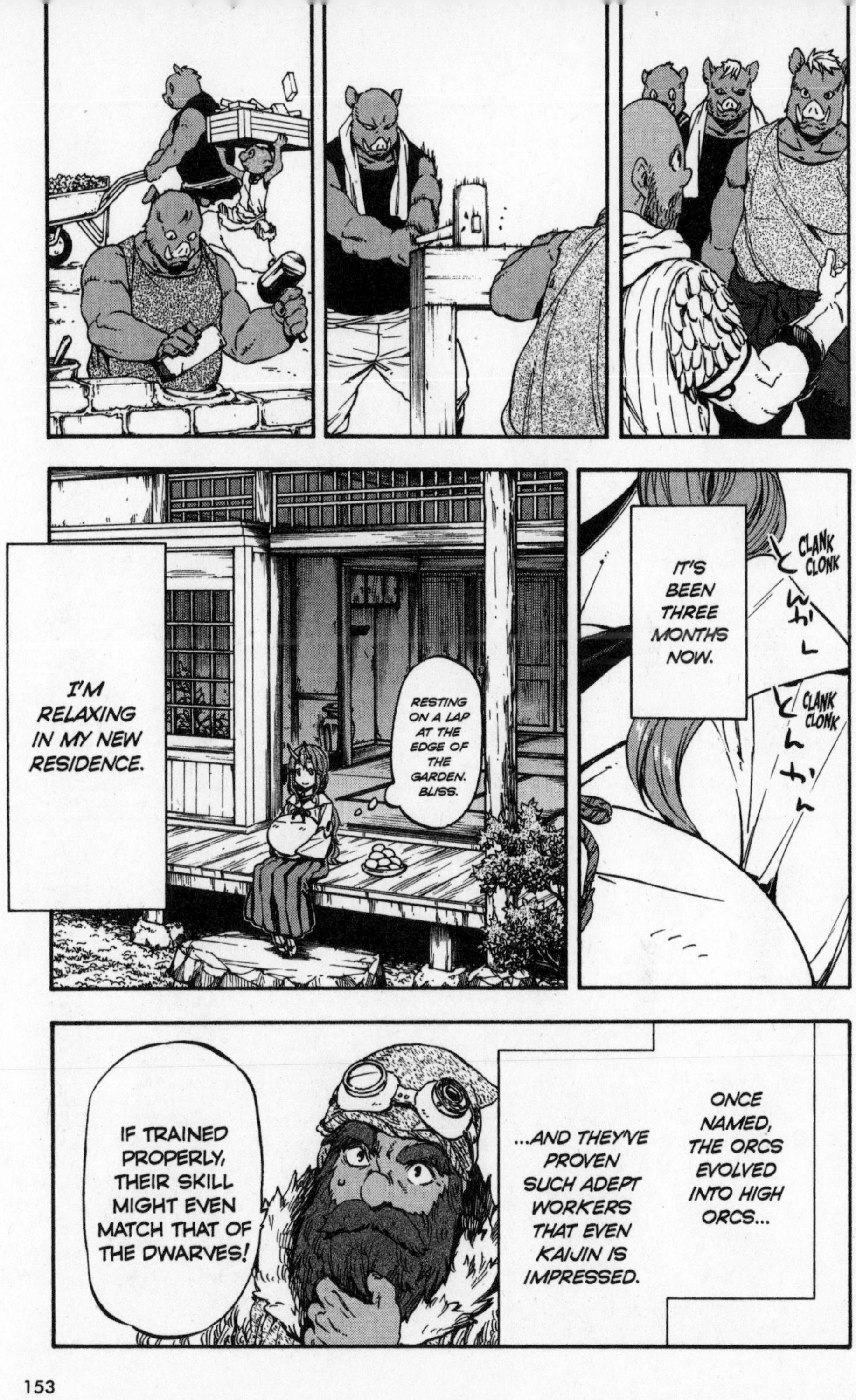
IT'S BEEN THREE MONTHS NOW.
CLANK CLONK
CLANK CLONK
I'M RELAXING IN MY NEW RESIDENCE.
RESTING ON A LAP AT THE EDGE OF THE GARDEN. BLISS.
ONCE NAMED, THE ORCS EVOLVED INTO HIGH ORCS...
...AND THEY'VE PROVEN SUCH ADEPT WORKERS THAT EVEN KAIJIN IS IMPRESSED.
IF TRAINED PROPERLY, THEIR SKILL MIGHT EVEN MATCH THAT OF THE DWARVES!

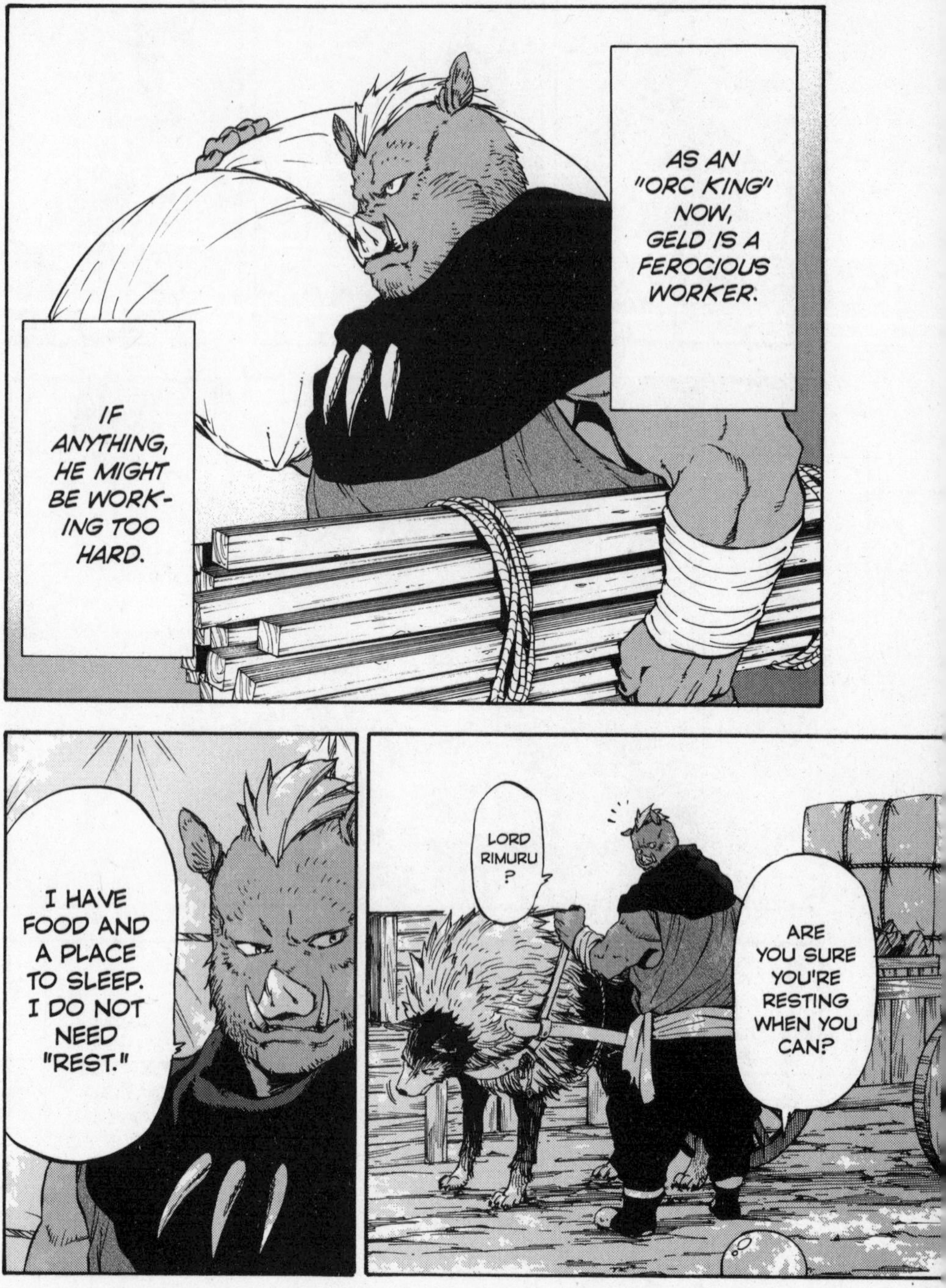
AS AN "ORC KING" NOW, GELD IS A FEROCIOUS WORKER.
IF ANYTHING, HE MIGHT BE WORK-ING TOO HARD.
ARE YOU SURE YOU'RE RESTING WHEN YOU CAN?
LORD RIMURU?
I HAVE FOOD AND A PLACE TO SLEEP. I DO NOT NEED "REST."

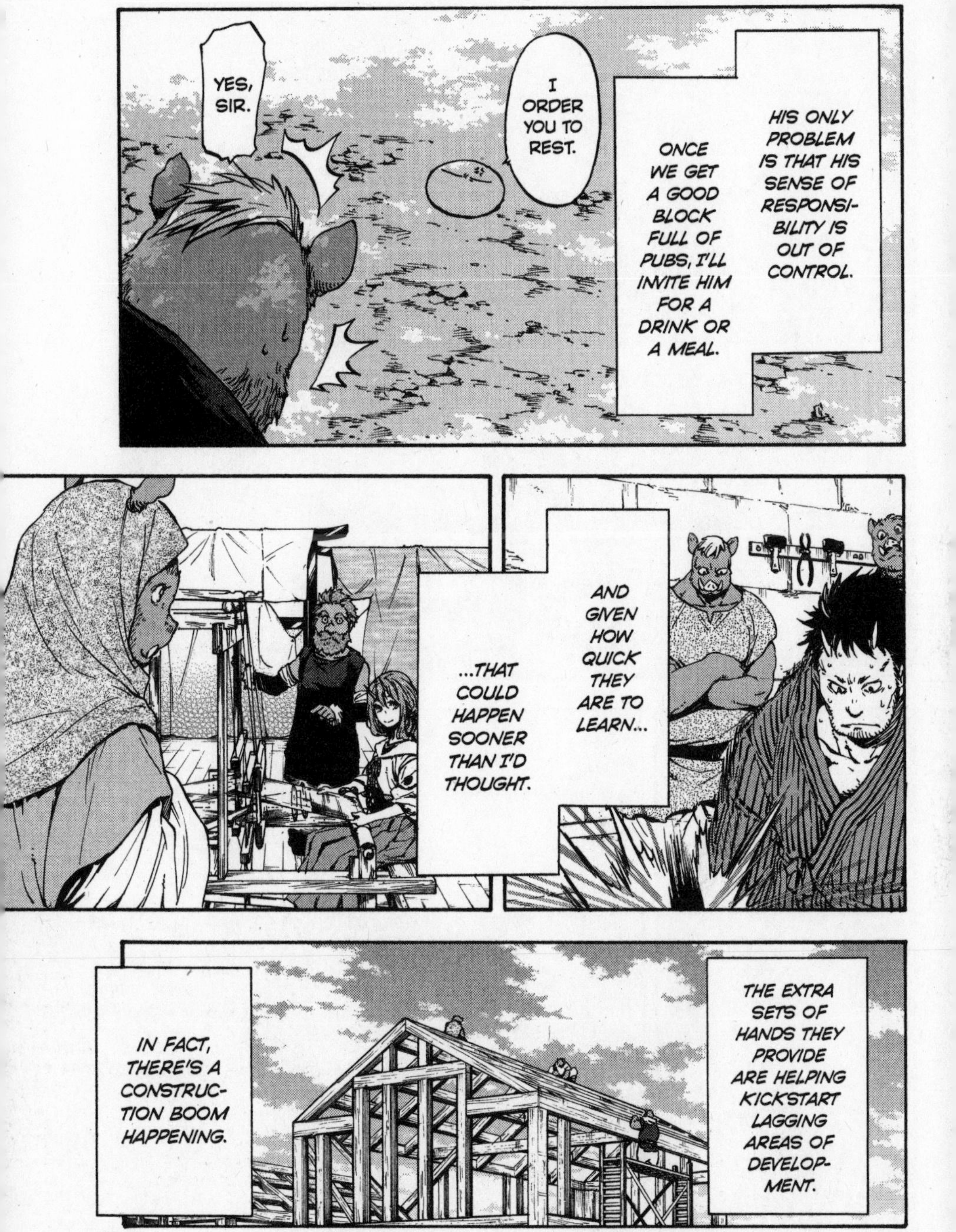
HIS ONLY PROBLEM IS THAT HIS SENSE OF RESPONSIBILITY IS OUT OF CONTROL.
ONCE WE GET A GOOD BLOCK FULL OF PUBS, I'LL INVITE HIM FOR A DRINK OR A MEAL.
I ORDER YOU TO REST.
YES, SIR.
AND GIVEN HOW QUICK THEY ARE TO LEARN...
...THAT COULD HAPPEN SOONER THAN I'D THOUGHT.
THE EXTRA SETS OF HANDS THEY PROVIDE ARE HELPING KICKSTART LAGGING AREAS OF DEVELOPMENT.
IN FACT, THERE'S A CONSTRUCTION BOOM HAPPENING.

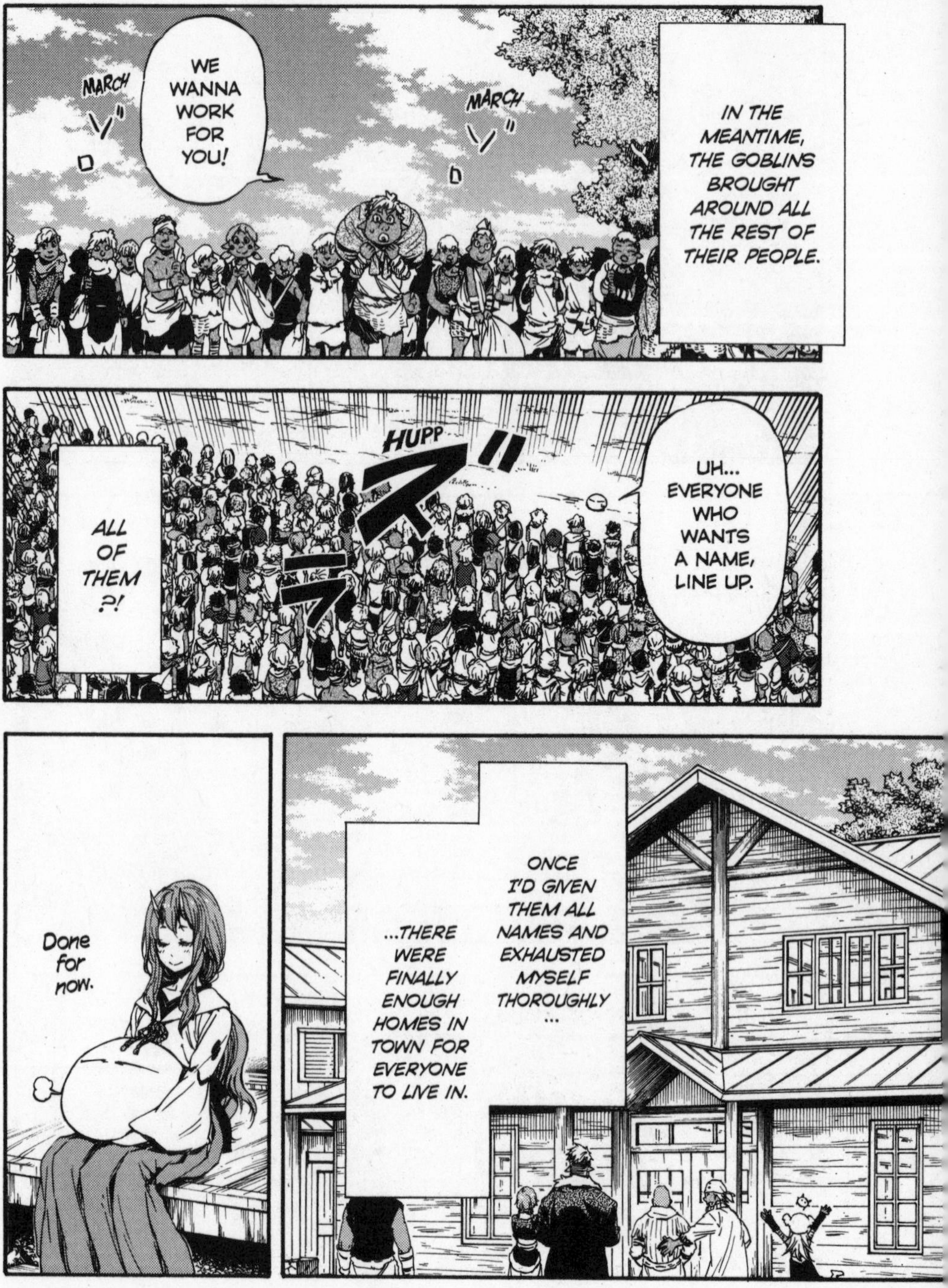
IN THE MEANTIME, THE GOBLINS BROUGHT AROUND ALL THE REST OF THEIR PEOPLE.
MARCH
WE WANNA WORK FOR YOU!
MARCH
UH... EVERYONE WHO WANTS A NAME, LINE UP.
HUPP
ALL OF THEM?!
ONCE I'D GIVEN THEM ALL NAMES AND EXHAUSTED MYSELF THOROUGHLY...
...THERE WERE FINALLY ENOUGH HOMES IN TOWN FOR EVERYONE TO LIVE IN.
Done for now.

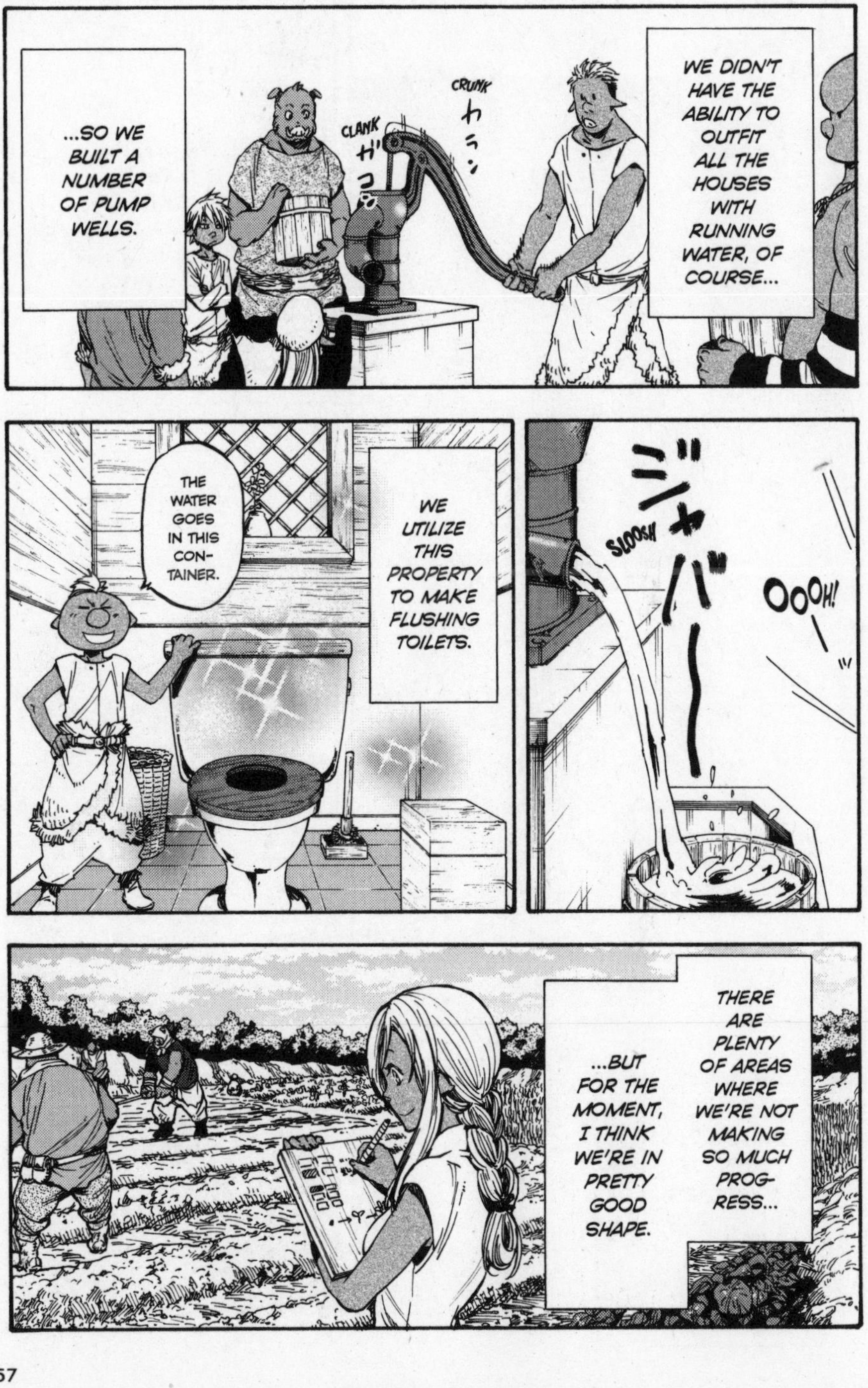
WE DIDN'T HAVE THE ABILITY TO OUTFIT ALL THE HOUSES WITH RUNNING WATER, OF COURSE...
CRUNK
CLANK
...SO WE BUILT A NUMBER OF PUMP WELLS.
SLOOSH
ジャバー
OOOH!
WE UTILIZE THIS PROPERTY TO MAKE FLUSHING TOILETS.
THE WATER GOES IN THIS CON-TAINER.
THERE ARE PLENTY OF AREAS WHERE WE'RE NOT MAKING SO MUCH PROG-RESS...
...BUT FOR THE MOMENT, I THINK WE'RE IN PRETTY GOOD SHAPE.

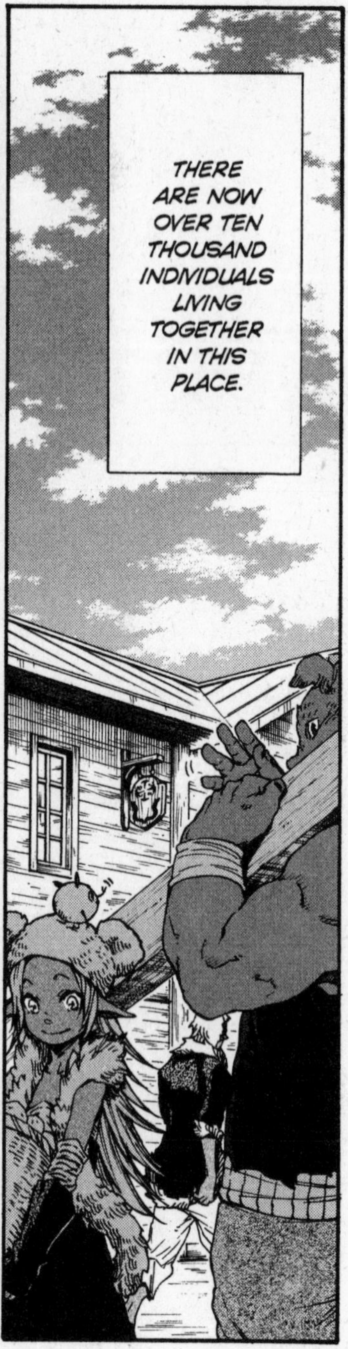
THERE ARE NOW OVER TEN THOUSAND INDIVIDUALS LIVING TOGETHER IN THIS PLACE.
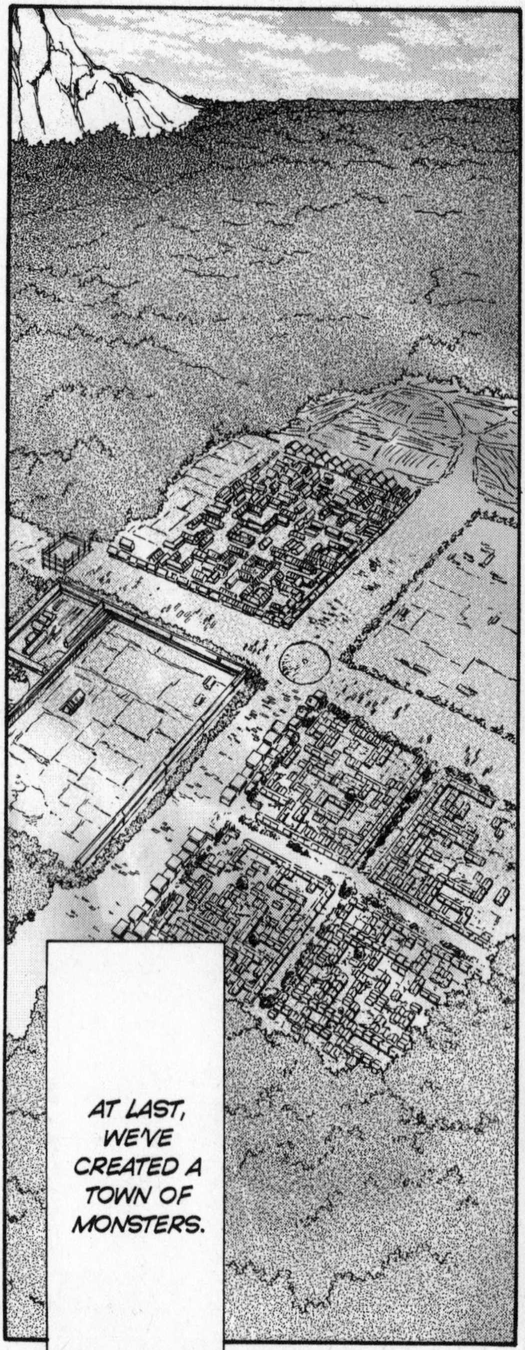
AT LAST, WE'VE CREATED A TOWN OF MONSTERS.

Reincarnate
in Volume 6?

→YES

NO

Bonus
Short Story

Veldora's Slime Observation Journal
~FULL STOMACH~

Veldora's Slime Observation Journal
~FULL STOMACH~

◆ORC DISASTER◆

Admittedly, it is starting to get difficult to find titles for these journal entries. Regardless, how is everyone else these days?

I am fine.

"Yes, Master Veldora, but you're still trapped in here..."

Silence.

Do you think I am not aware of my captivity at all times?!

But I suppose this does not matter. What is of more importance now is the fact that Rimuru's battle is entering its climactic stage.

With the help of his kijin companions, Rimuru has laid waste to the greater officers of the orcish horde. The horde itself cannot be ignored, of course, but it is largely toothless as a fighting force now.

The orc lord still remains, but his dullard nature does not inspire much fear, if you ask me.

Before long, however, the situation grows much darker. Now there is some kind of majin wearing a silly mask prancing about the scene.

"What is the meaning of this?!" he screeched at Rimuru. He is panicked and nervous, a sure sign that he is small of heart.

And yet he calls himself "the Great Gelmud." Not to mention that he is explaining all of the details of his plan. What an embarrassing display.

"This majin is no match for Lord Rimuru," said Ifrit, agreeing with me.

However, he is mistaken in one respect, so I corrected him: "Ifrit, fellows like this one are most beneficial, in fact—he will tell you all his secrets before he is destroyed. If we simply killed him right at the start, we would not learn all the facets of this plan he is blabbering about."

"Ah, I see! And that is why Lord Rimuru sits back and observes, rather than taking action?"

"Precisely!" For Rimuru is a clever fellow. Not at all like this fool, Gelmud.

As I expected, he has revealed all sorts of important information. His goal in this campaign is to create a new demon lord in this land.

In my opinion, however, the truly pitiful ones are the orc lord and the lizardman Gabiru. They have been the unwitting tools of such a small-minded, would-be demagogue.

"Ah, yes! I understand! I can see why Gabiru is so worthy of pity, despite his proud, draconic element. Could it be that being named by such a small, petty man has warped his personality?"

Hrm?!

I see. That would certainly line up with the facts. You do me proud as my chief of staff, Ifrit.

"I suppose there is some merit to what you say. In fact, it is exactly what I was thinking," I said happily. Clearly there can be no other reason. If Ifrit had not put that thought together, someone else would have eventually. But enough about that.

"...Gabiru. His timing is excellent."

Surprisingly enough, Gelmud cast an attack spell, Death-march Dance, on Gabiru, who might as well be like a son to him. It is a piddling spell, just a few magical projectiles controlled with aura, but even Gelmud's energy is far beyond Gabiru's. A direct hit would surely be fatal.

"It seems he wants to feed Gabiru to the orc lord so that the lord's powers can grow further," Ifrit surmised. "He is wreaking havoc in your territory, Master Veldora. It is unforgivable."

He is correct, of course, but something in that statement caught my attention.

"But Ifrit, were you not wreaking havoc in my forest as well?"

"...Erm, er, was I? I don't seem to recall..."

Is it me, or has this elemental been getting much saucier in recent days? He was perfectly well-behaved at first. I cannot imagine whose behavior has been rubbing off on him.

"You and I are the only ones here, Master Veldora. Sometimes we hear Lord Rimuru's voice, but that is a one-way communication only, through one of his skills."

"That is true. I can read Rimuru's thoughts, but it seems that it requires a considerable amount of effort for Rimuru to make his will known to me. It is not easy for us to communicate, alas."

Of course, I am under no obligation whatsoever to reveal to Ifrit my secret correspondence with Rimuru about playing shogi.

"Yes, which would mean that I am being influenced by..."

"Hrm?! Ah, g-good point. You are under no one's influence. It is my mistake. Indeed, it was all a mistake. *Kwaaaa ha ha ha!*" I laughed, to hide my embarrassment.

Indeed, I was very nearly in danger of promoting the idea that my influence causes others to be rude. That would be impossible.

Best to change the topic. Time to see what is happening outside. This Gelmud will not last long, I suspect.

Rimuru is furious that Gelmud sacrificed Gabiru for his own

ends. Some demon lord or another ordered Gelmud to go around naming monsters in the Jura Forest, we've learned. Now there is no longer any excuse for allowing Gelmud to leave alive.

Hostages are meaningless to a demon lord, and this confession alone has little evidentiary value. He can simply claim that he has no idea what this is about, thus denying the statement is evidence of anything.

It is certainly what I would do, were I to be accused of anything.

Ages ago, when I destroyed the city of the vampiress, I insisted that I had nothing to do with it. And nobody believed me, so it was quite the disaster, really.

"…So…you got what was coming to you?"

"Did I?"

"Yes. It's a surprise to me that you thought anyone would believe you."

Hrm. This is news to me. But not everything goes one's way all the time, and this was long in the past.

"I don't think that saying it happened a long time ago means you weren't in the wrong…"

Ifrit is certainly clinging to this topic, isn't he? He seems upset about it, but if I worry about that, I've lost the argument. More important is the matter of Gelmud.

Rimuru wasn't the only one in a righteous fury. The same could be said of Benimaru, Shion, and Hakuro! The kijin companions bore open rage at Gelmud. It must be because of the sacking of their village.

For his part, Gelmud is a higher majin who performed many namings. If he had not lost so much of his magical energy through that process, he might have found a better outcome for himself. However, the difference between one who manipulates others and those who put themselves on the line for vengeance is vast.

"Th-this can't be happening! H-how can I be trapped like this?!" Gelmud squealed.

He tried to escape, but the entrance of the swift, blue-haired Soei put a stop to that idea. The contest was all but over at this point.

"We've won. *Kwa ha ha ha!*"

Rimuru left Gelmud to the kijin and turned his attention to the orc lord instead. The leader of the orcs was in the thrall of his own power. It was all he had in order to protect his population of two hundred thousand. No wonder it was causing his own consciousness to grow thin.

And yet, it seemed clear that he stands no chance against Rimuru. But what happened next stunned even me.

"H-help me, orc lord! I mean…Geld!!" screeched Gelmud, who abandoned all of his pride as a higher majin and scrambled for his life. But the orc lord's distorted mind responded to his summons in a distorted way. It is hard to believe, but I suppose this is how the namer and the named are bound.

The orc lord attempted to grant Gelmud's wish. With one fell swoop of his meat cleaver, he freed Gelmud's head from his shoulders.

To be honest, I expected this to happen. Naming a monster is, by its nature, a dangerous act. Placing a being stronger than oneself beneath you upsets the order of the strong eating the weak. It was inevitable that this would happen.

Confirmed: the individual Geld is evolving into a Demon Lord seed.

Hmm. That was the "Words of the World." And demon lord seed, you say? That means he is growing into that dreaded being.

Gelmud's ambition was to bring about a new demon lord

in this land. And the surest way to grant this wish was for Gelmud himself to be devoured in order to bring about that evolution.

It was the correct choice. And the orc lord's decisiveness in carrying out that choice is worthy of merit.

…Complete. The individual Geld has evolved into the demon lord "Orc Disaster."

Orc Disaster, eh?

So the orc lord has evolved into the rank of demon lord. One never knows what might happen on the battlefield.
He does not appear to be the type of foe that requires great sacrifice to overcome, but who can say?

Frustrated that I could not jump out to take part in the fight, I was forced to stay put and watch the outcome with Ifrit.

◆THE SUBMISSIVE DEMON LORD◆

The Orc Disaster's magical energy is far beyond anything he had before evolving. Now he devours the bodies littering the battlefield to satisfy his raging hunger.

But more importantly, I have made an incredible discovery! Much as a pawn may be promoted in a game of shogi, I feared that the orc lord was about to undergo a similar change. I laughed the feeling off, thinking my powerful imagination was getting away from me, but in retrospect, I might as well have prophesied the evolution of the orc lord in that moment.

"They call that a 'flag,' apparently."

"What?"

"According to Lord Rimuru's wisdom, making knowing statements in the midst of battle is forbidden. Just like how

you said, 'We've won, *kwa ha ha ha!*' earlier, Master Veldora.
That's called a flag, and it's one of the reasons things turned
against us in dramatic fashion."

Could this be? That would mean that I am essentially respon-
sible for this situation.

Well done, me.

No one can accomplish the great and mighty deeds that I
bring about. The extent of my incredible capabilities almost
frightens me! Even locked behind this damnable seal, my will
is capable of affecting the entire world around me.

"Well, if you're happy with that, I'm not going to complain,
Master Veldora," Ifrit said. He seemed a bit peeved, but that
is surely just my imagination.

As for the battle, by evolving into the Orc Disaster, the orc
lord has regained his senses. He knows enough to introduce
himself as Geld, and now makes full use of the power that he
was barely aware of before.

He will be a fearsome enemy now.

While a demon lord *seed* is merely a step on the way to being
a fully-fledged demon lord, it is still a dreadful being far
above the average monster or majin. And the first to recognize this change were the battle-hardened kijin.

Shion was the first to strike. Those bountiful breasts of hers
are always resting upon Rimuru like a cushion. It drives me
mad with jealou—erm, pardon me.

Shion struck at Geld with her tremendous power. Normally,
this would be the end of it, but the enemy is now a Disaster-
class foe. It will not be as easy as it was before.

Geld took the brunt of her blow without flinching, and
emerged superior. I am not surprised. In fact, I relish a good
fight.

"You do know that it's not about whether the fight is 'good' or 'bad,' but the fact that if Lord Rimuru dies, you're going to die too…right?"

"Perhaps. But in that case, a new storm dragon will be born elsewhere."

"I see. Well, that's a relief—"

"But while the new dragon shall inherit my memory, it shall not receive my will and personality. My soul will vanish here, while a new soul will inhabit the reborn storm dragon. *Kwaa ha ha ha!*"

"Wait, why are you laughing about that?!" asked the Ifrit.

My point is that he ought to worry more about himself than about me. "It is not such a surprise. I swore an oath to believe in Rimuru. So I can leave all of this to him now. If he fails and proves himself unfit for the task, then that was simply my fate."

"…?! Er, right. That is correct, I suppose. In a sense, it is only because of your whims that I have been granted extra life, Master Veldora. I do wish that I could see Lord Leon once again, but I suppose that will never happen now. It's important to recognize reality for what it is, and accept it."

…He makes such grandiose exaggerations, this fellow.

Still. Though this is not exactly my view, he is correct in the broader sense. There is little need to set him straight. In my case, I merely wish to enjoy my life, but this is not the situation to deliver a speech to that effect.

It would seem that Shion's attack was meant as a distraction to unbalance Geld and allow Hakuro the chance to strike. The elderly fellow's skill with the blade is of the highest caliber. Something in it reminds me of the legendary hero that fought me. It would be weak against the rare creature with Physical Resistance, but his technique alone places him as the strongest of the kijin, in my opinion.

Hakuro struck off Geld's head. *Brilliant!* I thought, but in no time at all, Geld picked up his severed head and stuck it back on.

"I'm telling you, those assumptions are flags..."

Oh! Whoopsy, daisy.

Perhaps my idle thoughts have strengthened Geld yet again. Still, this is not yet the time to panic.

The strongest attack available to the kijin comes from their leader, Benimaru. And Soei did the hard work of immobilizing Geld so that the full brunt of Benimaru's strength can strike true.

Given enough time, Geld should be able to escape Soei's "Sticky Steel Thread," but Benimaru has ample opportunity to unleash his best.

The wide-area conflagration attack: "Hell Flare."

Because he had already used it multiple times, the scale of it was smaller than usual. Still, it was more than powerful enough to burn a single target to a crisp.

"See that, Ifrit?! Not even Geld's incredible regenerative ability can withstand such superheated flames! That hellfire even contains elements of my Black Flame ability, so surely he must be dead now!"

"I told you, you shouldn't say things like—"

Oh! Now Ranga has joined the fray! On Benimaru's orders, he released a "Death Storm." Every last ounce of his magicule energy went into it, with a pinpoint attack against Geld.

"It's over now."

"Well, let's hope so..."

This Ifrit truly cannot keep himself from worrying. There is no way that a newborn demon lord seed could withstand such a furious consecutive assault!

"There, you see, Master Veldora? He's still alive."

"What...?!"

I could not believe my ears and eyes. By expelling all of his energy at once, Geld neutralized the damage, then devoured his own blood and flesh to power his healing ability. Only this mad tactic could allow him to withstand that combination attack.

It would seem that I have underestimated the Orc Disaster and his unique skill, "Starved."

Geld suffered great damage, but eating helps him recover from it. He ate his own followers to heal his wounds. If there is anyone who can hope to defeat Geld at full health...

"Lord Rimuru is stepping forth."

...then it must be you.

Go, Rimuru!

He must be confident, because he spurned Benimaru's help and insisted on facing Geld alone. What will happen now?

With one swipe of the sword, Rimuru severed Geld's right arm. This time, it showed no signs of re-growing. With perfect "Black Flame" control, he covered the wound to prevent Geld's regenerative ability from kicking in. This seems like a promising strategy.

In any case, everything I have is riding upon you.

Go forth, Rimuru, and show us your true power!

Rimuru sprang into action, nimbler than ever before. Surely
this is due to my emotional support.

His plan must be to slice Geld into fine pieces, and use "Black
Flame" to prevent the Orc Disaster's regeneration. But when
did Rimuru get so adept at utilizing his skills? Even the kijin
seem amazed.

Sensing that a close positioning was to his disadvantage,
Geld switched to employing long-range attacks. This adap-
tive use of strategy shows him to be far smarter now than in
his previous state.

"Deathmarch Dance!!"

Geld is using the same attack as that of the diminutive majin,
Gelmud. But in this case, each little magical projectile has the
power of the unique skill "Starved" attached. In other words,
this "Chaos Eater" intends to devour its targets. Needless to
say, the force of the attack is terrible.

"This Orc Disaster Geld is beyond what I imagined…"

"Indeed. He's got even more magical energy than you, Ifrit."

"He does. Nearly twice as much, I imagine."

"Your estimate is accurate. And for your information, I have
over a hundred times your energy!"

"I see. But that isn't really very interesting, so…"

What? Ifrit, did you know that you are allowed to express
your shock and admiration at this fact? It makes me sad to be
dismissed so easily.

"More important, they've caught Lord Rimuru, Master!"

"Whaaaat?!"

I'd been preparing a very good boast, but the situation outside demands attention. Geld's severed arm had regrown, and he grabbed Rimuru with it.

That means Rimuru can no longer take advantage of his superior fleetness. Could this be a moment of life or death?!

"It's a shame that your life will end in my belly. Whatever 'Starved' corrodes becomes our food. You will melt to your death."

"...Negative."

So it's...*not* a moment of life or death?!

If anything, Rimuru's attitude suggests that this was all according to some kind of plan.

"Flare Circle."

Oooh!! Yes, now I see. Rimuru let it appear as though Geld had caught him, but in fact, it was he who was absorbing Geld. By enacting a Flare Circle, he simply ensured that there will be no escape.

"That's one of my better attacks, only more powerful than before," muttered Ifrit, a bit sadly. I can understand that—it hurts a little to see one's own proud technique utilized by others to greater effect.

"That's no surprise. Rimuru simply has more energy than you. But do you really think this is the end?"

"The instantaneous power of Hell Flare is tremendous, but it only lasts a few seconds at best. But Flare Circle will continue until the target is incinerated. No matter how incredible the Orc Disaster's regeneration is, there is little he can do now," Ifrit opined.

But I think differently. What I've learned from this fight is that a battle of historical proportions is completely unpredictable. One cannot know what will happen. I think Rimuru is of the same mind; his expression is tense, with no hint of ease.

Confirmed: Orc Disaster Geld has gained Flame Attack Resistance.

I knew it. I knew this would happen!

"Master Veldora?"

"Do not panic, Ifrit. This is another of your 'flags,' yes? But I presume that Rimuru foresaw this coming as well."

"So you trust Lord Rimuru to handle this?"

"Of course." I trust him far more than any story flag.

"It seems your flames do not affect me," boasted Geld.

"Is that so? I dunno, you might've been happier just burning into ash," said Rimuru, grinning confidently. Of course he has some plan in mind.

Oh! Look at that!!

Rimuru melted and clung to Geld all over. At that point, strength alone cannot pull him loose. This was the meaning behind Rimuru's actions!

"Quite the master stroke. At this point, there is no way for a power-type monster to counteract him."

"I agree," said Ifrit. "With my spiritual body, this would not be a problem, but for those monsters stuck in a material body, this would be impossible to overcome."

Indeed. Power is meaningless in this context. Geld has the ability to eat his foes, but in this situation, it is merely a contest of strength. Each one has regenerative ability, and devouring others is a central part of their power. Whoever can eat the other more quickly will win.

While they might seem evenly matched at a glance, Rimuru is sure to triumph at this point. For one thing, he has such a vast stomach that he was able to swallow me in a single gulp. "Wouldn't that also be a flag?"

"Ifrit, flags are meant to be broken. Victory only comes to those who seize it!"

He had to grimace and agree with me.

I needn't elaborate upon the outcome.

"I've won. Rest in peace," Rimuru announced, a momentous statement in the midst of the now silent battlefield.

◆THE JURA FOREST ALLIANCE◆

After Rimuru devoured Geld, I attempted to reach out to him.

However, Geld's consciousness rejected my call. He claimed that he was satisfied—that he was full.

Geld went to sleep within Rimuru's body, and his soul vanished. In my opinion, it was a brilliant end.

Through Rimuru's heroics, the Great Forest of Jura's crisis was averted. And, as though she had planned it all, Treyni the dryad appeared just then. But of course, she would have been watching it all unfold.

Treyni wanted Rimuru to fight the orc lord to find some weakness in the brute, but then he evolved into the Orc Disaster, only for Rimuru to topple him in that greater form. Surely she could not have calculated that all of this would happen.

But her idea to scoop up the pieces is a credit to her role as manager of the Great Forest of Jura. I was so unconcerned with things of this nature that I'm certain I caused her grief. So I cannot speak with great conviction here, nor do I intend to.

But then Treyni forced the duty of chancellor of the talks

upon Rimuru. She must be plotting something.

Rimuru seems uncomfortable with the idea, and of holding a council for talks. But I am sure he is thinking that if nothing is done here and now, worse consequences will occur later. Such a softhearted goody-two-shoes, he is.

And thus began the council for peace talks.

"First of all, I want to be absolutely clear: I have no intention of judging the orcs for their crimes," said Rimuru. Just as I expected, he is entirely too soft! He must have been thinking of this statement all night.

He even made sure to gain the understanding of the kijin, who bear a deep and reasonable grudge against the orcs. It is both a careful measure to eliminate the roots of hatred, but also a soft and considerate idea that is unbecoming of the truly powerful.

"Master Veldora, perhaps *you* should spend more time think-ing about how to minimize damage to others around you—"

"Silence, child! Even I am still developing as an intelligent being. Why can't you take the long and generous view and overlook my shortcomings?!"

"Umm... So you have a hundred times more energy than me already, and you're still looking forward to growing fur-ther...?"

"But of course. I am always striving to be better."

"Oh...okay..."

Ifrit fell silent for a time, no doubt moved by my inspira-tional example.

As for the council, Rimuru understood the details of the orcs' plight, likely because he read Geld's memories. He explained that the orcs were dying of famine, and only accepting the effect of "Starved" would enable them to survive longer. He also explained that Gelmud had been manipulating this series of events to his benefit.

Moving on to practical answers, he explained that the orcs would not be capable of paying any kind of reparations for their actions. When this was done, Rimuru pointed out that this was all a polite excuse.

"I have accepted all of the orcs' sins. If you have any problems with that, you come to me," he declared. Everyone was stunned.

Only the kijin took it in stride, as they had already heard the idea from Rimuru. To those who were unsettled by it, Rimuru explained, "That was my promise to Geld, the Orc Disaster."

Keeping his promises is one of Rimuru's ironclad rules. So nobody could possibly complain to him about this decision. If there was one thing to be said...

"The strong eat the weak."

It would be what Benimaru just stated. If they had a problem, their only recourse would be to defeat Rimuru. And nobody there could feasibly do that.

The chieftain of the lizardmen, unlike his son, has a calm and collected head on his shoulders. He attempted to understand and accept the entirety of Rimuru's decision. This is the proper way of action for a creature possessing elements of dragonkind.

His question was a very practical one: "If you do not judge the orcs for their sins, then do you intend for all of them to stay in this forest?"

There are over a hundred and fifty thousand orcs remaining. To welcome them all at once would wreak havoc on the forest's food supply. It would lead to unnecessary chaos and squabbling over what little food there is.

It is natural that the leader of a people would be wary of such a situation.

Rimuru replied, "What if all the different races living in the forest formed a kind of alliance?"

Surely knowledge of the orcs' situation led him to this idea, but it is clearly folly. Attempting to shoulder everybody's burdens in search of common ground is noble, but I find it unlikely that all others present would follow his example.

But to my surprise, the actions of all present gave lie to my presumption. They've all been infected by Rimuru's idealism.

You must see reality, people. Such a thing is clearly impossible!

And yet, a part of me couldn't help but be excited. If anyone can do it, perhaps it is Rimuru…

I suppose this sensation was shared by everyone present at this momentous meeting. Did they, like me, find Rimuru's words unrealistic—a wild fancy—and yet worth dreaming for? I imagine that this was the case.

Thus, on this day, the Jura Forest Alliance was formed, with Rimuru as its chancellor.

◆A PLACE TO RELAX◆

I must admire the clever way that Treyni arranged all of this. She very naturally foisted the most annoying and troublesome role upon Rimuru. I must learn from her example.

But Rimuru! When will you ever learn? Now his softhearted ways have got him naming the orcs.

One hundred and fifty thousand orcs! Perhaps even more. They keep coming and coming—I estimate their true number at roughly a hundred and sixty thousand now. He cannot handle such a number with his source of energy alone.

Even if I were to lend my help, I feel this would still be a fool's game.

However, he found a method that reuses each individual's magicule energy instead. The aftereffect of Geld's "Starved" skill put the orcs into a state of magicule over-absorption. Over time, these would descend to the normal level, but Rimuru had the idea to reuse them for the naming process while they were still active.

I could scarcely believe my eyes as I watched the process unfold. Can you really do that? Well, it went off without a hitch.

"I cannot believe it."

"I understand, Master. He has just overturned so much of what we take for granted."

For one thing, if this idea got out, it would make the process of accruing strength so much easier for demon lords.

Instead of risking the danger of naming one's subjects, it is possible to dope them up with extra energy, then name them with that excess value. I suspect the soul bonds are weaker than that of a proper naming ceremony, but in the pursuit of greater military power, this is no real issue.

"...But it is so difficult that even I cannot attempt it."

"Even you, Master Veldora?"

"Indeed. The magicule wavelength differs by individual. Because you cannot simply reuse the magicules, one must absorb them into oneself first. And normally, it is not possible to take in another's energy. Even if it were possible, no more than half of it or so could actually be repurposed for other uses. And yet Rimuru..."

"Is reusing the power with at least ninety...if not a full one-hundred percent efficiency..."

"You see what I mean? I could not do such a thing."

Despite his daft looks, Rimuru often achieves nearly impossible feats with the greatest of ease. As the news of this gets around, more will seek to utilize him to their own ends.

He himself seems totally oblivious to this, and while I doubt that anyone would run about spreading the tale, I do fear that if nothing is done to prevent this possibility, it will one day lead to some catastrophic failure.

It is no easy feat to inspire fear in me. Will your surprises never cease, Rimuru?

On top of that, the last orc was one of the officers of Geld the demon lord. And Rimuru went right ahead and gave that one the name of Geld to carry on!!

"Glarrbbggh!!"

Blast! He took my magicules again!!

Luckily for me, I was ready for this to happen, but I would have appreciated a word of warning first.

Understood. This will be taken into account next time.

Y-you fool! I don't want it "taken into account," I want him to stop naming monsters!

He made quite the miscalculation this time. It hurt a little bit, which is a sign that he took more than his share from my energy.

Sometimes I cannot believe this slime.

But very well. I suppose that I can be magnanimous and forgive him in repayment of all the excitement he provided.

This was the end of the chaos in the Forest of Jura. The various races returned to their home habitats, and peace returned to the woods.
Three months later, Rimuru's village had undergone a dramatic change. Through the naming process, Rimuru had evolved the orcs into high orcs. The resulting increase in

power led to a massive surplus of physical labor.

Thus the residential area expanded and developed at a rapid pace, which brought more and more residents to the area. Excitement flooded into the village, and the thrum of anticipation of a happy future is everywhere.

A place where all monsters can gather: Rimuru's ideals have come to fruition in this remarkable town.

Even I cannot hide my elation. When I am free of this damnable prison, I will build a home in this place, too. Then everyone will praise and compliment me, as I deserve!

I am awaiting this day, Rimuru. My eyes shall not leave your exploits until it happens!

To be reincarnated in Volume 6!

EXTRA ILLUSTRATION

*This was a rejected chapter cover-page design.

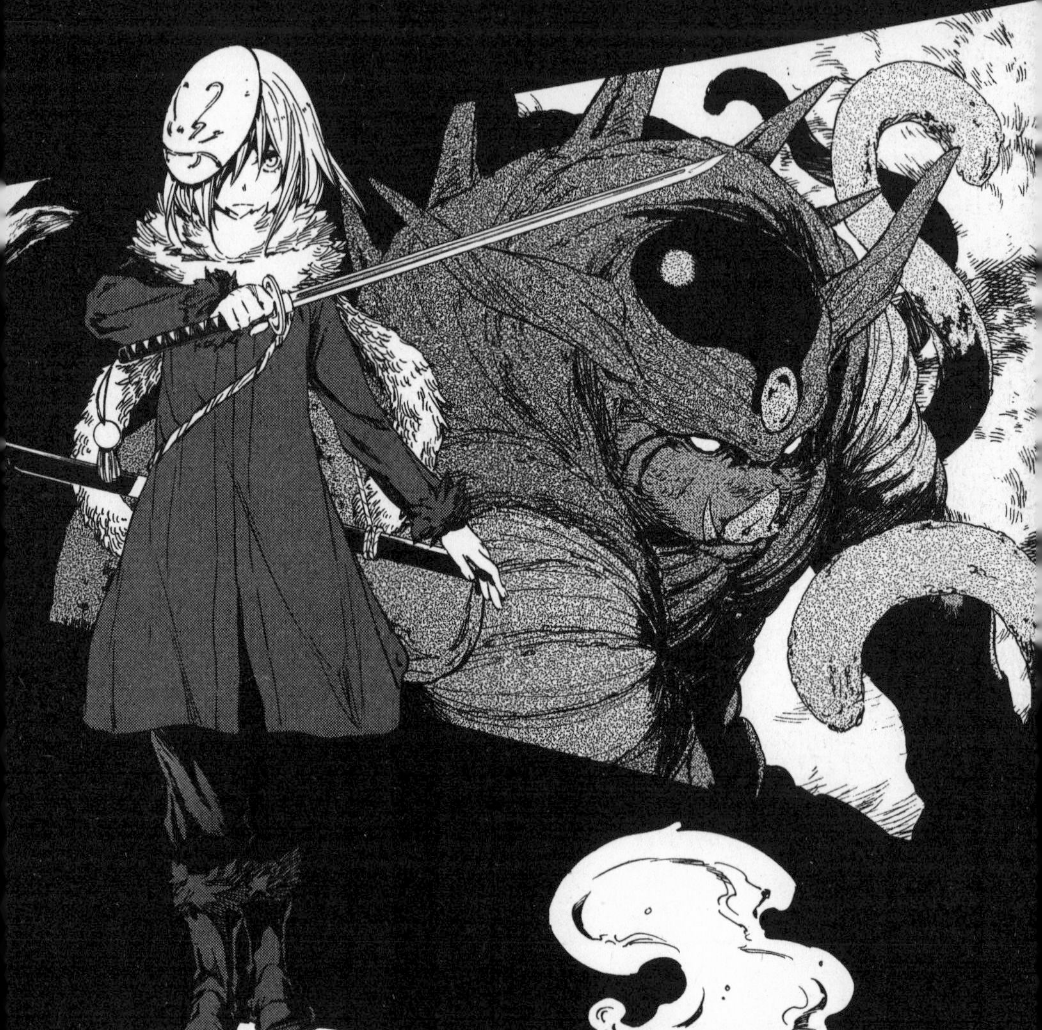

A HUGE FAD IN THE MONSTER KINGDOM

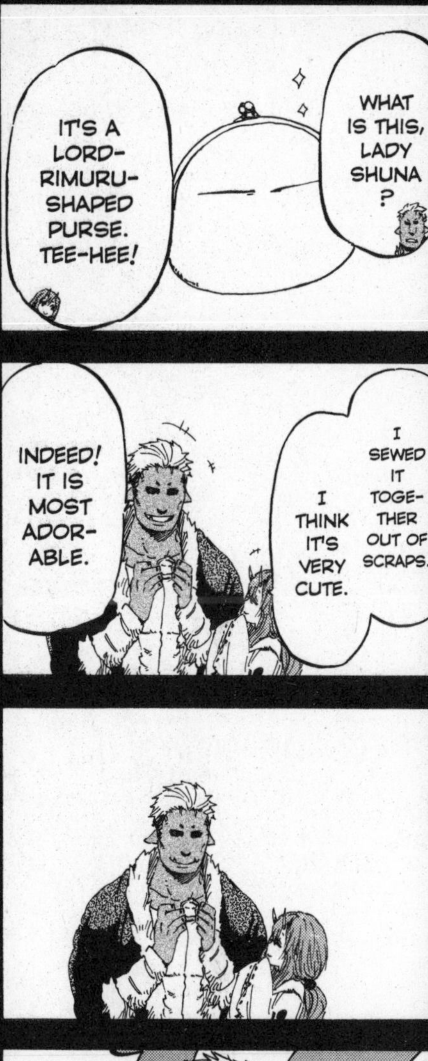
WHAT IS THIS, LADY SHUNA?
IT'S A LORD-RIMURU-SHAPED PURSE. TEE-HEE!
I SEWED IT TOGETHER OUT OF SCRAPS.
I THINK IT'S VERY CUTE.
INDEED! IT IS MOST ADORABLE.
...WOULD YOU LIKE ME TO MAKE ONE FOR YOU, TOO?
YOU WOULD DO THAT FOR ME?!

MOSTLY BENIMARU, SOMETIMES GOBTA

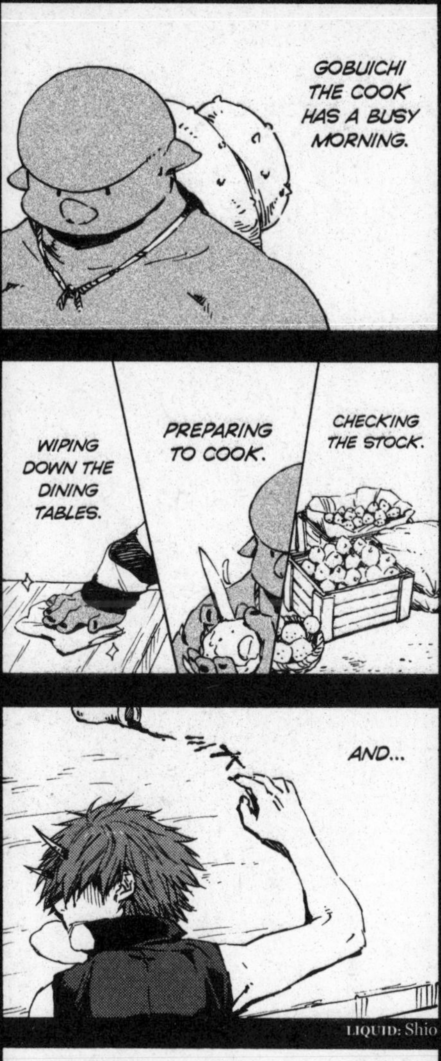
GOBUICHI THE COOK HAS A BUSY MORNING.
CHECKING THE STOCK.
PREPARING TO COOK.
WIPING DOWN THE DINING TABLES.
AND...
LIQUID: Shio
HERE'S SOME HEALING HERBS, BENIMARU.
Th... Thanks.
...SAVING THOSE HARMED BY SHION'S COOKING.

GABIRU THE IDOMITABLE

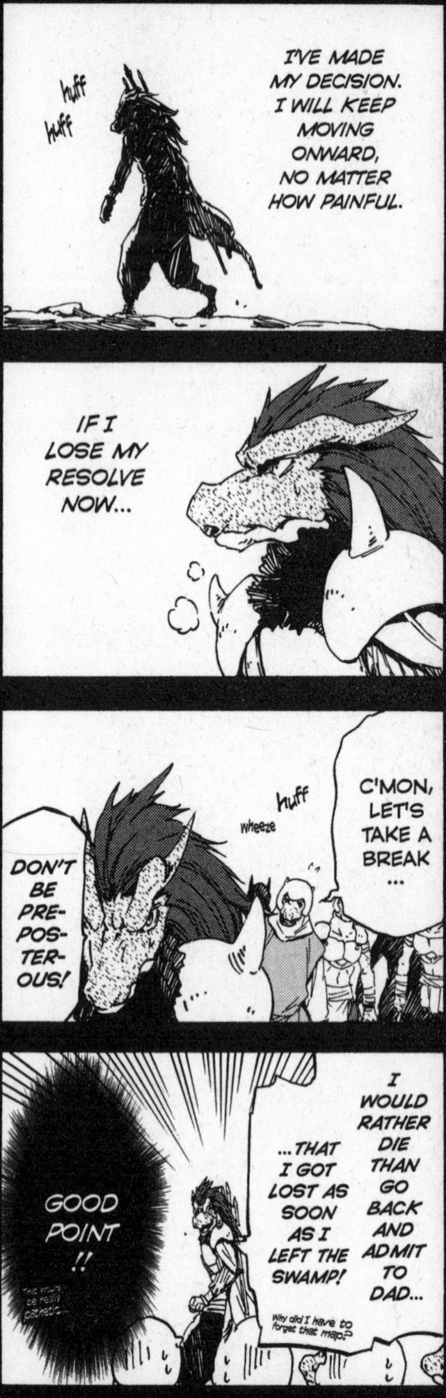
I'VE MADE MY DECISION. I WILL KEEP MOVING ONWARD, NO MATTER HOW PAINFUL.
huff
huff
IF I LOSE MY RESOLVE NOW...
C'MON, LET'S TAKE A BREAK ...
huff
wheeze
DON'T BE PRE-POS-TER-OUS!
I WOULD RATHER DIE THAN GO BACK AND ADMIT TO DAD...
...THAT I GOT LOST AS SOON AS I LEFT THE SWAMP!
Why did I have to forget that map?
GOOD POINT!!
That would be really pathetic...

COSMIC TRUTH

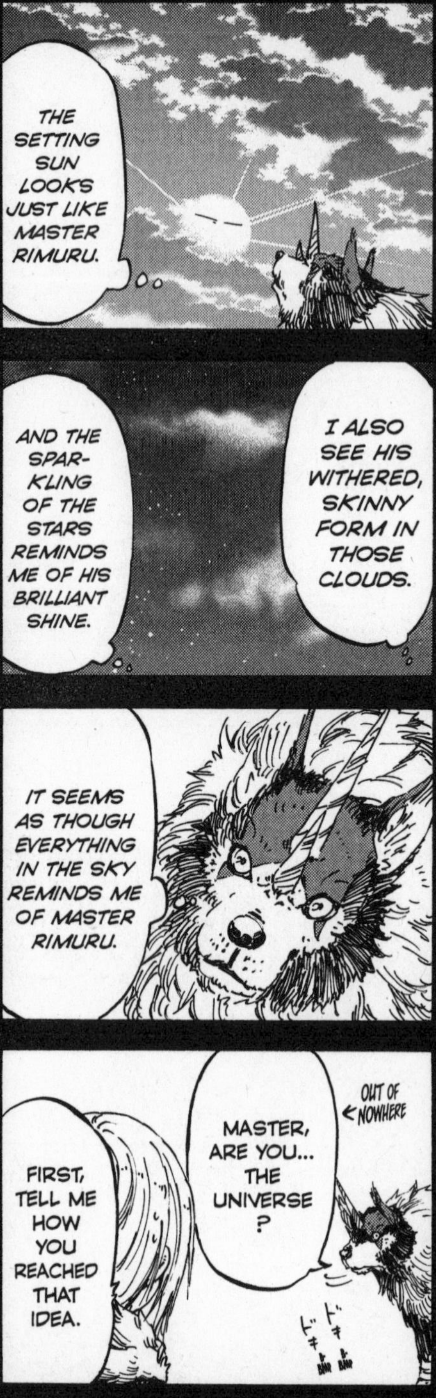
THE SETTING SUN LOOKS JUST LIKE MASTER RIMURU.
I ALSO SEE HIS WITHERED, SKINNY FORM IN THOSE CLOUDS.
AND THE SPAR-KLING OF THE STARS REMINDS ME OF HIS BRILLIANT SHINE.
IT SEEMS AS THOUGH EVERYTHING IN THE SKY REMINDS ME OF MASTER RIMURU.
OUT OF NOWHERE
MASTER, ARE YOU... THE UNIVERSE?
FIRST, TELL ME HOW YOU REACHED THAT IDEA.
ドキ
B-BMP
ドキ
B-BMP

THE HORN PROBLEM

P58
HANG ON TO MY MASK, SHION.
IT'S VERY PRE-CIOUS.
LORD RIMU-RU'S MASK ...
RIMURU VS. ORC DISASTER
WHOOSH
FSHAA
JUST FOR A SECOND ...
CLANK
BA BA BA BA BA BA BOOM
BOOMF
P72
LORD RIM-URU!
H-HE RE-GREW HIS ARM!
WATCHING THE FIGHT

LIST OF ACKNOWLEDGMENTS

AUTHOR:
Fuse-sensei

CHARACTER DESIGN:
Mitz Vah-sensei

ASSISTANTS:
Muraichi-san
Daiki Haraguchi-san
Masashi Kiritani-sensei
Taku Arao-sensei
Takuya Nishida-sensei

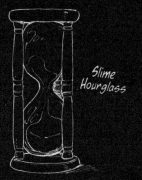

Congrats on getting your own series !!

Everyone at the editorial department

And You!!

Slime Hourglass

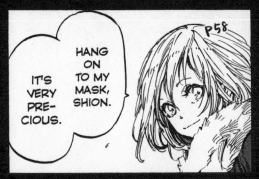

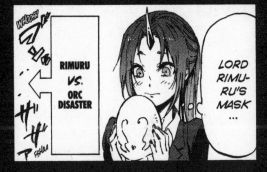

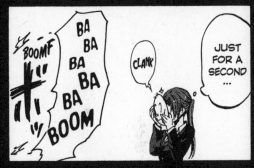

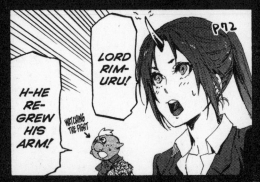

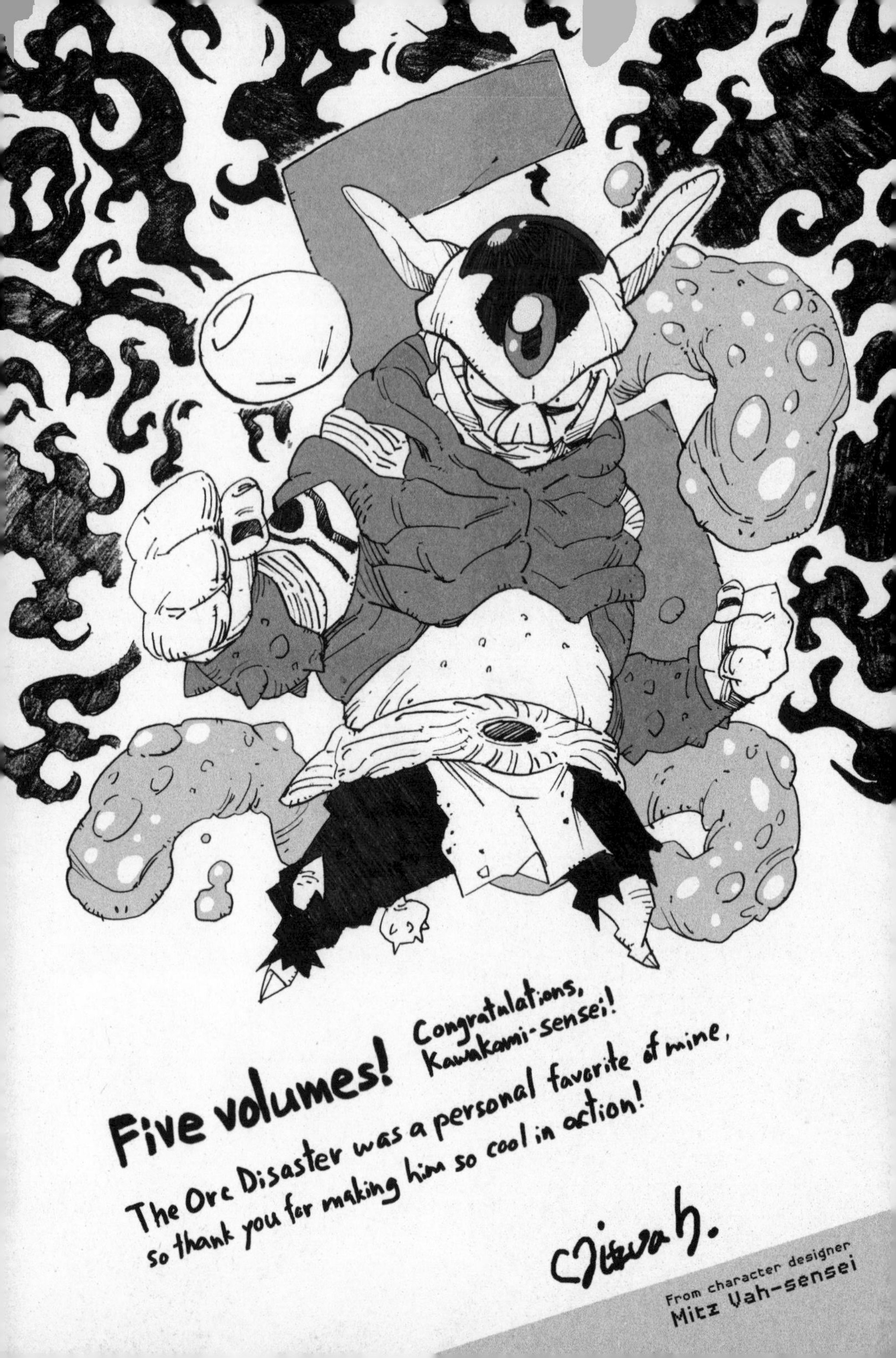
Five volumes! Congratulations, Kawakami-sensei!
The Orc Disaster was a personal favorite of mine, so thank you for making him so cool in action!
Mitzvah.
From character designer
Mitz Vah-sensei

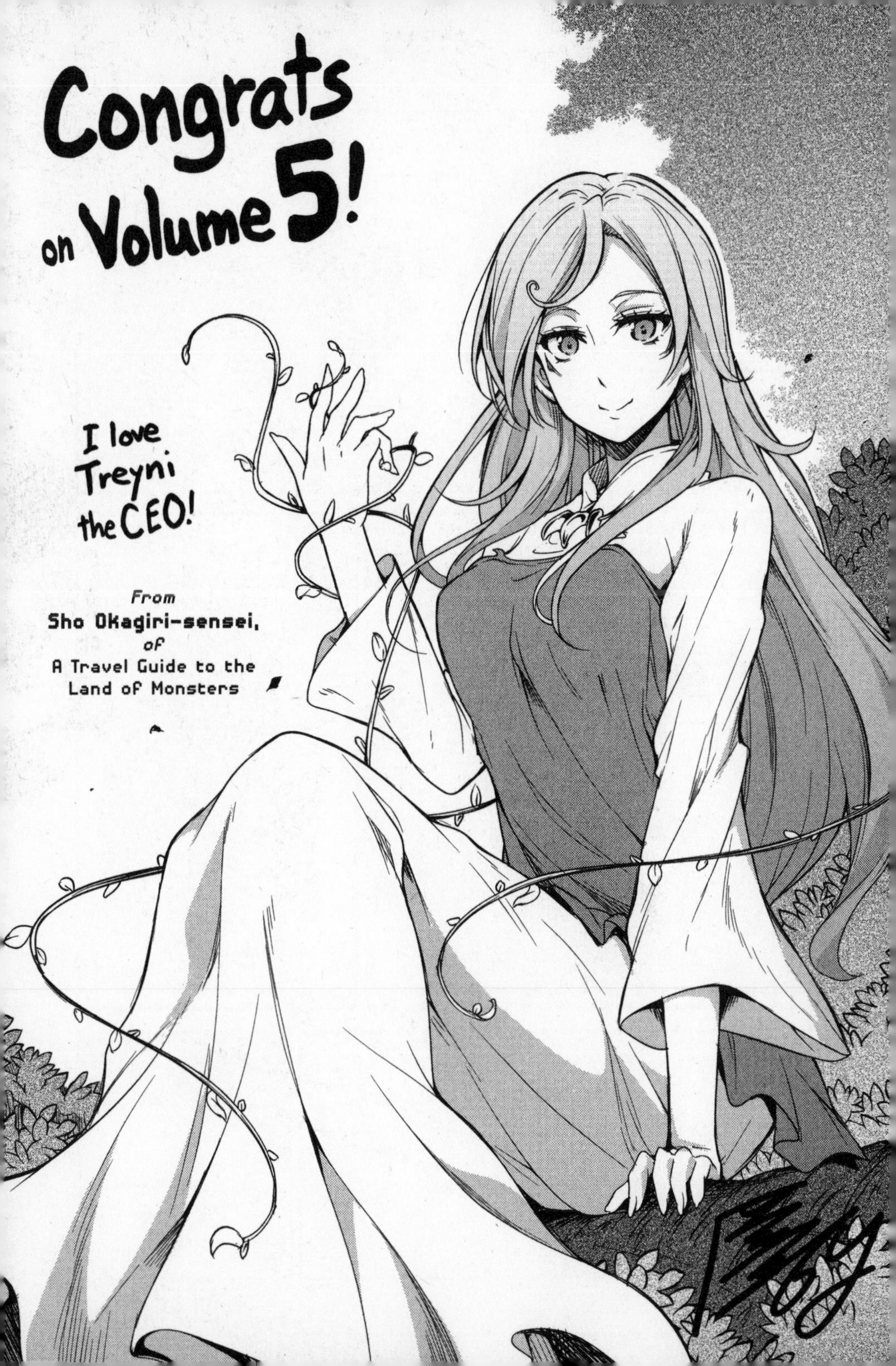
Congrats on Volume 5!
I love Treyni the CEO!
From Sho Okagiri-sensei, of A Travel Guide to the Land of Monsters

Straying Off Course

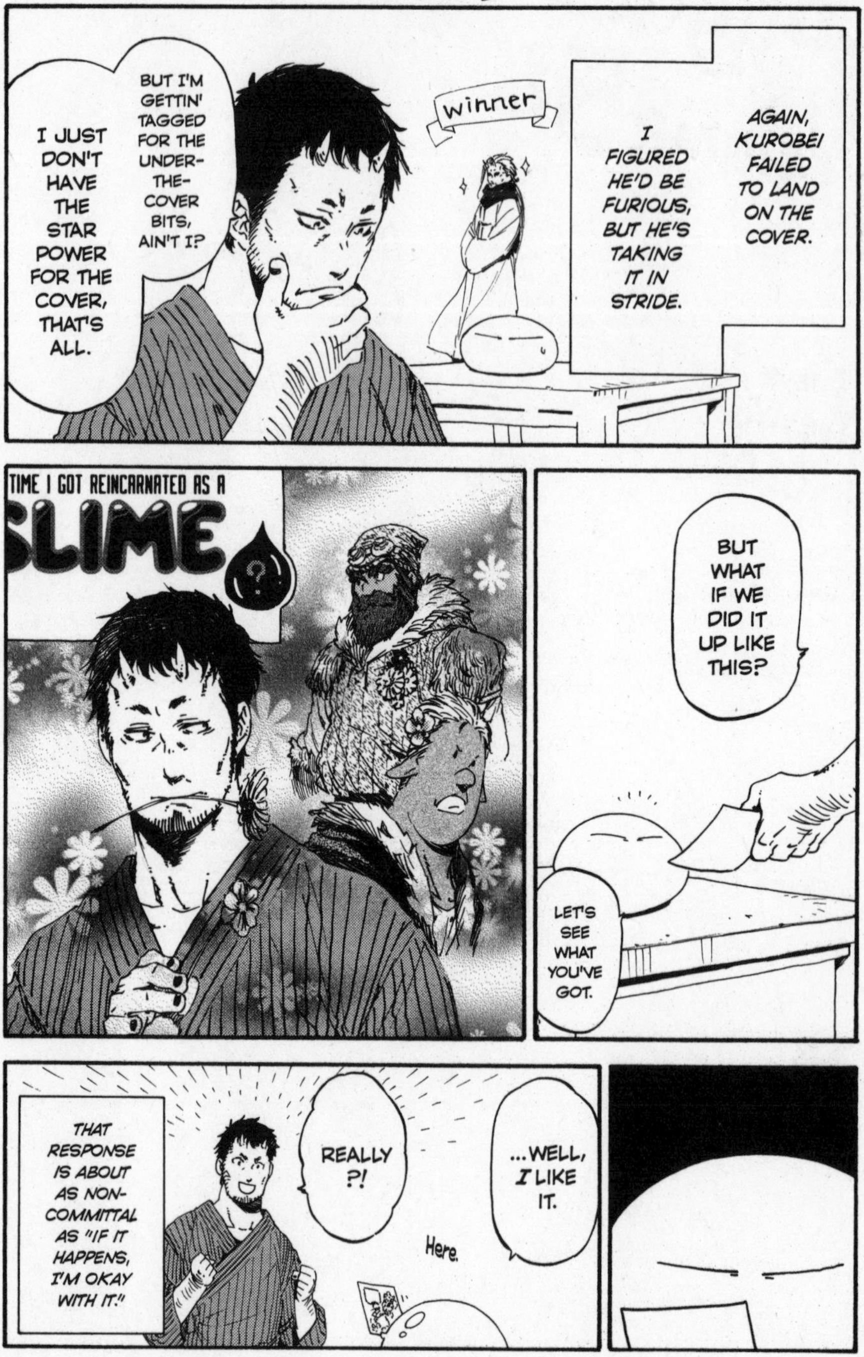
AGAIN, KUROBEI FAILED TO LAND ON THE COVER.
I FIGURED HE'D BE FURIOUS, BUT HE'S TAKING IT IN STRIDE.
winner
I JUST DON'T HAVE THE STAR POWER FOR THE COVER, THAT'S ALL. BUT I'M GETTIN' TAGGED FOR THE UNDER-THE-COVER BITS, AIN'T I?
BUT WHAT IF WE DID IT UP LIKE THIS?
LET'S SEE WHAT YOU'VE GOT.
TIME I GOT REINCARNATED AS A
SLIME
...WELL, I LIKE IT.
REALLY?!
Here.
THAT RESPONSE IS ABOUT AS NON-COMMITTAL AS "IF IT HAPPENS, I'M OKAY WITH IT."

Candy Apple.

Well, the candy part.

TRANSLATION
NOTES

HIGH ORCS

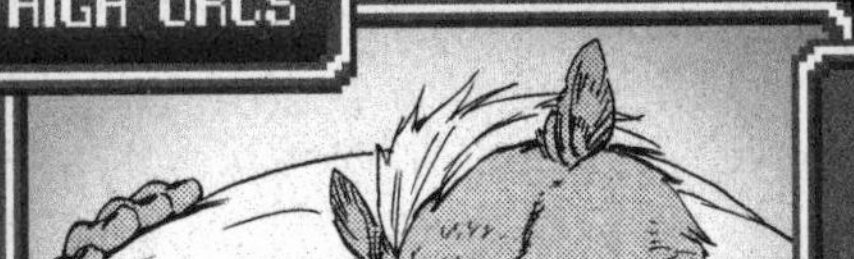

page 153

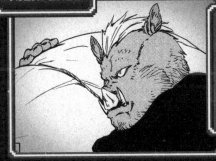

Much like the Kijin, who have a different set of *Kanji* from their "ogre" foundation, the orc and high orc terms have their own *Kanji*. The word orc is written as "pig-head clan," while the high orcs are "boar people clan," which again suggests that evolving has brought them a greater human influence. Similarly, orc King is simply written as "boar people King."

A Kodansha Comics Trade Paperback Original.

Published in the United States by Kodansha Comics,
an imprint of Kodansha USA Publishing, LLC, New York.

Publication rights for this English edition arranged through Kodansha Ltd., Tokyo.

First published in Japan in 2017 by Kodansha Ltd., Tokyo, as *Tensei Shitara Suraimu Datta Ken* volume 5.

ISBN 978-1-63236-639-9

Printed in the United States of America.

www.kodanshacomics.com

9 8 7 6 5 4 3

Translation: Stephen Paul
Lettering: Evan Hayden
Editing: Ajani Oloye
Kodansha Comics edition cover design: Phil Balsman